THE GREAT HEART OF THE REPUBLIC

THE GREAT HEART

of the

REPUBLIC

ST. LOUIS AND THE CULTURAL CIVIL WAR

Adam Arenson

HARVARD UNIVERSITY PRESS

Cambridge, Massachusetts
London, England

2011

Library of Congress Cataloging-in-Publication Data
Arenson, Adam, 1978–
The great heart of the republic : St. Louis and the cultural Civil War / Adam Arenson.
p.   cm.
Includes bibliographical references and index.
ISBN 978-0-674-05288-8 (alk. paper)
1. Saint Louis (Mo.)—History—Civil War, 1861–1865.   2. Saint Louis (Mo.)—History—
Civil War, 1861–1865—Social aspects.   3. United States—History—Civil War,
1861–1865—Social aspects.   4. West (U.S.)—Politics and government—19th century.
5. United States—Territorial expansion—History—19th century.   6. Slavery—United
States—Extension to the territories.   I. Title.
F474.S257A74 2010
977.8'6603—dc22   2010018704

To my family

Contents

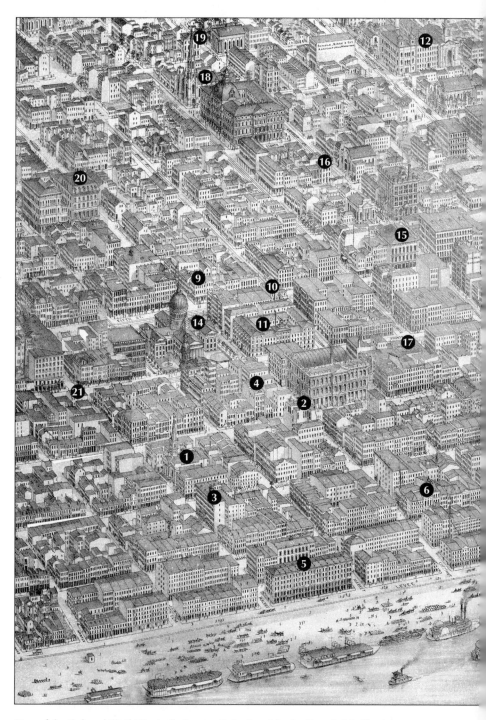

Sites of the Cultural Civil War in St. Louis, 1848–1877. Map by Dennis McClendon, Chicago Cartographics. Bird's eye composite courtesy of the David Rumsey Map Collection, from plates of *Pictorial St. Louis, the Great Metropolis of the Mississippi Valley; a Topographical Survey Drawn in Perspective AD 1875*, by Camille N. Dry, designed and edited by Richard J. Compton (St. Louis: Compton & Company, 1876).

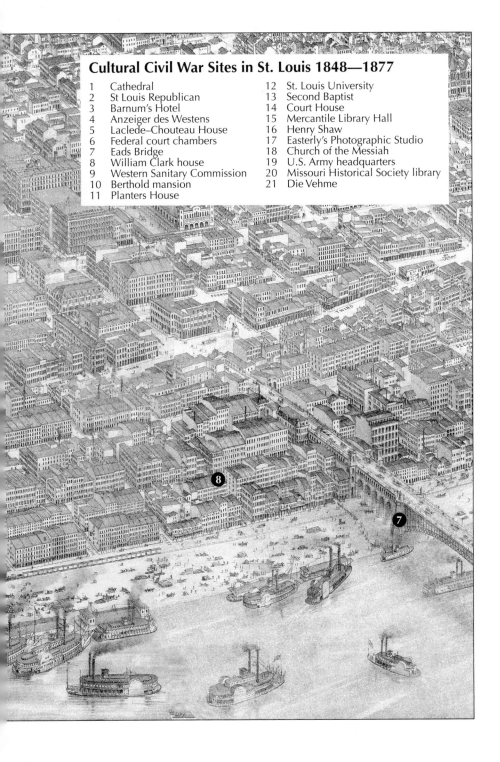

Cultural Civil War Sites in St. Louis 1848—1877

1   Cathedral
2   St Louis Republican
3   Barnum's Hotel
4   Anzeiger des Westens
5   Laclede–Chouteau House
6   Federal court chambers
7   Eads Bridge
8   William Clark house
9   Western Sanitary Commission
10   Berthold mansion
11   Planters House
12   St. Louis University
13   Second Baptist
14   Court House
15   Mercantile Library Hall
16   Henry Shaw
17   Easterly's Photographic Studio
18   Church of the Messiah
19   U.S. Army headquarters
20   Missouri Historical Society library
21   Die Vehme

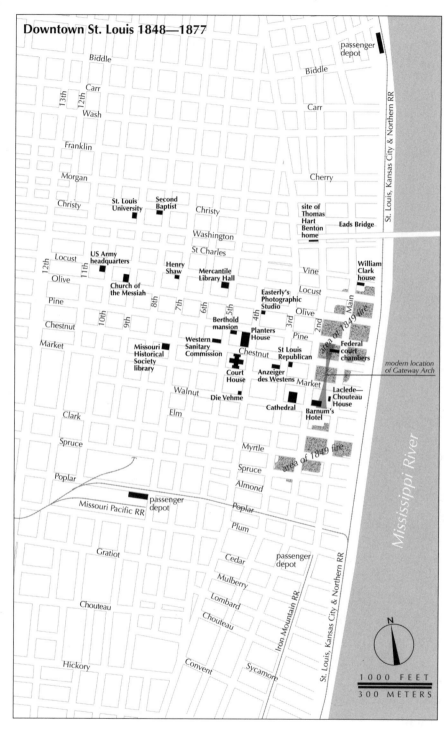

Downtown St. Louis 1848–1877. Map by Dennis McClendon, Chicago Cartographics.

I was a Metropolis when Chicago was a trading post;
I was a cosmopolitan on the bank of a moody river when Philadelphia and
Boston were pulsated only by town-criers;
Along my levee French and Spaniard and Aborigine and African met and
understood each other.
I was founded upon a hardy brotherhood.
I became asylum to a horde of freedom-bent Germans from an oppressive
Fatherland;
I was bosom to the shorn lambs of Ireland.
When Gold polarized the West, through my bounden limbs converged the
Argonauts of 'forty-nine.
Frugal Yankees and touchy Southrons came and fetched their feud over slavery;
Slave pens and a public mart are among my relics in limbo, but I supplied
History with the cause celebre named for black Dred Scott.
I was a Union City in 1861, yet I gave succor and occasion to Confederate
sympathizers—(I should be the most liberal city in the U.S.A.).
. . .
I am the center of the Continent. I am the centripetal capital of these United
States, for I am a parcel of all sections; . . .
I am the American City of manifest destiny—I am St. Louis.

—Nathan Benjamin Young Jr., " 'Your St. Louis' Speaks," 1937.

The Three Sides of the American Civil War

Samuel Langhorne Clemens was not proud of his Civil War experience. As Clemens recounted it decades later, he had been "strong for the Union"—before joining a Confederate militia, organized in his hometown of Hannibal, Missouri. He had believed in the gallantry of a soldier's life—for about two weeks, before his unit agreed to disband. "We were the first men that went into the service in Missouri," Clemens later wrote, and "we were the first that went out of it anywhere." Did this brief tenure make Clemens a secessionist? Was he a deserter for leaving, or merely a coward? Clemens waved off such questions. "There was a good deal of confusion," he insisted, "during the first months of the great trouble." Rather than choose sides, Clemens wished to avoid the war's conflict. And so, as the battles began, he took a stagecoach to the Nevada Territory. There, through his journalism, his fables, and his tall tales, Samuel Clemens made a name for himself, as Mark Twain.[1]

Throughout his stories, Twain offered his personal history as national amusement: tales of rural childhood and riverboat adolescence, memories of scampering after California gold and exposés of the fraud in what he termed "the Gilded Age." Yet when it came to the Civil War, Twain was far more reticent. "In the war," he later wrote, "each of us, in his own person, seems to have sampled all the different varieties of human experience." In the waning decades of the nineteenth century, Twain lived in Hartford, Connecticut, a cultural southerner spinning stories of the West while making his home among the Yankees.[2] Though Samuel Clemens may have escaped the fighting, Mark Twain was surely a veteran of the cultural civil war.

One hundred fifty years ago, on the morning of April 12, 1861, Confederate partisans fired their first salvo against Fort Sumter, the federal installation in Charleston Harbor, South Carolina. Almost four years later, on April 9, 1865, Robert E. Lee surrendered his troops to Grant at the Appomattox Courthouse. In the battles that came between, more than three million men marched under arms, and more than 620,000 soldiers died. Yet the American Civil War did not end at Appomattox, any more than it began at Fort Sumter. The four-year military clash was only an intensification of the cultural civil war, the already-smoldering battle of ideas, clashing moral systems, and competing national visions that revealed what united as well as what divided the United States in the mid-nineteenth century.

The cultural civil war was an all-encompassing conflict, decades in coming and generations more in consequence. It included the question of secession and the resulting military engagements, but it was not contained in the minutiae of military maneuvering or defined by battle outcomes. Its skirmishes were fought within and among U.S. states and regions; within cities, communities, and families; and, at times, within individual hearts. And the cultural civil war was more than just a conflict between North and South, fighting over the West as a prize. The cultural civil war was the clash among three incompatible regional visions, as leaders from the North, South, and West argued about the definition and importance of Manifest Destiny and slavery politics. As Mark Twain came to understand, this three-way conflict was at its most intense in the center of the continent—in Missouri, the first state across the Mississippi River, and in its metropolis, the city of St. Louis.

Considering the full breadth of the cultural civil war changes our understanding of the American Civil War in two important ways. In this book I craft a cultural history of a cultural war, utilizing the interpretive power of events seemingly outside of politics.[3] Pairing battles and triumphant architecture, elections and university origins, it contextualizes the entire era from 1848 to 1877, from the conquering of millions of new acres in the U.S. War with Mexico through the Civil War and Reconstruction to President Rutherford B. Hayes's inauguration. Casting a wide net for political, ideological, and economic details, this research draws upon letters, diaries, court records, and newspapers in English, French, and German, along with paintings, engravings, daguerreotypes, and other artifacts. The result is a nuanced, intimate history of the Civil War era from the heart of the republic.

The cultural civil war that preceded, accompanied, and followed the military battles had three sides, as advocates of the North, South, and West each balanced shifting alliances and growing oppositions. For too long the Civil War has been understood as merely a two-way conflict, between advocates of the North arguing for cheap, slavery-free land across the continent for free white laborers, and "fire-eaters" in the South seeking to expand and strengthen slavery and resist governmental interference. This misses the crucial third side to the Civil War, that of the West. In the mid-nineteenth century, residents of a vast region—including parts of Arkansas, Indiana, Illinois, Kentucky, and Michigan as well as California, Missouri, Iowa, Wisconsin, and federal territories from Minnesota to Oregon to New Mexico—considered themselves westerners. Regional advocates—including Henry Clay *and* his opponent Thomas Hart Benton, Abraham Lincoln *and* Stephen A. Douglas, and more—fought for the distinctive economic, political, and cultural agenda of the West, despite their other political differences.[4]

Seeking federal funding for the transcontinental railroad and free land for prospective settlers, western leaders engaged their counterparts in both the North and South. Crossing party lines, they brokered compromises to contain the slavery debate, allowing for the orderly admission of more western states and the incorporation of western territories. They envisioned the day when both the North and South would be subservient to the economic and political might of the West. This western agenda caused few Civil War battles, but it had caused the war itself. Though the West had no specific role in the surrender and Reconstruction, the definition of expansion and Manifest Destiny held by the victors shaped the peace.

Embracing cultural and urban history methods, I reveal the effort by those in the North, South, and West to define expansion and slavery politics in the years before, during, and after the nation was forever transformed by civil war. I describe the connections between Reconstruction and homesteading, railroad-building and free-labor ideology, as ideas of Manifest Destiny were embraced across the Civil War's dividing lines. And I conclude that, ultimately, impossible visions of expansion stymied all three regions of the country, as advocates in the North, South, and West each tried and failed to attain Manifest Destiny's promise.[5]

In the first decades of the nineteenth century, the population of the United States grew at a rate never seen before or since—doubling by 1825, and more than doubling again, to 23,191,876 residents, by 1850. Advances in transportation and communication revolutionized economic patterns. Both grand visions for the nation and the humdrum fabric of everyday life were dramatically altered. In this moment of change, European explanations for the pace of modern life seemed unsatisfying or outdated. From poets to politicians, American leaders sought uniquely American ideas. And no narrative of American exceptionalism proved more powerful than the vision of Manifest Destiny.[6]

"The right of our manifest destiny to overspread and to possess the whole of the continent which Providence has given us for the development of the great experiment of liberty and federated self-government . . ."—that was the claim that appeared in the *United States Magazine and Democratic Review* in 1845, coining the phrase. Yet the idea of Manifest Destiny—the existence of a specific American mission in the world, one that justified expansion into lands held by others—had been a central tenet of American identity since the days of the Pilgrims. Manifest Destiny was a theory of empire, and thus an ideology of connection. It provided a rationale to unite disparate groups of settlers, drawing together established cities and new settlements, remote frontiers and the centers of business, politics, and culture.[7]

Ironically, Manifest Destiny convinced Americans they were unique—while, around the world, other imperial projects believed their own assurances of providential benevolence. As the officers of the British Empire expanded their reach in the nineteenth century, they defended their control of Birmingham factories and Jamaican plantations, South African mines and Canadian forests, and imagined governing Cairo's streets to be as easy as patrolling a London suburb. Other European empires also grabbed banners to unify their exploits—whether inclusive ideas such as science, industry, or modernity, or exclusive barriers such as racial or linguistic discrimination. This was a cultural as well as a political domination, a social program as much as an economic one. And, more often than not, these attempts at globe-spanning unity failed.[8]

What *was* the promise of Manifest Destiny? How was it lived, not only in the moment of conquest but as millions of old and new U.S. residents sought to shape its progress? The history of St. Louis can provide some revealing answers. As a political idea, Manifest Destiny was conceived in New York and implemented from Washington. Its economic bounty enriched Chicago, Denver, and San Francisco. Yet for decades, the cords connecting the cities of the North and South to the lands of the West passed through St. Louis.[9] Immigrants from all over Europe and North America disembarked every day, adding their skills and their dreams to the cosmopolitan city. French and German were heard in the streets almost as often as English, as St. Louis appeared similar to other rapidly growing cities of empire around the globe. They arrived just as Manifest Destiny and the city of St. Louis were tested by the cultural civil war.

To tell the story of the cultural civil war, one could easily follow the traditional hopscotch of Civil War history: Wilmot Proviso, Compromise of 1850, nativism, Bleeding Kansas, *Dred Scott,* Harpers Ferry, Fort Sumter, Antietam, Appomattox, Ford's Theater, Andrew Johnson's impeachment, Promontory Point, and the Colfax riot—keeping an eye to national politics but ignoring the connections between events and locales. But, as Henry David Thoreau realized, one can also travel widely while remaining in Concord. The turning points of national history are bound up in the culture and politics of so many local places.[10]

To describe the full panoply of the cultural civil war, I have pursued my research around the nation but I have also traveled widely in St. Louis. In this largest city along the border of slavery and freedom, the Civil War era looks different: it is a struggle with a different chronology, a different emphasis, different turning points. And in St. Louis, the war has three sides, as proponents of the North, South, and West all argued for their vision of the nation. This has made the city a place of lively contradictions. All justified their proposals in the language of Manifest Destiny: while rhetoricians caricatured the Civil War as a fight between Boston, Massachusetts, and Charleston, South Carolina, no newspaper editor could so easily capture St. Louis or Missouri.[11]

Northerners and southerners, European immigrants and free and enslaved African Americans—as a booming metropolis in a border state, St. Louis's demographic stew mirrored the nation's regional, political, and ethnic diversity as no other city did. Given the richness of the stories to be told in

St. Louis, it is remarkable how the city's history has been foreshortened in popular memory, skipping from the 1804–1806 Lewis and Clark expedition to the 1904 World's Fair. Situated on so many regional borders, the city was home to complex political and cultural allegiances that more often than not have been ignored. I embrace that complexity in order to describe the cultural civil war where ideology intersected with place, on the streets and wharves of St. Louis.[12]

Founded by the French, governed by the Spanish, and sold to the Americans, St. Louis was always a borderland city on the edge of empires. A hub of western movement, a destination point for immigrants, and the beacon of moderation in border-state politics, the gateway city of St. Louis was an ideal place to view America changing. The city's history reveals the national transformation.[13]

The cultural civil war was far more intimate in St. Louis than in New York or Washington, Charleston or New Orleans, San Francisco or Chicago. National crises were precipitated in St. Louis, and national initiatives gained strength there. Universities named for both George Washington and Abraham Lincoln were founded in St. Louis, and the very name of Missouri was a talisman of the slavery compromise that held the nation's fractious politics in place for a generation. A nominee from St. Louis was considered in every presidential election from 1856 to 1872, and in 1876 the city hosted the Democratic National Convention at the moment of the party's resurgence. Events there precede national parallels, demarcating new periods in the history of Civil War and Reconstruction policies.[14]

"At St. Louis, they talk St. Louis incessantly," wrote the great American thinker Ralph Waldo Emerson during his visit there in 1852, marveling at the local confidence. In the nineteenth century, promoters of every city predicted success. Advocates envisioned St. Louis as a potential capital—a capital of agriculture, of economic opportunity, of rail lines, of cultural influence, and of political power—while boosters in Cincinnati, Memphis, Chicago, and Denver did the same. But not every city can win, and dreams in the American West often ended in collapse. While engaged with the local ramifications of the cultural civil war in St. Louis, I have balanced the excesses of local puffery with a sober assessment of how the cultural civil war was faring throughout the nation in these decades.[15]

Through technical breakthroughs, artistic and educational innovations, and a unique brand of compromise politics, the leaders of St. Louis embraced the challenges of their moment, setting forth a dramatic new vision of American history and destiny. From John C. Calhoun to Frederick Douglass, Walt Whitman to John Brown, the nation's political, cultural, and moral leaders tracked the progress of the cultural civil war by monitoring events in St. Louis. They observed how the city's leaders tried, briefly succeeded, and ultimately failed to control the national destiny.

St. Louis's central role in the cultural civil war began when it burned down. In the 1849 Great Fire, an outdated French business district was destroyed, and insurance paid for the creation of the state-of-the-art commercial district ready to profit from the bounty of the Mexican Cession. An influx of political and cultural capital as well as economic investment followed, raising the stakes for St. Louis and the entire West after the Compromise of 1850 was enacted. Senator Thomas Hart Benton promoted the transcontinental railroad, declaring that it would become "a band of Iron, hooping and binding the States together." Yet proslavery interests elsewhere saw the developing program—new western states, a federally funded transcontinental railroad, and proposals for gradual emancipation—as a threat to the traditional political balance. Slaveholders worked to frustrate both these policies and the city that embraced them, blocking the railroad and enforcing further strictures on slavery when the case of a St. Louis slave, Dred Scott, went from a back alley to the U.S. Supreme Court.

After Abraham Lincoln's election, the outbreak of fighting renewed St. Louis's prospects. Without the seceded states, Congress approved the Homestead Act and funding for the transcontinental railroad. St. Louis, a Union city in a slave state, became the nation's western administrative center, where ironclad ships were built, injured soldiers were brought to hospitals, and the regional command was based. John C. Frémont's local emancipation order in 1861 caused debilitating riots among Union troops, but he placed the question of emancipation at the forefront of war concerns. And the begrudging cooperation of local Confederate sympathizers with the military government in St. Louis provided a national model for a gradual reinstatement of those who would take an oath of loyalty to the Union.

After the war, St. Louis leaders grappled with problems of technological failure, political deadlock, and racial conflict as they struggled to define the principles of Reconstruction. The fledgling Lincoln Institute, a university founded by freedmen for the education of all men, pioneered a radically new racial compact. In 1869 local visionary Logan Uriah Reavis declared St. Louis "the future great city of the world"—and advocated disassembling the government buildings in Washington and moving the capital to St. Louis, where each region of the country could feel truly represented. Yet as Reconstruction faltered and the locally devised Liberal Republican movement failed, St. Louis leaders faced setbacks. In 1876 city leaders dedicated Forest Park, a grand new "Central Park for the West," and tripled the city's area through annexation. But these were the last grand actions, as many influential St. Louisans sought their fortunes elsewhere. Despite the growth of western cities and the completion of the transcontinental railroad, those in the West failed to bargain equally with the North and South until well into the twentieth century.

Events in St. Louis revealed the course of the cultural civil war at its fiercest, in the years between 1848 and 1877. As regional leaders pressed their beliefs to the extreme, this border-state metropolis embodied the strengths and contradictions of the nation, grappling with the hopefulness of Manifest Destiny and the controlling interests of slavery politics. In St. Louis, the interplay of local ambitions and national meanings revealed the wider cultural transformation brought about by westward expansion, political strife, and emancipation in the era of the Civil War and Reconstruction.

St. Louis's leaders dreamed of leading the nation. They began with their city in ruins.

I

The Destruction of the Past

At this critical moment the fire came and swept away the old tenements, leaving vacant the ground lately occupied by the principal business houses of the city—an opportunity was thus afforded . . .

—"First Ward," Letter to the *Missouri Republican,* June 10, 1849.

It began with the wind. On a normal St. Louis evening, the breezes would carry scents and sounds from the barges and steamboats floating in the Mississippi River onto the wharves, into the city's counting houses and mercantile showrooms. Yet on the night of May 17, 1849, the fierce gusts released a carnival of sparks from a passing steamboat. One lodged in the still-wet paint of the *White Cloud,* the boat docked at the northernmost end of St. Louis's commercial levee, upriver from the downtown district.[1] One errant spark unleashed an inferno.

The *White Cloud* was soon engulfed, and the flames danced to the neighboring steamer, the *Edward Bates.* Both boats soon burned across their anchoring ropes. Floating loose, they spread fire as they drifted downstream, until twenty-three of the massive commercial haulers were aflame. Tongues of fire followed the paths of commerce, up the gangplanks and onto the St. Louis levee, where hemp, cotton, and other goods stacked for transshipment became tinder. The Great Fire, as it would be known, was already large, and still growing.[2] Where would the conflagration lead?

The wooden buildings of St. Louis, crowded together on the narrow streets of what had once been a small French American village, faltered before a wall of fire. Those that collapsed sent up a tremendous roar. With the aid of the winds, the flames traced the downtown blocks, creeping uphill among the offices and storehouses, tenements and workshops. They soon threatened the cathedral on the bluff and the unfinished courthouse buildings nearby.

Growing brighter and mightier in the increasing winds, the Great Fire lit the sky for miles. In the residential neighborhoods of the city, safely removed from the flames, children sat on the porch reading a newspaper by its light, even as ash rained down around them. Yet others could not revel in the marvel of light at night. The illuminated horizon was "an awful spectacle," Sally Smith Flagg recalled later, since "some of my fellow creatures might be perishing there."[3]

With the winds blowing and the ominous light lining the levee, the urgent ringing of alarm bells only confirmed the suspicions of worried proprietors. Owners and white workmen gathered into their amateur fire companies. (In the moment of crisis, it was assumed that the city's slaves, many of whom labored in warehouses along the levee, would attend to their own safety.) The drifting steamboats had created one long sheet of flame. The extreme heat kept the volunteers from the waterfront, while the rudimentary hydrant system provided too little water. The business district would be lost.[4]

With the boats sunk, all the goods along the levee lost, and the very existence of the downtown district threatened, St. Louisans despaired for their city. "Appalling Calamity!" screamed the headline of the *St. Louis Reveille*, its editors setting the type even as the flames licked at the doorframe. The *People's Organ*—which, like the *Reveille*, lost its offices that night—described the efforts of men on the rooftops, "throwing water in puny quantities," helpless against the blaze.[5]

Desperate to save something, merchants snatched their goods and offered large sums to those willing to cart them to safety. At street corners, furniture sat heaped, women slumped among their belongings. They waited for husbands to hire draymen—yet often the flames reached them first, the women forced to flee as the fire incinerated the keepsakes of a lifetime. One river merchant, William M. Hall, recorded how "the heart and business part of the city is destroyed," while "goods of every description are scattered in wild confusion, all over the ballance of the City."[6]

Up the hill, blocks inland, the cathedral and the courthouse still stood, though now in the Great Fire's path. As the warehouses crackled, the fire companies regrouped, planning to fight back with fire if not water. Under the

command of Captain Thomas B. Targée, a well-liked merchant and auctioneer, the men lugged barrels of gunpowder to the corner of Market and Second streets. As the firebreak was set, however, there was a fatal miscommuni-
cation: unbeknownst to each other, two teams had prepared to implode the
corner's music store. Targée entered with a keg of powder on his shoulder, but
the blast came too soon—Targée remained inside. Aghast, the firemen began
searching the rubble.[7]

At the cathedral, flames scorched two sides of the church as the two arms
of the Great Fire met. Grappling with their commercial losses and now the
fire-company casualties, the men struggled to hold their ground, drawing the
conflagration into a stalemate, the cathedral and courthouse still standing.
Late in the night, the wind changed: the fire turned back toward the river,
burning itself out. With the flames dying down and the sun rising, the firemen trudged home, the evidence of their failures smoldering around them.[8]
Yet within the city's debris were the seeds of a momentous rebirth.

Despite millions of dollars in damage caused by the Great Fire, St. Louisans came to see how its destruction improved their city. Though it was
feared hundreds had died in the Great Fire blaze, only the firefighter Targée
and two others lost their lives in the night, as they worked to save the city.[9]
All other St. Louisans had escaped with their lives, and many with their
goods. Others received substantial insurance payments, and soon businessmen were capitalizing on the catastrophe. St. Louis was not lost. The opportunities created by the Great Fire allowed the city to profit economically,
politically, and culturally, for itself, for the West, and for the entire nation.

In nineteenth-century cities, when heating, cooking, and manufacturing
all required fire constantly, urban conflagrations were commonplace. But it
took economic acumen and political agility to turn a disaster into an opportunity for a city's refounding and redefinition, a chance to reassert or refor-
mulate a city's place in the national fabric. In the previous few decades, New
York, Detroit, and Pittsburgh had been similarly engulfed—and each found
the opportunity to form a stronger city through the process of rebuilding.
Though practically unknown outside the city today, the Great Fire of St.
Louis became just such a perfect refounding.[10]

St. Louis's Great Fire occurred at the start of a new era, stamping an
American future over nearly a century of French settlement at the confluence
of the Mississippi and Missouri rivers, a new imprint on top of thousands of
years of an American Indian presence. At a moment of global upheaval and

migration, as famine and failed revolutions in Europe sent tens of thousands more emigrants to seek a new life in the United States, the Great Fire removed the hindrances of St. Louis's colonial past and the uncertainty remaining from Missouri's uneasy admission to statehood.

As the United States absorbed the Mexican Cession, the aftermath of the Great Fire reshaped St. Louis as the Gateway to the West, the primary entrepôt for immigrants, entrepreneurs, and American ideals traveling into its new lands. The Great Fire enabled the reorientation of St. Louis from the world of the Caribbean and its slave society to the possibilities of becoming a western metropolis, profiting from the transcontinental vision of Manifest Destiny. By emphasizing the city's advantages to the newly continental United States, the Great Fire brought St. Louis out of its French and Spanish colonial legacies and squarely within U.S. national history, placing the city at the center of the cultural civil war.

The Great Fire was merely the most recent crisis to shape St. Louis's history. On February 15, 1764, a party of French fur-trading voyageurs alighted on the western bank of the Mississippi River. Finding the current strong, a high bluff rising near the shore, and the confluence point of the Missouri River nearby, Pierre Laclède Liguest, the head trader, and his assistant and adoptive son, thirteen-year-old Auguste Chouteau, ordered their mixed-race group out of the boats. Laclède and Chouteau laid out a town grid and began work on a trading post. But their work had no air of celebration: founding a city in the cold of winter held the chill of imperial collapse.[11]

In 1763, at the conclusion of the Seven Years' War, the French had lost their North American empire. In the first centuries of the European presence in the Americas, French traders had managed profitable relationships with American Indian nations in Canada and the Great Lakes region, with voyageurs extending their reach down into the Illinois country and the Mississippi and Missouri river valleys. French trading posts, Catholic missionary activity, and annual trading rendezvous had provided a profitable exchange for the French empire—and for their American Indian allies, who utilized the French to strengthen their negotiating position with the Spanish to the south and the English to the east. Yet in 1763 the Treaty of Paris transferred the lands of New France to the British, and representatives of King Louis XV revealed that they had given the vast lands of Louisiana (encompassing the western watershed of the Mississippi River and including the crucial port at New Orleans) to Spain a few years earlier, in order to keep control out of British hands. Thus, though the French founders of St. Louis established a refuge for French traders expelled by their English competitors, they operated in land claimed by Spain.[12]

While French farmers downriver scoffed at the new settlement's shortcomings in agriculture—calling it *Pain Court,* or "short bread"—those who lived in early St. Louis saw their occasional shortages as a point of pride. Instead of farming, they busied themselves with commercial and diplomatic affairs among the American Indian nations. The lands north of the new settlement at St. Louis had been the southern reaches of Montreal's fur-trading territory, but the British government disrupted those patterns and agreements. In 1764 Laclède and Chouteau had come upriver instead of down, and reconciled the renewal of American Indian connections with the needs of the French imperial officers in Saint-Domingue, the rich Caribbean colony that served as a hub for French ventures in the Americas after 1763.[13]

Thus, seeking after the lost fur-trading reaches, St. Louis was founded as the northernmost city of the Caribbean and governed as part of the remnant French empire there. Even without the sugar plantations and ocean breezes, St. Louis had its Caribbean traits: African slaves soon arrived, and the complex racial mixing of Native American, French, and African bloodlines that had long held sway from Guadeloupe to New Orleans also became a reality in St. Louis. Illegitimate white children—such as those born to Pierre Laclède and Auguste's mother, the still-married Marie Thérèse Bourgeois Chouteau— also benefited from the disruption of traditional European categories and assumptions. As the Laclède-Chouteau clan and their associates built St. Louis, they profited from the advantages inherent in a colonial outpost: at once tied closely to the economic and political priorities of the empire, it was nevertheless far from its social and religious minders.[14] The Caribbean legacy in St. Louis was one more element that American conquest would erase.

After a period of uncertain fortunes, St. Louis prospered in the renewed fur trade. Reestablishing connections with Native American leaders from Minnesota to Arkansas to Santa Fe—as well as illicitly back into the Illinois country to the east—the city grew, its profits self-sustaining and remote from the concerns of Spanish administrators or French American compatriots.[15]

In the decade after the United States won independence from Britain, France itself was engulfed in a revolution against monarchy. In those tumultuous years, Napoleon Bonaparte busied the nation in wars of empire on the European continent, yet the swapping of American territories continued. In 1800 Napoleon secretly required Spain to sell back the Louisiana territory. Soon after, the former slave François-Dominique Toussaint-Louverture utilized the French Revolution's language of natural rights to lead a successful revolt in Saint-Domingue, wresting the Republic of Haiti from the emperor. As his war efforts faltered, Napoleon again sought to unload New Orleans, St. Louis, and all of the Louisiana Territory. On March 9, 1804, the abstract European geopolitics of the Louisiana Purchase were enacted in St. Louis: in a triple flag ceremony, Spain formally gave the Louisiana Territory back to the French so that Napoleon's representatives could sell it to the United States.[16]

As new U.S. territory, St. Louis was reoriented from the Caribbean South to the American East. Fur trading continued, but when local leaders petitioned for statehood, the fears and questions of the United States about its West came to dominate. Those living in the West had their own questions—they wished for further advantages in the competition with Indian nations for land and resources, and fervently desired to be integrated into the commercial and political patterns of the settled eastern states.[17] Yet, across the Appalachians, the acquisition provoked both elation and alarm. With few thoughts for the indigenous Indian nations already living on the land, President Thomas Jefferson wrote that this new territory would soon be farms, ensuring an "empire for liberty." Whether free men or slaves would work those fields, however, soon drew the new territory into controversy.

In antebellum America, Missouri had been as much talisman as place. The territory's request for admission as a state in 1819 brought the demographic and political realities of the nation's remote western border into focus. Initially concerns about statehood centered on the potential influence left by monarchical, imperial, Old World French practices. In his 1835 *Plea for the West*, Calvinist preacher Lyman Beecher spoke for Cincinnati, insisting that Catholic practices were deeply rooted in the former French territories and that they threatened what he saw as the Protestant promise of the United States. Far more worrisome for national politicians was the status of slavery in the new state. In the fifteen years since 1804, states in the Northwest Territory had joined the Union as free forever from slavery. In the southern backcountry, new states enshrined the right to hold slaves. The balance in the Senate held at eleven states each. Attitudes on slavery's expansion reflected regional economies and societies, and Missouri's petition set the stage for a showdown over slavery in the West. After a tumultuous debate, the western senators Jesse Thomas of Illinois and Henry Clay of Kentucky agreed on a Missouri Compromise that established the state's baseline of 36°30' as the line to forever divide slave and free territory across the United States—with the exception of Missouri, a slave state, jutting north. This was politics at work: the state's geographical and political status was rarely brought to mind, its place still peripheral and its residents still somewhat suspect.[18]

As St. Louis was a French-founded city grappling with American precepts, it is a shame that Alexis de Tocqueville, the Frenchman so interested in the state of democracy in America, did not pass through the city as he traveled across the United States in 1831. Charles Dickens did venture to St. Louis during his tour of America, traveling through in 1842, but he was thoroughly unimpressed. As the novelist wrote in his *American Notes,* Dickens found St. Louis's downtown district—"the old French portion of the town"—filled with "crazy old tenements with blinking casements." Dickens saw a mix of the original French buildings and the new wharves and warehouses under construction by American-born businessmen. Calling them "lop-sided with age," Dickens wrote that the French buildings "hold their heads askew besides, as if they were grimacing in astonishment at the American Improvements." The city held no allure for him: "It is not likely ever to vie, in point of elegance or beauty, with Cincinnati," Dickens concluded.[19] In 1849 the new geography of the United States and the transformation wrought by the Great Fire proved Dickens wrong.

By the 1840s a gradual change in St. Louis was under way, and the city's most nostalgic already found cause to object. In 1841 the city's first permanent structure—the combination house and trading post that Laclède and Chouteau had ordered built in 1764—was targeted for demolition. In response Matthew C. Field, editor of the *St. Louis Reveille,* composed a ballad for the building, asking city leaders to "Touch not a stone! . . . Spare the old house! . . . Yield not your heritage for 'building lots.'" Perhaps the Chouteau family, still dominant in the city they had founded, appreciated the sentiment, but they soon profited from the destruction, as they owned the land under the new, large American-style municipal market building that rose in its place. On balance, city leaders agreed more with Dickens and Joseph

Nicholas Nicollet, a French scientist and early historian of the city. Nicollet wrote in October 1841 that the destruction of the Chouteau House might have been regretted, "did it not make room for more modern buildings, better suited to the commercial extension of the place."[20]

As the old French buildings gave way to new business designs, more chroniclers of St. Louis took an interest in the region's fading French and American Indian past. The Swiss artist John Casper Wild arrived in 1839 and began sketching the Mississippi River valley for a panorama. Wild would dramatically unspool his rolled-up canvas before theater audiences, condensing the weeks-long journey down the river into the marvel of an hour. Combining past and present, Wild sketched the abandoned Fort Chartres in Illinois, included the destroyed Chouteau House, and imagined the St. Louis courthouse complete; he depicted both the wildness of the uninhabited prairie and the bustling streets of St. Louis. Reviewing the sketches as they were published in 1842, the *Missouri Republican,* the long-established local newspaper, praised Wild's work, noting that "in less than five years each [sketch] will be of double value, as showing something of what St. Louis *was.*"[21] Even before the Great Fire, newly arrived St. Louisans had enveloped the city's French and American Indian history in the gauze of nostalgia.

As new development rose around the old French downtown district, something ancient kept getting in the way. St. Louis's founders had chosen a high, flat bluff for their city—flat, that is, except for earthen mounds that dotted the cardinal directions, in line with the sun at solstice and the rising of the moon. Nineteenth-century residents did not know it, but St. Louis sat atop an abandoned city. It was a satellite of the grand Mississippian city of Cahokia, just across the Mississippi, which had once been the largest city in North America before being abandoned for reasons unknown centuries before the arrival of the Europeans. St. Louisans called the largest temple terrace there Monks Mound, because it had been home to a group of Trappist monks when Illinois was under French control, before they abandoned it again. The mysteries of the mounds enthralled St. Louisans, but these funerary and ritual spaces did not receive respectful devotion. Scientists and early archaeologists performed a few investigations, and they debated whether the mounds were natural formations or shaped by human hands—but they never objected as the earthworks were leveled for agriculture and construction.[22]

St. Louisans embraced the nickname of the "Mound City," but they did not understand the sites' true significance. The Big Mound, once at the corner of Broadway and Mound Street, was the largest such structure on the St. Louis side of the river. It first held a flagpole, and then it was made into a beer garden with a shady terrace at its height. The Big Mound revealed its secrets when children scouted its terrain with sticks and shovels, and then when men with picks and crowbars hemmed it in for road expansion and carted away its debris for fill. Over the decades, these processes destroyed St. Louis's most impressive pre-Columbian monument, but no nostalgic local writer composed as much as a poem in memorial.[23]

The American Indian past was obliterated in St. Louis—a situation sadly repeated in many parts of the United States. While changing the French face of the city was an active topic of conversation, the destruction of American Indian ruins went on without debate, a constant fact of life in the first century of St. Louis history. The city's "creative destruction" was physical, cultural, and political, allowing for a new, American St. Louis to emerge on

In a series of more than a dozen images, Thomas M. Easterly recorded the process of the Big Mound's dismantling—and the average citizens who freely discarded of the American Indian relics they found within. Thomas M. Easterly, *Destruction of the Big Mound*, c. 1869. Missouri History Museum, St. Louis.

its own terms, ready to capitalize on the nation's mid-nineteenth-century transformation.[24]

In May 1846 a group of St. Louis traders encountered the cultural civil war. With a wagon train packed for Santa Fe and Chihuahua, the French-speaking entrepreneurs and their American-born business partners were ordered to halt their annual trek at Fort Leavenworth, in a territory not yet called Kansas. The U.S. Army had closed the Santa Fe Trail to mere mercantile travel. The United States deserved more land, President James K. Polk reasoned, and under the banner of Manifest Destiny he saw to its conquest. Santa Fe, northern Mexico, and the entire western half of North America was about to change. As the delayed merchants looked across the lines, they were surprised to see their fellow St. Louisans—boys from French and American families, from their classes at St. Louis University—come down the trail as this self-important military force.[25] Continuing together, the St. Louis traders and soldiers helped usher in a new era of American history.

As the U.S. War with Mexico progressed, even the ideologues of Manifest Destiny were surprised at the ease with which U.S. forces conquered California, forced the Mexican army into retreat, and occupied Mexico City. The newly acquired territories shifted the geography of the United States. St. Louis, once a western outpost, now stood at the center of the newly continental nation, at the gateway to this new West. Though they had not instigated the war, St. Louis's merchants stood to profit from the bounty of the new territories, even before gold was discovered in California.[26]

The momentous change presaged by the U.S. War with Mexico was likely an impetus for the first public celebration of St. Louis's founding, held on February 15, 1847. Ninety-six-year-old Jean Pierre Chouteau, the son of Pierre Laclède and Madame Chouteau, presided over the ceremony, somewhat awkwardly marking the city's eighty-third year. With him were dozens of children and grandchildren, carrying on the family legacy with American-born business partners, many of whom had married into French fur-trading lineages. Before becoming completely American, the founding families wished to commemorate the city's French roots. French patterns and traditions went into eclipse; American patterns and visions would guide St. Louis in the generation to come. While the full implications would not be obvious until after the Great Fire, St. Louis remembered its past while its young men enlisted in creating the nation's continental future.[27]

In the U.S. War with Mexico, Polk had seized half a continent—receiving with the desired land hundreds of thousands of inhabitants, only a few hundred of whom spoke English and only dozens of whom welcomed U.S. conquest. From the first months of the war, Polk's opponents questioned the wisdom of such an acquisition. Presciently, Ralph Waldo Emerson noted in his diary that "Mexico will poison us," while his protégé Henry David Thoreau went to prison to protest the taxes paying for the war. Would slavery be allowed in any or all of this new western territory, most of it south of the Missouri Compromise line? What would it do to the delicate national balance of North and South? How would it increase the power of those cities already established in the West?

On August 6, 1846, first-term Pennsylvania Whig congressman David Wilmot proposed tying the war's settlement funds to a guarantee that none of the new land be open to slavery. Eyeing the Spanish-speaking Catholic residents with the unease once engendered by St. Louis's French, Wilmot wedded his embrace of free-labor ideology to doubts about those of different racial and cultural heritages. Wilmot's proviso rallied Whigs against the national land grab; among its supporters was another first-term congressman, Abraham Lincoln of Illinois. But by February 1848, proslavery Manifest Destiny advocates won the political victory to cap their military conquest. Funding for the Treaty of Guadalupe Hidalgo was approved without the proviso, and Wilmot and Lincoln were among those war opponents who did not stand for reelection.[28]

The questions created by the Mexican Cession intensified the global impact of the 1848 European revolutions. As the United States was taking possession of its new territories and their inhabitants, radicals in Europe tried to remake their continent. In Switzerland, Germany, Austria-Hungary, Italy, Ireland, and France, populist movements arose under banners of nationalism and calls for democracy. The new movements briefly challenged traditional elites but eventually were squashed, co-opted, and delayed, starved by famine, and neutralized by meaningless elections. With the hope for change in their homelands lost and the democratic leaders facing expulsion, thousands decided to seek new opportunities in the New World—whether economic or social options, or, in the case of the Mormon migrants, religious refuge.[29]

When compared to their fellow immigrant groups, the German speakers were particularly prosperous. For decades, those in *Mitteleuropa* had dreamed of Missouri, thanks to the writings of Gottfried Duden. In 1829 Duden detailed the lush vegetation, the burgeoning business opportunities, and what he claimed was extremely mild weather to his German audience. While many came to find his praise overstated and his enthusiasm oversold, German immigrants filled the city of St. Louis, the Missouri countryside around Hermann, cities such as Cincinnati, and settlements from Wisconsin to the Texas hill country. In St. Louis two newspapers and a half-dozen churches catered to the growing population; the *Deutsche Tribüne* directory listed hundreds of businesses. As diehard free-labor advocates, most German immigrants condemned slave labor as an unfair advantage to their competitors. Though the Germans opposed slavery, they were not always sympathetic to rights for African Americans, preferring colonization to Africa or South America over coexistence and racial equality.[30]

In the early months of 1849, the global turmoil of 1848 rippled onto St. Louis's shores. Crowded together and exhausted from travel, the immigrants were easy prey for cholera, an annual threat along the rivers. When the suffering became epidemic in early 1849, St. Louis leaders quarantined the new immigrants. The prosperous port came to a standstill. Merchants sent their families away from the city, while ship captains—like the crew of the *White Cloud*—repaired their steamboats and applied new paint, waiting for an uptick in business.[31] But then on the night of May 17, 1849, the winds and the still-wet paint engendered the flames. The global wave of changes, from California to Prussia, crested just as St. Louis's transformation from a French-colonial fur-trading depot to a wide-ranging mercantile center was complete. The Great Fire became a rallying point, conquering the fear of disease and opening an era of new opportunity in St. Louis.

The morning light of May 18, 1849, revealed the Great Fire's full impact. In the downtown warehouses, wooden floors had burned away, while bricks had cracked and crumbled in the heat. Only the salvaged cathedral and the not-yet-completed courthouse gave any sense of hope, as the church spire broke the desolate horizon. Along with the firemen, the city's Unitarian minister, William Greenleaf Eliot, had been up all night, shuttling cholera patients from downtown out into the neighborhoods. "Our streets [were] like the ruins of Pompeii," Eliot later recalled, "and the people were amazed at the greatness of their loss."[32]

One need not imagine the desolation Eliot described, because its image remains. Along with the era's profound political and social changes, new technologies were ready to change how the world was recorded and remembered. On the morning after the fire Thomas M. Easterly, the city's first professional daguerreotypist, set out to record the ruined details. Over the decades Easterly recorded images of the Big Mound as it eroded toward oblivion; on the morning after the Great Fire, its destruction seemed dwarfed by the city's wreckage, prostrate in full sunlight, the minutiae articulated by the daguerreotype's long exposure.[33]

At first the sense of devastation was immediate and consuming. In the official investigation report, issued two weeks after the fire, the losses were tallied: fifteen square blocks destroyed and twenty-three steamers burned up and sunk. At least 310 businesses and 430 houses were lost, the total more than $3 million in damage. Newspapers from New Orleans to New York printed the lists of affected business, but others had not waited for the accounting to bemoan the disaster: "St. Louis will be prostrated, and its commercial energies paralyzed for years to come," predicted the *Louisville Courier*. The city of Pittsburgh sent $1,000 for the relief of St. Louis, unsure how terrible the costs; fellow steamboaters in Cincinnati also gathered funds.[34]

In the disruptions of the Great Fire, thousands lost their jobs when their places of employment were destroyed. Hundreds became homeless. While large businesses could often establish new operations, the small, informal traders and workers along the waterfront lost their routines and their small accumulations of credit or profit. Before cholera slowed business and the Great Fire halted it, every day on the levees saw "negro roustabouts rushing back and forth . . . a husky second mate, standing by with club in his hand, making the air blue with profanity; second clerks reviling late comers; and captain on forward deck ringing the bell," as Eliot's son later recalled. Among St. Louis's slaves, some lost their livelihood in the Great Fire—while others took the opportunity of confusion to flee across the river and begin a journey into freedom.[35]

The Great Fire affected all businesses. For months afterward, James Green, editor of the city directory, provided updated listings. Reconstructions of the two hardest-hit blocks, at the northern and southern ends of the downtown district, reveal the disparate effects of the Great Fire's damage. North of Market Street, the fire burned mercantile warehouses and heavy manufacturing businesses but affected few residences. For example, the block bounded by Main, Chestnut, Second, and Pine streets, which lost thirty-two buildings, had housed four attorneys' offices, a doctor, two drugstores, two drapers, two shoemakers, an auctioneer, a wholesale merchant, and "furniture ware-rooms." Among the addressees were four men listed as clerks (indicating four businesses prosperous enough to employ them) and at least five of the proprietors owning homes in the posh western section of town. Two blocks farther north, on Locust Street, some the city's most valuable properties were held: the slaves in Lynch's Slave Pen, crowded by the hundreds, sold by the thousands. Though a delicate maneuver, Bernard Lynch was sure to evacuate his property carefully, biding his time for the river trade to be reestablished, so that his profits could again be made in Memphis and New Orleans. Three months later, when Green published a definitive new city directory, the northern blocks had already been rebuilt "with tenements . . . good, and ornamental to that part of the city."[36]

In the southern part of the burnt district, workmen's stores were interspersed with family residences. The most damaged block in the city was in the southern section, bounded by Main, Myrtle, Second, and Elm streets, where thirty-seven buildings were destroyed. Six here listed their occupation simply as "laborer," while five were carpenters, coopers, or sawyers, four were tailors, and three worked the river. In a further indication of class status, there were no clerks or separate dwellings listed, but six lived "at rear," three upstairs, and two were listed as boarders.

The fire reached the downriver southern blocks later, after the city's fire-fighting equipment was already in use. Thus the southern district's residents, already a poorer class, suffered disproportionate losses. Even in the city directory, Green felt compelled to describe how the "ample means" of those in the northern blocks "enabled them to pay dray and carmen any price asked," while those "of more humble means, below Walnut, were thus deprived." The Deutsche Tribüne related the story of a man who obtained a dray and saved his belongings but his coattails were burned—such was the margin of escape. In this neighborhood, the Trinity German Evangelical Lutheran Church recorded more than $17,000 in losses for its immigrant members and began a special collection for the community's uninsured. The fire's dislocations, especially for working-class St. Louisans like the former residents of the southern district, were often long-lasting.[37]

Despite the evidence of loss and destruction, however, St. Louis's newspapers rejected the sympathy of editors in other cities, reading the laments as crocodile tears for a resurgent urban rival. Although the Deutsche Tribüne, the Missouri Republican, the St. Louis Reveille, and the People's Organ had lost their offices, all were back in production in less than a week, filling their columns with defiant optimism. The mix of reporting and bravado on the pages of the *Missouri Republican* was typical: "The fire, it is true, produced heavy losses, and much inconvenience," the editors admitted, "but it has not destroyed the city, neither has it checked the enterprise or energy of our merchants and manufacturers." Looking ahead to the opportunities the destruction offered, the *Republican* declared that St. Louis "will rise, Phoenix-like, from her ashes."[38] The speed with which the city was able to fulfill that promise brought it to the center of the national economy, politics, and culture. The new business district would be the setting for St. Louis leaders to make their case for the strength of the West to soon overshadow the older North and South. The city's leaders gladly placed themselves at the center of the coming conflict.

On the prosperous northern blocks, thoughts of recovery quickly grew into a full program for desired improvements. The ruined French-colonial buildings should be replaced with a state-of-the-art commercial district, property owners reasoned, to serve not only St. Louis but the Mississippi River valley, the overland trails to the West, and hence the entire nation. Owners petitioned the city, demanding an expanded levee, with easier entry into new, larger warehouses. Sunken steamboats should be raised, the city's entrepreneurs urged, the shipping channels dredged, drainage at intersections improved, and streets widened. Only fireproof buildings should be erected—with no lumberyard allowed in the district to kindle another fire. The local newspapers, regardless of their underlying political disagreements, cheered on the economic revival. The *Reveille* called for "immediate improvement on a liberal and noble scale" five days after the fire; another week later the *Republican* wrote, "We have already recovered from the first stunning blow."[39]

In May 1849 Frances Sublette was still acclimating to the life of a trader's wife when the Great Fire occurred. As she wrote her husband Solomon on May 21, she noted their first wedding anniversary, with "you in Mexico and I in St. Louis," and shared the awful news of the fire. Frances thought she was pregnant and then worried at any symptom that might be cholera; with her husband away half the year, she also struggled to manage the family real estate and the family slaves, bought on many occasions from Lynch's Slave Pen. The Sublettes' insurance papers had been lost when the fire burned down their trading house, Sublette & Campbell. But it left the Sublettes with an unexpected asset: the bare downtown block was now worth more than when it contained the older, French-style building. With the help of Micajah Tarver, a business associate of the firm, Frances Sublette sold the property for a $7,000 profit, enough to pay off business and family debts. A few months later she could admit how "Saint Louis commences looking like itself again"—a reflection of older prosperity in the mirror of a new commercial landscape.[40]

Insurance payments were essential to St. Louis's renaissance. In their first articles, St. Louis newspapers assured outside investors that the city's business risks were mostly secured. One contemporary account estimated that $2.5 million in insurance payments were made, covering the vast majority of the losses. As the cholera epidemic ebbed, skilled and unskilled workers streamed into the city to participate in the boom. Sublette's associate Tarver could not contain his sense of glee as the Great Fire produced "a grand speculation." As "most of the real estate belongs to the rich men of the city," Tarver concluded, "there were but few poor people who lost any thing." While his summary ignored the suffering in the southern sections of the city, Tarver's confidence was reflected throughout St. Louis's business community. And the local boosters were gaining a national audience: the *New York Herald* agreed that "excepting New York, St. Louis has the elements of recovering from such a disaster to a greater extent, perhaps, than any other city in the Union."[41]

Mann Butler, a lawyer, historian, and former university president, was the primary investigator of the fire for insurers. Tallying the losses, he nevertheless felt drawn to historic parallels and the sense of national opportunity. Citing the Great Fire of London in 1666, "which at once freed it from plague and from the embarrassment of crowded buildings," Butler hoped the St. Louis fire could end the cholera epidemic as well as reinvigorate the city. "American energy never tires," Butler wrote—though he then qualified the statement, suggesting, "I had better say the energy of freemen, confident in the protection of Almighty Providence." Butler cited the ingenious dams of Holland, where the Puritans had first sought refuge, and then the success of American settlements in New England. Other commentators joined the chorus to stress the nationalistic differences between the older French-built environment and the new American construction and its possibilities. Butler lived in what he still saw as a "western wild," but he predicted it could succeed like the first settlements of the Northeast—a Yankee prejudice in the multicultural, multi-regional city, but one that found increased local influence.[42]

The Great Fire offered St. Louis a commercial rejuvenation but also a cultural refounding. The slow destruction of the American Indian mounds and the smoldering ruins of the French-built environment in St. Louis were paved over by a new American foundation. In 1848 and 1849, as the nation expanded into new western territories and welcomed hundreds of thousands of European immigrants, many river cities found their prospects waylaid by the cholera crisis, yet St. Louis entrepreneurs used their Great Fire to both obliterate the past and obscure present tragedy. All fortunes would derive from the new downtown district. All other narratives of St. Louis's origins and identity were replaced with the Great Fire.[43]

By the end of 1849, local observers projected that all traces of the fire would be obliterated before the start of 1851. Construction continued at a pace "unprecedented in the history of any city in the Union," declared the *Review of the Trade and Commerce*. Otis Adams, a Massachusetts resident traveling through St. Louis in October 1849, declared that "it is now universally acknowledged that the 'Mound City' . . . must eventually become the New York of the West." The editors of the *Reveille* proclaimed the rebuilding a battle for the new shape of the United States, and that foresight now would be "an example of moral courage as noble as any example of physical courage ever exhibited by the soldier on the field of battle."[44] Less than a year after the U.S. Army had fought its way to Mexico City and months since European armies had shot into the crowds of democratic protesters, such language was a high call to action indeed. With its new commercial district nearing completion, St. Louis would be ready to control the path of Manifest Destiny, to champion the needs of the West in the newly expanded nation.

As they rejoiced at the pace of rebuilding, St. Louisans celebrated by watching it burn again on paper. Three months after the fire, two talented German immigrants, the engravers Julius Hutawa and Leopold Gast, captured both the drama of the Great Fire and the confidence in St. Louis's refounding. Their hand-colored broadside displayed the fire in progress as seen from the Illinois shore. As the smoke billowed in perfect, beautiful spirals, Gast's image displayed the fire but showcased its survivors. The cathedral, the courthouse, and the iron-framed city market buildings all appear, standing through the flames. Confronting the conflagration again, the editors of the

Missouri Republican urged citizens to purchase the imprint "for future reference," as "this view of the city, we predict, will be esteemed of great value in future years."[45]

Hutawa and Gast preserved the Great Fire as a moment of transformation. By including a street grid of the burnt district, they provided a level of detail that allowed purchasers to point out exactly where they lived or worked, and where the fire reached. The broadsheet oriented the lived experience of the fire to the abstract blocks, and outlined the fire's footprint as the refounding began. So successful was the image that New York engraver Nathaniel Currier created a derivative version the same year. And as late as 1857 another itinerant artist, Henry Lewis, was still reproducing the spectacle of St. Louis's Great Fire in his studio back across the ocean in Düsseldorf. Contrasted with

This engraving became an important memento of the Great Fire, enabling survivors to celebrate their city's re-founding. Julius Hutawa and Leopold Gast, *View of the City of St. Louis, Mo. The Great Fire,* August 1849. Missouri History Museum, St. Louis.

Easterly's first daguerreotype of the ruins, these images demonstrate the contrast and force of vision used to remove the French and American Indian past and celebrate the dramatic emergence of an American St. Louis.[46]

"The work of rebuilding began before the ruins were cold," the minister William Greenleaf Eliot later recalled. "To the experience of that fateful year we owe the fact that St. Louis is now one of the most substantially built cities of the United States."[47] St. Louis stood ready for the commercial, political, and cultural tasks at hand. The ideology of Manifest Destiny had gained vast new territories for the United States. Now patterns for integrating and profiting from that land were needed, whether for slave society or free labor. The rebuilt St. Louis should be the most important city of the West, promoters urged, guiding this new phase in the history of the nation. Despite French origins and older conflicts over statehood, Missouri should be the new keystone state, they argued, a symbol of national compromise and harmony ending the disagreements between North, South, and West. No one was more confident of these hopes than the senior U.S. senator from Missouri, St. Louis resident Thomas Hart Benton. And no one suffered more from its failures.

2

Thomas Hart Benton's Failed Compromise

> Our Atlantic and Pacific coasts will be competitors for the seat of that empire. Both will look to the [Mississippi River] valley for succor.... Occupying the position of neutrals in this Oceanic contest, accessible to both of the rival parties, caressed by both, dependent on neither, we may dictate our terms.
>
> —Josiah Dent, *Lecture on the Mississippi Valley, Delivered before the St. Louis Mercantile Library Association on the 18th February, 1853.*

On a mid-November evening in 1850, Missouri Senator Thomas Hart Benton rose to address the St. Louis Mercantile Library Association. Standing in Wyman's Hall, the gaslit concert auditorium just across from the courthouse and only blocks from the burnt district, Benton laid out his vision for "The Progress of the Age." In his characteristically soaring rhetoric, Benton united the bright future he envisioned for the newly expanded United States and the place for St. Louis as its pivotal political center. In "this middle year of the nineteenth century," as Americans took stock of their half century of growth and accomplishments, "the world was never so enlightened . . . never before so humane, social, and benevolent," Benton declared. Despite the worldwide revolutions and disruptions in 1848, Benton insisted that "wars were never less frequent" and "national, religious, and social prejudices were never so subdued."[1]

Speaking knowingly to his audience, Benton avowed, "This is to be the theatre of the St. Louis merchant—a city such as this will be, not only fifty, but five hundred, and thousands of years hence—an american territory which can neither be diminished nor divided," with "connexions over the globe." The past was urban prologue: "In the year *One* of the century," Benton recounted, St. Louis was "a small village; in the year *Fifty* of the century, a great city." St. Louis would be the very "illustration of the Progress of the Age," Benton told the audience of city leaders, exceeding their own confident and rosy projections for the accumulation of economic, political, and cultural power in the city. In a final flourish, Benton concluded that the St. Louis Mercantile Library would be there to see it—"destined, I hope, to live long, to flourish continually, and to realize the hopes of its founders, and of my own cherished anticipations."[2]

The eight hundred men and women of St. Louis's leading citizens who had heard the visionary predictions of their senator rose to cheer his vision. The speech was astonishing; as the *St. Louis Daily Union* wrote, its "striking" views "reflected credit even on Senator Benton, great as his ability for public speaking is already known to be." Given the speech's eloquence, the importance of their speaker, and the striking nature of his message, the library's board of directors quickly asked Benton for a preservation copy. As a U.S. senator from Missouri, Benton was a busy man, traveling back and forth from Washington and plotting the nation's future. Normally he would have had no time even for this most solicitous request. Yet the manuscript arrived just five months later, carefully lined and written in a large, beautifully clear hand. By spring 1851 Benton found himself, for the first time in thirty years, out of office, without obvious prospects.[3]

The progress of the United States in the first half of the nineteenth century was a truly astounding transformation, whether measured in the rapid population growth, the revolutionary industrial advances, the admission of a dozen new states, or the millions of acres purchased, conquered, or otherwise seized for the nation. Adapting to new circumstances, newly democratized party politics was built upon the confluence of new communication technologies, differentiating regional economies, and expanded white male suffrage. Elections moved from knowing affirmation among elite peers to an effort to market hard drinking, Indian fighting, and humble origins to those once dismissed as mere democratic rabble. Andrew Jackson is often given singular credit for these momentous changes, but longtime senators of the era—John C. Calhoun of South Carolina; Henry Clay of Kentucky; Daniel Webster and John Quincy Adams, opponents from Massachusetts; and Benton—were as influential in shaping the nation's political program in this era. While Webster, Clay, and Calhoun have been celebrated as "the Great Triumvirate" in the era's politics, and Adams singled out as the era's most insightful political leader, Benton has faded from view because of the unique conflict that developed between Benton, a Democrat, and the Democratic Party in Missouri.[4]

Thomas Hart Benton had begun his career as an erstwhile ally of Andrew Jackson, from the battlefield to the political scene. Born in Orange County, North Carolina, in 1782, Benton followed his father into law school and in managing the family estate. Attracted by the opportunities for better land farther west, Benton acquired land near Nashville, finished his law training, and was elected a state senator. During the War of 1812, Benton served as aide-de-camp for Jackson, Tennessee's preeminent political and military leader, earning Benton his oft-used title of colonel. After the war Benton felt constrained by Jackson's control of Tennessee politics—and a perceived insult between two men with prickly personalities led to a crisis: in 1815 Benton assaulted Jackson and narrowly avoided getting shot.[5]

That year Benton moved west again to St. Louis and took up employment as a political newspaper editor. Espousing ideas similar to those Jackson had formulated and advocating for Missouri statehood, Benton turned his knack for understanding voter sentiment and an interest in regional advancement into a platform for seeking political office. Once again the path was bloodied by violence: in 1817 Benton and Charles Lucas, the rival newspaper editor and scion of a long-established local family, engaged in a duel in which Benton shot and killed Lucas. Yet these events did not hurt Benton's political prospects; to observers at the time, Benton's violent past merely testified to the strength by which he held his convictions. Decades later the itinerant Swedish writer Frederika Bremer merged Benton's history of duels with his political techniques, referring to one legislative battle with Henry Clay as "a single combat between the lion of Kentucky and the hawk of Missouri." Benton's first political success was in ushering his new home into the Union.[6]

For two years Missouri's 1819 petition roiled Congress. The Founders still alive to observe the debates reflected on the proceedings with a growing sense of dread. "I had for a long time ceased to read the newspapers or pay any attention to public affairs," Thomas Jefferson postured, honing his image as a simple gentleman farmer ensconced at Monticello, "but this momentous question, like a fire bell in the night, awakened and filled me with terror." Jefferson's onetime rival and now fervent correspondent, John Adams, similarly felt that the slavery question "hangs like a Cloud over my imagination."[7]

The new generation of political leaders became the Great Compromisers by solving the quandary, making Missouri's baseline, at a latitude of 36°30', the dividing line between slave territory and free, with only Missouri itself the exceptional state in the northwest of the nation. Henry Clay engineered an agreement with John C. Calhoun, representing southern interests, and Daniel Webster, for New England, while the delegate-turned-senator of the territory, Thomas Hart Benton, ensured its acceptance with the Missouri merchants and landholders. With the Missouri Compromise in 1821, the state symbolized the stability of an America learning to evolve half-slave and half-free.[8]

In the ensuing decades, the Missouri Compromise was celebrated as an important marker of union, a success at continuing the radical experiment of the United States. As the founding generation passed away, the Great Compromisers rose in prominence. In an emergent culture of celebrity, the men themselves became symbols of the greatness of American democracy, to be toasted and celebrated, mobbed with adoration and commemorated along with the Founders. The compromise held for twenty-five years—a third of the history of the young nation.[9] Yet the Mexican Cession was far too large a territory to be easily digested under these old principles.

Thomas Hart Benton was a savvy and pragmatic politician who realized both the potential and peril of the Mexican Cession for his hold on power. In a continental United States, Missouri would be the new keystone state, bridging the customs, politics, and economy of the established states and the uncertainties of the new territory. Benton had made his name as a hard-money advocate, seeing the interests of the common man of Jackson's Democratic Party in bullion, access to homesteading land, and a growing but not overextended United States, with rights of honest labor protected alongside those of slaveholding.

In the run-up to expansion, President Polk and others claimed the Jacksonian mantle for a vast extension of territory, demanding Oregon lands to the 54°40' line and considering whether to annex all of Mexico and negotiate the purchase of Cuba. Yet Benton began to doubt the wisdom of an unchecked expansion of slavery. He became convinced that the promise of the new territories could be assured only by government action—not to ensure the spread of slavery, but to finance access along a transcontinental railroad.

"I was born to the inheritance of slaves," Benton freely admitted; he maintained house slaves in St. Louis and on the estate his wife had inherited in Virginia. Benton did not dispute the right to hold slaves, though his years in St. Louis, amid the city's entrepreneurial rebirth, led him to question the wisdom of slavery as an investment in the newly continental nation. While Andrew Jackson and his other longtime allies in the South were ever more vocal in their support of slavery, Benton found comfort in the actions of the nation's Founders, stating that his desire to limit the spread of slavery reflected the ideas of Jefferson.[10]

Though in previous decades Benton had opposed national railroad plans as government meddling and unnecessary competition for St. Louis's riverboats, with the new government lands of the Mexican Cession ready to benefit his constituents, Benton promptly changed course. In February 1849, before statehood petitions and acts for territorial organization for the Mexican Cession were ready, Benton introduced legislation to fund a transcontinental railroad on government bonds. In the wake of the Great Fire, Benton supported the call for a national railroad convention in the city, to demonstrate its vitality and secure its place in the changed national circumstances.[11]

Benton's political transformation was both tactical and heartfelt, both piecemeal and absolute. Too savvy a politician to announce his intentions before gauging public sentiment, Benton was a dealmaker, a compromiser. At the moment of continental expansion, Benton sought to harness the power of Manifest Destiny, to empower the West and unite the regional agendas of his fellow lawmakers, to find the ground for compromise that would also be advantageous to his constituents in St. Louis and the rest of Missouri. Benton saw in the transcontinental railroad line a full political program: the necessary centrality of St. Louis; the guarantee of national stability and regional compromise, and then a new era in world peace.[12] Yet Benton's opponents, local and national, saw such changed positions as a weakness—not the road to a lasting national compromise but a path to southern ascendency.

As a long-serving politician with a known penchant for indulging his temper, Benton already had a raft of enemies, even before his political evolution. When Benton began to speak about limiting slavery, his opponents in the newspapers were suspicious of his motives and biting in their criticism. The *Missouri Republican,* a Whig-leaning newspaper that had opposed Benton since the days when he edited the competing *Enquirer,* saw Benton's growing reticence as a sign of national ambitions. "Ever since he became a candidate *in utero* for the Presidency," the editors claimed, Benton had resolved neither to appear locally nor to speak to unfriendly audiences. They wrote that any talk of abolition, gradual emancipation, or colonization was antithetical to Missouri's interests, as it would "engender discord, arraying . . . county and State against town and city." As the editors in St. Louis realized, if urban support for slavery eroded, the very basis for the state's political parties would be at risk.[13]

In the months after the Mexican Cession, the political parties of Missouri splintered, a harbinger of national changes to come. Alongside the local Whig Party, advocating the internal improvements and tariffs of Henry Clay's American System, once there had been a united Missouri Democratic Party, ranging from the studied, lawyerly compromises favored by Benton and his St. Louis allies to the rougher and more raw-edged politics of the western frontier of the state, and the plantation owners in Boon's Lick, the region of central Missouri later to be nicknamed "Little Dixie." Yet after 1848 many of the outstate Democrats looked to John C. Calhoun rather than Benton, embracing fiery arguments that any aid to free white labor or any compromise on the future extension of slavery endangered the enshrined property rights of slaveholders. When Benton and his moderate allies called this an ultimatum that would lead to disunion, the Calhounites returned the charge: Calhoun himself called them "traitors to our cause, who hope to conceal their treason by the cry of disunion."[14]

In March 1849 laws authored by Calhounite Claiborne Fox Jackson passed the Missouri legislature, declaring that only a special convention of the people could set a new course on the legality of slavery. This early pronouncement of popular sovereignty was squarely aimed at Benton. Supporters of these Jackson Resolutions knew Benton opposed such local efforts as antithetical to the kind of national compromise he sought, and hence tried to entrap their senator into condemning his own electorate. As predicted, Benton denounced the resolutions, calling them "fundamentally wrong" in speeches around the state. Yet after the first flush of rhetoric, Benton pledged to obey his constituents' will and present the resolutions to the Senate—though not to support them.[15]

Calhoun was ecstatic: "Benton has fanned his doom," he wrote to his Missouri supporters, and newspapers aligned with the Calhounites began to actively identify themselves as "anti-Benton Democrats," opposed to their most senior party member. So extreme was the new measure, the *Republican* felt it worth defending its old nemesis, protesting that the Jackson Resolutions threatened "to connect Missouri with any effort to dissolve the Union," and hence Benton was in the right. Benton planned visits to St. Louis regularly, seeking new allies for what he knew would be a tough reelection campaign in his splintering party.[16]

Faced with discord over slavery, Benton trumpeted ever louder his belief that the transcontinental railroad would make all existing patterns of labor and land use obsolete. In October 1849, just five months after the Great Fire, Benton brought the national questions of the transcontinental railroad into the divisive politics of St. Louis. As the convention of nearly nine hundred assembled in the rotunda of the courthouse, delegations from thirteen states came to agree on the value of a transcontinental railroad—and to argue about which route was best.

As early as 1843, when Chinese ports had been officially opened to Americans, New York trade magnate Asa Whitney had begun advocating for a railroad west, suggesting that a connection be built between the existing commercial network of the Erie Canal and Great Lakes and the Anglo-American territories around Puget Sound. In the same years, Benton's forcefully opinionated teenage daughter Jessie had fallen in love with a young army officer, John C. Frémont, while Frémont was in Washington to write up the report of his latest western exploration and to seek funding for another. Seeing a marriage of motives as well as personalities, Benton commissioned Frémont to map the passes through the Rockies, west from St. Louis to the San Francisco Bay.[17]

After the Mexican Cession, when such plans seemed far more likely to succeed, southern interests loudly offered the alternative of shipping passengers and goods from New Orleans to an isthmus route across present-day Nicaragua or Panama, or creating a land route from New Orleans to San Diego or from Memphis to California's Monterey Bay. Stephen A. Douglas, the junior senator from Illinois, was the second-most powerful advocate at the St. Louis convention, though Missouri interests initially maneuvered him into a parliamentary role. Douglas advocated his own kind of compromise, suggesting that federal funding reach from San Francisco to Council Bluffs, Iowa, and that local interests could then build branches from there to St. Louis, Memphis, or to his constituents, in the still-small city of Chicago.[18]

The map accompanying Whitney's promotional pamphlet showed a criss-cross of possibilities for the transcontinental railroad, with possible hubs in Sandusky, Ohio, and St. Joseph, Michigan, and two dozen other cities, large and small. Driven by local and sectional interests, the effort seemed too fragmented to succeed; Memphis even had a rival railroad convention that would follow closely after the one held in St. Louis, and some of the southern delegates had only technically been credentialed to gather there.[19] As the sectional questions about integrating the Mexican Cession swirled in Washington, Benton saw the same forces at work in the railroad planning—and the same solution, a transcontinental railroad west from St. Louis, as the answer to both.

After "the most rapturous applause," Benton began his speech with a move intended to highlight his unique status as expert on the West, gained from

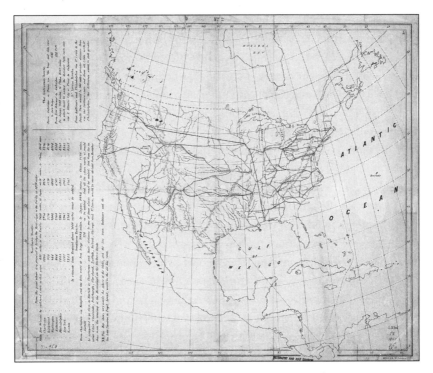

Asa Whitney's map imagined a number of possible routes and termini for the transcontinental railroad. Asa Whitney, Railroad Route to Santa Fe and San Diego; the central route through South Pass and on to San Francisco and "Puget's Sound," and connecting railroads east of the Mississippi, 1849. Library of Congress.

familial ties as well as political service. As he spoke, Benton pulled out a letter from Frémont and read his latest dispatches from the Rocky Mountains. Benton outlined a route touching the northern edge of the New Mexican settlements, the southern end of the Mormon settlements, and the potential for a branch line to Oregon, playing to the local fur traders by assuring that his plan reflected the geography as "all the men of the mountains knew it." In his element, Benton spoke to a local crowd about an issue of national importance, demonstrating his political acumen and his power of showmanship. Yet while the railroad route was important, its consequences for the nation were what truly mattered, Benton argued.[20]

"Discarding all sectional and all local considerations, Mr. B. was for a national road in character, as well as in name," the *Missouri Republican* reported; "national in its location, by being central—national in its construction, being made by the nation—national in its title, by belonging to the nation—national in its use, by being used by the people free of tax." Such a road, Benton argued, could be "a band of Iron, hooping and binding the States together east and west . . . a cement of union north and south." The railroad could solve the conflict between slaveholders and free laborers, advocates of expansion and established interests, because its lines would unite their people in commerce, and hence harmonize their politics and foment a truly national culture.[21]

With pitch and pace rising, Benton moved beyond the national frame to global, millennial terms. Just as "God had placed the Father of Floods," the Mississippi, at the center of the continent, Benton said, "so let it be with this great road—in the middle of the Union!" Providential in its design, Benton argued, the proposed road would allow all to "feel again, as their fathers did in the time of the revolution," united in work that was "the consummation of Washington's plan." According to the reports, the response was electric, and "the cheering immense"—but Benton's speech held one last rhetorical gem.[22]

"We live in extraordinary times," Benton intoned, "and are called upon to elevate ourselves to the grandeur of the occasion." The railroad would not only unite the country, not only fulfill the vision of the Founders. It would complete the entire history of the New World. "Three and a half centuries ago, the great Columbus . . . departed from Europe to arrive in the East by going to the West. Now," Benton revealed, "mechanical genius enables his great design to be fulfilled," the dreams of a king to be completed by a republic. In his "grand conclusion," Benton offered his final flair: the railroad—completed, harmonized, globally successful—"shall be adorned with its crowning honor, the colossal statue of the great Columbus . . . hewn from the granite mass of a peak of the Rocky Mountains . . . Pointing with outstretched arm to the western horizon, and saying to the flying passenger, there is the East! there is India!"[23]

Immense cheering, an indelible image, rhetorical acclaim—the railroad speech had been all Benton could have hoped. His oratory that night echoed across the nation's newspapers, providing a spotlight for the railroad effort. It was an era of golden phrases, and his Romantic, emotional appeals infused policy positions with a drama of government, joining with the speeches of Webster, Clay, and Calhoun to weave the United States together—and potentially, to tear the Union apart. As Elias Lyman Magoon declared in his book *Living Orators of America* that same year, "We live in an age which demands the services of men as industrious, resolute, and magnanimous as Mr. Benton." Yet in the light of day, the political realities returned; delegates returned to their squabbles over routes and adjourned with a resolution simply to convene again.[24]

As St. Louis rebuilt in the final months of 1849, Benton's railroad speech was again overshadowed by talk of slavery expansion. "[Benton's] friends in the city think the people will sustain him. His enemies are sure that he will be crushed," Otis Adams wrote to his Massachusetts friends, in the same letter where he predicted the future of St. Louis as the New York of the West. "A few months will probably determine," he concluded.[25] With the state election less than a year away, Benton returned to Washington, hoping to champion his railroad plan as a solution to the growing stalemate between the politics of slavery expansion and the vision for embracing the new western territories.

How should the Mexican Cession be integrated into the United States? How many territories did it encompass? Were the region's residents fit for citizenship? Where were the boundaries of Texas? On what terms could the prosperous new California territory be admitted to statehood? Should the Missouri Compromise line be extended farther west, or was there another way to determine the status of slavery in the new territories? What would be the fate of slavery in these thousands of acres? These questions, impossibly broad, echoed in the halls of Congress as the members gathered for the first session of 1850, with an election looming and the Great Compromisers gathered for the last time.

Democrats and Whigs, regional spokesmen and party leaders, attacked these questions with the fervor that had brought renown to the Senate. The sessions began with longtime legislative leader Henry Clay introducing a proposed compromise, balancing the perceived benefits for Whigs and Democrats, and those in the North, South, and West. In Clay's plan, California's statehood petition would be approved, and it would enter as a free state; Texas would be compensated $10 million for giving up claims on its western and northwestern borders; the lands between California and Texas would be organized as two territories, Utah and New Mexico, without mention of the status of slavery there; the slave trade would be abolished in the District of Columbia; enforcement of the Fugitive Slave Law would be tightened; and the list went on, with encouragements for Whigs seeking higher tariffs, and slaveholders wishing for an explicit rejection of federal interference in interstate slave trading.[26]

Clay's plan had its distasteful elements for all sides. For those in the North who opposed slavery, finding federal officers compelled to enforce the Fugitive Slave Law, and allowing for the possibility of slavery in the Utah Territory, a vast expanse above the Missouri Compromise line, were difficult measures to stomach. For slaveholders in the South, losing potential slave territory in the transfer of land from Texas to New Mexico, and the admission of a free California and having the D.C. slave markets closed, were alarming restrictions of their perceived property rights. Clay spoke boldly for the necessity of passing legislation for the good not of one region or party, but the nation; the western Democrat Stephen Douglas of Illinois joined the older statesman in speaking in the language of union.

Not just the principle of compromise, but the Great Compromisers themselves were faltering: John C. Calhoun, dying of tuberculosis, had to be carried into the Senate chamber, and his March 4 speech was read by others. Still, Calhoun's words were the most bitter, an uncompromising rejection of any restraint on the slaveholders' property. Missouri's other senator, David Rice Atchison, supported Calhoun's denunciation, linked as he was to the slaveholding politicians of central Missouri and their alignment with the South. On the seventh of March, 1850, the aged Massachusetts Whig Daniel Webster announced his anguished decision to support the bill, arguing that the endurance of the Union was paramount, even if it necessitated expanding the power of slaveholders.[27] In the North–South divide of eastern politics—in the standoff between Calhoun and Webster—Webster had blinked.

When his turn came, Thomas Hart Benton also rose in protest, speaking against the planned legislation. His fellow Great Compromisers had faltered, Benton argued, for the proposed bill was a false compromise, a political calculation without truly national support that would only sow more conflict.[28]

Envisioning himself as the last faithful friend of the West and as the last true Jacksonian Democrat, Benton turned to the unifying vision of the transcontinental railroad, of the stability of the Missouri Compromise's geographic dividing line to aid the West and to quell the slavery debate between North and South. Drawing again on his decades of experience in the new territories, Benton produced Mexican law books on the floor of the Senate and read how slavery had already been abolished in these territories, and the American treaties had promised to maintain these citizens' rights, in this case to free labor. As he would do again in the fall campaign, Benton argued the time spent on this complex bill delayed the necessary attention to California land-title resolution, harbor bills, and the railroad, measures that would truly improve the new lands. Instead of innovation, he claimed, Clay and Douglas offered a mixture of existing ingredients—resulting in a concoction as dubious and haphazard in its effects as patent medicine.[29]

Despite the humor, Benton sensed that his arguments were being ignored. He then took a parliamentary tack, attempting to stop the compromise with amendments and procedural votes. When Benton was ruled out of order by the presiding officer of the Senate, Vice President Millard Fillmore, the two men nearly came to blows; Senator Henry S. Foote of Mississippi worsened the fray by turning a gun on Benton, at which point the three were finally separated and tempers calmed. After Zachary Taylor's sudden death sent Fillmore to the White House, the new President continued to press the alliance of Webster, Clay, and Douglas to produce a compromise; when the effort for a vote on a comprehensive omnibus bill faltered, Senator Douglas provided the solution, allowing each measure to be voted on separately, finding its own regional and factional coalition without truly forming a national consensus.[30] Thus the Compromise of 1850 was effected.

Thomas Hart Benton had voted the agenda of the West: admitting California, organizing Utah and New Mexico without a firm policy on slavery, and opposing concessions to Texas for relinquishing its grandiose land claims. Benton voted to end the slave trade in the nation's capital and he abstained from the vote on the Fugitive Slave Law, demonstrating his continuing doubts about that institution. Either prescient, stubborn, or some mixture of the two, Benton charged that the compromise would not hold. No such deal, he said later, could work if it did not "make anybody President."[31]

Having failed to convince the Senate that a transcontinental railroad would bind the nation better than the expansion of bonded labor, Benton prepared to return to St. Louis for the election season, aware that his job was on the line. Yet Benton remained firm. As he repeated over and over, he sought to build "a high wall and a deep ditch!" between himself and the Calhounite faction, to save the Democratic Party and the West from the undue influence of slaveholders.[32]

In November 1850 Benton returned to campaign in St. Louis—after the general elections. As the *Anzeiger des Westens* explained to its German readers unfamiliar with the procedure, "You can not give your vote for a United States

Amidst the Compromise of 1850 debates, this cartoon showed a puffed-up Thomas Hart Benton, lording over his fellow senators. It indicated his temper but also his power. E. W. C., "Scene in Uncle Sam's Senate, 17 April 1850." Library of Congress.

Senator *direct.*" The message was important enough to print in English as well. Before the ratification of the Seventeenth Amendment in 1913, the Constitution gave this privilege to "the *State Legislature,* which, in *your name,*" the *Anzeiger* informed, "elect your Representatives to the Senate of the American people." Thus, while Benton could advocate to the general electorate, his true audience was the state senators, who held the only relevant votes.[33]

The Democratic Party in Missouri, divided by the Jackson Resolutions, was more vulnerable than ever. That Democrats had been in office during the Great Fire and the cholera epidemic had not helped their popularity, either. In the fall elections, the antislavery Democrats—including the newly powerful German immigrant vote—remained with Benton, but the split in the party statewide resulted in a Whig Party victory.[34]

The results did not immediately spell defeat for Benton. His railroad advocacy and cautious efforts to curtail slavery were closely in line with Whig policies. And staggered state senate elections meant that only some of his allies had been turned out of office. Still, Benton had to plan his campaign carefully, wooing a new coalition while maintaining faith among his old loyalists. To do so, Benton paired two prominent events within the course of a week—a November 9 courthouse rally and the November 14 address before the St. Louis Mercantile Library—working to find any audience that might sway the newly elected state senators to his side.

Benton's speech at the courthouse rally was classic Jacksonian populism. The rotunda was full; "hundreds, some say thousands more" stood outside, unable to hear, according to the *St. Louis Daily Union.* Its editors could not wait until Monday to produce a speech transcript, as the public interest—the inquiries from those who "although it was Sunday . . . besieged our office to read the speech"—was so intense. The speech transcript, closely read in newspapers from Louisville to New York to Boston, revealed Benton's mastery: his words were at once personal and consummately political, forthright yet perfectly pitched. Knowing that many proslavery Democrats had come to hear him defend his votes, Benton first offered tribute to the late John C. Calhoun, who "in health and vigor" was a longtime opponent, "but dying" when Benton saw him last in the Senate, "became a sacred object in my eyes." Yet Benton still renounced the Jackson Resolutions, linking the defense of slavery with threats to the nation. What had begun in the Missouri legislature reached the nation and "the whole Union was waked up to the danger of disunion!" Benton proclaimed.[35]

Continuing the theme as he turned to the Compromise of 1850, Benton argued, "I was no compromiser in a case of disunion," and hence he stood against the hateful clauses of the omnibus bill. Now, back in Missouri, his opponents offered only a "compromise upon any man but Benton," Benton said, while he stood for what Missouri needed. "You want rail roads, and safe rivers and swamps made dry," he said, promising success. Standing before the over-capacity crowd, Benton fought for his proper place in Missouri politics and his place as spokesman for the West.[36]

In days that followed, partisan newspapers found partisan lessons in Benton's speech. The *Daily Union,* dedicated to reconciling the Bentonite and anti-Bentonite factions of the Democratic Party, chronicled how Benton's opponents, "congregated there to annoy and disturb him, shrunk abashed from his presence, as meek and humbled as sinners." The Democratic *Burlington* (Iowa) *Telegraph* reprinted Benton's speech, arguing that the senator's electoral fate was a national issue, and cheering his "firm, unflinching and uncompromising" approach. Yet the Whig newspaper, the *St. Louis Intelligencer,* was not convinced. It claimed that Clay and Webster were truly "the 'eminent men who really did all in their power to restore tranquility,'" and Benton deserved no credit.[37] Thus Benton's speech before the Whig-leaning audience of the Mercantile Library was crucial.

When Senator Benton rose to speak before the St. Louis Mercantile Library on November 14, he knew his audience, and they knew him. The Mercantile Library represented its own kind of revolutionary compromise. From its founding in 1846, its leaders sought to create a place outside of workplace competition, household duties, and overt politicking for clerks and aspiring entrepreneurs to congregate, learn, socialize and relax—and, its supporters hoped, absorb some philosophical and moral precepts of the "better sort." St. Louis in the nineteenth century was an exceedingly diverse place, as slaves and freed blacks, Irish and German immigrants, and working men of all stripes populated a contentious, changing landscape. Yet the Mercantile Library, like other institutions of its time, saw the whole of its public as middle- and upper-class residents—lily-white, with the participation of women limited and African Americans, free or enslaved, completely excluded.[38]

But library membership was regionally and politically diverse. Though the Mercantile Library officers often favored the Whig Party platform, their guidelines to lecturers such as Benton insisted that "no particular political or sectarian views of the Lecturer, be suffered to make a part of his address."

The year Benton spoke, both Clay and Douglas, the actress and author Fanny Kemble, the Harvard scientist Louis Agassiz, and the Concord sage Ralph Waldo Emerson also received invitations. Those invited often were hesitant— "It will be very tedious, cold, and unpleasant, travelling in December to St. Louis," one such invitee, the Irish nationalist Thomas F. Meagher remarked— and hence many invitations to still-remote St. Louis were declined. Yet Thomas Hart Benton happily accepted, seeking the glory of the lectern to add to his political calculations. In August he had set the time, knowing it must be "*after* a political speech" at the courthouse but before the new state senate was seated.[39]

Benton knew to frame his appearance with the referents of the lecture hall, not the political rally. He cited the example of Alexander von Humboldt, the great scientific philosopher and explorer, then in his eighties, who was still regularly seen attending lectures in Berlin. In front of the Mercantile audience, Benton took the invitation to leave the immediate political context, to dream of a world to be made when compromise held, when the uniting railroads would be built. Railroads from Atlantic to Pacific and from Hudson's Bay to the Gulf of Mexico would make St. Louis "the continental crossroads," Benton explained. Despite the political roadblocks, Benton promised, "many who are now present, and hear me with incredulity, will see this road, and will ride upon it."[40]

Reflecting on the opportunities available for St. Louis's business leaders, Benton declared, "You have a grand theatre, politically and geographically, for the exercise of mercantile interest." Benton hoped his political direction could guide their success on this new stage. Though not mentioning slavery, sectional conflict, or the Compromise of 1850 explicitly, these remained his essential subtext. Benton instead spoke of history. "The American Revolution," Benton explained, was "that *Event* which I consider, next after the revelation of the christian religion, the most potential in ameliorating the condition of man upon earth." Impassioned and eloquent, Benton paid tribute to the Founders, whom he credited with the roots of all American successes. "Honor to their names! Gratitude to their memories! Perpetuity to their work!" Benton declared. If the current crisis could be surmounted, Benton implied, it was through the timeless founding principles.[41]

"I have stood upon the Missouri Compromise for above thirty years," Benton later declared, "and mean to stand upon it to the end of my life." He had rallied his political supporters and challenged his detractors at the courthouse; at the Mercantile Library, he had courted, gently, those fervently opposed to the Calhounite Democrats and perhaps open to his path of compromise. The *Daily Union* was convinced the sentiment was there—the people of Missouri simply had to demand that their representatives in Jefferson City return Benton to the Senate. William Barclay Napton, a Missouri Supreme Court justice from a slaveholding and anti-Benton region of central Missouri, came to a different conclusion: "Unless the public will be defeated by some gross fraud," Napton wrote, "T. H. Benton cannot be reelected to the Senate."[42]

The fight over compromise and region, national and local positions, was fought through proxies in the Missouri state senate session of January 1851. For twelve days and thirty-nine ballots, the Bentonite Democrats and the anti-Benton Democrats wheedled the Whig majority, to no avail. On the fortieth ballot, the anti-Benton Democrats endorsed the Whig candidate, St. Louis lawyer Henry Geyer, as U.S. senator. Wayman Crow, a St. Louis dry grocer, a founder of the Mercantile Library, and a Whig state senator, relished the victory, with an "almost irresistible impulse to gush up & Shout aloud" in the face of "our Anti friends, & the Bentonites." The editors of the *Daily Union* could only mutter that "mere political hostility" was allowed to cloud political principles. Political opposites had joined together to reject Benton's compromise vision; traditional political allegiances crowded out Benton's futuristic vision of a transcontinental railroad and a rededication to tri-regional unity and compromise. After thirty years in office, Thomas Hart Benton had been defeated.[43]

Benton sought to learn from his defeat—and return quickly to office. During the 1851 session, the lame-duck senator read his political obituaries with disdain. As the other Great Compromisers faded from the scene, Benton was not ready to relinquish his mantle as champion for the West. In the week that the great western Whig Henry Clay died, in June 1852, Benton was in Jefferson City, denouncing corruption. In a deft political move, Benton served as one of the honorary pallbearers at the local Clay memorial. Returning to St. Louis, "he makes his speech at the Rotunda," the *St. Louis Daily Evening News* reported, reiterating his platform of "*'union and harmony.'*" That summer Benton announced himself a candidate for the St. Louis seat in the U.S. House of Representatives. Looking to 1852, Benton declared that his comeback attempt would have national importance, again pressing the agenda of the West and the possibilities of compromise on slavery. "The eyes of America are turned to our elections to see which way she is going," he said. A correspondent for the *Daily Cleveland Herald* agreed that the heart of national politics lay in St. Louis—and that "the people of the North opposed to Slavery extension can hardly appreciate how much is due to Col. BENTON for the stand he has taken in behalf of freedom."[44]

Just two years after the theatrics of the Compromise of 1850, Benton alone remained of the vaunted regional leaders: Calhoun, Clay, and then Webster had died, each memorialized and mourned throughout the nation. In St. Louis the Mercantile Library acquired statues, busts, and daguerreotypes of these men as mementos of compromise. The student debate society at St. Louis University regularly considered the question, "Which did more good to his country, Calhoun or Clay?" Theirs was a closed political era—one into which Benton ultimately could not fit. Yet Benton, still active, would not rest in the history books: he returned to promoting the railroad, championing his St. Louis vision, a moderate, balanced view intended to stitch the nation together.[45]

When the St. Louis electorate returned Benton to Washington that fall, he gained a measure of vindication. He became ever more convinced that success would come from a new and firm compromise, one that both united the regions of the country and fostered St. Louis's success. "Benton . . . goes fearlessly forward in his own path," one political observer noted. "He reaches his position, and takes his stand there, waiting for public opinion to come up to him." Given the times, the commentator added, "such a man must necessarily for a long time stand alone." Benton stood not quite alone in championing western expansion and the construction of a national railroad as the true source of national unity. Despite his prickly personality, he attracted political protégés in St. Louis, beginning with his son-in-law, John C. Frémont, and a new generation of newspaper editors, including Benjamin Gratz Brown, Francis P. Blair Jr., and his erstwhile German ally, Heinrich Börnstein. Benton raised new options and considered new coalitions, keeping the railroad at the forefront of his thinking. With a new start in the House of Representatives, Benton worked to revive the compromises he felt lay at the very foundation of the United States' promise.[46]

After the physical reconstruction of the Great Fire came a political reshaping around the Compromise of 1850 debates. Thomas Hart Benton's vision, proclaimed in speech after speech, revealed the new fault lines in Missouri and national politics as old alliances broke apart. With an imperfect compromise stabilizing national politics nonetheless, St. Louisans could hope Benton's rhetoric would reach fulfillment, that the world, ever more peaceful, would radiate prosperity from St. Louis. Reverence for the Great Compromisers and the Founders provided a unity of vision of Americans in heaven; on earth, they revealed the difficulties in promoting a national vision from the West.

3

Building the National Future in the West

Which is more admirable, the discovery of America by Col[u]mbus or the achievement of its Independence by Washington.

Col[u]mbus	Washington
F. Desloge	M. Pallen
J. Hinsler	A. Menard
	V. Pujos

Those that sustained Washington turn out victorious.

—St. Louis University Philalethic Society debate, January 7, 1853

Reflecting back on the events of February 22, 1853, Unitarian minister William Greenleaf Eliot could not help but register his surprise. In the afternoon he had attended the city's celebration of George Washington's Birthday at St. Louis University, the city's established—French Catholic and Jesuit—center of higher education. The city had no expansive park or open square, and wintry weather could practically be guaranteed in late February, with the Mississippi River still frozen over for the season. The auditorium of St. Louis University was the perfect place for recitations and literary exercises, a chance for students to connect themselves to pride in U.S. history and veneration of its hero—even as they lived in territory remote from that history, territory that had still been held by a European monarch when Americans won their independence.[1]

Yet it was what followed that provided the shock. Eliot had been called to a meeting of his most prominent congregants and allies. There, his mind on his many obligations, Eliot found another presented to him: state senator Wayman Crow had presented Eliot with the charter for a new institution, a university, to be run by "our Society" in St. Louis. Crow had named seventeen personal friends as directors, and Eliot as their leader; modest, ambitious, deeply committed, and eternally curious, Eliot was unsure how to react. "'Eliot Seminary' has been incorporated by present legislature, but I know nothing of it," the minister protested to his journal.[2]

"A few earnest, enterprising, and munificent citizens of St. Louis"—that was how Judge Samuel Treat, one of those selected as an Eliot Seminary trustee, later described the university founders. For the most part staid businessmen, they left few papers and no statements of their intents and aspirations.[3] Repeating origin stories of happenstance and modesty, Eliot, Crow, and others would profess to have had no predetermined plan for their institution, which changed names often in the early years.[4] Yet planning continued for Eliot Seminary, for Washington Institute, for O'Fallon Institute, and finally, definitively, for Washington University in St. Louis. This cadre of St. Louis leaders, with overlapping affiliations as members of the Unitarian church, officers of the St. Louis Mercantile Library, and advocates of the Whig Party, consciously sought to make St. Louis a preeminent center for culture, reform, and education.

The founders of Washington University had chosen their meeting day carefully—with the national holiday favoring their intentions, and the location of the city celebration revealing the present danger. These men with Yankee, Puritan roots saw efforts to further Americanize St. Louis as key to the city's success within the continental nation—and they worried that the American Indian presence and French Catholic roots might mark the city as too foreign, too unmanaged to be the great cultural capital of the nation. In line with political currents washing over the nation, some embraced nativist policies. Targeting new immigrants as scapegoats, they imagined a new political consensus, as brewing sectional conflict caused the traditional political parties to falter.[5]

The new university would provide a cultural as well as educational alternative in St. Louis, its founders argued, by uniting the North, South, and West in a school of national scope, and one committed to nonpartisan and nonsectarian advancement. Washington University promoted a vision of the future for St. Louis and the nation that hid its exclusions in the rhetoric of universality.

The story of Washington University is in many ways the story of William Greenleaf Eliot. The school is the clearest repository of his energy and his vision—though one daguerreotype does compete. In the 1850s Eliot sat for Thomas M. Easterly, creator of the devastating images of the Great Fire and the Mounds. Eliot wore a proper coat and cravat, but his hair, unconstrained, shot out over his ears; his jaw was tensed, ready to open. With a gaze at once distant and direct, Easterly's image captured the vibrant energy and broad vision of the minister in his prime, a sharp contrast from the sweet-cheeked young scholar or the bearded, bent older Eliot displayed in other images. Despite his deep involvement in charity work, in education—and, to his unease, in influencing politics—Eliot always insisted he was simply the head of a church. He led not a "Lyceum, nor Benevolent Society, nor Reformer's Association, but a church—and that distinctly Christian," he wrote in his notebooks. Eliot's words were always unassuming, but his visage was far more forthright. He lived a public life and one dedicated to serving St. Louis.[6]

Descended from a family that had come to the Massachusetts Bay Colony in the first Puritan migration, Eliot was born in New Bedford, Massachusetts, but was reared in Washington, D.C., where his father, also William Greenleaf Eliot, worked as chief auditor for the U.S. Postal Department. Eliot attended the Columbian College (now, coincidentally, George Washington

Hair unkempt and gaze direct, this photograph projects William Greenleaf Eliot's unbridled energy for social-relief and educational-reform projects. Thomas Easterly, *William Greenleaf Eliot*, c. 1850. Missouri History Museum, St. Louis.

University) in the nation's capital and then returned to the Boston area to enter Harvard Divinity School. Reminders of family tradition were on practically every street corner, as Eliot's ancestors included a deacon of the Old South Church, the last Tory sheriff of Boston, and the first patriot sheriff, who had read the Declaration of Independence proudly from the Massachusetts State House balcony. Ordained in William Ellery Channing's flagship Boston church in 1834, the young minister seemed prepared to live another distinguished Eliot life in New England.[7]

Yet William Greenleaf Eliot went west, arriving in St. Louis in 1834 after enduring twenty-four days of travel from Washington. As evangelists of a cerebral, increasingly liberal theology, Unitarian ministers in the American West sought less to convert American Indians than to recover lapsed Christians, maintaining and promoting Protestantism among the souls drifting out of settled areas. Eliot had taken on a difficult task. As one early traveling preacher put it, "St. Louis is no more fit for a Christian than hell is for a powderhouse." Eliot himself lamented, "St. Louis is very far," reflecting on both the cultural and physical distance from the familiar. Native English speakers were still a minority in the city, and many of them had married into French families, and at least nominally adopted their Catholicism. On November 29, 1834, Eliot first convened services in the borrowed space of a classroom and met on occasion in the courthouse. Irish Catholic workmen were agog. "Did ye hear now about this young bla-gard that has come to preach in St. Louis who does not belave in God Almightly, bad 'cess to him," one said to another, as Eliot's colleagues later told the tale. "Oh, niver moind," was the purported response, "Father O'—— will soon drive him out of this."[8]

Yet Eliot was not run out of town or off of his beliefs. During his first year in town, Eliot spoke to the Franklin Society, an early lyceum; so recent were his East Coast origins that Eliot himself could serve as "guest," relating the latest from the centers of learning. Eliot's welcoming, earnest style as well as the city's changing demographics brought success, and Eliot's church soon constructed a building at Fourth and Pine. In June 1837 Abigail Adams Cranch, the daughter of a D.C. judge, traveled her own daunting route to distant St. Louis to greet her new husband. But when she arrived she was pleased to see the Benton and Bates families, familiar faces she had known in Washington, where Jessie Benton had been a schoolmate. Even Charles Dickens noticed the change the Eliots had made. Just after deriding the style of French St. Louis in 1842, the great author had praised Eliot as "a gentleman of great worth and excellence," representing his denomination well and aiding the poor "without any sectarian or selfish views." Ever overmodest, Eliot eschewed the compliment, but the foothold for Yankee elite culture Eliot had established in St. Louis quickly became a firm foundation with national reach.[9]

Eliot's charity efforts demonstrated the universal reach of his convictions. Routinely contacting all the ministers and priests in town—whether Protestant or Catholic, English-, French-, or German-speaking—Eliot coordinated relief and arranged homes for orphans, the blind, and the destitute. Eliot sat as a trustee on the board of the Medical Department of St. Louis University from its founding in 1836, despite its Jesuit auspices. As Eliot served as the board secretary in its first years, many of the early documents, including the medical department's constitution, are in his hand and over his signature. Eliot offered relief during city tragedies without parochial regard, and his Great Fire ministrations to cholera victims were not divided by religious affiliation. "I regard the minister as part of his own society," Eliot declared in his notebook. "He preaches to himself as well as to others." No wonder that Ralph Waldo Emerson, who encountered Eliot in St. Louis while lecturing before the Mercantile Library in the winter of 1852–1853, found him truly to be "the Saint of the West."[10]

Eliot freely admitted that his efforts relied on the willing participation of able partners, "generous men who have hidden themselves in their work & to whom the praise of my seeming success really really belongs," he wrote. Most were his congregants, inspired to share his worldview. The families of Wayman Crow, Seth Ranlett, James Smith, George Partridge, Mann Butler, Samuel Treat, and John How—all founders of the Eliot Seminary—were members of Eliot's church, and they were also active in its charity efforts. These businessmen provided the financing and management, while the women of the church often were the physical hands distributing relief and providing instruction. In his role as legislator, Crow secured state funding for Eliot's Blind Institute; James Smith had befriended Eliot on his very first day in St. Louis and had been active in his efforts ever since. Ranlett, a merchant and banker, served for decades as both secretary and treasurer for Washington University—and, for thirty-three years, as principal of the church's Sunday school. Eliot also found allies in other denominations: James E. Yeatman, an iron merchant and business entrepreneur from Tennessee, remained active in his Presbyterian church, but he nevertheless became an important member of

Eliot's circle. Eliot's children warmly remembered these men as neighbors and friends committed to their father's "adventures in idealism."[11]

Eliot's church building was expanded in an extensive renovation in 1842, and by 1846 the mortgage was paid off. Having completed two capital projects for the church, Eliot's circle turned further outward. At the first meeting of the St. Louis Mercantile Library that same year, James Yeatman was elected president and Seth Ranlett corresponding secretary, with many of the same cohort among the founding members, again adopting leading roles. With implicit racial and class restrictions, the directors sought to help what Eliot openly called the "better class" of newcomers to the city: both Americans and foreigners destined to "ultimately give the tone to public feeling, and set the standard of public morality," as he later wrote. Eliot arranged evening sessions at his church, where he offered advice to these strivers in a format somewhere between a lecture and a sermon. Their interests and beliefs would shape the future of St. Louis and the nation. It had become a clerk's republic, and those who could provide social and cultural opportunities to these clerks would gain their political and economic loyalties. While the river trade thrived, Eliot's congregation reaped the profits of the maturing West. They invested in institutions that would ensure that their outlook would also prosper.[12]

Decade after decade, more of these "better" immigrants appeared on the streets of St. Louis; as the clerks began to have families, they sought out educational opportunities for their children. Soon after the establishment of the Mercantile Library, Protestant St. Louisans began wondering about alternatives to the long-established Catholic schools. Over the decades there had been a few sporadic, ad hoc arrangements, but in 1848 Eliot pioneered a new and lasting effort, adding the office of school board president to his many duties. Securing funding through a public schools tax voted on mere weeks after the Great Fire, Eliot's congregation had achieved another accomplishment: a system of public schools for boys and girls.[13]

While welcoming of Eliot's charity and relief efforts, when it came to his educational innovations, the Catholic fathers were none too pleased. The Church had long been the primary teacher of St. Louis's children, and its leaders actively opposed the establishment of public schools. The old system had united St. Louis's youth as they learned French and formed friendships that became business partnerships and social relationships; in line with Jesuit practice, St. Louis University had long allowed a rather open consideration of even political and religious questions. The Philalethic Society, the school's composition and debate club, considered topics from the political (October 16, 1838: "Would a Division of the Union be beneficial?") to the sectarian (December 6, 1851: "Which has done more harm to the world, Mohamedanism or Protestantism?") to the perennially controversial (November 24, 1850: "Which is the more to be pitied, the slave or the Indian?") to the humorous (January 2, 1856: "Is the moustache an ornament to the human face or does it tend to deform it?"). Members included not just scions of the long-established fur-trading families but also sons from newly arrived families—some of whom had Protestant fathers hired to teach at the university.[14]

Yet the establishment of public schools forever altered this pattern. As the *Missouri Republican* charged, Catholic leaders were dissatisfied with a system "wherein loyal native-born children are trained to be republican, and 'nothing else.'" Eliot's son Henry recalled how the Lucas family, with children his age, lived just across from the Unitarian church, but he rarely saw them. Catholic schools even took off Thursday instead of Saturday "to prevent association with heretics," Henry wrote. Other children watched both populations longingly: as elite white girls in St. Louis found educational opportunities, more heavy domestic work fell on the city's slaves. Though many in Eliot's congregation began to hear his call and free their slaves (including the Crows, in 1853), most maintained domestic servants—both hired and slave—to allow the household economy to function.[15]

In July 1850 the growth of Eliot's church success led to an even further extension. The cornerstone for a larger church was laid at Ninth and Olive, and the new building was opened to a capacity crowd of 1,600 on December 7, 1851, under the new, expansive name of Church of the Messiah. Eliot allowed himself a moment of pride in a private note to a fellow minister, describing both the beauty of the new spire and the power of faith he found in his congregants. This building too was quickly paid for—the mortgage was canceled in December 1852, just in time for Wayman Crow to return to the state legislature with ideas for incorporating a new institution. That January, Eliot wrote to Seth Ranlett declining a raise. Perhaps he knew the congregation would soon have other projects on which to spend the money, not just to change their community but to shape the nation.[16]

While Eliot's congregation welcomed newly arrived Yankees, Irish and German immigrants remade St. Louis according to their own cultural and religious needs. The landscape of St. Louis had changed to the point that the editors of the *Missouri Republican* declared, "We found it almost necessary to learn the German language before we could ride in an omnibus or buy a pair of breeches," the city was so "inundated" with breweries and beer gardens, Swiss cheese and sausage shops. While the *Republican's* comments were rather lighthearted, others found the newcomers a threat as immigrants gained political power: James G. Barry had been the Irish Catholic Democratic mayor who had faced the Great Fire and the cholera outbreak, and in 1853 Henry Overstolz became the first German elected to citywide office, as controller. With the addition of these foreigners, local Whig leaders sensed that their vision for St. Louis leading the nation was slipping back in favor of Democrats and Catholics.[17]

The city was growing, but not in ways the nativists could welcome. The *St. Louis Daily American* noted with disdain that the old Frenchtown, in south St. Louis, was becoming a "Dutchtown," overrun with the *Deutsch,* or German, peoples. The editors urged politicians to make the immigrant question a key issue in that year's elections. Anti-Catholic sentiment had long contributed to how Protestant Americans. came to terms with French Catholic St. Louis. Elijah Lovejoy, known today as a martyr of abolitionism, had first caught the attention of St. Louis readers through his virulent nativism. Before proslavery mobs threw his presses into the river and set fire to his house, Lovejoy first faced off against the city's German leaders, who vociferously protested his claims. The issue of foreign exclusion and changed naturalization laws was debated on the streets and within St. Louis University. In October 1854 the Philalethic Society considered the proposition: "Would the Alien and Sedition Acts be of benefit to the country at the present time?" In one such nativist action, temperance and Sabbath activists packed a grand jury and sought charges against German beer halls open on Sunday.[18]

As early as 1844 a mob chose Washington's Birthday to express their nativist patriotism by attacking the St. Louis University medical college, after improperly buried cadavers there renewed rumors of Catholic misdeeds. The medical branch had explicitly sought a board of diverse religious leaders to prevent sectarian suspicion, and William Greenleaf Eliot was once again included on the board. On the very evening that Eliot received the educational charter, he had attended a medical school trustees' meeting. Thus the questions of education, immigration, nativism, and national politics were already on Eliot's mind when he and his circle gathered at Wayman Crow's request.[19]

William Greenleaf Eliot himself was no nativist. He read German, insisted on an ecumenical approach to charity relief, and earnestly believed in acting outside the web of partisan affiliations. Yet, with immigrants under threat precisely as Eliot's congregation flourished, he became a target of suspicion. In 1853 the Catholic *St. Louis Leader* claimed that the "Minister of the Poor" from Eliot's church, a Reverend Ward, had turned away Catholics, "telling them . . . to go to the College [St. Louis University], and ask them to melt down their church-plate." Eliot quickly responded to defend his church and its officers, pledging that "the language imputed to him [Ward], he never used, nor anything like it." Eliot further said he had calculated that five-sixths of his church's charity work went to Catholics, and he would not stand for "unjust prejudices."[20]

As Eliot stood to address his newest board of directors one year later, on Washington's Birthday 1854, he called their efforts "the beginning of a great work."[21] With the Mercantile Library, Washington University would contribute to changing the cultural landscape of St. Louis to promote Yankee ideals under the guise of nonpartisanship—a rhetoric that shared adherents with the anti-Catholic, anti-immigrant nativist rhetoric.

In 1854 the Native American Party stood for election on a brashly anti-immigrant platform, seeking supporters in St. Louis, Boston, and many other large cities across the nation. The faction, also known as the Know-Nothing Party because of ties to a secretive anti-immigrant group, drew most of its support from the Whig Party, reviving prejudices by spreading evergreen rumors about dastardly Jesuit practices and Catholic corruption and endlessly repeating stereotyped depictions of German and Irish drunkenness and profanity. In St. Louis a new publication, the *Native American Bulletin,* served as the movement's political organ, and its rhetoric achieved immediate results. On a visit to St. Louis in 1854, former President Millard Fillmore broke with tradition and did not visit St. Louis University, as Webster, Clay, and Van Buren had done before him. Fillmore's snub set a course for removing St. Louis University from its traditional place as host for the city's holiday gatherings.[22] William Greenleaf Eliot stood on a shrinking island of tolerance as the swells of nativism rose up around him—even within his own institution.

In the school's constitution, adopted on Washington's Birthday 1854, Article VIII declared that "no instruction, either sectarian in religion, or partisan in politics, shall be allowed in any Department of the Institute, and no sectarian or partisan test shall be used in the election of professors, teachers, or other officers of the Institute, nor shall any such tests ever be used in said Institute, for any purpose whatsoever." These safeguards made the eventual Washington University "a national work . . . of unquestionable and rare importance," Eliot wrote, escaping the "merely local or sectional interest" that increasingly plagued American culture and politics. Eliot considered his school "an American University," seeking "to address itself to the every-day working world of a republic."[23]

The motivations for a minister with a politically active Whig following to found a university forever divorced from politics and religion demonstrated how Eliot thought of the nation's promise and St. Louis's problems. Beginning in 1853 Eliot served as a trustee of the State University of Missouri, which was beginning to construct a campus at Columbia; at the same moment, however, a state legislative committee was investigating charges that the "teaching of party politics or sectarian doctrines" was affecting governance at the university. Thus, for practical reasons, Eliot wished to avoid such scrutiny.[24]

In later years Eliot often credited the "accident" of their meeting date, Washington's Birthday, as inspiration for the school name. As Eliot later noted, the new name "indicat[ed] the unsectarian and unpolitical, but yet American and Christian, basis on which we had determined to build." Washington, not the minister, would be the model for nonsectarian and nonpartisan ideals—allowing the ever-modest Eliot a chance to efface his role in the Eliot Seminary. A convenient story, but the naming committee had already made the choice in early February, before the Washington's Birthday meetings became a tradition. And, meeting once again after festivities at St. Louis University, the choice of names had a pointed quality. When a Presbyterian group briefly controlled the state license for a "Washington College at St. Louis," an anguished Eliot personally telegraphed the governor to prevent the state from renaming his school the Lafayette Institute. The desired name taken and Eliot still reluctant, the board changed the name briefly to the O'Fallon Institute, to honor the first major donor.[25]

The Washington name was eventually returned to the school, an easy symbol of national aspirations and supposedly nonpartisan and nonsectarian commitments. But what were the politics of that nonpartisanship? In later notes, Eliot sketched "the need of a /Protestant/ Univ^y or rather *American* University," using the terms interchangeably, to replace "the difficulties in State University and in sectarian colleges." Through these values, Eliot declared, the university stood as "an Institution worthy of the great name it bears," the "name which is the symbol of Christian civilization and American patriotism, and to which, therefore, no thought of sectarian narrowness or of party strife can ever be attached." Eliot called his vision of a university "at once conservative and progressive," and emphasized its broad foundations in all kinds of knowledge. Such claims sounded universal enough to the Unitarian Whigs in Eliot's circle and to their backers in New England.[26]

While Eliot's papers reveal no thirst for politics, his nonpartisan, nonsectarian university was inherently political. His Whig Unitarian circle saw their beliefs as reasonable, moderate, accepting, and reflecting a consensus cleansed of unhealthy elements. While Eliot professed wide acceptance, his directors often promoted the free exchange of ideas by excluding vocal adherents of immigrants, of slavery expansion, and of Catholicism. Such inconsistencies were more evident amid the lived reality of political, ethnic, and regional diversity in St. Louis than in the more homogeneous northeastern academies, where such principles were regularly espoused.[27] The election of 1854 served to combine the specter of nativism with the unanswered question of slavery's expansion in the West.

After the Compromise of 1850 set forth the rules for the lands of the Mexican Cession, politicians north, south, and west turned their attention to the quadrangle of unorganized land remaining from the Louisiana Territory. Stretching from the southern edge of the reserved Indian territory (now Oklahoma) up to the border with Canada, bounded by the Missouri River to the east and the Continental Divide in the Rockies to the west, the territory had been crisscrossed by emigrant trails and railroad pathfinders for decades. Yet its formal organization as a territory had been delayed repeatedly by regional disagreements.

A southern bloc—including Missouri's David Rice Atchison—stymied organization because they wanted to see the area open to slavery, regardless of its location north of the Missouri Compromise line. Free-labor advocates in the North objected. And western leaders like Stephen Douglas, the Democratic senator from Illinois, agonized that the deadlock was preventing the construction of the transcontinental railroad, the settlement of valuable agricultural lands, and the political and economic rise of the West. Just as he had split the omnibus bill to create the Compromise of 1850, Douglas now hoped that splitting the territory could bring the proposal enough votes. Douglas's innovation was radically simple: create two territories, Kansas and Nebraska, and let those who settled the territories vote on the status of slaveholding once a certain population was reached. Debated through the first months of 1854 and passed on May 30, the Kansas-Nebraska Act roiled national politics.[28]

In St. Louis, now U.S. Representative Thomas Hart Benton once again opposed what he saw as an illegitimate compromise. Supporting the bill would bring his railroad dreams closer to reality, yet doing so would have allowed for the expansion of slaveholding, enshrining popular sovereignty as the mechanism for slaveholders' ascendance. Benton saw the value for the West in the bill eclipsed by this boon for proslavery advocates of the South. "We have a northern and a southern party, but no western party," Micajah Tarver, the St. Louis investor, Benton ally, and editor of the *Western Journal,* complained. "Instead of gaining political influence with increase of population," he wrote, "the West is now more completely under the control of the East and South than it was twenty years ago." As in 1850, Benton voted against the proposal, placing himself even further outside the norms of the Democratic Party.[29]

Rallying his supporters with thunderous speeches, Benton again worked to turn opposition to a national compromise into momentum for his personal vision. As Senator Atchison's term was up, there was talk that Benton could be returned to the Senate if Missouri were to swing in his favor. Alienated from traditional Democratic voters, Benton relied heavily on support from the German community for his 1854 campaign. Henry Boernstein, the energetic editor of the German *Anzeiger des Westens* newspaper, published a broadside in both German and English, hoping to swell the ranks of free-soil, "anti-Nebraska" voters and urging them to rely on Benton. The *Anzeiger* called for the dissolution of old political parties, declaring that "the state of Missouri will strike the first blow" for a new political order, by electing Benton as "the *people's Candidate,* of the *progressive Democracy.*" The Philalethic Society faced the dire question: "What would experience more of the calamity of disunion, the Southern or Western States?"[30]

While the Democrats splintered, Whig politicians found that the Know-Nothing Party had captured their constituency, outflanking them with Protestant bona fides and a hard line on Sabbath blue laws and temperance. The minister's brother, Thomas Dawes Eliot, had been the U.S. representative for New Bedford, Massachusetts; after facing a nativist challenge, he declined to stand for reelection. In Missouri Edward Bates and Luther Kennett were among the longtime Whigs who ran on the American Party line, seeking the next political advantage. Bates spoke openly of fears that Americans "may find themselves, in another generation, outvoted by the heathens whom they have conquered or bought," raising the racial legacy of the Mexican Cession, while Kennett also alternated between courting and condemning immigrant voters as needed at political rallies. Kennett's allies feared that *we shall be literally 'sold to the Dutch.'* Linking the Germans to the former senator, the nativists urged that "every man of character & influence in Missouri should esteem it his especial business to do all in his power to kill off Benton."[31]

While the Whigs, nativists, and Bentonite Democrats considered how to garner the Senate seat, the incumbent, David Rice Atchison, remained unconcerned. Most Irish-born voters remained devoted to the mainstream, proslavery Democratic Party—and, at the *Anzeiger,* the free-thinking Boernstein spread rumors about Jesuit influence, further blurring the political lines for his free-soil but devout adherents. Atchison found Benton's shifting positions easy to refute. Planning his campaign, Atchison told Samuel Treat, a Washington University trustee and a proslavery ally, that "my theme will be 'Nebraska' & the 'road to India,' taking up Benton's words to use against him." Atchison intended to defeat Benton's vision once and for all.[32]

Atchison intended to make the election a referendum on the Kansas-Nebraska Act, while nativists sought to place the supposed immigrant threat at the center of debate; for Benton's supporters, this attack from both sides seemed particularly worrisome. The cousins Frank Preston Blair Jr. and Benjamin Gratz Brown edited the city's newest political newspaper, the *Missouri Democrat.* Despite its name, it was an "anti-Nebraska" organ, stressing Benton's free-soil vision, not the proslavery platform of the national party. Blair and Brown had won election to the state legislature in 1852 on a Bentonite ticket, and they would not countenance "the unfortunate introduction of religious differences into partisan struggles."[33] Yet their high-minded rhetoric and political acumen faced the insurmountable challenge of election-day violence and intimidation.

On August 7, 1854, the barrage of nativist threats culminated in bloody riots at the polls. When an Irish immigrant was denied the vote in "Battle

Row," the contentious collection of boardinghouses at the northern end of the levee, twenty buildings in the neighborhood were demolished in the resulting melee. Violence spread to the area of St. Louis University, where businesses were looted. The school itself was saved only by the quiet heroism of its president, Father John B. Druyts, who paced in front of the school reading psalms in order to dissuade the rioters from attacking. More prosperous German voters bore the brunt of the violence, and the *Anzeiger* offices were attacked; the militia, ordered to protect the immigrants, instead provoked new standoffs with the drunk and rowdy nativist crowds. In all, shootings and knifings left ten dead and many more injured.[34] Sectarian and political divisions were ripping the city apart.

Waves of nativist threats, rumors, and violence had washed over American politics before, but what made 1854 different were the nativists' successes. Nativists won congressional elections, gained control of state legislatures in Massachusetts, California, Pennsylvania, and Louisiana, and took over city offices in Boston, Philadelphia, New York, Baltimore, New Orleans—and St. Louis. In the year of nativist victories, Thomas Hart Benton was once again a casualty. In a four-way race for his House seat, the St. Louis proxy for the Senate election, Benton came in second, with 44 percent of the vote, while Luther Kennett, carrying the Whig and nativist endorsements, won with 52 percent. The 1854 election had transformed American politics—but it was nativism, not free-soil Bentonite Democracy, that shattered the old political parties.[35]

Unwilling to accede to an unchecked expansion of slavery or to condemn immigrants seeking their fortune in America, Benton had been defeated for the second time in three elections, after three decades of victories. Though Benton seemed unwilling to admit it, his protégés Blair and Brown realized their shifting positions fit ever closer with those advocated by new free-soil, anti-Nebraska groups in Michigan and Wisconsin, who founded what they called a Republican Party in that election year.[36]

Even in Missouri the Bentonite vision was not completely defeated. When Blair and Brown again took their seats in the state legislature, Bentonites outnumbered proslavery Democrats, with the Whig-nativist alliance holding a plurality. They gained at least a symbolic victory by preventing David Rice Atchison from returning to the U.S. Senate: with the state legislature so divided as to be deadlocked, one of Missouri's seats in Washington remained vacant until 1857. It would also take that long for Washington University to be dedicated, to finance and construct a college building.[37] In the meantime,

Eliot's circle shaped the St. Louis Mercantile Library into an institution of national significance.

From the moment of Washington University's founding, its relationship with the Mercantile Library was symbiotic. The two institutions shared political principles, collections, and officers, and both were intended to showcase the cultured refinement and intellectual advancement possible in the West. To accomplish these successes, Eliot allies Wayman Crow, Hudson Bridge, and John How brought their knack for institutional funding to the Mercantile Hall Company. They worked in earnest on the library construction from when the Church of the Messiah was completed, in 1851, to just before Washington University was chartered. They repeated their successful efforts, canvassing the city to sell bonds and sign up new library members; with the money raised and a design competition finished, the library's exterior was completed in 1853 and the building was formally opened in 1854. Seating 600 in the smaller lecture hall and 1,500 in the larger auditorium, and including book stacks, a reading room, librarians' offices, a directors' boardroom, and rental property at street level, the Mercantile Library Hall was instantly a

Within easy walking distance of the entire central business district, the St. Louis Mercantile Library Hall provided an essential meeting place for business, education, and socializing. Leopold Gast & Bro., *St. Louis Mercantile Library Hall*, from John Hogan, *Thoughts about the City*, 1854. State Historical Society of Missouri.

St. Louis landmark.[38] The elegant space was crafted proportionate to the size of its leaders' ambitions.

Soon after the library building was finished, Eliot inquired about renting space; the inherent ties made it easy for Eliot's school to hold classes at the Mercantile Library Hall. As Washington University professors were hired, they often were on hand at the Mercantile Library as lecturers. When Wayman Crow endowed the first scholarship to Washington University, he gave the Mercantile Library the privilege of selecting the recipient; later an agreement converted the university's share of Library Hall bonds into permanent membership privileges for a certain number of students each year. Studying among the busts of the Founders and the Great Compromisers, the joint trustees of the Mercantile Library and Washington University found cause to memorialize one another in marble as well. The founding Mercantile Library president, James Yeatman, arranged for a bust of Wayman Crow to be given to Washington University—but no objection was raised to housing the work at the Mercantile Library.[39]

Committed to their intellectual pursuits, the Mercantile Library directors invited all qualified lecturers to their podium, maintaining their learning and sociability with guidelines for nonpartisan and nonsectarian presentations similar to what Eliot and his board of directors provided to their university. Both Benton and his opponent Kennett had been invited to lecture, a mark of the library's political latitude; along with Reverend Eliot, Father Cornelius Smarius, professor of rhetoric at St. Louis University, and James Shannon, president of the University of Missouri, had each been repeatedly invited to speak. Father Druyts was familiar enough with the Mercantile Library directors to recommend one of his students to be assistant librarian, noting in his letter how the young man had already "frequented the Mercantile course of studies" for several years. The library also sought and received German patronage. In 1853 the library received German books and a collection of newspapers documenting the 1848 French Revolution from *Anzeiger* publisher Henry Boernstein, and that same year published the directors' annual report in German as well as English.[40]

Yet, in 1854 both Mercantile Library staff and patrons evinced the tones of nativism in their correspondence. In September of that year, Mercantile librarian William P. Curtis suggested that St. Louis University was not worthy to be a repository of Smithsonian Institution publications, as it was not open to the public and, though it went without saying, it was run by Jesuits. In

November, when ardent Irish nationalist Thomas F. Meagher presented a series of lectures, he wrote ahead to assure that he wished to appear "simply and solely as a private citizen," with "no manifestations of a political nature." Yet, after the first lecture an anonymous note came to warn Meagher that "the blood of some of our best citizens which was shed by irish assassins" during the election melee "still crys too strongly . . . for us to endure extravagant laudation of irish character."[41] The lecture hall was not immune from the passions of politics. Eliot's circle had built their Whig, Unitarian, Yankee institutions and declared themselves open to all opinions shared in a nonsectarian and nonpartisan manner. But the realities of nativism, like the fears of slaveholding politicians, pulled against the fragile facade of neutrality.

"Institution-building is and must be a slow work," William Greenleaf Eliot concluded on April 22, 1857, as the first Washington University building was dedicated. Yet Eliot was proud of his fledging university. In its first days, the *North American and United States Gazette,* in Philadelphia, noted the school's intention "to be equal to the best in the United States." When noted orator Edward Everett—the former Massachusetts governor, senator, and Harvard president—delivered the inaugural address for the occasion in the Mercantile Library Hall, he traced the trajectory of that day's significance from the European discovery of America, through the establishment of St. Louis, forward to how Washington University would endow "one of the foci of this great western world" with its proper sense of intellectual and cultural significance.[42]

George Washington was never president of a United States that included St. Louis.[43] Yet as St. Louis grew, the city's aspirations were tied up in national progress, from economic growth to political compromise to cultural efflorescence and educational advancement. Reverend Eliot insisted he only led a simple church, but he and his congregation were instrumental in transforming St. Louis, whether founding relief organizations, ensuring the permanence of the Mercantile Library, or establishing a new university with national ambitions. Whether wittingly or not, their actions displaced the traditional role of Catholic community in St. Louis, garnering prestige at the expense of St. Louis University at the very moment Catholic and other immigrants were being confronted by nativist voices in national politics.

By the end of 1854, the economic, political, and cultural transformation that resulted from the U.S. conquest of Mexican territory in 1848 was thoroughly evident in the streets of St. Louis. Across the Nebraska Territory, the tri-regional debate on slavery would continue on, joining with construction of the transcontinental railroad. St. Louis leaders felt confident that they could lead the nation forward, balancing concerns of the North, West, and South along those rails to the Pacific. The railroad was to be a salvation; slavery was to fade away. Yet events proved that many more challenges lay between St. Louis and its ambitions to lead the nation—and, as it turned out, between St. Louis and the new territory of Kansas.

4

Antislavery Derailed

It is a fearful thing to think, that so many and so noble and so good should have been invited upon a pleasure excursion only to be left at the river Gasconade, only to cross that other river that is called Death.

—*Rock Island Daily Republican,* November 6, 1855.

Those who gathered in the state capital waited fruitlessly in the rain. Thursday, November 1, 1855, had been chosen in advance, the day on which Jefferson City and St. Louis were to be connected by rail. It would be a historic day on the road through the Kansas Territory, over the Rockies, and to the ultimate goal, the Pacific coast. Just a few years before, Thomas Hart Benton had embraced the completion of the transcontinental railroad as Manifest Destiny incarnate, the crowning achievement of the West, to bind the states together.[1] Now, despite the inclement weather, the crowd gathered to see that vision fulfilled. The bunting was up and the band ready. But the train did not come.

Between six hundred and eight hundred passengers rode in the railroad cars that day, a collection of St. Louis's most distinguished and most eminent having been invited for the festivities. Prominent ministers were aboard to bless the voyage, and a group of musicians waited in Jefferson City to trumpet the arrival. Where was the train? Anxious to find his brother and brother-in-law, one man canoed down the Missouri River, seeking news. One woman, Hannah Ramsay, later recalled the dread that grew all afternoon, as those in Jefferson City waited and waited before joylessly eating the banquet feast the next morning. Just about noon that Friday, the crowd's worst fears were confirmed: the Pacific Railroad Company excursion train, on its inaugural run between St. Louis and Jefferson City, had plunged into the Gasconade River.[2]

With the power of hindsight, it is obvious that nineteenth-century financiers, in St. Louis and elsewhere, had no business chartering a Pacific Railroad Company. As decades of failure would prove, privately financed railroad companies, managed by boards of interested but untrained entrepreneurs, had no hope of completing a transcontinental railroad. Railroads simply required too much capital and carried too much debt. They could not make a profit until the entire expanse of rail was in place, and such a network was never under local control.[3] Yet in the first decades of railroading, investors all over the nation could not and did not know these hard realities. They simply had sought to harness the power, and potential profit, so evident in railroads.

Starting in 1837 St. Louis's civic and business leaders, from Yankee entrepreneurs to French landed families, signed the charters of the earliest railroad companies in Missouri. Though the Pacific Railroad Company was part of a second wave of foundings, in 1851, its inaugural board amply displayed these connections. Thomas Allen, whose name would become virtually synonymous with railroad efforts in St. Louis, was the Pacific's first president, investing funds accrued by his wife's old-line St. Louis family. Luther Kennett, the incumbent mayor, was the railroad's founding vice president. And the aptly named Hudson E. Bridge demonstrated the strong links between social institutions and business investments as a stove-works magnate, a guiding force of the Mercantile Library and Washington University, and the second president of the Pacific. Meanwhile, John F. A. Sanford, the husband of Emilie Chouteau, represented his French in-laws as a founding director of the Illinois Central Railway.[4]

The new railroad companies sported such names as the Pacific, the Illinois Central, the Ohio & Mississippi, and the St. Louis and Iron Mountain; the visions were grandiose. Despite this nominal confidence, actual construction proceeded slowly and with difficulty. Partly this was due to the nature of railroad construction. Since lines needed to be joined together, certain specifications had to be shared, but adjudicated agreements were no match for the speed with which competitors copied hard-earned innovations. The boom-and-bust cycle of canal building in the 1830s had left state legislators leery of committing funds, unsure whether they would fuel innovation or merely pad stock-jobbers' profits. For example, in 1840 Illinois had only half-finished, nonfunctioning railroads to show for its $13 million debt. But soon these Illinois roads were completed, and Missouri legislators understood the nature of the threat. They began to bond debt as well, seeking to maintain the advantage in lands farther west.[5]

In the decade after 1850, Missouri spent more on rail construction than any other state. By the Civil War the state had built more than nine hundred miles of track, at the cost of the fourth-largest state debt burden.[6] But the burgeoning rail system lurched to a halt when a political roadblock was thrown in front of St. Louis's railroad prospects, for between St. Louis and California lay Kansas.

St. Louis had long sought to control settlement in the West, dictating the patterns of political compromise and multiethnic cooperation as far away as New Mexico and California. In 1854, however, Congress had brought the action closer, creating the Kansas and Nebraska territories along Missouri's western border. Senator Stephen Douglas, Democrat of Illinois, hoped to side-step the entrenched Missouri Compromise line by introducing popular sovereignty as a seemingly neutral solution to the question of slavery's expansion. Yet instead of peace, the Kansas-Nebraska Act invited violence.

From his inauguration in 1853, President Franklin Pierce courted unity among the regional factions of the Democratic Party. Despite being a northerner, Pierce's actions empowered an ideologically committed proslavery cadre within the party, bent on conquering not only Kansas but also Cuba and even Central America for American slaveholders. This faction also opposed western railroads, in part to stymie the program of internal improvements espoused by the rival Whig Party. After 1854 popular sovereignty added a new angle to the regional conflict: since settling the new Kansas and Nebraska territories was a demographic competition between proslavery forces and antislavery Free-Soilers, southern Democrats had no interest in providing an easy connection for those coming from the Northeast. "The slave States do not begin to compete with the free States in the building of railroads," the *Missouri Democrat* argued, and antislavery newspapers across the North ruefully agreed. Slaveholders used their vision of Manifest Destiny to block the westward expansion of antislavery adherents.[7]

Sextus Shearer understood the connections with a rare continental perspective, having moved from Massachusetts to St. Louis and then to San Francisco. "Rail roads increase the facility of traveling so much," Shearer wrote to his St. Louis real estate agent, James Bissell, in 1854, "that it will almost destroy the value of slave property on the frontier of the slaveholding states." Shearer spoke from personal conviction; his slave Fanny had desired to join him in California and promised to be a faithful servant if her transportation was paid. Shearer demurred; he did not trust that given a release she would truly arrive by wagon train, and he felt technological advances would only multiply these doubts. "With the rapidity of the rail road [slaves will] be in Canada before you are aware that they had started," Shearer concluded.[8]

Notorious filibusterer William Walker spent much of the 1850s planning invasions of Mexico and Nicaragua to add to the "natural" territory of U.S. slaveholders. But after the passage of the Kansas-Nebraska Act, Walker valued the conflict in Kansas as a crucial battlefield, understanding the outcome there would affect conditions across the upland South. "Virginia, Tennessee and Kentucky ought to send her hardy sons out to claim their rights and maintain them too," Walker wrote to Missouri's ardent proslavery senator, David Rice Atchison. They should fight lest newly arrived Free-Soilers (whom Walker called the "offscourings of the East and Europe") come to "pollute our fair land, to dictate to us a government, to preach Abolitionism and dig underground Rail Roads." Atchison in turn wrote to Mississippi Senator Jefferson Davis, assuring him that western Missourians knew how to stop an unwelcome invasion. He reminded Davis they had done it in the 1830s, when Joseph Smith had brought his followers to the region. "We intend to 'Mormonise' the Abolitionists," Atchison wrote. "We will be compelled to shoot, burn & hang, but the thing will soon be over."[9] Kansas settler or local Whig businessman, underground railroad or tracks above ground—the distinctions fell away. All were equal threats in the correspondence of the proslavery leadership.

Beyond the rhetoric, those affiliated with St. Louis, both proslavery and Free-Soil, began to settle the Kansas Territory. Slaveholding French Catholics, tied by language and family, founded Lecompton. The Massachusetts Emigrant Aid Society, recruiting Free-Soil immigrants, noted the importance of a new path across Missouri. "The railroad across that State, [would] afford ready access," the society predicted—and St. Louis would be the vital entrepôt.[10] As settlers on both sides of the slavery question streamed into Kansas, the elegant simplicity of the popular sovereignty theory turned far uglier on the ground.

When Pierce appointed Jefferson Davis as secretary of war, southern Democrats scored a particular coup. The American West was a military zone, full of forts and outposts; with the need for rights-of-way and survey data, many railroad questions fell under the military's purview. With the backing of Senator Benton, John C. Frémont and the other military and scientific explorers had already mapped much of the West to determine the best routes. Yet Secretary of War Davis used his position to order further reports, comparing sites, documenting routes, and collecting flora and even providing ethnographic detail.[11]

The scientists on these expeditions happily greased the wheels of patronage, and politics clouded more than clarified. As one botanist wrote to his St. Louis colleague George Engelmann in September 1855, "Can you not gratify Capt. Whipple by naming some one of our new Opuntiae [cacti] after the Hon. Secretary of War Jeff. Davis?" Engelmann complied; the namesake Davis's hedgehog cactus is still on the books. The scientists' data were compiled in beautiful volumes, providing remarkable portraits of the American Plains just before the railroad transformed western lands. But they were also effective in delay, allowing cities firmly in the slaveholding South to become viable alternatives for any planned transcontinental railroad route across the middle or northern reaches of the continent.[12]

This program of delay was most forceful in St. Louis. Between the city and the chosen route west lay the St. Louis Arsenal and Jefferson Barracks. By the 1850s the locations of these army installations were hardly strategic— Manifest Destiny had spread American borders far beyond the posts—but the vicissitudes of military oversight gave Jefferson Davis leverage. On November 8, 1853, Secretary Davis made it clear to the railroad executives that specifications for the route and conditions for distance from government buildings "must be rigidly adhered to"—and that the railroad must bear any costs involved. In long and detailed letters, Thomas O'Sullivan, the railroad's engineer, pressed Davis to approve "the right of way which is made necessary by the laws of nature, and authorized by those of Congress." O'Sullivan argued that the work must follow the original route, for one day soon it would be a crucial link "of the greater *Mississippi Valley Rail Road.*" Yet Davis would not budge. St. Louis's mayor and city council had to file a protest with President Pierce before concessions were finally made. A later state investigation, however, revealed that righteousness did not rest with the Pacific Railroad in this debate: directors had insisted on the marked route in part because they had invested heavily in land between St. Louis and the barracks, and thus needed the approval in order to profit from side deals.[13]

Two years later, on February 10, 1855, the first train departed the Pacific Railroad depot. Though its destination was Washington, Missouri, merely fifty-four miles west, it revived the promise for St. Louis, a chance to garner California's riches and guide the world's trade with India. First came Kansas, and St. Louis's Free-Soil newspaper was ready, arguing that "Missouri will best consult her interests by assisting in making Kansas a free State," finding an avenue to profit beyond slavery.[14] Making the railroad west from St. Louis a funnel of Free-Soil migrants and a conduit of the city's pragmatic, moderate politics, could unite the desires of the North with another conduit for western control.

In March 1855, when the first elections were held for the Kansas territorial legislature, Missouri's leading proslavery legislators crossed the border to vote their politics. David Rice Atchison, just vacated from his U.S. Senate seat by the deadlock in the Missouri state senate, joined the leading anti-Bentonite Democrat in that chamber, Claiborne Fox Jackson, in illegally voting in Kansas. They proudly bragged about their illegal actions on their return. Their supporters saw the tenor of the whole region at stake: "If Kansas be settled by Abolitionists, can Missouri remain a slave state?" asked western farmer and state legislator J. Locke Hardeman. "If Missouri goes by the board what will become of Kentucky? Maryland, Virginia?"[15]

That same month the noted northeastern minister Henry Ward Beecher gave an antislavery speech in New Haven and received a rifle for emigrants to Kansas; the gift formed a connection between the New York preacher and these so-called Beecher's Bibles, shipped west with their necessary ammunition. Free State partisans were pouring into the territory, with St. Louis their key transfer point—and within months all kinds of goods sent from St. Louis to Kansas were being destroyed on suspicion of containing Beecher's Bibles or other tools of abolitionist interference. In June 1855 a prominent northern senator came to investigate. He carefully signed his name in the St. Louis Mercantile Library guest book: "Charles Sumner Boston." Missouri was certainly a good place for Sumner to judge sentiment about Kansas, since the rhetorical conflicts in Missouri fueled the increasing violence in the Kansas Territory. St. Louis moderates urged peace and compromise, while virulent defenders of slavery in western Missouri fed the conflict.[16]

Could the railroad be completed fast enough to allow Free-Soilers to travel west without interruption? Those on both sides increasingly wondered whether the Union itself would survive the mounting tensions in a place too remote for quick intervention. St. Louis railroad interests worked feverishly to extend the lines, hoping to change the political and social realities in Kansas by providing a sense of order and national perspective. One young passenger that summer captured the excitement of the moment: "I had the honor of going with them on the Pacific rail road on the route to *California*," Louisa Hull gushed, noting that "we went to Washington [as] the cars do not go any farther *at present*." Describing her picnic and day of sightseeing on the plains, Hull concluded, "Every thing went in very pleasantly *indeed*."[17]

Louisa Hull was not a regular passenger on a regular train, and she did not reach California. But even as a special guest on an excursion train to Washington, Missouri, she could feel the revolutionary nature of railroad travel, opening new vistas and breaking all conventions of speed and freedom of transport. The excitement was doubled on the morning of November 1, 1855, as ticketed passengers gathered to travel from St. Louis to Jefferson City. Tragedy would strike in the afternoon.

"We may congratulate our fellow citizens," one column of the *Missouri Republican* began on Friday morning, November 2, 1855, "that the road is an accomplished fact—that from this time forward, the commercial and political capitals of the state, are brought within a few hours' distance of each other." Carefully laid out ahead of time to quickly go to press, the celebration of one column was joined by the anguish of the next. "How little do we know what an hour may bring forth!" declared the same issue. "The magnificent train of cars which left our city yesterday morning . . . is now a heap of ruins, and infinitely worse than this, many of the noble hearts that participated in the pride of the occasion, are now stilled in death."[18]

Thomas O'Sullivan, the Pacific Railroad's engineer, had personally signed each of the numbered railroad passes. They announced a departure time of 8:30 a.m., a scheduled arrival in Jefferson City just after three in the afternoon, and the option to return the same evening. A cross-section of St. Louis's ministers, politicians, and business leaders, among them the railroad board and investors, gathered that morning—though, it being All Saints' Day, no Catholic clergy joined the excursion.[19] As the banquet arrangements were made at the state Capitol, almost everything was prepared. Everything, that is, except the bridge.

The bridge over the Gasconade River was not completed. Running behind, the builders, Stone & Boomer of Chicago, had only completed the abutments and the piers of the planned iron truss bridge by the appointed date. Instead, they built a wooden "falsework" bridge for the occasion, with timbers laid across the piers and rails nailed onto a pine lumber base. Afterward the newspapers pilloried it as a "pasteboard structure," but this had been a routine practice for unfinished crossings. As a construction engineer later testified, the company had proven the bridge's worthiness earlier that day by running a full gravel train across it. Running the train across a temporary trestle, in the pouring rain—the portents could be seen only in hindsight.[20]

As the excursion train approached the Gasconade River it was behind schedule, but O'Sullivan planned to make up time on the straightaways ahead. The whole ride had been a marvel, with celebrations in the stations despite the rain. The train had even slowed on approaching the bridge, early accounts reported, "to make the passage more secure, and give the persons on board an opportunity for viewing the structure."[21] It was to no avail.

What came instead was a slow-motion horror. With ten of the fourteen cars on the falsework, it gave way, sending them crashing down into the rocks and mud of the riverbed. The engine was catapulted into a headlong dive; other cars twisted and turned, many of the last being pulled down the embankment by their connectors. A survivor remembered the "crash—crash—crash—as each car came to the abutment, and took the fatal plunge." The rain continued, "the merciless pouring of the rain," as the *Missouri Democrat* put it, "the roar and flash of the angry tempest mingling with the cries of the wounded and dying." Survivors sought out the injured and searched the rubble for their buried companions. Groans came from within the "indistinguishable mass of wooden beams, seats, iron wheels and rods." The cars had come apart, revealing devastation. Some of the militia companies aboard began the sad work of collecting the dead.[22] No triumphant entry into Jefferson City would occur that day.

"TERRIBLE CATASTROPHE," rang out the headline in St. Louis. Soon after the accident, steamers on the river rushed the news to St. Louis, but no details were forthcoming. Everyone knew that leading merchants, politicians, judges, and militia leaders were missing. The Catholic newspaper, the *St. Louis Leader,* stopped the presses, removing type to make notice of the accident and remind its pious readers to pray. The editors nervously recalled "our dear friend, Capt. O'Flaherty, we saw at Church the same morning." The *Missouri Republican* reported that less than 10 percent of the passengers emerged without injuries, leaving hundreds unaccounted for. Crowds gathered at the Seventh Street and Fourteenth Street depots, waiting for the next train from the west, hoping against hope for more survivors and fearing to learn the names of the dead. And even then, as they waited, the rain began again.[23]

At five o'clock that evening, the wounded and the few unhurt accompanied the dead back along the same tracks, through the same storm, to the previous station at Hermann, the seat of Gasconade County and the modest capital of the *Deutschheim*. An agricultural community founded by a German settlement society, Hermann represented a far different America than either St. Louis or Kansas. German vernacular buildings, German varietals, and spires over German-speaking churches personified Hermann, a hamlet only beginning to grapple with its rail connection to St. Louis and the greater world. And yet St. Louis's tragedy intruded as the Hermann station was converted into a makeshift morgue.[24]

"Where on information has ben given to the Subscriber Coroner of said County that the Death body of _____ has ben found near the mouth of Gasconade and one now lying at the depot of Hermann, you are therefor commended to sumon der Hausehaldern and Citizens of said County, to appear forthwith at the same place," the Hermann coroner wrote that Friday morning, struggling to express himself in English for the later benefit of the St. Louis courts. Neighbors were impaneled as an inquest jury, to determine "by whom or by wat cause the Persons wo here before us lies death." The cost to St. Louis became clear: Thomas O'Sullivan, the railroad engineer, "his head being almost severed from his body." Thomas O'Flaherty, expert steamboat captain, dead at the scene. E. B. Jeffries and Thomas J. Mott, state legislators. E. Church Blackburn, president of the city council. Reverend Artemus Bullard, the dedicatory speaker.[25] And the sad litany continued.

Two dozen others—workers, dignitaries—also lay dead; newspaper accounts in St. Louis and around the country filled in the details. Samuel Best, a fire man in the engine car. Patrick Barry, a wood passer. Cyrus Melvin, a policeman, "found with a bowie-knife, which he had on, thrust up to the hilt in his body." Adolph Abeles had been a merchant and a rare German member of the Whig Party. Emilie C. Yosti owned a shoe manufactory. Thomas Gray was remembered in Euclid, Ohio, as the local blacksmith who had gained prosperity as a St. Louis industrialist. Calvin Case, formerly of Sackets Harbor, New York, "had attained a position of influence and high respect among his fellow citizens at the west," running an omnibus line. Reverend John Teasdale, another of the speakers. Mann Butler, the historian and Washington University trustee who had conducted the investigation after the Great Fire. Then, the man whose presence created the need for an inquest: Henry Pierre Chouteau, scion of St. Louis's most powerful family. Chouteau "was so disfigured," the *Democrat* mourned, "he was identified only by his invitation ticket."[26]

Needing an eyewitness, the jury called on Erastus Wells, listed with slight wounds, to testify. A member of the city council and founder of the first omnibus lines within the city of St. Louis, Wells combined political authority with technical expertise. He had been aboard with his wife, Isabella, who did not yet know she was pregnant. The only woman on the train, Mrs. Wells had escaped unscathed—she told a friend that her clothes caught on a hook and held her in place—though their elder son was "severely contused." In the inquest transcript Erastus Wells recounted that "we proceeded in safety until we reached the cropping of the Gasconade River, about eight miles beyond the town of Herman[n]." Then it happened so fast: "I suppose it could not have been more than a minute or two from the time the accident happened until I was out of the cars," he explained. "The car bursted open at the top and I went out at the aperture thus made."[27]

When the coroner concluded, the train started again for St. Louis—and the trauma continued. Running off schedule and with the telegraph wires down, the train of the injured risked a collision if another scheduled train came in the opposite direction along the single track. Nervously making their way, survivors endured yet another bridge collapse—debris from the Gasconade River falsework had weakened a downriver crossing. Though this was a low bridge with a modest span, the second collapse came at night, the surprise intensifying the physical and psychic injuries to those aboard. "Fatality seems to attend this road," the *Democrat* felt compelled to conclude, the latest accident adding to the horrors. Even a few days later, the editors wrote how "the extent of the disaster is by no means fully comprehended by our citizens."[28] The train had not reached Jefferson City—could it truly reach Kansas and the Pacific?

The Gasconade tragedy enveloped St. Louis. The seventy severely injured mirrored the thirty dead in status: state legislators Joseph S. White and William A. McClain; John M. Wimer, the former mayor of St. Louis; Madison Miller, the mayor of Carondelet and former president of the Iron Mountain Railroad; Washington University and Mercantile Library trustees Hudson E. Bridge and Wayman Crow; and members of the *Missouri Republican* and *St. Louis Mirror* staffs. Wilson Primm, the St. Louis lawyer and avid local historian, was "injured about the head." Singled out by race among the injured were "James Kelly (a colored man)—leg broken" and "Frank Carr, a black man—badly wounded."[29]

Some of the injured grimly returned to the tasks at hand. One survivor related how Reverend Truman M. Post "went home that night and washed the blood and dirt off him and retired not saying a word or letting his wife or family know," so as not to worry them. The next day the minister delivered an unforgettable account to his congregation, with the prayer of Jonah in the whale as his text. Hearing him, "you could almost see and feel the dreadful crash," the survivor wrote, as a "chilled feeling" welled up inside him.[30]

As the disaster seeped into the psychology of the merchant community, a general numbness was evident. Men gathered in small knots along the streets, their confidence shed in the murmuring of mutual fears. Normal business was replaced with resolutions of mourning for their fellow religious, business, and political leaders. William Hull had received the excited account of the earlier excursion from his daughter Louisa; now his business associates in the East wrote to express their condolences. The St. Louis Bar closed the Circuit Court for the funerals of their colleagues. The Pacific Railroad directors put it most starkly, acknowledging their responsibility for the moment when "twenty-nine of our citizens were suddenly hurtled from existence."[31]

Mayor Washington King, himself a Gasconade survivor, declared Monday, November 5, 1855, a day of mourning in St. Louis. But this was merely a formality in a city already at a standstill. In accordance with the proclamation, all businesses were closed, and churches held services of commemoration for the dead and of thanksgiving for the survivors. Reverend Bullard was brought into First Presbyterian in a metallic coffin, into the new church building he had dedicated just two weeks before. The requiem Mass for Henry Chouteau was held Wednesday at the cathedral. The archbishop buried Thomas O'Flaherty on Sunday afternoon, and the Washington Guards, his militia company, attended. The *Democrat* made an explicit analogy to the Great Fire and cholera epidemic of 1849, noting that "fire and flood and pestilence they have withstood," but the news from Gasconade "caused a panic that we have never before witnessed." The newspapers, aching from the crushing details, could only wish that "the pageant of woe has ended."[32]

With the dead buried, the investigations began. Who or what was to blame—the falsework bridge, the stormy conditions, the decisions of engineer Thomas O'Sullivan? "The man-trap over the Gasconade was no bridge at all," charged newspapers as far away as Cleveland and Philadelphia. "It was a scaffolding on which a bridge was to be erected." The *Missouri Democrat* pushed this question, wondering how safe the other fifty-odd bridges on the road from St. Louis to Jefferson City might be. Rumor had it that Hudson E. Bridge, on the locomotive at the time of the crash, had requested that the train stop and the passengers walk over the bridge but that O'Sullivan was overconfident. In a letter to the editor, Bridge called the charges "wholly and entirely untrue," defending the dead O'Sullivan. "To me," he wrote, "it seems a miracle that either of us escaped instant death." Even as the official Pacific Railroad Company report was issued, doubts persisted. City engineer Henry Kayser—the only member of the committee to visit the crash site—described finding bridge piers leaning and not drilled to sufficient depth. Kayser wrote that the attempt to use such a bridge "can only be ascribed to incompetency, recklessness, or infatuation," emphasizing the enormity of the failure.[33]

By failing a key test, the Pacific Railroad and its backers in St. Louis and throughout the state lost ground both economically and politically. Delegates from all over the state had awaited the train; with the legislature back in session and the state liens coming due, the opening of the railroad to Jefferson City was to be a decisive event.[34] A successful railroad link would have eased more state support, and the promise of the railroad across western Missouri, Kansas, and finally to the Pacific would have kept St. Louis business interests and Missouri politicians paramount in shaping the future of the continental nation. Instead, discussions returned again and again to the accident at Gasconade, to the hopes dashed.

"The prosperity of St. Louis and of the State of Missouri received a terrible shock," the *Leader* wrote, as if the effort "to connect the two oceans by a road of iron, had provoked the anger of heaven."[35] The dream of a transcontinental railroad soured; proslavery politicians, seizing the advantage, openly questioned whether railroad investments should continue at all. Wrangling consumed the legislature while conditions in Kansas and then at Rock Island, Illinois, transformed St. Louis's prospects.

While St. Louis and the city's antislavery leaders recovered, their allies from Kansas to Washington suffered from the Gasconade disaster. As one Free-Soiler in the Kansas Territory warned, men mentioning antislavery moderates Frank Blair or Benjamin Gratz Brown, or caught carrying the Free-Soil newspaper from St. Louis, were "marked objects." The politics of slavery erupted into violence as a band of proslavery border ruffians crossed from Kansas into Missouri and looted the U.S. arsenal in Liberty. In response, a Free State faction led by the newly arrived John Brown gathered to protect Lawrence. Speaking on the Senate floor of the "Crimes against Kansas," Massachusetts Senator Charles Sumner declared all supporters of popular sovereignty to be "in championship of human wrongs," given the violence it sowed.[36]

On two days in May, proslavery forces redoubled their efforts, leveling the Free Soil Hotel in Lawrence and then attacking their detractors in Washington. Preston Brooks, a representative from South Carolina, approached Sumner's Senate desk cane in hand. While accomplices prevented interference, Brooks beat Sumner until he bloodied the floor, until Sumner ripped his desk out of its bolts, until Sumner was long unconscious, until Brooks's cane was broken. Carried from the Senate floor, Sumner would not return for three years. A few nights later, in reaction to the news, John Brown and his sons killed five men along Pottawatomie Creek upon mere suspicion of slaveholding sentiment. Horace Greeley's *Tribune,* seizing on sensation to sell newspapers, labeled the carnage "Bleeding Kansas"—even though far more people had died in the Gasconade disaster.[37]

In the fall sessions of Congress in 1856, two desks in the Senate sat vacant: the Missouri seat held in political limbo, and the seat of Sumner from Massachusetts. Thus two seats were made empty by the rhetorical and real violence of slavery politics.[38] The railroad had not come. St. Louis had not been able to bring its moderate politics to Kansas. What else would be derailed?

In the months after the disaster, the locomotive was salvaged from the Gasconade River and the state railroad funding renewed. On March 12, 1856, the first regular train successfully ran from St. Louis to Jefferson City without ceremony. In the aftermath of the Gasconade disaster, further progress on the Missouri Pacific was slow, and the railroad did not reach Kansas before the Civil War. St. Louis interests were forced to cede the first stage of the railroad race to upriver rivals. In 1859 Chicago interests completed a railroad across northern Missouri, the Hannibal and St. Joseph; it connected to St. Louis only by spur line.[39]

Even more important for Chicago was the railroad bridge at Rock Island, Illinois. The bridge's story was parallel to but very different from that of St. Louis and the Gasconade bridge. Rock Island is as it sounds: an island, an outcropping of Illinois in the Mississippi River alongside Davenport, Iowa, which has held a federal arsenal since 1816. Like Thomas Hart Benton did for Missouri, a powerful Democratic senator, Stephen Douglas, championed the Illinois–Iowa line, his politics generally in line with those of the western advocates in St. Louis. Though Jefferson Davis raised objections to a railroad easement at Rock Island, early construction and a favorable legal ruling found a way around this roadblock. At Rock Island, the firm of Stone & Boomer—which had failed so spectacularly at Gasconade—succeeded with a wooden trestle bridge. The first train rumbled across the Mississippi River on April 21, 1856, opening direct communication between Chicago and the Platte River, a feat celebrated from Cleveland to Maine.[40] Suddenly Chicago had the first piece of a transcontinental railroad in place and the best route from the East Coast into Kansas, while trains from St. Louis could only reach Jefferson City, the goal so dearly sought just months before.

Even accidents at the Rock Island Bridge were more manageable. When the freight steamer *Effie Afton* hit the bridge in its second week of service, no lives were lost. (It did take awhile to collect all the cattle left swimming in the Mississippi, though, and a few weeks to repair the bridge damage.) In the resulting lawsuits, the St. Louis Chamber of Commerce backed the *Afton*'s owners, hoping to build up their own rail connections while delaying those of Chicago. Yet opposing them in the suits was a local lawyer and sometime Whig politician by the name of Abraham Lincoln, who carefully studied the intersection between western railroads and the failures of popular sovereignty in Kansas. In 1859 a desperate Josiah Bissell, agent of the St. Louis Chamber of Commerce, attempted to set the bridge on fire; he was arrested and put on trial in Chicago. As all-expenses rail-and-steamboat packages for New York's wealthy transferred at Rock Island, no such tours left from St. Louis.[41] Instead, the link between railroads and disaster burrowed deep into the collective psyche.

The Pacific Railroad bridge collapse and the resulting deaths would long haunt St. Louis. Two weeks after the accident, the *St. Louis Leader* published a poem titled simply "The Gasconade." A dialogue between mother and son, it recorded the moment she told her son that the "manly soul" of the boy's father "hath fled," and his body "lies with the mangled dead." In later generations the Gasconade disaster remained the shorthand for unforeseen calamity, the worst of a series of rail disasters somberly named when any new mishap occurred. After the Civil War Joseph Keppler's cartoons for the German magazine *Die Vehme* visualized these fears, as the specter of a railroad train falling off a bridge—in some images, the cars clearly marked "Pacific RR"—propelled nervous passengers to purchase policies from the nearest insurance salesman.[42]

The death of one Gasconade victim, the steamboat captain Thomas O'Flaherty, cast an even longer shadow on his daughter Catherine, age five at the time of the disaster. The shock kept her away from school for two years. Only decades later, after she had married and established herself as a writer, could Kate Chopin return to the events of that day. In Chopin's short story for the December 6, 1894, issue of *Vogue,* "The Dream of an Hour," tragedy is compounded when the report of death in a railroad accident much like the Gasconade disaster comes in error. When the husband of the protagonist arrives home, quite alive, she dies of "the joy that kills."[43] For Kate Chopin and all of St. Louis, however, there had been no mistake.

The collapse at Gasconade and the successful bridge at Rock Island symbolized how, after the passage of the Kansas-Nebraska Act, the missing railroad link from St. Louis prevented advocates from promoting a vision of westward expansion built on moderate antislavery in Kansas. By February 1857 the implications were obvious to St. Louis politician Benjamin Gratz

Brown. He rose in the state legislature to warn that commerce now flowed "into Northern and Southern routes," bypassing St. Louis and its program for the West. The national bounty was slipping away from St. Louis. "Soon its outpost will be at Council Bluffs," Brown intoned, "and its emporium at Chicago." Brown blamed this loss on proslavery Missourians and their meddling in Kansas.[44] And he proposed a radical response: a plan for gradual emancipation in Missouri.

In arguing that slavery would ruin St. Louis and cause the loss of the railroad route, Brown was shading the truth. Inadequate financing and sheer bad luck played their part, but Brown spoke only of the role of slaveholders. As when Horace Greeley turned the phrase and created "Bleeding Kansas," Brown pressed an image to incite action, not to document history. His immediate aim

A generation later, the Gasconade disaster still haunted St. Louis travelers. In this image, insurance salesmen hawk their wares to nervous passengers by reminding them of the risks of rail travel. Joseph Keppler, "Starting Westward," *Die Vehme*, June 18, 1870. Missouri History Museum, St. Louis.

was to prevent more roadblocks from proslavery politicians and to secure a federal commitment to a railroad through Missouri, not necessarily to free slaves. He responded to the sense that, in the era of popular sovereignty, conflict over slavery had swallowed all other issues. Brown's slavery proposal was prescient: at that very moment, the U.S. Supreme Court was ready to decide the fate of Dred and Harriet Scott and their daughters, a St. Louis slave family. Once again a national decree would overturn the hard-won balance in St. Louis.

5

The Limits of Dred Scott's Emancipation

There now appears . . . triumphant in the city of St. Louis, an emancipation party to contest for supremacy in the State, which declares that agitation of the slavery question shall never cease until Missouri is free.

—*Ripley* (Ohio) *Bee,* April 18, 1857.

News of the decision reached St. Louis before the end of the day. On the morning of March 6, 1857, Chief Justice Roger Brooke Taney gathered the U.S. Supreme Court to deliver the decision in *Dred Scott v. Sandford.* In the basement chambers, beneath the unfinished dome of the Capitol, Taney declared that his Court did not have the proper jurisdiction to decide the case, but then he read a lengthy majority opinion nonetheless.[1]

The result was telegraphed throughout the country all afternoon. "The act of Congress which prohibits citizens from holding property of this character north of a certain line is not warranted by the constitution, and is therefore void," Taney announced, "and neither Dred Scott nor any one of his family were made free by their residence in Illinois." Taney emphasized the point by recourse to history. Since the founding of the United States, the chief justice intoned, "the class of persons who had been imported as slaves [and] their descendants" were "regarded as . . . so far inferior that they had no rights which the white man was bound to respect."[2] The case of Dred Scott and of his wife, Harriet, of their daughters, Eliza and Lizzie, was denied, and the tradition of geographical compromise on slaveholding negated.

American slavery had been rife with contradictions long before *Dred Scott,* yet this case brought the balancing act of slavery into stark relief. Southern advocates cheered the expansive understanding of their slaveholding rights; northerners stood aghast at the lack of protections for escaping slaves; westerners despaired that the tradition of political compromises to determine what was free and what was slave territory had ended by judicial fiat. Yet, while the legal implications of the *Dred Scott* precedent have long been explored and debated, the local logic of the case—and the quite different local reaction to the *Dred Scott* decision—have been overlooked.[3] At the apex of connection between St. Louis and the nation, at the nexus of northern, southern, and western understandings about the limits of slaveholding, the *Dred Scott* decision transformed the intermittent outbursts of the cultural civil war into an all-engulfing crisis that could no longer be ignored.

Slavery in St. Louis had always been intimately tied to the Mississippi, Missouri, and Ohio rivers. Rivers offered employment: there was so much work along the docks—hauling and repairing, laundering and cooking—slaves were often hired to do these tasks independently, even accruing some money in their own name while remaining the legal property of others. Rivers also offered the gamble of escape: a quick trip upriver or across the Mississippi could provide slaves with a path to freedom. As the *Dred Scott* case proved, however, such freedom was not absolute. Fugitives faced a lifetime of uncertainty, not only worrying about the possibility of recapture but also fearing for the family and friends left behind.[4]

Rivers had once separated empires in the heart of the continent, and their contours could still lead to court victories. Along the border of slavery and freedom, African Americans in St. Louis experienced the layering of French and American traditions of slavery, and the contradictions of urban slavery. Between official doctrines and de facto differences, French principles and American precedents, there was a narrow space for negotiating under the constant threat of violence. The intensity and uncertainty have made its texture somewhat easier to reconstruct from scant historical records.[5]

For decades slaves who could prove (via white witnesses) that they had been taken to reside in free territory were awarded their freedom. Even as the Missouri Compromise was being finalized in Washington, the case of *Winny v. Whitesides* was being argued in St. Louis. The Whitesides family had

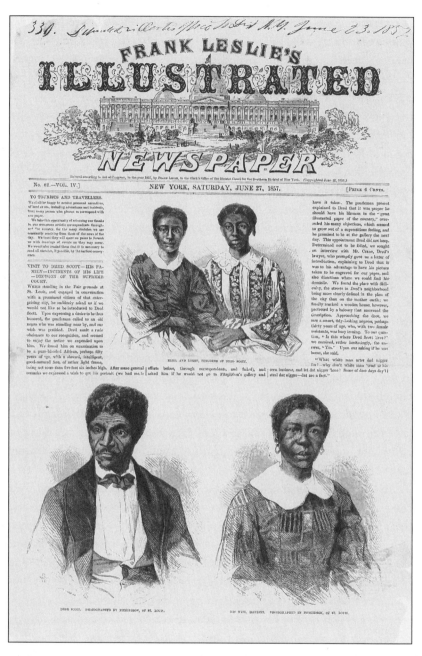

Dred Scott, his wife Harriet Robinson Scott, and their two daughters lived in a St. Louis alley, independent from slaveholders but not free. Note that the magazine had erroneously reversed the daughters' names. Lizzie, Eliza, Dred, and Harriet Scott, *Leslie's Illustrated*, June 1857. Library of Congress.

brought Winny from North Carolina to Illinois, residing there for a few years before relocating to St. Louis. In 1824 the Missouri Supreme Court proclaimed a doctrine of once free, always free, citing the prohibition of slavery in the Northwest Ordinance as grounds for Winny and her children to be freed. The principle became so well established in St. Louis that some slaveholders would negotiate with slaves to determine a price and method for obtaining freedom, rather than facing their claims in court. *Winny v. Whitesides* gave slaves who had resided north and west of Missouri a glimmer of hope for justice under antebellum law. It was still the controlling legal precedent in 1846, when Dred and Harriet Scott filed their freedom petitions.[6]

Yet rivers could also provide leverage to slaveholders. As a steamboat captain later recalled, "On the east side [of the river] in the State of Illinois, even, the slavery idea predominated. . . . A black man was a 'nigger,' and nothing more," he recalled, judicial niceties be damned. The prosperous Chouteau family worked vigorously to blur the lines, regularly ferrying their slaves between Missouri homes and Illinois plantations. Rivers also facilitated the routine transfers of slaves, sales terrifying in their banality. "My girl will be down in your city and county during the coming holydays," Thomas T. Pitts of St. Charles wrote to James Tower Sweringen, a St. Louis department store owner and financier, in December 1856, in reference to his house servant Ann; the price was $1,000. St. Louis merchants held profitable slave markets, selling both down the river, into the voracious arena at New Orleans, and directly into coffles, headed into the rich new cotton lands of Arkansas, western Louisiana, and eastern Texas.[7]

"Though slavery is thought, by some, to be mild in Missouri," William Wells Brown wrote in 1847, in his narrative of slavery and escape, ". . . no part of our slave-holding country is more noted for the barbarity of its inhabitants than St. Louis." Brown described what he experienced and what he saw in the streets. While carrying trays of newspaper type for Elijah P. Lovejoy, the nativist publisher of the *St. Louis Times,* Brown was taunted and pelted with snowballs by a crowd of white boys and then caned severely for reprimanding them. When the wheels of a slave-driven carriage splattered mud on a passerby, the driver was purchased and tortured for the offense. And then there was the time William Shelby Harney, a U.S. Army officer stationed in St. Louis, had simply whipped a slave woman to death.[8]

The possibilities for swift change along the river fueled ferocious outbursts of violence. In the late 1820s the free black proprietor of a "house of rendezvous" was tarred, feathered, and forced to flee the city for his life after a quarrel with a white customer. His tormentors took advantage of his illiteracy to seize his house and two prime city lots through fraud. In a "horror-striking scene at St. Louis" in 1836, as the young Whig legislator Abraham Lincoln told the Young Men's Lyceum of Springfield, Illinois in 1838, "a mulatto man, by the name of McIntosh, was seized in the street, dragged to the suburbs of the city, chained to a tree, and actually burned to death; and all within a single hour from the time he had been a freeman, attending to his own business, and at peace with the world." On April 28, 1836, Francis McIntosh, a free black boatman, had scuffled with police officers, fatally stabbing one; when captured that same night, he had been lynched. When Elijah Lovejoy protested the pro forma nature of the lynching investigation, the mob turned against his newspaper. On November 7, 1837, Lovejoy was killed across the river in Alton, Illinois, while defending his presses, his death marked as martyrdom by later white abolitionists.[9]

The McIntosh and Lovejoy killings were hardly the acts of hooligans. Many prominent citizens—including the mayor at the time—later related the events in great detail, suggesting their familiarity if not also their participation. As elsewhere, sporadic violence reinforced the legal strictures of slavery in St. Louis. In 1841 a group of black men were executed for their alleged role in an arson plot. In February 1843 a new ordinance to jail all free black steamboat employees while in the city further eroded black freedoms. A story of slave humor repeated among whites suggested the narrowed possibilities: a visitor, it was said, asked a slave in the streets of St. Louis why he was chained to a cannonball. "To keep de bad people ob de city from stealing it," came the purported reply. "Heaps of tieves, massa, about heah."[10]

Possibilities of freedom, threats of violence: this was the charged environment Dred Scott found when he returned with his family to St. Louis. The man known to us as Dred Scott (a name that does not enter the records until 1836) was born into bondage in Virginia around 1799. By adolescence he was held by the Blow family, who moved him with their other possessions into Alabama and then to St. Louis in 1830. (This was a typical story of internal migration, one slave among the millions moved from the spent agricultural lands of the upper South onto the slaveholding frontiers of the Southwest.) After the death of family patriarch Peter E. Blow, Scott was sold to Dr. John

Emerson, a U.S. Army surgeon, who in 1833 was transferred to Fort Armstrong, in Rock Island, Illinois, later the site of the crucial railroad bridge.[11]

Residence at Rock Island, Illinois—on federal property in a free state—gave Scott his first claim to freedom. When Emerson was again transferred to Fort Snelling, in the section of the Wisconsin Territory that is now Minnesota, this strengthened Scott's potential case. There, Scott met Harriet Robinson, servant to the Indian agent Major Lawrence Taliaferro; the fact that Agent Taliaferro later solemnized and recorded their marriage held intimations of the Scotts' freedom. The couple lived together in Dred's quarters at the fort, even when Dr. Emerson was away, and maintained a similar sense of independence when traveling with him, up and down the ports of the Mississippi River, to his postings at Fort Jesup, in Louisiana, and then again up north to Fort Snelling. In October 1838 Harriet delivered their first daughter, Eliza, on the return trip aboard the steamboat *Gypsy*, somewhere off Iowa. Only in 1840, with Dr. Emerson assigned to duty in Florida, did the Scotts come to reside in St. Louis County, on the farm of Irene's father, ardent antiabolitionist Alexander Sanford. Three slaves, each with a claim to freedom, experienced the harsh calculus of rural slavery anew.[12]

In 1843, shortly after returning from Florida, Dr. John Emerson died. While his will awaited execution, his widow, Irene Emerson, lent Dred Scott to her brother-in-law, Captain Henry Bainbridge. Bainbridge soon brought Scott to Corpus Christi, Texas, where they joined American troops massing along the border with Mexico, ahead of the U.S. invasion in 1846. As Scott himself later told a reporter, after his service in Texas, he attempted to purchase his family's freedom—with the arrival of Lizzie, sometime in 1845–1846, they numbered four—with his cash and the guarantee of an acquaintance, "an eminent citizen of St. Louis, an officer in the army," as security. Such an offer fits the local patterns of slave relations, and St. Louis court records show a spike in manumissions and the filing of freedom bonds just before and during the U.S.-Mexican War. Yet Irene Emerson refused. Only then did Harriet Scott insist they file petitions for freedom, seeking the established rights of Missouri slaves under *Winny v. Whitesides*.[13]

The Scotts' petitions came to trial in 1847. After the testimony of a key witness was disallowed, the Scotts lost—they had not proven their presence in free territory. Though *Scott v. Emerson* had begun with the actions of a very brave slave family, a raft of interested whites provided the necessary funds and expertise to keep the case going. Taylor Blow, the third son of Dred's original owner, financed the family's claims, enlisting the help of his brothers-in-law, the well-connected Whigs Joseph Charless Jr. and Charles Drake, and local lawyers sympathetic to the cause. These men succeeded in having a second trial granted, and in 1850 a jury found the Scotts should be freed.[14]

Now it was the defense's turn to appeal, sending out a call for help to slave-holders in St. Louis and throughout the state. Proslavery judges controlled the Missouri bench; one of their leaders, Judge William Barclay Napton, sat on the Missouri Supreme Court and had already drafted an opinion declaring the Missouri Compromise unconstitutional when he was ousted in a judicial election in 1851. Yet, in 1852 the court nevertheless followed Napton's logic. "Times now are not as they were when the former decisions on this subject were made," the majority opinion in *Scott v. Emerson* declared, overturning precedent. Dred, Harriet, Eliza, and Lizzie Scott, and with them all of St. Louis's slaves, lost their promised freedom; no court in the state could back their claims.[15]

During the lengthy trials, Irene Emerson had moved out of Missouri; she met and married another doctor, Calvin C. Chaffee, who lived near Emerson's sister in Springfield, Massachusetts. Throughout the years of the trials, the Scotts were left alone in St. Louis, in the custody of the sheriff, hired out as before. When the Missouri Supreme Court decision was made, the Scotts' advocates began the process again in U.S. district court, claiming absentee ownership created a diversity-of-citizenship claim and hence a federal case. The remarriage of Dr. Emerson's widow activated the laws of coverture and disqualified her as executrix of his will, and so her brother John F. A. Sanford, the railroad executive, fur-trade lawyer, and widower of Emilie Chouteau, became the nominal owner and named defendant.[16]

Sanford, who lived in New York, was hardly closer to the Scotts, but his work and family ties to the Chouteau family brought him to St. Louis with some regularity. Both Sanford and his in-laws were eager to utilize the case to overturn more precedents—for their part, the Chouteaus were known as particularly tenacious in fighting freedom suits and had already fought one ruling to the U.S. Supreme Court. After the Scotts' lawyers made preliminary arguments in the humble federal chambers over H. E. Dimick's & Co. Great Western Emporium for Shot Guns, Rifles and Pistols, they appealed directly to the U.S. Supreme Court, where the case was accepted and a clerk misspelled Sanford's name. *Dred Scott v. Sandford* was born.[17]

While Dred Scott—an older man, likely tubercular, with the aches from a lifetime of labor evident in every step—was "left to do pretty much as he pleased," according to the reporter who interviewed him, Harriet Scott had worked as a laundress and raised their two daughters. Young women of keen ability entering their childbearing years, the girls were Irene Sanford Emerson Chaffee's most valuable slave possession. Their release would most hurt Chaffee's finances, while their freedom would provide the greatest sense of relief for their parents. Eliza and Lizzie Scott would have commanded a high price on the slave market, trading as it did in sexual violence and calculating reproductive capacity as an investment factor. Any day they could be stolen from St. Louis, sold beyond recovery onto the slaveholding frontiers in Texas, Kansas, or the Indian Territory—*Frederick Douglass' Paper* ran lurid tales of such attempts experienced by the "best looking girls" in St. Louis. And so the Scott daughters hid while the case was being decided, young women shuttled about in secrecy. Unlikely rumors placed them in Canada.[18]

By the time the Scotts' case was argued before the U.S. Supreme Court in February 1856, this once-typical Missouri slave suit was national news. Prominent St. Louisans in Washington were tapped as counsel. Montgomery Blair, U.S. solicitor in the Court of Claims and brother of Frank P. Blair Jr., argued for the Scott family. Henry Geyer, the sole sitting member of the U.S. Senate from Missouri, argued for Sanford's position, with the help of Reverdy Johnson of Maryland, a former U.S. attorney general. Months after hearing the positions and reading the briefs, the Supreme Court requested the case be heard again; it was then reargued on December 16, 1856. The second time, George T. Curtis of Massachusetts, brother of a sitting Supreme Court justice, joined the arguments on the Scotts' behalf. Each delay, each change before the Court, added to the case's national following.[19]

By New Year's Day 1857, a decision was rumored. The *New York Herald* knew that "all the judges but two hold that Congress has no power over the question of slavery in the Territories," naming John McLean and Benjamin Robbins Curtis as the dissenters. The leak clearly ruffled some feathers: a few days later the *Herald* defended the scoop from official critique, saying that "time will fully prove the statement . . . entirely correct to every particular." In Missouri the proslavery Judge Napton felt confident that the U.S. Supreme Court would concur with his opinion as drafted six years before, finding the Missouri Compromise and all such agreements unconstitutional. The final announcement was delayed by the death of Justice Daniel's wife, and then held until after the March 4 inauguration of the new Democratic president, James Buchanan. National observers waited for word, as all depended on the Supreme Court, or so it seemed to those outside Missouri. Legislators in St. Louis had another idea.[20]

"In St. Louis it has raised quite a furor," Missouri legislator Benjamin Gratz Brown wrote to his political ally, the railroad promoter George R. Smith, on March 3, 1857—describing not the impending *Dred Scott* decision but the effect of his own emancipation proposal. At the moment that the U.S. Supreme Court was erasing the statutory limits on slavery, Brown, Frank Blair, and other Bentonite lawmakers were seeking to do precisely the reverse. Courting the young, white, working-class constituency—the "free labor" men, both native-born and immigrants—they committed themselves to preventing slavery's expansion.[21]

"It is the 'manifest destiny' of slavery to be pressed *southward*," declared the *Westliche Post,* a new German newspaper in St. Louis. While its editors dreamed of an ever-enclosed slave power, or its slow extinction from North America, the *Richmond South,* in Virginia, took comfort in the defeat of John C. Frémont, the Republican Party, and its similar antislavery program a few months before. Yet those editors warned proslavery advocates that by no means had the 1856 election "settled the slavery controversy, quieted agitation, and rescued the South, from danger of future attack!"[22] The exclamation point gave voice to how the anxiety was heightened when the emancipationist effort originated in St. Louis, the premier city of the talismanic slave state, tipping ever further against their slaveholding rights.

White emancipation proposals were bolstered by the example of free black residents, often responsible for attaining their own freedom, through purchase or lawsuit. Black ministers were instrumental in enabling the freedom suits or purchasing the freedom of their parishioners in St. Louis. Since 1818 the Reverend John Berry Meachum had worked all week as a cooper and ministered on Sundays, eventually preaching in a church he had built himself. After being harassed for holding classes for blacks in St. Louis, Meachum supposedly purchased a boat to teach in the middle of the Mississippi River. On land Meachum purchased his fellow slaves and contracted them to work off the cost—an arrangement that on occasion led to Meachum's being sued for freedom, like any other slaveholder.[23]

The Reverend John Richard Anderson, Harriet Scott's minister at the Second African Baptist Church, was among those ministers who solicited sympathetic whites to sign freedom bonds, financially guaranteeing the "good behavior" of free blacks, as state law required. On these bonds, the names of such antislavery adherents as William Greenleaf Eliot, Wayman Crow, and James Yeatman appear alongside those of large slaveholding families, including the Chouteaus, Carrs, Lucases, and Campbells. These documents testify to the white-black personal relationships that set the parameters of slavery and freedom for African Americans in St. Louis.[24]

Courageous white St. Louisans also had long provided aid and comfort to the local black population—but quietly. "If I were not a red-hot abolitionist, bent on cutting every body's throat," a jocular James F. Clarke wrote to his divinity school classmate William Greenleaf Eliot in 1852, "you would naturally invite me to be your colleague at St. Louis, which now you could not properly do." While Clarke's strident approach would have caused conflict in the city, Eliot was able to aid the slave community by choosing action over pronouncements. Occasionally giving speeches or writing pseudonymous letters to the editor, Eliot watched how slavery politics threatened to split other local churches. In his case, slavery brought churches together: "Nigritia, the colored Sunday School," Eliot recalled later, met in his church building every week, without interruption, beginning in 1856.[25]

While quiet, church-based antislavery efforts continued, in the mid-1850s proslavery forces still held the balance of power in St. Louis, making themselves known in cultural as well as political settings. Given the universality of racial prejudice, even those fighting for free labor or emancipation found humor in crude ethnic and racial stereotypes—the end of slavery was a goal far different than racial equality. For example, a minstrel version of *Uncle Tom's Cabin* was performed in St. Louis during a number of theatrical seasons in these contentious years. While the true plot of Harriet Beecher Stowe's original antislavery novel would have been volatile, the play stripped away the novel's moral compass, using the characters—and local personalities—as merely another frame through which to belittle the enslaved and attack those attempting to assist them. In April 1854 a playbill in St. Louis listed the roles of "Professor Crow," "Mrs. Harriet Screecher Blow," "Hon. Horace Squeely," "Baronness Bierhausen," and "Rev. Susan Facesche." Alongside references to such national abolitionist figures as Stowe and Horace Greeley were local antislavery advocates (Wayman Crow, with Taylor and Susan Blow) and local ethnic stereotypes (German beer and French clergy), feminized to heighten the satirical effect.[26] The inclusion of local names sharpened minstrelsy's barb.

Antislavery author Harriet Beecher Stowe would not recognize her novel in the stage version of *Uncle Tom's Cabin*. But local antislavery leaders would recognize the names added to mock them. *Uncle Tom's Cabin*, April 24, 1854 playbill, New Varieties Theater. Missouri History Museum, St. Louis.

While the Supreme Court deliberated, while the everyday tensions of slavery continued, Benjamin Gratz Brown rose to speak in the Missouri legislature on February 12, 1857. The measure under consideration at the time asked the assembly to declare emancipation—in the gloriously inclusive terminology of legislation—as "inexpedient, impolitic, unwise and unjust." On the contrary, Brown argued. Holding the floor for close to two hours, Brown rejected the prevailing defenses of slavery and presented a radical new proposal: St. Louis and Missouri would be best served by the gradual emancipation of all slaves.[27]

Emancipation, Brown urged, would be "out of regard for the white man and not the negro." In 1857 only the most radical voices, such as William Lloyd Garrison and his *Liberator,* and the bravest of fugitive slaves, such as Frederick Douglass and Sojourner Truth, called openly for the immediate and total abolition of slavery. In contrast, Brown's proposal would free the last of Missouri's slaves late in the nineteenth century. Releases would be acts of Christian charity, and the state would compensate slaveholders. Emancipation would be a good investment, because former slaves would be colonized in Liberia or elsewhere, and hence would no longer compete at the mechanic's bench or in the hauling trades. (Free and enslaved blacks would of course object to these white free-labor visions. But the debate over emancipation was, first and foremost, an abstract conflict over white rights rather than a verdict on black lives.) In his speech Brown cited census statistics showing that free white men were already displacing slaves with their labor in the maturing counties of the Missouri frontier. To complete the process would set Missouri itself free, Brown said, and give St. Louis the power to "hold the balance between the North and South."[28]

Brown's proposal jolted the city's political alliances. While free-soil Germans and those brave enough to use the Republican name in a slave state were enthusiastic, traditional Democratic and even Whig powerbrokers worried over Brown's influence. "Twenty four [legislators] left themselves on the record in favour of emancipation," an incredulous George M. Williams wrote to Dr. John F. Snyder, a fellow southern Democrat, on the day of Brown's speech. "What a disgrace to St. Louis," wrote A. W. Mitchell, a Whig and member of the extended Farrar family, in February 1857, complaining that the new Bentonite congressman, Frank P. Blair, was "becoming a leading man among the Abolitionists." Blair and Brown had so enraged the standard bearer for southern-rights Democracy in St. Louis, U.S. Attorney Thomas C. Reynolds, that Reynolds challenged Brown to a duel—St. Louis's last such political affair, and an affray both were lucky to escape alive. Brown, though forever lame afterward from a bullet to the knee, kept his political positions intact, pressing his case with fiery editorials in the *Missouri Democrat,* and confident of the coming Free-Soil victory in Missouri.[29]

Then Taney's decision finally arrived.

At first the Supreme Court's message was garbled. Chief Justice Taney took nearly three hours to read the majority opinion, and did so "in a tone of voice almost inaudible," according to the Associated Press reporter; it was so lengthy that the Court had to reassemble on Saturday to hear the dissents from Justices McLean and Curtis. As McLean averred, "A slave is not a mere chattel. He bears the impress of his Maker, and he is amenable to the laws of God and man." Curtis challenged Taney's dismissal of black rights directly. "It is not true, in point of fact, that the Constitution was made exclusively by the white race," Curtis wrote, citing instances of "free colored persons" with state citizenship at the time of the Constitution.[30] The acrimony the case would cause the nation already had begun within the Court itself.

Strident declarations quickly filled the partisan newspapers. "The miserable and *political* decision," the *Daily Cleveland Herald* called it, while the *Cincinnati Gazette* said, "The suicide of slavery has begun," given how the decision must surely lead to greater conflict. Horace Greeley's *New York Tribune* called the decision an invitation to violence, a "Bowie-knife sticking in the stump ready for immediate use if needed," while the *Charleston Mercury* reprinted the *New York Herald's* view that "the importance and comprehensive bearings of these decisions cannot be over-estimated," as the Court's words "strike at the root of the mischief," painting the case as one "against Massachusetts and her colored citizens, and in favor of South Carolina" and its strident proslavery politics.[31]

Sensational headlines were the everyday ephemeral work of newspapers, of course, but citizens beyond the pressrooms also noted the momentousness of the decision and speculated on its consequences. "Coming so close upon the murderous rages in Kansas," wrote Donn Pratt of Cincinnati, "the Dred Scott decision . . . sinks deep into the minds of the American people." Abraham Lincoln, the Rock Island Railroad's lawyer, was again aspiring to political office, and jotted down his understanding of the decision when Taney's words reached him. "Soon as the Supreme court decides that Dred Scott is a slave, the whole community must decide that not only Dred Scott, but that *all* persons in like condition, are rightfully slaves," Lincoln wrote. If the decision permitted slavery everywhere, free-soil advocates had either to acquiesce to slaveholder rule or rise to denounce the decision—either Massachusetts or South Carolina would rule, with no chance for moderation. The vision of compromise in the West was collapsing.[32]

After the decision the Scott family remained slaves. Yet the notoriety of the case soon raised them up from the anonymity of their race, their condition, and their menial work. The one reporter who seemingly received Dred Scott's cooperation described him as about fifty-five, "of unmixed African blood, and as black as a piece of charcoal." The reporter also added some tantalizing details, noting that Scott had been married before and his wife sold away—and that he had had two sons, both now dead. Escape to freedom had often been available, the reporter said, but Dred Scott was now resigned to "abiding by the principles involved in the decision." The reporter asserted that Dred Scott was "not ignorant," and as a slave had "traveled considerably, and has improved his stock of common sense by much information picked up in his journeyings."[33]

In the only known words attributed directly to Dred Scott, he described how the prolonged nature of the case had provided him "a 'heap o' trouble,' he says, and if he had known that 'it was gwine to last so long,' he would not have brought it." Scott was "tired of running about," and anxious to again work to purchase his family. In the final sentence, the reporter agrees with Scott "that he could make thousands of dollars, if allowed, by traveling over the country and telling who he is."[34] This briefest hearing of Dred Scott accentuates how even the most famous of slaves are lost to history.

What did the *Dred Scott* decision mean for the fabric of life in St. Louis, for its greater projects for the West and the nation? Taney's decision denied the history of free and enslaved St. Louisans of African descent and limited their horizons, yet immediate reactions seem so subtle as to be nonexistent. Despite the increasingly heated rhetoric in national newspapers, the *Dred Scott* decision seemed to change hardly anything in St. Louis. Manumissions and filings for freedom bonds did not significantly increase or decrease. The St. Louis University Philalethic Society proposed the question: "Has congress the right to abolish slavery in the territories?" at their first meeting after the decision was announced, but then they did not debate it for months. A correspondent of the

Milwaukee Daily Sentinel visited a St. Louis slave pen and, with the biases of a northern Democrat, found "no handcuffs, chains nor instruments of torture, no disconsolate wives . . . nor weeping children." He felt inclined to see slavery *itself* as the "abused institution"; he could hardly resist "throwing up my hat and giving three cheers for the U.S. Supreme Court and Nigger Slavery." In local newspapers, other concerns predominated. Conflict in Kansas continued, and the effort to rebuild railroad lines and sue for rights at Rock Island remained a priority.[35]

But the most shocking reaction came during St. Louis's April elections, with Benjamin Gratz Brown's and Frank Blair's emancipationist victory. St. Louis's leading politicians were not burdened but defiant: even in the face of the *Dred Scott* decision, they still sought a compromise on slavery they hoped could sweep the entire nation. The effort to portray gradual emancipation as the moderate course succeeded through an alliance between the remaining Bentonite Democrats and the first Missouri Republicans—and thanks to the votes of white workingmen, native and immigrant. Virginia-born John M. Wimer, who had been listed as an "emancipation Democrat," won a return to the mayoral office by 1,700 votes. St. Louis "is henceforth The Free City of the Valley of the Mississippi," a jubilant Brown declared.[36] The symbolism of the election could hardly have been greater: one month after the Supreme Court decided the most important slavery case in its history with claimants from St. Louis, the city chose a free-labor, antislavery platform.

This is not "a joke, a hoax, this abolition triumph in the capital of a first-class slave State," the *Richmond South* informed its readers, calling it "the first time slavery has been routed in one of its own strongholds." The Richmond editors actually agreed with William Lloyd Garrison and *The Liberator,* as both argued that the violence in Kansas had redounded into St. Louis politics. The *Ripley* (Ohio) *Bee* observed with glee how "the Missouri Republican, the organ of the effete conservatism of Missouri," had to announce the antislavery results. The *Bee's* editors wondered whether the true pioneer of western compromise, Thomas Hart Benton, might be persuaded to run again in the 1858 elections. Only the *New York Herald* could find a promising message for proslavery forces, excusing the election by claiming Missouri's climate had never been ideal for slavery. The editors felt assured "there is no danger that South Carolina or Louisiana will ever undergo the change" to free labor, "which is inevitable in Missouri"—but proslavery ideologues never wished to find out.[37]

All this attention to the end of slavery benefited the Scott family on May 26, 1857, when they finally attained their freedom. After Taney's decision,

Irene Emerson's second husband, Calvin Chaffee, now a Republican representative from Massachusetts, claimed horror to learn that he might be the
owner of Dred Scott. His fright was likely staged—an aftereffect of allowing
his wife's St. Louis allies to continue the case all those years. Yet, after the
newspapers had raised him to ridicule, Chaffee worked quickly with the Blair
family to gain clear title to the Scotts and provide for their manumission.
"Let Dred select the person to whom the transfer shall be made," the final
note advised, and Dred Scott's longtime friend and patron Taylor Blow was
chosen to finally make it official. With their freedom, the Scott daughters
could emerge publicly; "their father knew where they were," the *St. Louis
Daily Evening News* assumed, and "will doubtless recall them now." Yet, after
the *Dred Scott* decision, what could freedom mean for the family? The *Hartford Daily Courant* stated the contradiction directly. "Dred Scott is a slave no
more," the editors wrote. "Being a freeman, in spite of Chief Justice Taney,
we suppose he now has no rights which white men are bound to respect."[38]
After the *Dred Scott* decision, what did a vitiated freedom mean to anyone of
African descent?

Whether or not Dred Scott was free, he was a celebrity. The *St. Louis News*
wrote of regular sightings along Third Street; a minister traveling to Iowa met
him in church and invited him back to the steamboat—though, aboard, "some
high-toned southerners" found the gesture of respect "strange indeed." In an
encounter with a correspondent for *Frank Leslie's Illustrated Newspaper* at the
Scotts' alley address in June, Harriet's rebuke—her only known words—
suggested she at least was tired of the attention. "What white man arter dad
nigger for?" the dialect depiction reads. "Why don't white man 'tend to his
business, and let dat nigger 'lone?" Harriet was adamant that Dred would do
no touring and that "she'd always been able to yarn her own livin, thank God,"
and the family needed no such scheme. The *Leslie's* reporter did succeed in ca-
joling the Scott family into the local photography studio, and the result made
the front cover of the newsmagazine. In the only known images of the family,
they appear dignified but seemingly without joy, their frustration displayed in
slow exposure.[39] Even unbound, the family was not free from the *Dred Scott*
decision—which, despite the April opposition victory, constrained all African
Americans.

With the *Dred Scott* decision and the emancipationist victory, conditions in
St. Louis were the topic of conversation around the world. Missouri's master

painter and sometime Whig politician, George Caleb Bingham, spent 1857 ensconced in art studios in Düsseldorf. There, German artists fascinated by America shared space with American artists glad for their attention. As studio mate Henry Lewis finished his views of a timeless Mississippi River valley, punctuated by his image of the 1849 Great Fire, Bingham kept abreast of the latest news with letters from James Rollins, the Whig planter and instrumental supporter of the University of Missouri. Despite the distance, Bingham continued to follow Missouri politics and the unrest in Kansas closely.[40]

When he wrote to Rollins in June 1857, Bingham was still smarting over what had seemed, from European news, as the likely victory of Frémont and the Republicans the previous fall. "Tell our friend Blair that I hope he will muster a strong part for emancipation by the time I get back," Bingham urged, finding new hope in the initiative. Regarding the brouhaha over the *Dred Scott* decision, Bingham had two reactions, one overtly political and one painterly. "The ultraists of the South will soon discover that in their attempt to grasp all, they have endangered that which they already possessed," Bingham predicted, providing a thoroughly western and pragmatist reading of the situation. And in the same letter, Bingham mentioned his latest work, "a large picture of 'life on the Mississippi' . . . far ahead of any work of that Class which I have yet undertaken."[41]

That new painting, *Jolly Flatboatmen at Port* (1857), reflected the impact of the *Dred Scott* case. In the earlier *The Jolly Flatboatmen* (1846), a young man danced on the top of the flatboat, arms spread carefree over the wide expanse of river. Working from the same portrait sketches of "types" with their straw hats, corncob pipes, and jugs of liquor, Bingham here constricted the river panorama with scenes of dock life. He multiplied the hints of nostalgia: the noonday sun replaced by a sky reaching sunset, children playing on the docks, and then the steamboat in the right background, suggesting how the flatboat had long been an outdated technology.[42]

Bingham heightened the contrast by placing a black dockworker among the new figures in his 1857 painting. He stands with a relaxed pose, his face breaking into a smile, his height equal to that of the fiddle player on the opposite side of the compositional pyramid. (This was no casual decision: the work of William Sidney Mount, an earlier master of American genre painting whom Bingham admired, had used the sharing of music to suggest connections between workers across the barriers of race and class.)[43] For an expatriate Missourian sympathetic to antislavery, the *Dred Scott* decision intimated narrowed horizons and change along the river. It is no coincidence that the white man's pole, coming up between the dancer and the African American enjoying his performance, gives the silhouette of a rifle pointed to the sky.

Though the Scott family soon disappeared from discussions of the *Dred Scott* decision, local and national politicians grappled with the emancipationist ideals espoused by Brown and Blair. In the 1858 midterm elections, the Republican Party mounted its second attempt at a congressional presence. In Illinois Abraham Lincoln, another midwestern politician with a cautious program of general emancipation in mind, spoke about the *Dred Scott* decision to the Republican State Convention in Springfield on June 26, 1857, as he prepared to challenge Stephen Douglas for his Senate seat.[44]

Laying out his own vision for African-American life in the United States, Lincoln rejected Douglas's charge that "because I do not want a black woman for a *slave* I must necessarily want her for a *wife.*" Lincoln averred, "I need not have her for either, I can just leave her alone. . . . In her natural right to eat

Though he was in Düsseldorf when the *Dred Scott* case was decided, the politically active Missouri painter reacted by adding two Africans Americans to the dancing flatboatmen, reflecting the change along the river. George Caleb Bingham, *Jolly Flatboatmen in Port*, 1857. Saint Louis Art Museum, Museum Purchase 123: 1944.

the bread she earns with her own hands without asking leave of any one else, she is my equal, and the equal of all others." To work and be left alone—Lincoln's vision reflected the simple but revolutionary goals that Harriet Scott had established with her petition. The "ultimate destiny" of America's slaves, Lincoln said, "has never appeared so hopeless as in the last three or four years," but he told the convention that he remained optimistic that the Court might overrule its own decision, as had occurred before.[45]

Thomas Hart Benton also took a keen interest in the *Dred Scott* decision and the emancipationist victories, just as the newspapers had predicted. Benton interrupted the compilation of Senate debates to publish a scathing, three-part, 130-page commentary on the case. The *Dred Scott* decision did the United States no favors, Benton argued. "Far from settling the question, the opinion itself has become a new question," Benton wrote. He called the Missouri Compromise "a *political enactment,'* . . . not to be reversed afterwards by judicial interpretation," again reflecting his stance as a tactical opponent of compromise terms but a stern defender of completed compromises. Slowly dying of cancer, Benton knew himself beyond the power to run again, but he actively followed Missouri politics, urging that his vision be championed by his protégés.[46]

Even Judge Napton, despite being a southern-rights Democrat, mulled the possible emancipation schemes. In his diary Napton noted the scheme of the National Compensation Society, which floated the idea of paying for a complete emancipation with western lands. The last major discussion in a southern state over a negotiated end to slavery, in Virginia in 1831, had considered a similar proposal. "National indemnification," wrote the society's founder, Elihu Burritt, "would not be a mere compromise, but an earnest and brotherly partnership between the North and South . . . which would bless equally both sections of the Republic." Such a proposal became preposterous when Napton wondered at where "the four millions of slaves now in the United States" would go, and how any colonization scheme would be financed.[47] The compensation plan might be equal in northern and southern eyes, Napton found, but it was unjust for those Americans already settled in the West, pursuing their own agenda.

Despite garnering national headlines, the cause of emancipation made slow progress in Missouri—until an international financial crisis removed support for the idea altogether. The Panic of 1857 swept across the nation as bankers tightened credit and discounted the value of investments, from crop futures to railroad bonds. Economic hardships brought awkward conversations: *Anzeiger des Westens* editor Heinrich Boernstein noted with irony that "the same people who had desired to devour my paper and all Germans" now "meekly crept to my editorial office" to request help. The "dashing ladies of St. Louis," another observer wrote, were borrowing "at 2½ and 3 per ct." to the season's extravagances. Among the state legislators active in proposing new specie and new investments was Benjamin Gratz Brown; his emancipation proposal had been shelved.[48]

When the Panic began to settle in the spring of 1858, the unresolved political conflicts of Kansas-Nebraska, railroads, slavery, and emancipation all returned in force. Kansas voters rejected the proslavery Lecompton constitution in January; Free Staters regrouped in Lawrence to attempt to craft their own document. The conflict began to split the Democratic Party, just as it had laid waste to the Whigs. Illinois Senator Stephen A. Douglas, Lincoln's opponent, was rapidly becoming the standard-bearer of the national Democratic Party, but southern-rights partisans in Missouri eyed him warily.

"The democracy of St. Louis were all Douglas men," state senator Benjamin F. Massey wrote, but a plurality of city residents had supported emancipation in the last election. "Who is it that expects a real democrat to succeed in St. Louis?" he wondered. The Democrat James S. Green, who was finally elected in 1857 to fill Missouri's long-vacant U.S. Senate seat, took a pragmatic stand. "There are some things which I must condemn in Douglas," Green told Samuel Treat, the St. Louis judge and Washington University trustee, "but as long as he defends the South and the Democratic party, and sustains the constitution against Black Republicans, I cannot hesitate in my preference for him over the opposition." Yet hard-line Democrats felt Douglas was offering too much, especially given the Supreme Court's strident declaration of slaveholder rights. "Since the Dred Scott decision a Negro is a head of cattle like any other," the radical editors of the *Westliche Post* mournfully noted on the decision's one-year anniversary, "and cattle have no standing in court."[49]

Cyprian Clamorgan, however, maintained a far different analysis of St. Louis political power in the wake of the *Dred Scott* decision. The mulatto grandchild of a trader from Guadeloupe who chose only black wives, Clamorgan was born into a wealthy but marginalized St. Louis Creole family with branches on both sides of the color line. In his pamphlet *The Colored Aristocracy of St. Louis,* published in 1858, Clamorgan profiled the cream of St. Louis's free black community. He modeled his bons mots on the musings in similar works published in New Orleans. Mostly mixed-race free individuals who traced their ancestry into the French period, Clamorgan's subjects maintained a lively culture apart from both white and slave society, proudly bearing French Catholic names that repeated in the pews below their "African balcony." Referencing the canon in literary allusions yet making a living as a barber, the author embodied the precariousness of the community he wished to celebrate.[50]

After describing Mrs. Pelagie Rutgers (a wealthy widow, her house staffed with a French gardener and a white nanny, her time spent with the two white children she had adopted) and Samuel Mordecai (a river steward and inveterate gambler, with a daughter at school in England), Clamorgan detailed how the political power of "colored" families like his functioned. "The colored men of St. Louis have no votes themselves, but they control a large number of votes at every election," Clamorgan wrote, for white voters rented houses from landed black families. It was "an easy matter to say . . . 'Mr. Blair and Mr. Brown are our friends—vote this ticket or seek another place of abode,'" he declared.[51]

Clamorgan begged off a direct statement on the *Dred Scott* decision—but only because, he proceeded to suggest, "the learned Chief Justice . . . has in this State kindred of a darker hue than himself." Such political power and racial innuendo gave southern-rights Democrats heart palpitations, but was it reality or exaggeration? It is impossible to know. Clamorgan's portraits overturn many assumptions about the lives of blacks in a slave-state metropolis, but the defiant pride also held a tinge of mournful nostalgia.[52] Free African Americans were buffeted by the same forces that limited their slave brethren and eclipsed the power of French-speaking St. Louisans generally—and they, too, watched the contest between Lincoln and Douglas anxiously.

Amid the bustle of economic recovery and the bombast of political contests, however, those in Missouri paused to mark two momentous passings in 1858. On April 10, 1858, Thomas Hart Benton succumbed to intestinal cancer. The previous day Benton had attained one final accomplishment, completing his *Abridgement of the Debates of Congress,* the authoritative accompaniment to *Thirty Years' View,* his firsthand history of three decades in the Senate. Magnanimous toward his longtime rivals, in the volumes Benton saw the actions of Clay, Calhoun, Van Buren, and others in the light of history, reading higher purposes in the place of just political scheming. By 1858 the events he recounted—the deaths of the Founders; the brokering of the Missouri Compromise; the squabbling of the second party system—all belonged to an era long departed.[53]

After President Buchanan, numerous congressmen, and members of the cabinet paid their respects in Washington, Benton's body traveled by special train to St. Louis, where it lay in state at the Mercantile Library Hall, draped in black for the occasion. More than 25,000 mourners came throughout the day and into the early afternoon to file past the body. In death Benton held his characteristically "lofty, tranquil, and gentle expression," Benjamin Gratz Brown declared. Newspapers around the nation reported on the funeral procession—how it took forty-five minutes to pass a given point, and how relatives, friends, militia companies, firemen, benevolent societies, and members of the courts and city government continued to join in "an immense concourse of citizens" until the streets pointing toward Bellefontaine Cemetery became impassable.[54]

St. Louis business was suspended for Benton's funeral, as it had been after the Great Fire and the Gasconade disaster. Flags were lowered and heads were bared. But this observance held a far different feel: a long and noted life was being commemorated. A crepe-edged image of Benton appeared in a storefront near the courthouse with the inscription: "Among the foremost men in all this land / The great Missourian stood pre-eminent. . . . He snapped asunder party rules and ties / As Samson did the cords which bound his limbs." In the seven years since Benton had spoken on "The Progress of the Age," a lifetime in elected office dissolved into a string of defeats, as political constituencies fractured and re-formed. Benton's vision of technological progress and national unity fell victim to the weakness of western compromise in the face of slaveholders' intransigence. For Benton's funeral, those accustomed to denouncing their partisan enemies gathered for a fleeting moment, with politicians of every stripe trading stories about their final conversations with the ill man, seeking after his mantle.[55] Benton's significant contributions and political prowess kept him fondly in memory. But whether his vision could be sustained remained to be seen.

On September 17, 1858, Dred Scott died, a victim of the tuberculosis that had long plagued him. No grand funeral was held, businesses were not closed, no newspaper described the procession as Scott was laid to rest. Scott's grave in Wesleyan Cemetery was unmarked. Both Dred Scott and "Sandford" were then dead: John F. A. Sanford had passed away a year before at a New York insane asylum, having suffered a breakdown in the months before the Supreme Court decision and never aware of its result. Perhaps owing to his deteriorated condition, Sanford's death went mostly unremarked.[56] Not so the death of Dred Scott, which was announced throughout the country.

The most prominent national political newspapers noted his passing with column-length obituaries. "Few men who have achieved greatness have won it so effectually as this black champion," the *New York Times* declared, reviewing his life circumstances, the family left behind, and the sour way in which Dred Scott became "accidentally but ineffaceably associated" with Taney's decision. "His name will live when those of CLAY, and CALHOUN, and BENTON will be feebly remembered or wholly forgotten," the *Times* predicted, with bombast that proved prescient. "The adverse decision he encountered here will there meet with reversal," in "the Supreme Court above," the editors concluded confidently. Left earthbound, however, was the *Dred Scott* case; as the *Daily National Intelligencer* opined, most would welcome it if "all the useless strife connected with his name . . . also died," yet the political climate made that impossible.[57]

"What does Senator DOUGLAS say of Dred?" asked the *Daily National Intelligencer,* turning from the obituary to the coming fall elections. Two weeks after Scott's death, Lincoln and Douglas met for their final debate in Alton, Illinois, just across the river from St. Louis. As he had at each debate, Douglas referenced Lincoln's claim to the Republican State Convention, that the controversy "will not cease until a crisis shall have been reached and passed," placing Lincoln's words in the context of the *Dred Scott* decision. "'A house divided against itself cannot stand,'" Lincoln reaffirmed. "I believe this government cannot endure permanently half Slave and half Free. I do not expect the house to fall—but I do expect it will cease to be divided. It will become all one thing, or all the other," Lincoln concluded.[58] Practically within sight of Thomas Hart Benton's grave, both Lincoln and Douglas sought the vision of union and compromise. Yet detractors saw each as portending radicalism and dissolution.

All one thing or another—Taney's *Dred Scott* decision had made slaveholders' rights the duty of the entire nation, further cheapening the idea of black freedom by negating the history of black citizenship. Yet in the city where the case originated, legislators and their allies sought a different vision, the promise of national unity through a dedication to free white labor and the eventual end of slavery. In 1857 the people of St. Louis demonstrated that the Republican Party held out a new and popular vision of universal free labor and antislavery, unhinged from nativism. Emancipation plans were being seriously considered around the nation for the first time in a half-century. Their constituency was growing, and its influence was great; but in the 1858 elections, these forces would not yet triumph.

Benjamin Gratz Brown and Frank Blair lost their bids for reelection in the fall of 1858. Cousins and until now political allies, Blair and Brown quarreled about control of the *Missouri Democrat,* their Republican mouthpiece in St. Louis, and soon parted ways. Across the river, Illinois Republicans won the popular vote, but owing to outdated apportionment and opponents in the middle of their terms they could not control the state senate. Thus Abraham Lincoln lost, trapped by indirect election as Benton had been in 1850. Despite these losses, proslavery Democrats understood that the intensity of the emancipationist challenge showed little sign of waning. "There is no chance of success for the democratic party in 1860," Missouri state senator Massey concluded in June 1859, "but by occupying something very much like Douglas' positions." What had once seemed too moderate for triumphant southern-rights Democrats became a welcome alternative to the increasing constituency of antislavery.[59]

After John Brown's daring but doomed raid at Harpers Ferry, slaveholders saw the balance shifting again, and predicted that a moderate consensus for a sensible expansion of slavery, coupled with colonization, could remain a formula for electoral success. "We shall at no distant day get rid of our free negro population," Waldo P. Johnson, a lawyer and former jurist in Osceola, Missouri, wrote to fellow Democrats in December 1859, "certainly a great pest to the citizens of this state, and a nuisance every where." Johnson was so confident that the logic of *Dred Scott* would prevail, the following sentence ticked on to his next concern: "Nothing yet that indicates with certainty what the Legislature will do in regard to the Rail Roads."[60]

In contrast, slavery's opponents once again saw reason for despair. "What a blessing slavery is!" an exasperated Eliot wrote in his journal on May 22, 1860, reflecting on the power of the *Dred Scott* decision. He had spent most of the day rescuing Sarah Green, a freeborn young woman kidnapped from her parents' house by a local slave broker. Only with the payment of $950, the arrangement of a security guarantee by a congregant, and the promise of gradual repayment by her parents, was Green let out of the slave pens.[61]

The *Dred Scott* decision ended the older flexibilities of geography, race, and class that had governed slavery along the Mississippi River since the French era. Strict southern property restrictions supplanted principles of western pragmatism, and even as western politicians such as Douglas and Lincoln found national followings, they adjusted their rhetoric to the newly clear policy on slavery in the new western territories. When these senatorial opponents met again as leaders of two of the four presidential tickets in 1860, it only intensified the importance of the case as the conflict grew from a regional question to a national dividing line.

For St. Louisans white and black, however, the U.S. Supreme Court's *Dred Scott* decision remained only one opinion among many, as Missourians grappled with the limits of emancipation. Even as the Supreme Court constricted the freedoms and rights of African Americans, Benjamin Gratz Brown's gradual emancipation proposal sought to expand rights for white workers by loosening the bonds on the enslaved, restoring the space to negotiate freedom. With the Panic of 1857, political and tactical defeats ensued, but in 1860, with the election of Abraham Lincoln as president, this sense of possibility pervaded national Republican Party politics.[62] The cultural, economic, and political battles already under way between the North, South, and West were already evident on the streets of St. Louis; hardly a spark was needed to engulf the whole country in its flames.

6

Germans and the Power of Wartime Union

At the first call, all Germans unanimously reached for their weapons, risking family, position, fortune, and all private interests. Going to battle for the defense and preservation of a united republic, they succeeded.

—Henry Boernstein, *Memoirs of a Nobody: The Missouri Years of an Austrian Radical, 1849–1866*, 1881.

St. Louis surgeon Joseph McDowell thought that German artist Emanuel Leutze had it all wrong. In his masterpiece *Washington Crossing the Delaware*, Leutze portrayed General George Washington in the winter of 1776, leading his bedraggled troops across the ice-blocked river to surprise British forces near Trenton, New Jersey. This much was true. Completing the painting in 1851, Leutze focused on the heroism and leadership of Washington, fighting for independence from the increasingly tyrannical British Empire. Again, no complaint.[1]

Yet Joseph McDowell's father had served alongside Washington and crossed the Delaware River that day in 1776. McDowell knew no man would be foolish enough to stand in the wobbly rowboats, as Leutze depicted, attracting attention during the vulnerable crossing. Washington seemed to head west, but New Jersey was *east* of the Continentals' encampment in Pennsylvania. And why was a German painting this scene at all, claiming this history as his own? After all, Hessian contract soldiers camped with the British at Trenton, Germans sent by their sovereign to fight for their fellow monarch against the partisans of democracy. McDowell would have none of it.[2]

McDowell raised these concerns in an open letter he wrote on December 8. 1859, considering the crisis of the moment alongside Washington's crossing.

Earlier that week John Brown had been hanged for leading the attack on the federal armory at Harpers Ferry, Virginia, and McDowell felt impassioned to remind European idealists such as Leutze that "there still lives the same love of liberty in my bosom that impelled them to battle and to cross the Delaware." Any attempt to subdue the South, he declared, "would impel me to cross the Mississippi to battle the foes of this Union." In McDowell's opinion, Washington's troops should turn back east and defend the country again.[3]

Yet, when the fighting of the Civil War began, McDowell fled rather than fought. His medical college was seized and later converted by Union troops into the Gratiot Street Prison. Troops would cross the Mississippi like the Delaware, yet McDowell's southern partisans would be on the losing side. As the city's oldest residents withdrew and its conservative Unionists dithered, Germans in St. Louis and other immigrants throughout the Union seized the opportunities to shape the war that redefined the United States. Their political and military actions would keep St. Louis firmly under Union control.[4]

Emanuel Leutze was one of many German Americans expressing a newfound love for the United States in the years before secession. As they became established, German Americans prospered financially and could turn their considerable numbers to political advantage in states across the Midwest. Yet, as the contentious 1858 midterm elections portended the final collapse of interregional compromise in the election of 1860, they were astounded by the call for secession: memories of the *Kleinstaaterei,* or small-statism, that had doomed German unity for hundreds of years led to immediate suspicions.[5] How could the United States give up its greatest strength, its unity in diversity? German-American leaders joined the search for a national leader who could preserve the Union and limit slavery.

In the spring of 1859, the most likely candidate seemed to be a St. Louisan, Edward Bates. Born in Virginia, Bates had long since freed his own slaves. A onetime Whig representative, Bates had opposed the territorial expansion of slavery and had avoided controversy in his years as a local judge. In 1856 Bates stepped down from his judgeship to seek political office; that year he served as presiding officer at the last national Whig Party convention, where those remaining in the party nominated former President Millard Fillmore. In April 1859 Bates was announcing his positions in long public letters, carefully measuring the response from political newspapers in his diary; by July he was sitting for prominent St. Louis portraitist William Cogswell. That month the *Louisiana* (Missouri) *Journal* made its choice for the crucial election. The newspaper placed Bates in its masthead and declared, "He is the man to lead on to victory the columns of the mighty 'Union Party,' that is daily gathering strength all over the country."[6]

Entering the Republican Party convention in Chicago in 1860, Bates was the only candidate from a slave state. Like Thomas Hart Benton before him, Bates was a southern transplant, a moderate known for urging compromise. The Democrats met in Charleston, South Carolina, but the northern wing of the party rejected a proslavery platform; when they regrouped in Baltimore to nominate Stephen Douglas, they made permanent the party's regional split. Observing and prognosticating, some Republican leaders thought Bates, a former slaveholder who sought to limit slavery, would be a particularly promising candidate to face Douglas, a fellow westerner still defending slavery's expansion.

German Republicans, however, had their doubts. Bates had long supported Fillmore, who was tainted by his acceptance of the nativist American Party endorsement in 1856; memories of the former president's 1854 visit to St. Louis, and the nativist violence it fomented, also remained raw. Bates, too, had been on anti-immigrant tickets in those years, although it was an endorsement he had neither sought nor condemned. Understanding his weakness, Bates actively courted Germans by advocating more radically Republican views—calling for the admission of Kansas as a free state and voicing a hint of support for a general emancipation. Yet this strategy cost him moderates and changed few minds in the German community.[7]

Nineteenth-century presidential politics bore little resemblance to today's contests. The candidates, it was understood, would stay home and maintain a disinterested pose, while their teams of operatives lobbied state conventions and judged their support among the national delegates. At the Chicago convention, the Bentonite congressman from St. Louis, Frank Blair, presented the case for Bates to the nominating committee. However, Carl Schurz and Gustav Körner told the committee that Germans in the upper Midwest could not forgive Bates's nativist taint—and party bosses promptly removed Bates from consideration. In his place, another moderate midwesterner and a former Whig, Abraham Lincoln, who was never suspected of nativist beliefs, emerged as the surprise candidate for president. Unionist Germans would stand in defense of St.

Louis, but their first act of political influence on the national stage was to re-move the local leader from contention for the presidency.[8]

Though a resident of Wisconsin, Carl Schurz was among those political refugees of the 1848 revolutions who saw themselves as citizens of the world, seeking the path to greater freedom and liberty wherever it could be found. After Bates balked at stumping for Lincoln, Schurz readily came to St. Louis to rally supporters, giving speeches in English and German that were re-printed widely. "Although in a slave State, I stand on the soil of a free city," Schurz declared, crediting the unique political landscape for giving him "the privilege of expressing my opinions freely." Senator William Henry Seward of New York, who like Bates went from Lincoln competitor to Lincoln cabi-net member, endorsed Schurz's efforts, proclaiming that "Missouri must be Germanized to win the state for freedom." However, the U.S. attorney in St. Louis, Thomas C. Reynolds, would not let the city's German voters go so easily. Campaigning for the proslavery Southern Democrat in the race, Vice President John C. Breckenridge, Reynolds displayed such eloquence in Ger-man that some suggested he was actually European—the rumor said a Prague-born Jew—rather than merely a well-traveled South Carolinian. With Schurz's encouragement, though, and despite Reynolds's efforts, the German commu-nity came away enthusiastic for Lincoln.[9]

Despite the growing German influence, the larger politics of St. Louis and Missouri seemed to favor Stephen Douglas. When Douglas appeared in the city on October 19, 1860, the streets were thronged. Speaking in front of the courthouse, Douglas projected a shared identity with St. Louisans. "We are bound to the North and to the South by ties of blood and affection, as well as of commerce," Douglas boomed, in front of banners that read, "We are opposed to all sectional parties." A strong supporter of the transcontinen-tal railroad and a leading voice for a homestead act, Douglas championed the West while encouraging northern industry and protecting southern interests. Regional advocates hoped the election and the 1860 Census would each dem-onstrate the primacy of the West in American politics. "Massachusetts and South Carolina have dictated our politics long enough," declared John Rich-ard Barret, a St. Louis politician aligned with Douglas. A victory, along with the new population figures, "will place us in control of this great Republic," he predicted.[10]

When the presidential ballots were cast, St. Louis and Missouri again demonstrated their unusual politics. While Lincoln won the states in the

Northeast, in the Midwest, and along the Pacific, and the Southern Demo-crat Breckenridge won eleven of fifteen slave states, Missouri was the only state won by Stephen Douglas. Moreover, St. Louis went for Lincoln—the largest city in a slave state to vote for the future president, a plurality victory that mirrored the returns throughout the divided country. German Unionists and other antislavery St. Louisans celebrated the unlikely result—and pre-pared for the proslavery backlash.[11]

In the fall of 1860, as St. Louisans voted for Abraham Lincoln and Missouri's state electors were pledged to the northern Democrat Stephen Douglas, the governorship went to the proslavery Southern Democrat, Claiborne Fox Jack-son. The author of the 1849 proslavery resolutions that had challenged Senator Benton's vision of compromise, Jackson saw slaveholding as a fundamental part of Missouri identity.

At his inauguration on January 3, 1861, Governor Jackson emphasized how slaveholding states would determine the fate of the Union. "The weight of Ken-tucky or Missouri, thrown into the scale," could determine the balance, Jack-son proclaimed, either to boost the chances of success for the burgeoning Confederacy or to provide the resources for a northern victory. Until the crisis was resolved, Missouri would remain neutral, the governor affirmed, and he called the state militia to alert, vowing to protect the state from attack by either side. While publicly suggesting that an amendment to the U.S. Constitution guaranteeing slaveholding could prevent war, Governor Jackson also indicated his willingness to consider the invitation from South Carolina for Missouri to join the seven states already seceded. Placing the decision in the hands of the people but expecting a vote for secession, Jackson called for a state convention to debate the future of Missouri and therefore the fate of the nation.[12]

And so, with the 1860 election just concluded, a new round of politicking began for the February 1861 state convention delegate elections. Jackson and his allies had hoped for open support for secession, but the majority of delegates elected were conservative Unionists, many among them slaveholders anxious to seek a political solution. Proslavery forces faced a first setback when the dele-gates voted to move the convention from the state capital to the St. Louis Mer-cantile Library Hall, and another when they chose the date for reconvening: the first Tuesday of March 1861, the same morning Abraham Lincoln would be inaugurated as president, albeit of ever-fewer and less united states. Still, the

German editors of the *Westliche Post* despaired that "the pride and the power of the nation . . . has been broken," and, with the sectional crisis, "Manifest Destiny . . . now has vanished into thin air."[13] Missouri delegates gathered to debate secession and the proposed amendment while local partisans wondered what might lie ahead.

Then St. Louisans saw the flag.

On March 4, 1861, the morning of the convention meeting and Lincoln's inauguration, dawn revealed Missouri's first secessionist flag flapping over the St. Louis courthouse. Displaying the state's coat of arms and only one star, the unauthorized banner was quickly removed and replaced by the Stars and Stripes. Basil Duke, a Kentucky-born lawyer and political ally of Governor Jackson, was the man responsible; he had also organized a new militia of "Minute Men," named for the revolutionary heroes but ready to act against the U.S. government. In the solidly Democratic neighborhoods of central St. Louis, both elite French and working-class Irish men gathered to protect slaveholding rights. Newspapers as far away as San Francisco published details of the secessionists' plots, declaring them "so prompt and definite" as to force a confrontation.[14]

German observers saw that what had been rumored and feared now came into the open: secessionists would make a stand in St. Louis. "These people have christened themselves with the name of Washington and assert that they are friends of the Union and the Constitution!" the *Anzeiger des Westens* reported incredulously. "It would not be easy to be any bolder or any crazier," the editors concluded.[15] As the delegates convened, their resolutions were powerless promises in the face of the spectacle on the streets.

St. Louis contemplated the fate of the Union under the flags of secession. Another such banner flew over the Berthold mansion, the Minute Men's secessionist base. With the crescent from South Carolina's flag, a yellow cross, and a single star, the *St. Louis Daily Evening News* called it "every conceivable thing that was suggestive of a Southern meaning." Duke hungered for a provocation, a chance for his forces to disperse the crowd and besiege the U.S. Arsenal, demanding the surrender of its weapons. Just as he hoped, an angry Unionist crowd gathered in front of the mansion to demand the flag's removal. Duke's men sat in the second-story window, watching all day, but no chance came to defend their banner.[16]

But the resistance, too, was ready. Frank Blair prepared to battle for the Union. Since many of the old-line militia groups in St. Louis—the Grays, the Guards, and the Rangers—had affiliated with Duke, Blair created new groups to support President Lincoln and defend the United States. The year before, the Blair Rangers, also called Wide Awakes, would march to political rallies to prevent trouble for their candidates (while at times causing it for others). Now Blair redoubled the effort, drawing support from the German population. Duke's Minute Men were formally enrolled as a state militia and drew state support, while Blair's groups were unofficial, secretive, and hence feared. When one company took the common German name *Schwarzer Jägercorps,* or Black Rifles, local Democratic newspapers mistranslated the name ominously as "blackguards." The Wide Awakes drilled in breweries and turner's halls (the home of German gymnastic clubs), supplying themselves from private stocks of rifles.[17]

As winter turned to spring, Blair's efforts expanded, and he found both U.S. military and German community leaders to be ready allies. Franz Sigel had been a military commander in Baden during the German revolutionary effort and minister of war in the 1849 provisional government there; in 1861 he was a recognized community leader employed as a mathematics teacher in St. Louis. Nathaniel Lyon was a Connecticut Yankee and an outspoken abolitionist, recently ordered to command at St. Louis. He soon overcame his nativist prejudices to work with his new allies, advising the German militias. As the secret drills continued, Unionist forces won a political victory: on March 9, 1861, delegates to the Missouri state convention voted to reject secession by a vote of 70 to 23. They adjourned on March 21 with a pledge to seek national reunion.[18]

Unable to garner a political mandate, pro-secession leaders, including Governor Jackson, convention president and ex-governor Sterling Price, and leading state senator Daniel Frost, joined the efforts of Basil Duke, tightening control over German Unionists in an effort to create a flashpoint. In the April 1 city elections, a nonpartisan Union ticket replaced strident Republicans in city offices; soon after, the governor dismissed the local St. Louis law enforcement leadership and placed the city police under direct state control. They enforced Sunday-closure laws to shutter German beer halls, made English the only language of state business, reallocated education and poor-relief funds to finance state militia drills, and generally worked to offend Republican sentiments. *Anzeiger* editor Henry Boernstein saw the intimidation as a replay of the nativist riots, finding "that same anti-German and lawless element" among the Minute Men. Secessionists hoped they could pressure the officers of the federal arsenal in St. Louis to concede their post to the Confederacy, for slavery ideologues in South Carolina, Virginia, and Arkansas had captured their local stockpiles.[19]

On April 12, 1861, South Carolina secessionists fired on Fort Sumter. With war under way, both Union and secessionist forces understood the importance of controlling St. Louis. Those who held St. Louis controlled the access to the overland trails, the network of federal installations, and the mineral and agricultural resources of the Mississippi and Missouri river valleys. Seizing St. Louis would mean altering the regional balance by providing the bounty of the West to the Confederacy; holding the city laid the groundwork for the later Union victories throughout the western theater of the war. Both Governor Jackson and President Lincoln sought to gain this advantage by controlling St. Louis.

When President Lincoln requested volunteers from all unseceded states, including Missouri, Governor Jackson was ready with his retort, declaring the request "illegal, unconstitutional, and revolutionary in its object, inhuman and diabolical, and cannot be complied with." Under the guise of the declared neutrality, Jackson's allies prepared Missouri for secession. Basil Duke was dispatched on a secret mission to request cannons from the fledgling Confederate government; the secessionists understood that St. Louis would have to be coerced into the Confederacy. Meanwhile, Jackson and Frost called the state militia into encampment, just outside of St. Louis.[20]

As this was a legally mandated assembly of the state militia, not all those marching to Lindell's Grove—christened "Camp Jackson" to honor the governor—shared secessionist sentiments. Some assumed this would be routine training, followed by a quick dismissal. Members of a German-American militia company, recently back from service on the Kansas border, were shocked to find themselves lined up against their neighbors.[21] Allegiances were confused: Jackson, the duly elected governor, prepared to lead the official state militia out of the Union, while Blair, the duly elected U.S. representative, sought to provide U.S. weapons to a fervent but as-yet-informal military force made up of Unionist St. Louisans.

On April 17, 1861, Frank Blair returned to St. Louis with authorization from President Lincoln to officially enroll his forces, to sidestep the overall commander of the U.S. Arsenal, the slaveholding General William Harney, and to organize his troops under Colonel Nathaniel Lyon. The muster rolls for Blair's troops displayed the depth of German enthusiasm for the Union: all but 100 of the 4,200 enlisted were German Americans. Blair's militias chose community leaders as officers: Blair was made first commander, while the editor Boernstein and the teacher Sigel were made colonels. As yet without uniforms, these troops marched to orders shouted out in German and filled the air with German war songs. Though many of the volunteers had military experience, "one would have served in the Austrian army, another in the Prussian, and others with the Bavarian, Württemberg, Hessian," Boernstein recalled, and "had learned different grasps, movements, and commands." Thus Boernstein established a model company of officers, who learned American methods in the morning and then rushed out to instruct their own men that same afternoon. At the end of April, Boernstein's forces crossed the Mississippi on their own secret mission, ferrying federal guns and ammunition to Alton, Illinois, out of reach of the state militia. Secessionists called this the first act of war in Missouri.[22]

While Frost drilled the state militias at Camp Jackson and Blair's forces gathered at the U.S. Arsenal, another group of men, women, and children acted in response to the outbreak of war. St. Louis's free blacks swarmed to the courthouse seeking to file freedom bonds and receive state-issued licenses, paper protection from reenslavement offered in return for a promise of "good behavior"—and backed up with promissory notes from African Americans and their guarantors. Though enacted in 1840, Missouri's freedom bond law had been honored mostly in the breach. Only after precipitating events—a new law in 1843 threatening black riverboat men with jailing; the U.S.-Mexican War; and, most dramatically, the firing on Fort Sumter—did dozens of free men and women find sponsors and file the necessary paperwork. Of the 1,080 extant bonds from St. Louis, 334 were signed during the last two weeks of April 1861, about half as many as had registered in the eighteen years preceding. Among them was Eliza Scott, Dred's daughter, newly of age and anxious to safeguard her freedom.[23]

The effort by African Americans in St. Louis to guarantee their freedom overwhelmed routine business at the county court, annoying commissioner Peregrine Tippett. "Free negroes and mulattoes had crowded the room for several days," he wrote, erroneously believing the licenses were "certificates of citizenship." Tippett felt the process should be halted and, citing the *Dred Scott* decision as his authority, that all emancipations, licenses, and freedom bonds issued since 1840 be voided. Yet Tippett was overruled, and the registrations continued. In the midst of militia maneuvering, free African Americans understood the opening of the war as a clarion call.[24]

On May 10, 1861, Lyon's regulars, the German volunteers, and the loyal Home Guards—eight thousand men in all—marched through the streets of downtown St. Louis to surround the twelve hundred militia men gathered at Camp Jackson. German troops were cheered in their home neighborhoods and taunted in the Irish "Kerry Patch" and from the mansions of established French families. The troops passed St. Louis High School just as classes got out, so many curious teenagers followed behind. "Everything was oppressively silent, nothing being heard but shuffling of feet," one later recalled. Not knowing what to expect—a battle? a negotiation?—residents came out to watch, taking up observation posts in trees and on rooftops. By three-thirty in the afternoon, Unionist troops had Camp Jackson surrounded, and Lyon's officers presented Frost with a demand to surrender.[25]

At first, no fight came. While Frost called the order "illegal and unconstitutional" and Lyon's action an "unwarranted attack," he felt it best to comply. His officers and their troops would surrender their arms and be taken into custody. Onlookers packed close to see what was occurring; as the lines became confused, some of those assembled in the parade ground threw away their militia insignias and blended into the crowd. So tight were the streets that Union commander Lyon was temporarily knocked unconscious by a kick from a fellow officer's horse. The state troops, aligned with the secessionists, had surrendered peacefully.[26]

But it was the skirmish after the surrender at Camp Jackson that caused the first Civil War fatalities in Missouri. As the federal troops processed the surrendering militias, secession-minded members of the crowd began taunting the Union soldiers, pelting them with clods of dirt, stones, and tiles. "Damn the Dutch!" was the common exclamation, using the American bastardization of *deutsch;* cheers rose for Jefferson Davis. When the Union flag was hoisted over Camp Jackson, onlookers became enraged; soon after, an errant shot of unknown origin hit a German captain, Constantin Blandowski, in the leg. Warning shots were answered by gunmen hidden in the crowd; soldiers struck back with bayonets. In the crossfire and confusion, regiments fired toward each other around a bend in the road; officers frantically tried to stop the shooting. Minutes later calm prevailed, but thirty lay dead: only three members of the state militia were killed, but two dozen in the crowd, including at least five teenagers, had fallen. Twice as many were wounded; Blandowski's leg would be amputated and complications would kill him by the end of the month.[27] St. Louisans were among the first to experience how the Civil War would bring brothers, colleagues, neighbors, and friends to fire on one another. The Unionism of this border city was now complicated by violence and straining under duress.

Was Camp Jackson a Confederate surrender with a bloody aftermath, or a Union attack on innocent civilians? Two versions spread through St. Louis and the divided nation. "German Mercenaries Murder American Citizens," the conservative *Missouri Republican* had it, while the radical German *Westliche Post* wrote that the day's brave soldiers would be able to tell their children how they bore arms to save St. Louis. Both sides could agree that the events at Camp Jackson caused a momentous break, and many bystanders wrote to family and friends to record their impressions and predict the incident's significance.[28]

William Tecumseh Sherman, who had recently moved to St. Louis to become president of a streetcar company, was among those in the crowd at Camp Jackson. When the fighting started, Sherman pushed his son to the ground to protect him. Ulysses S. Grant—at that moment a retired army officer and failed St. Louis farmer, working in his father-in-law's leather goods store in Galena, Illinois—went out to the arsenal the following day to congratulate Lyon, his fellow West Pointer, on the capture of Camp Jackson. On the streetcar there, Grant encountered "a dapper little fellow" red in the face because the secessionist flag over the Berthold mansion had finally been removed. These two future leaders of the Union army witnessed the first standoff in St. Louis, and the events at Camp Jackson shaped their perspective on the war effort.[29]

President Lincoln was monitoring the events in St. Louis—though he, too, received contradictory reports from Camp Jackson. Blair and Lyon sent a defense of their actions and asked for Harney, the arsenal commander, to be removed; leading conservative Unionists (including Wayman Crow, James Yeatman, Hamilton R. Gamble, Robert Campbell, and newly elected mayor Daniel Taylor) decried Lyon's actions as foolhardy and urged the president to support Harney's moderate and cautious policies. Lincoln's cabinet members with personal ties to St. Louis lobbied him as well: Postmaster General Montgomery Blair backed his brother, while Attorney General Edward Bates believed his brother-in-law Gamble. Lincoln chose to side with the Blairs. He issued a removal order for Harney but cautioned Blair only to use it with cause. The German volunteers rejoiced at the news. "With this conversation and from then on," Boernstein noted, "Lincoln . . . seemed to evaluate the situation in Missouri correctly."[30]

German troops had been essential members of the Union forces at Camp Jackson, and the German community actively promoted their interpretation of the resulting bloodshed. In Turner Hall, Mrs. Gempp led a group of St. Louis *Frauen* in presenting "a fine silk Union flag" to Company A of Blair's regiment, as a symbol of their thanks and pride in their community efforts. Other St. Louisans singled out the German soldiers for blame. John P. Couran was arrested in September 1861 but he took the loyalty oath, telling military investigators that he acted "more against the Germans in this City than against the Government." Released, Couran's anger did not subside: two years later he was again arraigned for screaming that every drop of blood spilled at Camp Jackson would be revenged when "they would kill all the Dutch in town."[31]

The German militias again saw action in mid-June, when the détente between Unionist federal forces and the remaining secessionist state forces broke down. For the weeks since the Camp Jackson affray, General Harney, still nominal head of the U.S. Arsenal in St. Louis, and Sterling Price, the newest commander in the state militia, had agreed to separate spheres of action for state and federal forces, each nominally protecting Missouri from attack. Yet the mere fact of Harney's agreement with an obviously hostile state government led to criticism both from local radicals and national military leaders, and Frank Blair delivered Lincoln's order of removal and assumed command. On June 11, 1861, at one final meeting between Jackson, Price, and their aides with Blair, Lyon, and their staff, any lingering sense of agreement collapsed. With a flair for the dramatic, Lyon rose to declare, "This means war."[32]

The next day Jackson declared war on the United States and called for fifty thousand Missouri men to defend the state against federal troops. (In the course of the war, St. Louis saw more than twenty thousand of its residents march under arms, split between the Union and the Confederacy.) As Jackson and Price traveled back to Jefferson City, they ordered the burning of railroad bridges—including over the Gasconade—to slow the pursuit of federal troops. Potent symbols of federal power and the Unionist vision of Manifest Destiny, railroad tracks would be attacked again and again in Missouri throughout the Civil War. Severing these hardly delayed Union troops, however, so Jackson's allies were forced to abandon the state Capitol. The

German troops fanned out: Sigel's unit occupied the southwestern Missouri railhead at Rolla, while Boernstein's regiment proceeded from St. Louis to Hermann to Jefferson City by steamboat without incident. On as much an adventure as a military engagement, the German troops mostly stood watch; in a quixotic act of clemency, Boernstein's soldiers released one prisoner "solely on literary grounds," he wrote, after the man impressed his guard with knowledge of Schiller and Goethe. Yet the secessionist militias escaped at their full strength, regrouping for attacks in southern Missouri.[33]

As battles elsewhere in the state pitted St. Louis troops against the secessionists, St. Louis itself became ever more quiet, if not exactly calm. The day after the scuffle at Camp Jackson, shots had been fired at the newest German regiment from the steps of the Second Presbyterian Church, and four soldiers were among the nine dead. Many congregations were divided over the growing conflict, with some ministers admonishing congregants to avoid political questions, and others urging action from the pulpit. "The church is carried away too by the storm," lamented Minerva Blow, a conservative Unionist. Some members of the Second Baptist Church unsuccessfully sought to censure their minister, Galusha Anderson, for "the introduction into our pulpit of the political questions now agitating our distracted Country." The Catholic leadership urged priests and parishioners to remain neutral, yet ignoring the war was impossible; at the end of May, St. Louis University ended the academic term abruptly, unable to continue instruction when students feared for their families. For their part, members of the Trinity German Evangelical Lutheran Church participated in a Day of Prayer and Repentance called by President Lincoln after a string of Union defeats. In the months after Camp Jackson, the battles raged elsewhere. But the pressures of maintaining Union support weighed heavily on those controlling St. Louis.[34]

In the summer and fall of 1861, German St. Louisans cheered the brief but explosive command of General John C. Frémont. Frémont had been away from politics and away from St. Louis for four years. Having just arrived in California when news of Thomas Hart Benton's death came in 1858, Jessie Benton Frémont and her husband missed her father's funeral. When the Civil War broke out, the former explorer, temperamental commander, and first Republican Party presidential candidate had been in Paris, courting investors for his California mining operation. In July 1861 President Lincoln appointed Frémont commander of the Department of the West, leader of military operations from Illinois to the Rockies, and the couple returned to St. Louis to establish headquarters. On November 3, 1861, just as he was ready to engage Confederate forces near Springfield, Frémont received his order of removal. After less than four months in command, John and Jessie Frémont packed for New York. They would never return to power in St. Louis.[35]

During his Civil War command, Frémont attracted fervent followers and vicious detractors, much as he had done throughout his career. Frémont's military errors were evident: he failed to reinforce inexperienced German troops when they were vulnerable, and made tactical mistakes that gave the secessionist state militia its first battlefield victories at Wilson's Creek and at Lexington. The death of General Lyon at Wilson's Creek compounded Frémont's problems. His return to St. Louis was marred with mistakes: by establishing headquarters in the Brant mansion, home of an old-time family close to the Bentons, Frémont invited criticism; the choice reminded radical Unionists of Basil Duke's secessionist command, terrorizing the city from the Berthold mansion. Frank Blair, obstinate, felt he was already the commander in St. Louis, and so he refused to acknowledge any orders from Frémont. Throughout it all, Frémont constantly found support from the radical German-speaking community, on account of his long and fervent antislavery record. Responding to this favor, Frémont also included many German speakers among his headquarters staff. Their fealty was almost blind; as Boernstein recalled, these fellow Germans seemed not to mind that Frémont ruled "as a sort of dictator" over Missouri.[36]

In August 1861, with his support in the army leadership crumbling, General Frémont sought to boost his influence on the national war effort by issuing the most volatile declaration of the Civil War. After declaring martial law in St. Louis and extending it to cover all of Missouri, Frémont defined the entire southern section of the state as a war zone. There, to combat what he saw as "the helplessness of civil authorities," Frémont ordered armed rebels to be summarily executed—and "their slaves, if any they have, are hereby declared freemen." Radical Germans cheered and *The Liberator* happily reprinted the decree, but many others throughout the Union immediately condemned General Frémont's "Missouri Emancipation Proclamation." President Lincoln was irate. The declaration endangered Union control in all the loyal slave states. Troops in Kentucky threw down their arms in protest, and the administration of new Unionist Missouri governor Hamilton Gamble teetered toward disarray. Alexander Badger, a St. Louis–born soldier serving at Fort Vancouver on the Pacific, felt free to put it plainly: "The longer the numskull Fremont remains in command," he wrote, "the better it will be for the Southern Confederacy."[37]

After Lincoln urged Frémont to change his mind, he received a noncommittal answer from the general and a visit from his wife (whom opponents called "General Jessie"). "General Fremont should not have dragged the Negroes into it . . . he never would if he had consulted with Frank Blair," Jessie Benton Frémont recalled Lincoln saying in admonishment; she returned to St. Louis somewhat cowed. When John C. Frémont would not retract his order, Lincoln publicly repudiated it. After Frémont arrested Blair for his criticisms, dawdled in attacking Confederate forces in southern Missouri, and strained many of his remaining alliances with his arrogance, Lincoln had had enough and removed Frémont from command.[38]

Frémont's emancipation declaration freed only two slaves, Hiram Reed and Frank Lewis. Both were held as menservants by Thomas Snead, aide-de-camp to Governor Jackson; after Frémont's proclamation, it seems they escaped across the army lines in southern Missouri, making their way to St. Louis, where they were granted freedom. Yet even after it was revoked, Frémont's order maintained its resonance: one Confederate sympathizer was arrested months later for saying, "Genl Fremont ought to be hung, drawn, and quartered for issuing such a proclamation." Sympathizers were left with a hopeful uncertainty about the fate of slavery. In December 1861 Frederick M. Colburn, a conductor on the Terre Haute, Alton & St. Louis Rail Road, wrote his superintendent for clarification on whether African Americans could ride the rails, as he had been allowing them to ride "on proof of their freedom." Asking whether policies had changed, Colburn was told to refuse all black passengers.[39] Yet such strictures could only delay rather than deny the desires of African Americans to join the Union effort.

In the years to come, Frémont's command had its champions, even as the Blair family charged him with recklessness, corruption, and mismanagement. Given Frémont's strong attachment to the free-labor cause and the exploration and development of the West, the bold actions of his command inspired some St. Louisans to think beyond the war years, to the chance to reclaim a central role in American politics, economics, and culture for their region. On the grounds of military necessity, Frémont ordered the city's rail companies to unite their lines and allow the direct transfer of goods from the levee to freight lines headed in any direction. Not only would this serve the war effort, the *Anzeiger des Westens* wrote, it would provide an "enormous advantage" in peacetime, matching the transshipment capabilities of Chicago. Frémont's backers in Congress championed his actions, saying he left the state with "every mile" of the railroads in working order, and "the city of St. Louis a monument of his good sense."[40]

Despite his visionary actions, however, Frémont's arrogant behavior and impolitic style made many enemies. Frémont had "surprised and alarmed the semi-loyal," William Greenleaf Eliot told Lincoln in the fall of 1861, alienating factions until only radical emancipationists, the loyal Germans, and his family relations stood to support him.[41]

Those who had openly championed the emancipation of slaves and the flowering of the western agenda had to accommodate themselves to more conservative Unionist commands, raising suspicions about what continued in secret. "Germans too are as bad as Secessionists, since Genl Fremont was removed," a female informant told the military authorities in late 1862. Looking back, *Anzeiger* editor Henry Boernstein lamented that Frémont's tenure had split the German community in St. Louis between backers of Frémont and supporters of Blair—a division that led to continued infighting and diminished political power for St. Louis's German population. These divisions would prove instrumental in shifting St. Louis politics during Reconstruction, but during the war such differences did not prevent the German bloc from remaining stalwart in its defense of the Union.[42]

With the end of Frémont's command, emancipation was canceled, martial law lived on, and the city of St. Louis remained a placid island in the growing bloodshed. "So far as St. Louis is concerned we would not know that such a thing as war existed," prominent local businessman Samuel Cupples boasted at the end of 1861—though he was quick to note the rest of the state "is in an awful condition."[43] Frémont's emancipation proclamation revealed the stakes of the Civil War to those in St. Louis, in terms that would soon be obvious to those fighting throughout the nation. Abolitionists and secessionists, German radicals and delicately moderate conservatives could now agree: The fate of slavery would be determined by the progress of the war. For now, free and enslaved African Americans were left to dream, to check their papers, and to cheer Union troops.

*   *   *

As the war dragged on, Germans and other St. Louis Unionists sought to express their loyalty on the nation's symbolic as well as actual battlefields. In the center of the city, the most important civic building, the courthouse, had been under construction for a quarter-century. As the Civil War began, its dome was finally nearing completion, but the conflict produced a renewed uncertainty; could the project be completed, or would it be abandoned? In their own Civil War battle, a faithful American architect and a brilliant German-American painter brought the courthouse work to a triumphant finish.

William Rumbold had just been appointed official architect in September 1859, but it was a fateful tenure; he succeeded in completing the million-dollar, multidecade project. Before Rumbold's tenure, the courthouse construction had been a mess, an "immense unfinished pile," as the *Missouri Democrat* called it, a folly that reminded the editors of the Tower of Babel. War and martial law were not obstacles anyone could have expected, but Rumbold was still able to make progress. As the man who had brought

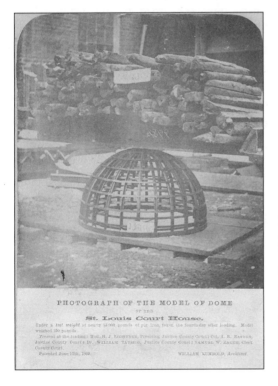

In the midst of fragile politics, courthouse architect William Rumbold held public tests of the dome's strength, encouraging St. Louisans with its physical and symbolic power. William Rumbold, strength test of iron dome, *carte-de-visite*, 1862. Missouri History Museum, St. Louis.

news of the Gasconade disaster to St. Louis, Rumbold understood the depth of adversity the city's other crowning projects had faced. Rumbold hired workers, reworked the design, and replaced the planned courthouse dome with his own iron-ribbed version that allowed for greater height without internal supports. In the midst of fragile politics, Rumbold held public tests of its strength—symbolically and physically powerful, the dome earned a patent and the attention of those working from a similar design for the unfinished U.S. Capitol. Coppered in the fall of 1860, the dome was an instant icon as well as a functional space for city, county, and federal officers. A completed courthouse symbolized the renewed strength of St. Louis's Unionism.[44]

As domes rose in Washington and St. Louis, each city sat at the edge of the war zone, commanding operations for the Union. Local officials imagined a race to completion with the U.S. Capitol, and hoped the administrative as well as architectural similarities would bring St. Louis further responsibility for governing the West after the war as well. Freed from the need for tri-regional compromise, western advocates in Congress advanced their agenda, funding the transcontinental railroad, passing a comprehensive homestead act, and establishing a system of land-grant colleges. Advocates hoped the combined political, military, and cultural opportunities of wartime administration offered lasting opportunities for St. Louis and the West.

When the dome scaffolding was removed in June 1861, a county court judge himself hoisted a fifty-foot American flag onto the flagpole. He reported how "all over the city, the appearance of the national ensign was hailed with delight—knots of men at the corners and along the principal streets waving their hats and cheering." The flag could be seen for nearly a dozen miles along the Illinois–Missouri waterfront, from Alton down to Carondelet. In January 1862, with the interior walls plastered and the basic painting completed, the Board of Commissioners sought the best local artists to fresco the dome. August Becker was hired, and he in turn engaged his mentor, Leon Pomerade, as well as his half-brother Carl Wimar, the master artist among St. Louis Germans.[45]

As Emanuel Leutze labored on murals for the U.S. Capitol dome, Wimar, his protégé, brought the high-art traditions of Düsseldorf to the courthouse commission, producing images that rivaled Leutze's in expressing the German fervor for the Union. "Concerning art America is 100 years behind

Germany," a disdainful Wimar had written in August 1854, yet in the decade that followed he built his renown by depicting American subject matter in the German high style. Wimar filled so many canvases with buffalo and encounters on the emigrant trails that he became known to his colleagues as "the Indian painter." Born in Bonn, Wimar moved with his family to St. Louis when he was fifteen, and, like his half-brother Becker, initially trained with Pomerade. "Everything Pomerade advised me to do I found right," Wimar wrote—whether to study in Paris and Munich, as he did, or to seek training in Düsseldorf, from Leutze.[46]

As much as it fired surgeon Joseph McDowell's anger, Leutze's *Washington Crossing the Delaware* was a touchstone for Wimar's artistic growth, "surpass[ing] everything I have seen before," he wrote. "Mr. Leutze paid a visit to me in my atelier, and brought along all the Americans who are here," Wimar wrote excitedly in October 1854. In 1855 Wimar painted *Washington as Ambassador to the Delaware Indians,* and, while in Düsseldorf, Missouri's prized artist George Caleb Bingham attempted his own version of Washington and his troops on the Delaware River.[47]

Despite his enthusiasm for the historical paintings, Wimar continued to produce scenes of the frontier inspired by the *Wildwestgeschichten,* or Wild West stories, he read. To that date, Wimar himself had never been to an American Indian encampment and had witnessed the rituals of trade only when Indian parties had encamped on the parks of St. Louis, an annual event at the time. In the winter of 1858–1859, Wimar returned to America, finally ventured up the Missouri River, and afterward stopped depicting imagined abductions. He began painting stark Plains landscapes, rituals of the buffalo hunt, and ethnographic portraits of American Indian leaders.[48]

The joint courthouse commission with Becker and Pomerade allowed Wimar a chance finally to attempt monumental history paintings. The resulting images offer a telling narrative of the past, present, and future imagined for St. Louis by a German-American master. As he crafted a design, the outbreak of the Civil War weighed heavily on Wimar's thinking. During the contentious 1860 election, Wimar had sketched *Reconciliation,* imagining the scene of reunion between North and South, regional hands grasped by a figure of Columbia and heralded by cherubs bearing the symbols of industrial and agricultural production. Though he never completed the commission, its imagery was echoed in Becker's work for the very height of the dome, where accounts described corn and wheat, the leading products of the North and

Midwest, joining pineapple and sugarcane, icons of southern hospitality and trade, to symbolize the reunited national harvest in this western metropolis.[49]

Yet Wimar also acknowledged the bloodshed that followed, creating a somber triple portrait at the end of 1861 showing Captain Blandowski (who had been Wimar's traveling companion among the American Indians), the fallen General Lyon, and the controversial and revered General Frémont. His first work at the courthouse, in the spring of 1862, was to complete allegorical figures of Law, Justice, Liberty, and Commerce, holding up the dome. Surrounding Liberty with an eagle, a shield, and an unaltered Stars and Stripes, Wimar sent a clear message of loyalty for the Union.[50]

In his four largest compositions, for the dome's semicircular lunettes, Wimar followed the suggestion of county commissioner Charles Taussig, selecting themes that "symbolize the discovery and development of the far West." For accuracy of detail, Wilson Primm, a longtime St. Louis resident and author of an early history, was consulted, and panels to the north, south, and east depicted the 1541 "discovery" of the Mississippi by Spanish explorer Hernando De Soto; the 1764 founding of St. Louis by French trader Pierre

This sketch, completed during the 1860 elections, imagined the scene of reunion between North and South, as regional hands are grasped by a figure of Columbia. Carl Wimar, *Reconciliation*, 1859. Missouri History Museum, St. Louis.

Laclède; and a 1780 attack on St. Louis by Indian tribes allied with the British during the American Revolution. Once before, St. Louis had repulsed amassed forces, Wimar implied, and now the city could celebrate its defense in another war that redefined the American nation.[51]

It was in the final lunette, however, on the western side of the courthouse, that Wimar expressed his vision of the nation's future and the place of St. Louis within the ongoing battles of the cultural civil war. Even before it was completed, a newspaper reporter could recognize Cochetopa Pass, "the natural gateway of the Central Pacific railroad," mapped by John C. Frémont through the mountains of Colorado. Wimar's scene showed a completed railroad, following the herd of buffalo into the West. In the same months when his mentor, Leutze, completed his own fresco, *Westward the Course of Empire Takes Its Way,* in the U.S. Capitol, Wimar finished his own masterwork of westward expansion under the same title, not a nostalgic image of wagon trains but a vision of future railroad routes. Yet the pass so far remained empty: owing to the influence of Chicago interests, the newly funded transcontinental railroad would run farther north, through Omaha. Yet the renewed excitement of the possibilities of the West encouraged St. Louisans to wonder whether the Civil War could finally provide an opening for the dream of Manifest Destiny and the concrete goals of the western agenda.[52]

Wimar stressed the national tenor of his composition by completing the work with portraits of four heroes of the Union, George and Martha Washington, Thomas Hart Benton, and Edward Bates. The Washingtons were icons of national promise, as celebrated by the namesake university nearby. The local politicians Benton and Bates had each played a role in promoting the uniting power of railroads. Each was recognized as a fervent patriot who had sought to prevent division over slavery through sectional compromise. The two men were heroes of St. Louis but failed national leaders, thus adding a reminder of the limits of St. Louis leadership even in its temple of Union strength. His vision complete, the ailing artist never finished another canvas; Carl Wimar succumbed to tuberculosis on November 28, 1862.[53]

From its innovative dome to its evocative murals of St. Louis history and national heroes, the completed courthouse was the iconic heart of St. Louis, a bold symbol of civic and national ambition created at a crucial time. As Union troops faced defeats and uncertain prospects, those military officers and civilians enduring the war in St. Louis could rejoice at the courthouse's completion, on the Fourth of July, 1862, just as promised. And there was no further threat of secessionists' hanging their flag over the edifice of Union: from the end of July, a "keeper of the Rotunda" was charged with maintaining clean and proper conditions, holding the key to the lookout, and, as "custodian of the Flag," seeing that only the proper colors flew from the courthouse dome.[54]

Wimar's marvelous frescoes reflected the vision of the German St. Louisans at the outbreak of war. They had nurtured freedom both in Germany and their adopted homeland, and in the first years of the war they maintained their commitment to antislavery even as they waged war for the reunification of the nation on any terms.

In the courthouse's western lunette, Carl Wimar provided a vision for St. Louis's future, with the completed railroad running through Cochetopa Pass. Below, Wimar added a portrait of George Washington, linking the scenes of St. Louis past and future to the iconic heart of the nation. Carl Wimar, *Westward the Star of Empire Takes Its Way* (*The Cochetope Pass*) and *George Washington,* 1862. Jefferson National Expansion Memorial Archives, National Park Service, St. Louis.

Of course not all Germans cast their lot with the Union. While Wimar and Leutze glorified the Union with their art, the German-born dentist and incisive political satirist Adalbert Johann Volck championed the Confederate cause in Baltimore. Under the pseudonym V. Blada, the one-time St. Louis resident produced images of Lincoln consulting with imps and devils, and depicted the Republican Party as a bacchanalia of atheism, free love, and "Negro Worship." Harshly criticizing his fellow Germans, Volck engraved "Valiant Men 'Dat Fite Mit Siegel,'" referencing a popular ditty while showing German soldiers plundering a Confederate home, with little regard for a woman begging for mercy. Volck even had a response to *Washington Crossing the Delaware* that would have made the secessionist Joseph McDowell proud. His engraving *Crossing the Potomac* mirrored Leutze's composition, but here Marylanders ran supplies across the river to aid Confederate forces. Their leader stood confidently as his sailors rowed the boat to safety, out of the range of a distant cannon.[55]

In St. Louis, the botanist and community doctor George Engelmann wrote in his personal correspondence of enduring "a horrible war of suppression," fought for hollow principles, and that death and discomfort would be the war's only result. Engelmann's son, a student at Washington University, shared his pessimism. In February 1862 George Julius Engelmann wrote in his diary that the city was experiencing "a reign of terror." And Jacob Miller was the rare German man arrested in St. Louis as a secessionist. In August 1862 fellow boarders at his hotel testified that he had just arrived from travel through the Confederacy, and seemed "a dangerous character."[56] Though Volck, the Engelmanns, and Jacob Miller were not the only German Americans to support the Confederate cause, they were in an extreme minority. Most of their countrymen were proud to express allegiance by providing political, military, and cultural manpower to the wartime Union.

In the early years of Civil War fighting, the stakes of the cultural civil war were obvious throughout St. Louis, from the ballot box, to the neighborhood streets, to the dome of the courthouse. During the 1860 election cycle, Edward Bates had represented the last chance for an outdated local tradition of compromise. Once the war broke out, John C. Frémont and his German allies unleashed the power of radical Union sentiment against ardent Confederates. Before Frémont's emancipation order was halted, a future without slavery became a real possibility, and the city filled with escaping African Americans. The fighting freed St. Louis leaders from the narrowed options and failed compromises that had crippled their efforts at national leadership for a decade. Fervent Unionists in a slave state, controlling access to the Mississippi River and the trails into the West, German Americans and others in St. Louis worked to redefine the national values.

As the war dragged on, the Germans and their radical allies faced reversals. Only in its later years would they learn that regional compromise had not been abolished, but merely shifted, as conservative Unionists and southern sympathizers had to be engaged in the creation of a workable neutrality.

7

Building Union from Neutrality

This Civil War is a painful theme which thrusts itself before us, at every turn. . . . Missouri is becoming more & more Sesesh every day—before the affair at Camp Jackson—full 9/10 of our People were for the Union—now more than that proportion are on the opposite side—Judge Gamble has stated the no. to be 19/20. . . . But enough of this harrowing theme.

—William Carr Lane to William Glasgow Jr., April 14, 1862.

The Unionists would all go to Hell, and the Secessionists to Heaven." That was what Catherine Bockman heard when she attended Mass at St. Vincent's, near the French market in the Soulard neighborhood of St. Louis, on May 27, 1862. Bockman was shocked. She had come to pray for the welfare of her husband, a soldier in the 5th Regiment, Missouri Cavalry, and instead heard the Union cause denounced. Returning home, Bockman shared her outrage with her neighbors, fellow Germans, and an account soon appeared in the German newspapers. While most of the community joined her denunciations, one man named Wachtel was more cautious. "She ought to be ashamed of herself for telling anything that her priest had said, outside the church," he reasoned—especially if she misheard or misunderstood the accent of the Irish clergyman.[1]

Cheers for secession, especially from a man of God, were just the sort of thing that interested the U.S. provost marshal, the chief of military police charged with maintaining peace and loyalty in the civilian population. After reading the newspaper accounts, the marshal's officers petitioned Archbishop Peter Richard Kenrick for an explanation, and he in turn contacted Father Hennessey, the parish priest of St. Vincent's. It was a misunderstanding,

Hennessey insisted, and he thanked the officers for asking questions before proceeding to arrests. Congregants soon came to his defense: young John Wessel *thought* he had heard the same condemnation, but "when I got home I asked my father why the priest spoke about 'secession,' and father said that the word was 'ascension.'" The investigators concluded that the German speakers misunderstood the priest's message—not a political message at all but a call to celebrate the ascension of Christ. The investigation concluded and the proper reports filed, a crisis was thus averted.[2]

In St. Louis the greatest Civil War battle was over the nature of neutrality. Though western Missouri was the scene of constant fighting, after the May 1861 skirmish at Camp Jackson, St. Louis remained quiet. Union supporters held firm judicial control, but conservative Unionists and southern sympathizers remained powerful, at the helm of many city businesses. After the initial shock of division, St. Louis recovered economically to function and even prosper during the war. St. Louis became a Union administrative center, where military bases were established, ironclad ships were built, and injured soldiers were brought to hospitals. Yet vital to success was the cooperation—willing, grumbling, or coerced—of the city's sizable population of Confederate sympathizers. City leaders drew on the local traditions of compromise to build a flexible neutrality, one that secured the loyalty of Confederate sympathizers and checked Radical Republican excesses.

St. Louisans lived out the war in a state of tense uneventfulness. Though battles did not come, Confederate forces often camped just a day or two away, with battlefronts possible on many sides. Throughout the war, refugees periodically streamed into the city, bringing tales of skirmishes to the north, south, and west. In its best moments, the enforced neutrality of St. Louis was something natural for Unionists and Confederate sympathizers, merely a new condition for doing business, a polite urging to leave some topics unmentioned. But essential to the maintenance of Union command amid this flexibility was the office of the provost marshal.

In St. Louis as elsewhere, provost marshals functioned as a military combination of mayor, district attorney, and police commissioner. When rumored allegiances and misunderstood phrases came to the attention of the provost marshal's office, the staff investigated, as their key weapon was intelligence gleaned from the civilian population. Newspapers were screened; mail was censored and seized. Daily they investigated rumors, solicited and recorded testimony, required oaths of allegiance, and made arrests. And each action left its paper trail, shards of information about neighbors reporting on neighbors.[3]

Over this hierarchy of surveillance lay a matrix of punishments. When no mere oath of loyalty would do, Confederate sympathizers faced fines and assessments against property. Forms were printed for the purpose, so that the provost marshal and his assistants needed only to fill in the name and the amount to be paid in "Clothing, Provisions or quarters" for military personnel or Unionist refugees driven from their homes in southwestern Missouri. Depending on how serious an offense was judged to be, acts of confiscation, imprisonment, and even banishment could follow. Targeted individuals rightly complained how the standards of justice were not absolute, as punishments often depended on the social stature of the accused and the perceived threat to the war effort. The provost marshal's office balanced the desire for uniform Union loyalty with concerns about political stability and economic viability. Over the course of the war, more men were arrested in Missouri than in any other state.[4]

As evidenced by Father Hennessey's rumored secessionist sermon, any public denunciation of the Union cause triggered a provost marshal investigation. A. R. Cazauran was arrested in the courthouse after he cursed the United States, declaring he owed it no more allegiance than he did "to the Sandwich Islands or to the Feegee Islands." George Mathews vowed to kill every Union man in St. Louis and he was "commanding influence in certain circles," according to the marshal's records. These cases seem spectacularly clear, yet most incidents were far more murky.[5]

Often accusers utilized allegations of disloyalty to twist ongoing conflicts grounded in ethnic or class tensions. When a group of teenagers, off from work at the tobacco factory, entered Louis Weil's store on the evening of July 28, 1862, they wanted beer and the privilege of charging their drinks to a tab, which Weil refused. "Go to Hell," they shouted, and he retorted, "You may go there yourselves." One worker knocked Weil down, Weil grabbed his revolver, and then another broke a chair over Weil's head before the group left. This conflict was not explicitly about the war, yet the next day, when Weil again refused the factory workers drinks, they called him "a Dutch Union son of a bitch" before continuing down the street to harass another German storekeeper—and Weil quickly reported them. The fervent Unionism of the St. Louis German population particularly rankled Confederate sympathizers, and nativists who spoke about cleansing the city of Germans were arrested for their anti-Union sentiments. Any momentary outburst could mean months in jail.[6]

As wartime enlistments drew away tens of thousands of the city's men, St. Louis women emerged into new roles and had their own encounters in the streets. The conflict between Margaret J. Knapp and her neighbor, Margaret Gay, began on Washington's Birthday 1862, when another neighbor hung out a Union flag for the holiday. "Damn the Union flag," Margaret Gay declared, vowing to burn it. Gay then called Knapp "a dirty bitch" and said that she wished to have "a sharp knife to cut off Abe Lincoln's head" and the heads of all his soldiers—Knapp was glad to turn her in. Maggie Melvin was investigated for taunting her neighbors, saying she "wished to see Union women have negro twins by a big buck nigger," stoking fears by linking the Union cause to miscegenation. Mary Ann Fitzgerald sang "The Bonnie Blue Flag" and other Confederate songs, and faced similar accusations of treason.[7] Such complaints reflected the power of gossip as a weapon in the wartime city.

From the fracas of women fighting in the streets to arrests for mere boasts and prattle, St. Louis's wartime social order was disorienting to William Carr Lane and his daughters. "Under our present abolitionist Yankee rule," Lane wrote in February 1862, "all rights not only of property but of person have melted away." Lane had witnessed most of St. Louis's history, having arrived in 1815 and, in 1823, having won election as the city's first mayor. A former New Mexico territorial governor, a master of business and political ties along the Santa Fe Trail, and a close associate of the founding French families, Lane was accustomed to development, but not to the dramatic reversals the war administration brought.[8]

Protected by his reputation and age, William Carr Lane recorded the perceived outrages against the St. Louis elite in detail. Assessments had been levied against the Benoist family, old-time French residents of the city, and against the widow of General Stephen Kearney; Lane remarked on the threats against George Engelmann, the rare German who opposed the war, and rumors that the government would arrest the archbishop. Lane despaired that the provost marshal, "that unscrupulous shallow pate Barny Farrar," came from a good French family in his social circle and yet still enforced the Union strictures—even forcing his own sister, Martha Farrar Sweringen, to flee the city. Lane clearly enjoyed writing fiery letters, railing against the "secret police & new night court of inquiry," condemning the property assessments. Yet he was also shrewd to send his letters out of the St. Louis region with trusted friends.[9]

Lane's daughters lived out the war on different continents. While Anne Lane, unmarried, endured indignities in her hometown, her sister Sarah Lane Glasgow and her family fled to Europe. They found Germany a welcoming place for southern sympathizers: "I was at a Confederate party at Mrs H's on Friday," Glasgow wrote from Wiesbaden in 1864. "None there but rebels," she said, and "we had a real American supper turkey ham & chicken salad." Sarah Lane Glasgow found it "almost like home"—yet at home in St. Louis, Confederate families had no such freedom to celebrate.[10]

After their father's death in early 1863, Anne Lane took up the cause to provide war news and to write disapprovingly of conditions. When a group of Confederate officers' wives were banished, she called it cowardly: the federal authorities "remind me of the boy who could not whip another boy but could make faces at his sister," she wrote. The garden of Eliza O'Flaherty, widow of a Gasconade victim and mother of Kate Chopin, had been vandalized by Union soldiers, the men "breaking the vases in her yard and the Shrubbery & hoisting a flag over her house," Anne Lane lamented. She found the intrusions increasingly farcical, as when a spy appeared in her sewing circle. "Nice country this is to live in," she observed sardonically.[11]

To succeed at neutrality, Confederate sympathizers had maintained uncertainty, their allegiances suspected but not revealed. After the Confederate surrender at Camp Jackson, William Tecumseh Sherman brought the news to his neighbor Eliza Dean, who promptly slammed the door in his face. Many hid in like fashion. Some women wore a white rose pinned between two red blossoms, to match the red-white-red pattern of bars on the Confederate flag—a symbolism obvious to some but also subtle enough. Discretion was key: as early as 1859 ardent secessionist John F. Snyder was warned to destroy his letters, and in 1862 former Missouri Supreme Court Justice William Barclay Napton went so far as to bury his diaries. Throughout the war, Confederate sympathizers registered their anguish and disdain at what they were certain would be remembered as an awful war of Republican extremism. Yet, for their own personal safety, they did so in private.[12]

In January 1862 suspicions of disloyalty engulfed the St. Louis Mercantile Library board elections. As business leaders fostering intellectual and cultural advancement, library directors considered their hall library a showcase for the best educational and social ideals, a very paragon of neutrality. They had always taken pride in their apolitical institution, and elections were normally humdrum, as incumbents merely moved up a rank, according to custom.

Yet, at the first annual meeting held during the war, the regular slate of officers was challenged by a self-proclaimed "straight Union ticket." The challengers argued that the incumbent officers seemed too apolitical, too neutral, given the circumstances. The dueling tickets split the membership, dividing business partners and even Oliver Filley, the former Free-Soil mayor, from his more ardently emancipationist brother Chauncey. As war spilled into a second year and martial law tightened, the challengers reasoned, could the library afford to court any suspicion?[13]

Charges and countercharges filled the newspaper columns. The fervently pro-Union *Missouri Democrat* labeled the regular slate a "Secesh ticket," while the more neutral *Missouri Republican* reported that hundreds of new members—including two named on the stridently Unionist ticket—had joined the library association solely for the election. One member writing in the *Republican* thought this introduction of "election politics" would destroy the tenor of the Mercantile Library, a place where hitherto "Protestant and Catholic, Democrat, Republican or Whig, formed a common platform." Others, however, found the insistence on a Union ticket necessary. Politics had already split the Merchants Exchange, and many St. Louis churches divided into North and South branches.[14]

When the regular ticket of Mercantile Library directors won a narrow victory on January 21, 1862, the Unionists were alarmed, and the result became a national issue. Allies of General John C. Frémont mentioned the library alongside the St. Louis Chamber of Commerce at congressional hearings defending his conduct, asserting that "a majority of the men of wealth and high social position there [in St. Louis] are disloyal" and that something had to be done. In response, Major General Henry Halleck issued Special Orders, no. 80, requiring new oaths of allegiance from all officers and employees of the Mercantile Library, Washington University, the Merchants Exchange, all churches, and other seemingly apolitical institutions throughout the city. James Edwin Love, an Irish-born Unionist from St. Louis posted to Fort Leavenworth, Kansas, was cheered to hear "Mercantile Library—Preachers—Lawyers—Doctors & Institutions of all & every kind, got to come up & take the Oath," calling it "only right & simple justice." Reading reports of arrests and ruminating on the rawness of secessionist sentiment, Love began to wonder whether even a decisive Union victory could heal the city.[15]

At the new board's first meeting, the Mercantile Library directors unanimously agreed to meet the next day to take the oath. At the same meeting,
they accepted the offer of an American flag for the building from stalwart
members Hudson Bridge and Albert Pearce. This was a peace measure of
sorts: Pearce had led the Unionist challenge, while Bridge's business partner
John Beach had been elected president on the regular ticket. Despite the hys-
teria, the Mercantile Library survived the challenge of allegiances—with one
symbolic casualty, its head librarian, Edward William Johnston. Born in Virginia in 1799, Johnston was a bespectacled, white-bearded gentleman and
much esteemed; his 1859 catalog for the St. Louis Mercantile Library collection was the first anywhere to use subject classifications, and it became a
regular reference in the Library of Congress. Yet Johnston was also unabash-
edly pro-Confederate, and he would not take the loyalty oath. He resigned
the next week.[16]

Could this old man be a threat? Might an exemption be granted? Anna
Ella Carroll, a self-appointed Unionist spy provocateur from Baltimore, confronted Johnston in the Mercantile Library reading room in the fall of 1861
and later recalled how he "expressed astonishment that I, a Southern woman,
should be working so vigorously against my section." Johnston's travails continued even as he cooperated with Union authorities, his health deteriorat-
ing. Johnston's cramped handwriting gave evidence of an increasing palsy,
and he suffered a relapse of erysipelas, an agony of rash and fevers. The provost marshal's office still demanded a medical certification and a personal
appearance from Johnston. In dire financial straits, Johnston begged the federal authorities to decide whether to banish him, and to make arrangements;
by the summer of 1863, after his wife had been arrested, he complained, "I
am shut out from all employment . . . made an alien if not an outlaw." Johnston was eventually sent through Kentucky to his home state of Virginia.
Scarred by the disregard and suspicion, Johnston nevertheless considered St.
Louis his home—he returned once again to work for the Mercantile Library
after the war.[17]

What Johnston called his "enforced journey" was a voyage through all
stages of the provost marshal's handbook: the demand for oaths leading to
his resignation, shunning, arrests, ultimatums, forced sales, delays, and finally exile.[18] Old, sick, and no more militant than a librarian, he was not
immune from scrutiny. The library's contested board election and the treatment of its former librarian revealed how tightening standards of neutrality

created uncertainty and the recourse to extreme solutions. Just as some library directors had shaded into nativism a decade earlier in a moment of anti-Catholic fervor, during the Civil War even stalwart members could come under attack if they offered anything less than a full-throated defense of the Union.

The firm Union control of Missouri made it unlike any other theater of the war. While federal forces faced defeat after defeat in Virginia and Lincoln searched for a general to stop the Confederate incursion into Maryland, Major General Henry Halleck kept St. Louis a quiet command. Able to keep the army neutral on the fugitive slave question, Halleck's local successes led to his appointment as overall commander of the U.S. Army. Missouri's condition was so stable that the principles for postwar government could already be considered in June 1862. Local Whig leaders, including the former slaveholders Samuel Glover and James Broadhead, discussed the merits of a gradual emancipation order and debated whether the disfranchisement of rebels would be a necessary condition of peace. Local elections were conducted according to schedule, despite the war, and candidates presented plans for the city's future and by extension the nation's prospects.[19]

In the 1862 elections, two groups of Republicans fought for dominance in St. Louis, foreshadowing the national divides of Reconstruction. The moderate faction, led by congressmen Frank Blair and Henry Taylor Blow, advocated a total but gradual emancipation linked to colonization. "The people of Missouri will require the removal of the blacks as a condition precedent to their liberation," Blair predicted. In contrast, the smaller and more radical faction led by Benjamin Gratz Brown and Charles Drake, and supported by most local Germans, argued that the time had come for immediate emancipation. After a close vote, Blow and Blair retained their seats and the policy of gradual emancipation linked to colonization seemed likely to carry the day.[20]

Yet Charles Drake found another avenue to power. The librarian of the courthouse law library, Drake had been an unsuccessful politician before the war, first as a western Whig and then as a proslavery Democrat. The Civil War made Drake a fervent Union man, and by 1863 he had become a leader of the local Radical Republican faction, making fiery denunciations of the Union leadership and even Lincoln himself. That spring Drake urged the provost marshal's office to redouble its scrutiny of local families, and he personally drew up a target list. Drake singled out prominent, long-established, slave-holding St. Louis families, including the Chouteaus and the Lucases, and recommended banishment for Elizabeth Frost, wife of Confederate General Daniel Frost, and her entire circle. Drake promoted his crusade through fiery speeches, and approved as a secret committee judged evidence and meted out punishment without offering the accused a chance at self-defense.[21]

With the tightening of the military regime, the provost marshal's office filled with signed loyalty oaths. Individuals wrote out the oath longhand, signing on company stationery; whole congregations signed together, under their pastor's guidance; courthouse employees signed long strips of legal-size paper, fastened together. Drake's approach fired up the Radical partisans, and the pressure revealed weaknesses among moderates. Even Taylor Blow, brother of U.S. representative Henry Taylor Blow and the family member responsible for manumitting Dred and Harriet Scott and their daughters, was charged with disloyalty. Blow had faced a series of business failures early in the war, and his behavior had become erratic. According to the report from October 1863, a clearly intoxicated Taylor Blow had "displayed a large knife" and declared himself a Union man—but had then damned the new government policy of arming African Americans. While four years before, gradual emancipation and colonization had been the liberal position, after the Emancipation Proclamation, doubts about the value of African-American soldiers were now deemed unacceptable and possibly traitorous. When sober, Blow approached the provost marshal's office to apologize for his behavior, and the case was dismissed.[22]

Drake's list caused acrimony because of its excesses. When Samuel McPheeters, minister of the Pine Street Church, was investigated, the complaints reached President Lincoln's desk. Lincoln chided the local command, asking why "the question of who shall be allowed to preach in a church in St. Louis, shall be decided by the President of the United States?" The provost marshal's office had overreached, and clergy were soon given a wider berth. Drake's renewed property assessments against suspected Confederate sympathizers raised his stature with the city's Unionists, yet their harshness and the secret, unassailable decision-making earned him opponents with long memories. Despite Drake's demagoguery, some conservative Unionists stood up to question whether there would be costs to neutrality excessively enforced.[23]

Other Unionists saw the value in soliciting cooperation from all St. Louis residents, rather than prosecuting some on suspicions. Working to keep

Washington University open and faithful to its nonpartisan and nonsectarian credo, William Greenleaf Eliot fervently defended neutrality on campus
and civility toward secessionists. In the aftermath of Lincoln's election, Eliot
had rebuked the school's chancellor after he had shown favoritism to the
anti-secession argument in a student debate. This was trouble, Eliot wrote,
"1st that such discussion sh^d be permitted at all in the Univ^y, and 2^d that an
evident leaning sh^d be manifested by you." Yet he was realistic about what the
war would require. "I had taken my stand firmly and plainly," Eliot later wrote,
"and, in my peaceful way, had enlisted for the war." Eliot resisted Drake's
actions as overreaching, and their secrecy as inconsistent with Republican
values. He was among those conservative Unionists who complained directly
to President Lincoln in December 1862, urging that the calm in the streets of
St. Louis was proof that the harassment was unnecessary. Within two weeks
General Halleck conceded there was "no present military necessity" for the
enforcement action, and he ordered his St. Louis colleagues to suspend it.[24]

In his congregation, Eliot encouraged those drafted to serve, and he cheered
the enlistment by his brother Frank. But Eliot welcomed the university's insu-
lation from the war. This was partly a function of wealth; the parents of many
Washington University students secured exemptions or hired substitutes for
their sons, as Eliot did for his own boys. It was only when General John
M. Schofield—on leave from his duties teaching physics at Washington
University—became district commander that Washington University students
began to conduct morning drills, and the Mercantile Library Hall was made
available for military exercises.[25]

George Julius Engelmann, the botanist's son and a student at Washington
University, tested the school's neutrality commitment. In January 1863, after
the promulgation of the Emancipation Proclamation, Engelmann literally
placed his allegiances on his sleeve. "I wore Confederate buttons on my coat
at drill to day," he recorded. Punishment was swift: "Our yankee teacher
Stone, immediately noticed it," the younger Engelmann wrote. "I was told
that if I wore them again, I should not see the inside of the school again." His
father wondered whether to send him to Germany, but both Engelmanns
endured the war in St. Louis.[26]

Eliot's greatest contribution to wartime neutrality, however, was the creation of the Western Sanitary Commission. In the first months of the war,
Union defeats revealed the inadequacy of federal plans for burying the dead
and treating the wounded. In St. Louis, hundreds of injured soldiers arrived

by train after battles in southern Missouri, quickly overwhelming the city's hospitals. Eliot saw soldiers suffer from the slow pace of care and the dearth of nurses. Dorothea Dix, the social reformer and adviser to President Lincoln, was working with Jessie Benton Frémont to provide relief, but by the time Dix arrived in St. Louis, Eliot's efforts were bearing fruit. On September 5, 1861, General Frémont issued General Orders, No. 159, formally establishing the Western Sanitary Commission on the model outlined by Eliot.[27]

The Western Sanitary Commission was a quintessential Eliot enterprise, beginning with its leadership structure. The commission's appointed board included Eliot; his ever-present ally, banker James Yeatman; local physician John B. Johnson; and the grocers Carlos Greeley and George Partridge. These men held all the expertise necessary for funding, purchasing, distributing, and healing, and all were integral members of Eliot's circle, with its interlocking boards of directors and trustees. George Partridge's loyalty oath illustrates the logic of Eliot's works nicely. Partridge listed his affiliations, as trustee of Washington University, the Church of the Messiah, the home for the blind, and the Union Merchants' Exchange, and as director of two insurance companies, a bank, a sugar refinery, and the Iron Mountain Rail Road.[28]

Eliot aimed for Washington University to be a national institution, and the directors of the Western Sanitary Commission considered their efforts in a similarly large scope. In October 1861 they refused entreaties to join the U.S. Sanitary Commission, a similar organization formed by a Unitarian minister in Philadelphia. "Whatever we could do as a sub-committee or branch of your Commission," Yeatman argued on behalf of the St. Louis directors, "we can do equally well, or better, retaining our present organization." When Frederick Law Olmsted, the antislavery activist, journalist, and designer of New York's Central Park, became the head of the U.S. Sanitary Commission in 1862, he was even more insistent on merging the organizations, arguing that the Western Sanitary Commission was dividing and hence weakening Union relief efforts. Olmsted even came to St. Louis to argue his case and found himself entranced by the city's streetscapes—elegant and substantial, "more so than New York on average," he declared, and not merely or "particularly Western" in their outlook. Olmsted also relented from his insistence on merger, once Eliot demonstrated how much work there was to be done across the Mississippi.[29]

The commission's work exemplified Eliot's robust neutrality. Wounded soldiers, regardless of their allegiances, were carried off railroad cars every afternoon, Eliot explained, and then "suppered, slept, breakfasted, & on the next day distributed to the hospitals." Funds came from a national network of supporters, especially in New England, and Eliot declared in 1864 how "at this moment no two cities are nearer each other than St. Louis and Boston." Close to $2 million in donations passed through the Western Sanitary Commission's distribution system, but the ever-modest Eliot preferred to focus on the details: the need for more slippers, more socks, and more blankets for military wounded and civilian refugees, the funds necessary for medical supplies, the prisons to be monitored, and the urgent need for direct relief for those on all sides of the conflict.[30]

The labor of women, too, was essential to the commission's successes. In New England, women rationed and knit and boxed supplies; in St. Louis, female members of Eliot's congregation joined other Protestants and the Sisters of Mercy in ministering to the wounded. The Ladies' Union Aid Society, formed by women from St. Louis's most affluent Union families, sorted incoming donations, arranged benefit concerts and fund-raising fairs, and broke social taboos by personally investigating conditions for the sick and wounded at Benton Barracks. These projects found a place in a celebratory lithograph that depicted the aid society's activities in tableau, where women standing in an immense pavilion nursed soldiers to the south while caring for widowed or stranded women and children in St. Louis to the north. Above, the Union flag flapped proudly while the American eagle ripped the Confederate banner to shreds. On the ground, a copperhead snake (mocking the antiwar northern Copperheads) lay dead and an African-American family kneeled to express their gratitude. Dating from the end of the war, the image crystallized the labors of the commission's female workforce and the fervent nature of their convictions—for Union and for universal aid.[31]

The commission's most lavish effort was the Grand Mississippi Valley Sanitary Fair, held in St. Louis in May and June 1864. Modeled on St. Louis's antebellum Agricultural and Manufacturing Fair but realized on a much larger scale, the Sanitary Fair combined patriotic fervor with a chance to satisfy pent-up demand for entertainment and consumption. The vast panoply of goods donated to be auctioned or sold revealed the continued strength of local manufacturing and arts and the influence of the commissioners and Union Aid ladies on a vast network of national leaders. Among the most treasured items were documents signed by twelve of the nation's sixteen presidents to date, as well as endorsements from noted literary figures and a complete photograph album of the sitting U.S. Congress. Mines in the Nevada Territory sent gold and silver bars; citizens of New Bedford, Massachusetts, sent whale teeth and "New Zealand war clubs"; General Sherman donated a quilt in a flag design; and noted reformer Catherine Sedgwick offered her cherished lock of Reverend William Ellery Channing's hair. Nellie Grant, the daughter of the general, proved herself a good-luck charm, selling the winning raffle ticket for a marvelous mantel clock in the shape of a locomotive, the flowing garments of the goddess Progress resting on its engine. At the Sanitary Fair, St. Louisans could experience the bounty of the entire nation, and dreamt they could continue to profit from it in the days of victory and peace.[32]

In keeping with the commitment to unity, political declarations were mostly absent: the fair "recognizes no State lines nor sectional divisions," its

This engraving celebrated the work of women: caring for soldiers, widows, children, and refugees and working to knit the country back together. Major & Knapp, engravers, "Memorial—St. Louis Missouri Ladies' Union Aid Society," 1868. Missouri History Museum, St. Louis.

organizers declared. This was a loyal neutrality, however, stretching more "from the East to West" than into the South. Photographs reveal the names of the Union generals displayed in foot-high letters at the back of the exhibit booths, promoting a poll of the fairgoers' favorite officer. (General Winfield Scott Hancock—long stationed at Jefferson Barracks, married to a favorite St. Louis daughter, and recently wounded at Gettysburg—won.) The soda fountain made a few hundred dollars, and the Committee on Swords $4,500. Even after accounting for the costs of building the large temporary pavilion and staffing it for three weeks, the fair had earned more than half a million dollars.[33]

The success propelled Yeatman to emphasize how, even though the city was "situated . . . upon the frontier of loyalty," St. Louis was providing a truly national contribution. The New York and Philadelphia sanitary fairs—the latter with the Liberty Bell on display and signed copies of the Emancipation Proclamation for sale—raised only about $1.67 per inhabitant, while the Mississippi Valley Sanitary Fair garnered $3.50 per St. Louis resident, even counting all those soldiers in the field, and the thousands in the city who opposed the war. The Western Sanitary Commission had once again bested the U.S. Sanitary Commission in friendly competition, Yeatman casually noted, and newspapers throughout the North followed suit. But all acknowledged that these calculations were secondary to the efforts to care for the sick and destitute—and to win the war quickly and decisively.[34]

By the time of the Sanitary Fair in 1864, Union partisans understood that neutrality on the slavery question was no longer possible. The underlying issues of the war broke through the placid surface of the fair when Henry A. Nelson, pastor of St. Louis's First Presbyterian Church, invited two black ministers to dine with him. The "young ladies of the highest respectability" at the fair's Laclede Café refused to serve the men, and they refused to leave, creating a tense encounter only defused when one young woman reversed course and volunteered to wait on their table. Nevertheless, the incident was a matter of conversation for weeks, with articles and caricatures appearing in the newspapers. The editors of the *Missouri Republican,* no friends to African Americans, called the ministers' actions "exceedingly repulsive." But they admitted that "if things go on as they have commenced, these scenes . . . will have to be endured."[35]

President Lincoln had issued the preliminary Emancipation Proclamation two years before, on September 22, 1862, but it hardly affected Missouri. Confederates had long since concluded that a Union victory would end not only the expansion of slave territory, but also the institution of U.S. slavery itself. Perhaps it would be immediate, perhaps gradual, perhaps compensated, proslavery advocates had long warned, but slave society would dissolve and the states built on the backs of black men and women would be thrown into disarray. On January 1, 1863, with no Confederate states offering to return to the Union in order to keep their slaves, Lincoln made his proclamation absolute—in enemy territory.

In loyal slaveholding states, such as Missouri and Maryland, and in Union-occupied areas, such as the ports of New Orleans and Norfolk, Virginia, there was not yet a new birth of freedom. On New Year's Day 1863, as multiracial crowds in Boston and Washington celebrated the declaration of emancipation, slave sales continued in St. Louis. Slaveholders who cooperated with Union forces could still negotiate their annual slave transactions, just as the law allowed. James Tower Sweringen had sold his slave Ann for $1,000 over Christmas 1856; at the start of 1863 he balked at selling another, Phoebe, for a paltry $200, but uncertainty and panic shook the slave trade. Sweringen's agent informed him that slaveholders had flooded the market, and too many women were hired out in the city to command a good price for a sale.[36]

In the field, such contradictions were even more stark. In June 1862 the St. Louis platoon of James Edwin Love exchanged guard duty in Kansas for an enforcement operation in Tennessee, where conflicts over slave status filled his days. On the steamboat trip downriver, Love heard the entreaties of "a jet black lady," who said a posse of white men had kidnapped her in St. Louis. He put her ashore at Cairo, Illinois, so the provost marshal could sort out the facts. Contrabands—escaped slaves, working around the Union camps and benefiting from their protection—soon gathered around Love's unit. One afternoon they brought slaves from a nearby field into the Union camp, but the slaveholder, "an old white headed *Secesh*," in Love's eyes, objected; he had taken the loyalty oath and hence Love had to return the slaves. Around the campfire, the soldiers debated whether African Americans escaping were freeing themselves or should be judged stolen property—even if they were stolen by fellow African Americans, still considered property under the law. Neither military statutes nor civilian attitudes had caught up with these new realities. Yet, by seizing their freedom and asserting their rights, African Americans ensured that the Civil War would change the fundamental nature of American society—and on that point, no one could remain neutral.[37]

The changing circumstances emboldened Reverend Eliot to fight for African-American freedom. For decades Eliot denounced slavery from the pulpit but tolerated it in the streets; he had witnessed the wrath of the white mobs that murdered Francis McIntosh and Elijah Lovejoy in 1836 and 1837, and did not court such violence. Eliot had done what he could personally: helping his congregants manumit slaves, making his church a welcoming place for African Americans to worship and seek an education. On one occasion, Eliot had purchased a slave, in order to free her. Yet the ongoing conflict offered Eliot new opportunities. In the war's early days, Missouri was "trembling in the balance, between loyalty and secession," Eliot later wrote. He bemoaned how Frémont's proclamation to free the slaves of Confederate sympathizers had been countermanded, but he understood efforts still had to be incremental. The struggle for freedom remained interlaced with the need to maintain the support of loyal slaveholders.[38]

After Lincoln's proclamation, Eliot still advocated an incremental approach to ending slavery, reflecting his decades of experience seeking compromise for St. Louis and the nation. Missouri remained "a state as large as England, in the centre of the Union, commanding the high way to the Pacific, controlling the mouth of the Ohio & Illinois Rivers," Eliot remarked in a letter to his brother Thomas, a Massachusetts congressman, in January 1863, "containing in itself all the requisites of a great nation." Compensated emancipation there would be a good investment, Eliot urged, and might provide a national model for stability, just as the Missouri Compromise had a generation before. Local slaveholders were far less sanguine about their options: "What old Abe does not do in the emancipation bill," one slaveholding farmer observed, "our Radical Legislature will accomplish."[39]

In February 1863 Eliot hired an extra hand who transformed his perspective on the plight of the slaves. Archer Alexander, about fifty years of age, offered his services in the city market; visibly nervous on the walk home, Alexander admitted to the Eliots that he did not exactly "belong to the city." After the family's Irish cook fed him, Alexander went to work in the backyard, mowing grass, trimming trees, plowing, and caring for the horse and cow. After a few days Alexander admitted to being a fugitive slave, telling

Eliot of his Virginia birth, how he was brought to St. Louis in the 1830s and then to a farm in St. Charles County. Though his father was sold away and he was separated from his mother at a young age, Alexander's enslavement had its leniencies. He was able to marry his love, Louisa, in a true Christian ceremony, and had been sold to her slaveholder, and he had a chance to rear many of his children—though some had been sold away. "The heart learns to bear inevitable burdens," Eliot reflected, grappling with this newly personal understanding of slavery.[40]

Alexander told Eliot he had run away at the start of 1863 because he had been punished for helping a nearby Union brigade avoid a planned sabotage, and now he feared for his family. Telling the details of his escape, Alexander provided lurid details and described near-misses, playing on the conventions of the abolitionist literature he knew Eliot would cherish. Whatever the truth, however, the fact was that this fugitive slave now worked for the Eliots. Eliot wondered briefly whether to follow the law of the land or to mount a moral defense. Prominent St. Louis slaveholders such as the Chouteaus still pursued any slave who escaped, and Eliot did not wish to court controversy. After consulting with the provost marshal's office, Eliot received protection for Alexander directly from President Lincoln—just ahead of an attempt by kidnappers to pluck the slave from the custody of such a prominent Yankee abolitionist.[41]

Missouri legislators approved a gradual emancipation plan in June 1863 that would free most of the state's slaves by 1870. Even Radicals did not yet equate freedom with rights—Charles Drake's plan, for example, included "apprenticeships" for the freed slaves. And slaveholders expelled for disloyalty were still allowed to bring their slaves with them. In September Congressman Henry T. Blow abandoned his hedging and joined the call for immediate emancipation in Missouri. That fall the allowance for slaveholders to be exiled with their slaves ended, and more slaves risked coming to the city. Thousands of escaped slaves marched into army service in 1863, though in Missouri they did so within a slave society faltering but not totally defunct. In rural areas slaveholders could still contemplate finding a local buyer, but in 1864 James Tower Sweringen gave up on his annual slave purchase, instead weighing the recommendation from Silas Bent for "Andre, [who] formerly belonged to me," to work for wages.[42]

Having Archer Alexander in the Eliot household further enmeshed the minister in the struggle of Missouri slaves. While the exile policy held, Eliot wrote to General Schofield to ask why army policies were "discriminating against freedom & strengthening the bonds of slavery." In the flood of new refugees, three of Alexander's daughters and his wife arrived, having been aided in escape by a German neighbor willing to drive his wagon after dark. From Louisa Alexander, Archer learned that his son Tom had enlisted in the army and that he had died fighting for the Union. Here too the newfound intimacy changed Eliot's thinking. The year before, Eliot had opposed arming former slaves, arguing in a sermon that the "notion of vengeance" would leave fugitives "not trustworthy" and "barbarous." But after Archer Alexander's arrival, Eliot became a passionate champion for their enlistment. He argued that the army should no longer seek the consent of loyal slaveholders or pay them the colored soldiers' commissions as compensation. Though Eliot still sought proper title to the fugitives to formally manumit them, the Alexanders found such dealings among whites increasingly irrelevant when freedom could be seized and fought for.[43]

As more and more African Americans joined the Union army, some wrote back to former slaveholders warning them not to threaten or punish family members left behind. "I have no fears about geting mary out of your hands," one of these African-American soldiers, Spotswood Rice, wrote to his former owner from St. Louis's Benton Barracks Hospital; "this whole Government gives chear to me and you cannot help your self." Elite Confederate sympathizers recoiled at the thought. "We thought dutch soldiers bad enough but negro ones are worse," Anne Lane wrote, as she watched colored troops drill outside her home. More cynical observers simply joined the new system: men who had been kidnapping fugitive slaves for bounties began arranging the entry of African Americans into the army. Skimming money off the top was of course illegal, and those "brokers" who could be found after the war were sued for breach of contract.[44]

Embracing newfound freedoms, St. Louis's African Americans came out of the shadows. James Thomas, a St. Louis barber born a slave in Tennessee, recalled the change as "the Ebony hued individual was allowed to go and come without disturbance . . . while the whites were required to prove their loyalty or show by a pass." When the Lindell Hotel grand opening ball reunited antebellum high society for a night in November 1863, "contrabands and colored gentry" were among the crowd in the streets, gawking and celebrating in their own manner. Two new schools were established for black children, and the city's six black churches coordinated their own relief efforts.

Members of the Colored Ladies' Union Aid Society worked alongside their white compatriots to serve African-American soldiers and refugees, and protested the requirement that they stand outside on the streetcars. As longtime St. Louis African-American minister Edward L. Woodson told a visiting federal delegation, "We don't like to have the white people think we can't take care of ourselves"—a statement he applied both to relief efforts and to the fight for freedom.[45]

Many of the escaped slaves arrived in the city in desperate straits: it was army policy to provide food but not clothing or shelter. Tens of thousands camped along the Mississippi River, and unless something was done, "hundreds of the blacks would gladly return to slavery," surmised Eliot, Yeatman, and the Western Sanitary Commission directors. The commission offered its relief services while Congress debated taking action. Escaped slaves overwhelmed the nearby Union outposts, and so General Samuel Curtis arranged to house them in the empty Missouri Hotel, and for contrabands to be hired out to work or sent on to free states. The American Missionary Association set up a school in the hotel's kitchen and finally received permission to send teachers into the contraband camps farther south, with the help of the Western Sanitary Commission. In these ways and others, Eliot's and Yeatman's efforts paralleled and often preceded the programs of Reconstruction, such as the Freedmen's Bureau.[46]

As slaves fled for protection or to fight for the Union cause, rural farmers faced increasingly dire choices: they could gather belongings and flee into urban centers, where suspicion would follow at every turn. They could stay on the homestead, eke out whatever could be harvested, and hope to avoid the internecine conflicts of western Missouri, where guerrilla violence had raged unabated since the mid-1850s. As the Civil War battles continued, William Quantrill's raiders joined such Confederate-sympathizing ruffians as Jesse James and Frank Younger and their brothers as evangels of terror in western Missouri and Kansas, disrupting shipments, sabotaging bridges, capturing escaped slaves, and, on August 21, once again sacking the Free-Soiler city of Lawrence, Kansas, killing more than 150 civilians. When the raiders wrapped sections of railroad track around trees, they left Union troops a poignant symbol of how national unity was twisted and broken, perhaps beyond repair.[47]

In response, General Thomas Ewing issued General Orders, No. 11 on August 25, 1863, erasing the distinction between civilian sympathizer and armed fighter in four western Missouri counties. Neutrality was dead. In order to isolate insurgents, Ewing cleared all homes and held residents in camps, a tactic that would shape American Indian reservation policy and later offer precedent for the concentration camps of Cuba, southern Africa, and Nazi Europe. These actions stoked more anger, and more violence. Confederate rebels intensified their attacks throughout rural Missouri. Union troops retained their edge, but more as a result of their numeric rather than strategic advantages.[48]

The noted artist George Caleb Bingham, then serving as Missouri state treasurer, was another conservative Unionist angered by the chaos. Despite his loyalty, the provost marshal in Kansas City had seized one of his houses to board female Confederate sympathizers. Bingham was sickened when the house collapsed, killing many of the women, and he blamed the destruction on the wanton carelessness and aggression of Union forces. After the war Bingham painted a large, angry painting to protest the inhumanity of Order No. 11 and the harassment of those he called Missouri's "best citizens."[49]

In the work, smoke rises as a white-haired father stands before his looted house. His daughters plead for mercy from stoic Union soldiers, their faces somber and illegible. A wagon train of fellow victims, bent beneath the painting's horizon, trudges east, toward St. Louis and away from their homes and the promise of the West. As with *Jolly Flatboatmen at Port,* Bingham here included an African-American man in a prominent position. But that figure, too, takes no delight in the Union action, covering his face with his hands.[50]

The war measures employed against civilians would discomfit many conservative Unionists long after the guns were silenced. While others justified the violence as necessary for a quick and definitive Union victory, Bingham made it clear that even victory could not justify these crimes. While many Republicans embraced the Radical platform, Frank Blair, unseated from Congress and increasingly at odds with party leaders, denounced the harsh tactics of Order No. 11 as "subterfuge of an imbecile." He openly wondered how the state's voting population—that is, its white males—could heal from such outrages.[51]

As the election of 1864 neared, Confederate troops under General Sterling Price invaded southern Missouri. They aimed to capture St. Louis, reshape the unfolding course of the war, and to end President Lincoln's bid for reelection. On September 26 Price launched an attack on the Union installation at Pilot Knob, less than ninety miles south of St. Louis. By coincidence, General Ewing was at the fort at the time, reviewing the troops; surprised and outnumbered, he nevertheless chose to fight Price's 12,000 men with the 1,500 soldiers and seven heavy guns he had available. Ewing was able to repulse the attack and, through the ruse of a slow-burning fuse, withdrew his troops under cover of night to seek further reinforcements. Price, furious, found his troops too weakened to pursue, and so they moved westward, eventually defeated at Westport (today within Kansas City) on October 23, 1864. Meanwhile, thousands of the poor and destitute fled into St. Louis, where the jails filled with prisoners and the streets with refugees.[52]

While Lincoln could easily dismiss John C. Frémont's short-lived challenge from the left—despite Frémont's vocal support from Charles Drake, Benjamin Gratz Brown, and many Germans in St. Louis—the challenge

Bingham opposed the Army's scorched-earth policies, and created this image in protest: Union soldiers remain stoic and illegible while a wagon train of victims trudge east. George Caleb Bingham, *Order # 11*, 1865–c.1868. State Historical Society of Missouri.

from General George McClellan and the Peace Democrats seemed far more serious. In the fall 1864 contests, Lincoln ran not as a Republican but as a National Union candidate, with War Democrat Andrew Johnson, the military governor of Tennessee, as his new running mate. But conservative Unionist and loyal slaveholders saw this gesture as too little and charged that Lincoln had violated their trust by ending the agreed-upon neutrality. "If Lincoln is going to do any thing for Missouri," one wrote to the provost marshal, "it is high time he was setting about it." Reverend Eliot also worried, writing to Lincoln that the 1864 elections in Missouri would be viewed as a referendum on emancipation. Victory there would be "important from a moral & social point of view" to the future of the nation, Eliot opined—but he also found himself unable to predict the result.[53]

In the final month, Lincoln supporters showed their support at a "Rally! To the Rescue of Your Imperiled Country," as the poster read, and by attending a courthouse speech by Carl Schurz, urging, "GERMANS AROUSE!" Far more important, however, were the efforts of St. Louisans far from home. General Sherman, the former St. Louis resident, led his troops into Atlanta, while St. Louisan and Commanding General Ulysses Grant guided the overall Union strategy, from the capture of Mobile Bay, Alabama, to General Philip Sheridan's successes in the Shenandoah Valley. Supporters in and out of uniform exulted, with soldiers predicting the South was now certain to surrender. On the heels of these victories, Lincoln won in St. Louis, in Missouri, and in the nation, and the Radical Republicans gained control of city government and the state legislature.[54]

In the hard years of the Civil War, St. Louis nevertheless was able to prosper. Stability and relative calm allowed the city to function as the key western administrative center, for the war's conduct and for relief efforts. Union control in St. Louis was absolute, so a vigorous debate between conservative and radical Unionists about the nation's future could continue throughout the war. The city was never shelled, burned, or destroyed, so it remained ready to unify proponents of the North and South into a new postwar reality, built in the West. Through these successes, St. Louis provided a model for the sort of moderate reconciliation President Lincoln envisioned.[55]

Following the Emancipation Proclamation, however, neutrality on the slavery question was a necessary casualty of war. Emerging from slavery free to advocate for themselves, African Americans surprised and troubled those white observers accustomed to inhibited slave behavior. The end of slavery made all

Confederate sympathizers feel like exiles, whether at home or abroad. In contrast, St. Louis Radical Unionist Isaac Sturgeon could celebrate the contributions of African Americans to the war effort, looking forward to when the nation would pay tribute by enfranchising every member of the colored troops—and perhaps all freedmen.[56] African Americans joined all others loyal to the Union cause in hoping that the war's end would provide a just reward. Instead, victory brought tragedy.

8

Abraham Lincoln's Lost Legacies

We your petitioners, colored citizens of the city of St. Louis Mo., . . .
humbly pray that the right of *"franchise"* may be extended to them, that,
this great republican principle may be carried out.

—Petition of Colored Citizens of St. Louis to the State
Constitutional Convention, January 31, 1865.

On the day after Easter, April 17, 1865, the St. Louis County Court instructed all its officers to dress in mourning. The gleaming courthouse, the very symbol of the Union in St. Louis, was to be draped in black for thirty days. As the Radical Republican newspaper, the *St. Louis Democrat,* described, with "the tolling of bells, the firing of half-hour guns, the National ensign everywhere floating at half-mast," the city grieved for the assassinated president.[1]

As Lincoln's funeral train made its slow journey across the country, a specially constructed hearse stood ready to transport the dead president's body from the riverfront to the courthouse. Inside, the city architect prepared an octagonal platform, ringed with Corinthian columns and covered with a black canopy. A circle of thirty-four white stars, for the states north and south, graced the velvet, with a large silver star in the center for the fallen leader. All was ready, as St. Louis awaited the chance to join the other major cities of the Union in marking the president's passing.[2]

Yet the mourners in St. Louis held a funeral without a body.

More than Lee's surrender at Appomattox, President Lincoln's assassination marked the opening of a new era in American politics. White or black, Unionist

or Confederate, men and women in St. Louis and throughout the newly reunited states continued the fight over Abraham Lincoln's legacy, the com-
memorations new battles to be won or lost. Their debates revealed the depth
of postwar divisions.

During the Civil War, Lincoln had held together a remarkable coalition:
conservative and radical white Unionists, newly freed slaves, religious activists, military leaders, political enemies, and foreign allies—all while commanding an army faced with a new kind of warfare and a painfully intimate
enemy. Lincoln's brilliance (and his luck) led to Union successes on the home
front as well as the battlefields, and allowed the nation to withstand both the
bitter years of fighting and the transformative decision to free the slaves. Assassination cut short Lincoln's chance to enact his announced plan for "amnesty and reconstruction," and instead intensified the conflict between the
extremist rhetoric of Congress's Radical Republicans and the personal vengeance sought by many War Democrats.[3] This we know from hindsight. In the
last year of the war, the rush of action and the topsy-turvy emotions made any
such perspective impossible.

St. Louis emerged from the war physically unscathed, the years of martial
law having left an atmosphere of suspicion but little physical destruction. The
military importance of St. Louis presaged postwar fortunes, as St. Louis remained vital to federal control, a key entrepôt for western forts and railroad
lines and the administrative center for the coming military occupation of
Arkansas, Texas, and Louisiana. The success of St. Louis's neutrality left an
unusually heterogeneous Reconstruction population, with ex-slaveholders
and ex-slaves, loyal Unionists and Confederate sympathizers, well-established
families and refugees. St. Louis's leaders had maintained order along their
wartime border, and now sought a peace dividend that would place the city
in the vanguard of the reunited nation's successes.[4]

In November 1864, five months before the end of the war, Missourians
had elected delegates to a constitutional convention, to oversee the transition
back to civilian rule. Convening in the St. Louis Mercantile Library Hall in
January 1865—where the secession convention had once met—the delegates
were a mix of Radicals and conservatives from all over the state, many of
whom had sacrificed dearly to preserve the Union. The convention's first order of business was a statute declaring complete and total emancipation. On
January 11, 1865, Missouri passed its emancipation act, superseding the 1863
gradual emancipation law. Even as the war raged on, those in St. Louis celebrated slavery's end. Fireworks were launched from the courthouse; churches

held special thanksgiving services; and a crowd "of both sexes and all colors," in the *Missouri Democrat*'s phrase, gathered before the patriotic transparencies in the windows of the Planter's House Hotel. Convention delegates were deservedly proud: in a special commemorative album, with a portrait photograph of each convention delegate, the title page bragged how members had outdone every governing document in U.S. history—from the Pilgrims' contract to the Declaration of Independence to the Northwest Ordinance to Frémont's and Lincoln's Proclamations—by definitively abolishing slavery. This was an accomplishment for the nation to celebrate, they argued, and newspapers from Milwaukee to Maine dutifully took note.[5]

Once emancipation was enacted, however, the convention delegates realized how difficult the tasks remaining would be. Now that African Americans were free from slavery, what should be the extent of their rights under the new state constitution? As delegates debated the new political order, old prejudices mixed with contemporary concerns. Should the franchise be extended, and to whom? Native-born Americans? Women? African Americans? How should other "outsider" groups within the United States, from German and Irish immigrants to American Indians, be considered? For citizenship, should an oath of allegiance to the Union be required? Should the test oaths be "ironclad," required of all judges, lawyers, priests, and ministers, excluding anyone who had provided aid, comfort, or sympathy for any rebellion against a duly elected government? Convention delegates found themselves grappling with fundamental questions of U.S. governance as no group had since the Founders met in Philadelphia.[6]

Charles Drake found his answers to these questions by pursuing a simple principle: those who had upheld the Union were true citizens, and those who defended slavery and secession should be viewed with suspicion. Drake parlayed his years spent browbeating, threatening, and pursuing punishment for wartime Confederate sympathizers into a position as the convention's policy leader. Yet Drake's extremism split the delegates; it seemed so different than what President Lincoln hinted would be a lenient policy after surrender.[7]

African Americans had no chance to vote themselves, so they were most dependent on convention allies. On January 31, 1865, St. Louis's black community delivered an appeal to Drake, in a petition signed by more than one hundred ex-slaves. In deferential phrasing, they endorsed forthright claims: "Your humble petitioners are capable of reading the constitution of the United States and of this state and also are able to write," the signatories declared.

Their patriotism was unquestioned; their taxes paid without complaint; they had volunteered to fight—and "because we consider this right inalienable and that we have been too long deprived of its exercise," these African-American men demanded citizenship and the right to vote.[8]

Also held at a distance were former Confederates, though they garnered their own measure of sympathy. When Drake proposed an ironclad oath to punish the former enemies politically, conservative delegates objected, urging that the rights of ex-Confederates be restored quickly to counterbalance any rights given African Americans. Others saw practical objections: Moses Linton, a Kentucky-born Catholic entrepreneur, worried how an ironclad oath might hamper trade with the former Confederacy, while Isidor Bush, a Prague-born Jewish merchant and leader in the St. Louis German community, suspected that Radical restrictions on ex-Confederates could easily be applied to immigrant groups by enforcement officials with nativist leanings.[9]

German-speaking delegates were especially vocal at the convention. They relished the chance to reshape a government, a dream long denied to the refugees of 1848. Yet the Germans split on issues philosophical as well as political. The freethinking Germans opposed the religious language in the proposed preamble, seeing no need to mention God; in contrast, the Catholic Germans objected to the proposal requiring clergy to swear loyalty oaths, arguing it smacked of the anticlerical extremism of the French Revolution. Germans had long been against slavery and for free labor but were divided on whether to grant African Americans full state citizenship. George Husmann, a Radical German politician from Hermann, sought to prevent "any distinction . . . between white, black, red, and brown" in the state constitution. But others still envisioned Missouri as for whites only.[10]

In the end, the compromises completed Drake's outline of loyalty while borrowing from the ugliest racial and political ideas of his opponents. Rural Missourians, many of them slaveholding Unionists radicalized by the terrorism of roving Confederate mobs, became the key voting bloc, passing proposals that angered Radicals and conservatives in turn. The convention maintained the word "white" to describe citizens—leaving African Americans as "free as a woman, a foreigner, or a minor," as Drake later phrased it. While some of the constitution's provisions—on popular ratification, compulsory public schooling, and curtailed private bills—were welcomed as good-government reforms, its central tenets were political. It ended slavery but maintained whites-only rule; it disfranchised ex-Confederates and required ironclad oaths, from voters, lawyers, teachers, jurors, public officials, and clergy to affirm their lifelong loyalty. The rather unlikable Drake became an easy target for later frustrations with the document that became universally known as the Drake Constitution—and sometimes pilloried as the "Draconian Code."[11]

The convention finished its work in the second week of April—just in time for Lee's surrender, and the joyous headlines shouting "WAR IS OVER!" So raucous was the celebration that the U.S. Arsenal commander had to write to the officers of the Mercantile Library Hall, reminding them to return the two mountain howitzers they had borrowed for the victory gala. On Saturday morning, April 15, 1865, residents of St. Louis awoke expecting a victory parade. Instead, they heard the incredible: President Lincoln had been shot and was close to death, and urgent telegraphs to and from Jefferson Barracks urged the apprehension of the actor John Wilkes Booth. St. Louisans looked once again to their weapons, worrying that they were witnessing the opening salvo of another round of war. The provost marshal arrested men and women heard praising Lincoln's death in the streets. By the next morning, Easter Sunday, the rumors were confirmed: Abraham Lincoln, emancipator of the slaves, victor of the Civil War, and presumed architect of Reconstruction, had been assassinated.[12]

St. Louisans experienced a sickeningly familiar feeling as plans for celebration were again crushed by news of death and injury. Far beyond the scope of a local railroad accident, Lincoln's assassination was a national loss, a scar on the body politic of the United States just as the healing at the end of the Civil War had begun. In his sermon Easter morning, Reverend William Greenleaf Eliot spoke openly of the murder. He urged his congregation to focus not on how victory colors were now shrouded, but on how the Easter lilies "remind us on this Resurrection Sunday that from seeming death the most glorious life must always, by the law of God, spring forth." The Catholic clergy, unable to mark a secular tragedy within their liturgy, tolled bells and hung a flag at half-mast at the diocesan offices. "Missouri joins hands with her sisters in a fresh and irrevocable pledge to forever maintain the Republic," the *St. Louis Democrat* declared. "Slavery, the would-be assassin of civilization, is having its last victims."[13]

The proposed state constitution, passed out of convention just days before and set for a ratification vote in June, was already obsolete. New compromises would have to be made, as the ascendency of Vice President Andrew

Johnson, the Tennessee War Democrat, former slaveholder, and brash political fighter, altered dramatically the plans for national Reconstruction.[14] Yet first Missouri mourned the nation's fallen president, and St. Louis leaders planned for a local funeral.

On April 19, 1865, St. Louis Mayor James S. Thomas, presiding judge of the St. Louis County Court William Taussig, and St. Louis's U.S. representative, Henry T. Blow, addressed their request to "Mrs. President Lincoln." Memorial planning was under way in Baltimore, Philadelphia, New York, and Chicago—there were to be "FUNERALS EVERYWHERE," one headline stated—and thus the three leaders asked the widowed Mary Todd Lincoln to let the train pass through St. Louis on its way to Springfield, Illinois, as to "grant to us, and the people west of the Mississippi," a chance for mourning. St. Louis's fortunes were intimately tied to Lincoln's leadership and to the fruits of Union victory. Thus, the leaders reasoned, the city should participate in the national parade of solemn funerals.[15]

In Washington the unprecedented task of planning the funeral procession for an assassinated president fell to George R. Harrington, an overworked assistant secretary of the Treasury whose resignation letter had been refused the month before. Harrington called an emergency meeting Easter evening, consulting with all parts of the executive branch as he planned the procession order and invited the proper members of the diplomatic corps to the Washington funeral. All the while, Harrington's office was besieged with telegrams: the German gymnastic association of Louisville sent "a wreath of rare flowers"; bishops and businessmen from New York and Washington gave notice of their intention to attend; newspaper reporters asked for access to the White House; the committee of colored citizens of Washington sought an assigned place in the procession.[16]

Yet more complex than arranging for Lincoln to lie in state in the Capitol was planning what would happen next. "Our rail road connections north & west of us are pressuring me for information as to route of remains & escort from Wash^n to Springfield & whether it is contemplated to stop over at principal points to allow people to pay respect to deceased," one station master announced, setting out the principal questions in the staccato of a telegram. Citizens of Philadelphia urged that the casket rest at Independence Hall, recalling how Lincoln's speech there "expressed his willingness to be assassinated on the spot rather than sacrifice the principles of Liberty." Generally following the route Lincoln had traveled to his inauguration four years before, an entire itinerary of quick ceremonies and true funerals evolved in hundreds of communities: Washington, Baltimore, Harrisburg, Philadelphia, New York City, Albany, Cleveland, Columbus, Indianapolis. But the final funeral before Springfield was scheduled for Chicago, a significant detour. Thus, as the train traveled, St. Louisans made their case for inclusion.[17]

"The authorities of St. Louis have made the most elaborate arrangements," wrote Blow, Taussig, and Thomas to Mrs. Lincoln. The *Anzeiger des Westens* detailed the hanging of black crepe, the readying of the hearse, and the preparation of the platform, describing for its readers the signs of mourning in an American funeral. "The President's coffin will stand there, if the request mentioned above is fulfilled," the *Anzeiger* explained. As the funeral train moved west, Althea Johnson captured the feeling of St. Louis in the streets in a lengthy letter. "This city for the past week has worn the habiliment of mourning," she wrote, describing the display of flags intertwined with black. "The sorrow seems universal." Living with the news for a week, Johnson was able to hope again, wishing that Lincoln's legacy could inoculate the nation against further ruin. "I sometimes think Lincoln's work was nearly done," she wrote. "He had performed all he said he would four years ago, well and faithfully, and his name will be handed down to future generations with that of Washington's." Time would tell; for now, Johnson waited for the planned St. Louis funeral, describing the "empty tomb arranged in the rotunda."[18]

Althea Johnson's husband, Stephen, doubted that the St. Louis funeral would happen—before the final route was known, he made plans to attend the burial in Springfield instead. His suspicions proved prescient: the funeral train proceeded from Indianapolis to Chicago to Springfield, where the hearse constructed in St. Louis carried the president's body. A delegation of St. Louis leaders and other bereft citizens made the trip to pay their respects. Those crowding around the bier became delirious in the last moments, ripping flowers from the wreaths and snipping lockets of Lincoln's hair, in "a great effort to get relics from this place," as one shocked witness recorded.[19]

The weeks of national mourning had ended, and St. Louis was denied the solemn honor of a Lincoln funeral. Why? The public letter to Mary Todd Lincoln is the only evidence of this request; no discussion appears in the administration records or in Mrs. Lincoln's personal papers, so no certain answer exists. St. Louis was not on the train route from Washington to Springfield, but then neither was Chicago or Harrisburg, and both held funerals. Would the extra day have been a concern? Lincoln's body had been embalmed, but imperfectly—though this fact was unknown to those in Washington planning the route.[20]

Was it geography? As St. Louis officials wrote, a funeral across the Mississippi would demonstrate the continental reach of the Union, and the chance to honor Lincoln in a former slave state once claimed by the Confederacy would have been momentous. Yet St. Louis still had no direct rail connection—all traffic was barged from Alton, or brought from Chicago across the Rock Island bridge. Perhaps organizers worried about a transportation accident. (Many of those pushing for a Lincoln funeral would add to the drumbeat for a bridge over the Mississippi River in years following.)[21] When the funeral train bypassed St. Louis, it demonstrated St. Louis's weakness as a national city.

Whatever the reason, St. Louis held its "funeral" for Lincoln without his body present. A bust of President Lincoln "crowned with a wreath of laurel and immorteles" was placed underneath the canopy, with evergreens below, a military guard on constant duty, and a gas-powered eternal flame lighting the display. (St. Louis newspapers discussed memorializing their commemoration with an engraving or photograph, but no extant image is known.) "The catafalque will remain thirty days standing in the Courthouse Rotunda," the *Anzeiger des Westens* announced.[22]

Thousands filed past to pay their respects, on special trips or as part of their daily patterns. St. Louisans from all walks of life reflected on the legacy of Abraham Lincoln. Sarah Williams noted her visit to the cenotaph in a housekeeping diary. Amid notes on her cooking and planting, Williams mentioned visiting the courthouse memorial when a dentist appointment brought her downtown. Decades later, Frank B. Cressy still recalled how "in 1858 I saw two slaves (men, 22 and 45 years old) sold on the steps of this Court House," in St. Louis. After years of army service and three times passing before Lincoln's coffin in Springfield, Cressy returned to St. Louis "and went up those same courthouse steps to see a Lincoln cenotaph within, saying to myself, 'There, on that very spot, is where I saw slaves sold; but now, thank God, they all are free, and our nation is preserved.'"[23]

After thirty days, John Wilkes Booth had been caught and killed, Jefferson Davis and the final rogue generals of the Confederacy were captured, and Congress debated proposals for national reconstruction put forward by "his Accidency," President Andrew Johnson. In St. Louis on May 29, 1865, the military guard was thanked and the black draping removed. William Rumbold, the courthouse architect, disassembled the memorial.[24] With the symbolic space emptied, St. Louisans wondered how the bond between Abraham Lincoln and St. Louis could be more permanently memorialized— and whether the political changes threatened their promise of postwar success.

Lincoln's death split the wartime Republican coalition, resulting in the fierce antipathies of Reconstruction politics. Split less along regional than ideological lines, the victorious Unionists found the pressing questions of peace as hard to handle as those brought about by war. Radicals hoped to provide security for the newly freed African Americans, with the power of suffrage; conservatives worried about the alienation of ex-Confederates. St. Louisans considered how a more perfect union of the disparate postwar groups could lead to local, regional, and national prosperity. Yet the issues raised were filtered through the state's racial, ethnic, and political divides. The anger and pain of four years of war, now topped by Lincoln's assassination, made radical political change painful if not impossible.

Who had killed the president? Before Booth was caught, politically motivated accusations flew. "The liberals etc." blamed the South for the murder, the French-born merchant Louis Fusz wrote, but he wondered privately whether the Radicals themselves might have had some hand in it. "They constantly sought to thwart his plans of conciliation," he wrote, "and now we hear some say that his death was a punishment from God for being too lenient!" Might they have committed murder, placing blame on southern sympathizers and therefore increasing the severity of postwar measures? Whether such a conspiracy was too farfetched, Fusz was confident the atmosphere of fear would push Drake's Radical constitution to ratification.[25]

Heinrich Boernstein, the former *Anzeiger* editor and army colonel, heard the news of Lincoln's murder in Bremen, where he served as a consul for the Union government. "I had been sure of Lincoln," Boernstein mused, "but how would it be with his successor?" Radicals immediately distrusted Andrew Johnson, and their caricatures and charges come down through history: Johnson wished to reenslave African Americans, Radicals charged; Radicals wished to enslave ex-Confederates, Johnson's supporters retorted. Radicals wished for Reconstruction to be a long and arduous punishment for the sins of war, while Johnson's allies claimed that Lincoln intended reintegration to be quick and lenient. So the charges flew, and the volume rose; within a year the disagreements between the Radical congressional leaders and the new president—from the technical to the substantial—led to an impasse and then impeachment proceedings, which became a political distraction at a crucial time of national soul-searching.[26]

Though they would take years to come to a head, these tensions were already simmering as the Drake Constitution awaited the ratification vote in June. Uncertainty ruled the day, whether for ex-Confederates or German-speaking citizens, economically ruined Union veterans or newly freed men and women. Who had earned, gained, or maintained rights became the central unanswered question—and political transformations as great as Drake's happened every day. "Some of our firmest radicals are in part those who 4 years back stood on the other side," wrote the conservative German botanist George Engelmann. As he contacted his fellow part-time scientists, "Lindheimer from Texas and Chapman from Florida," there was "much denying now, that they had ever any sympathy for the South." When the vote came, many Germans also reversed course: lacking confidence in Drake and lacking the assurances President Lincoln had provided, Germans throughout the state lobbied against the constitution's ratification. Every St. Louis voting ward rejected the new state constitution—and then they were bound by its terms nonetheless, as the Drake Constitution passed on a cushion of rural votes.[27]

With the terms of debate set, African Americans renewed their call for inclusion in the new political order. Newly free African Americans made the memory of the martyred president into an emblem of their freedom. Lincoln's name was treasured by ex-slaves seeking independent livelihoods, political and social rights, and the promise of equality at the ballot box and in the classroom. On October 12, 1865, the Equal Rights League of Missouri took up the banner, addressing a pamphlet "to every true, honest, and liberty-loving citizen of Missouri," this "redeemed Commonwealth." The league's executive committee included James Milton Turner, a graduate of Oberlin College; Frank Roberson, whose barbershop in the Barnum Hotel had given him a prewar fortune of about $5,000; and Moses Dickson, born free in Cincinnati in 1824, who had organized secret societies before the war and remained fervent in his vision of black self-help. Whatever meager advantages were available to African Americans in the wake of slavery, these men possessed them, and made their political statements boldly.[28]

No longer slaves, "no longer cowed," the members of the Equal Rights League declared, "We own ourselves, our families, and our homes," and "we mean to make our freedom *practical*." Wishing "that the skeleton of liberty may be clothed with flesh and blood," the men undersigned urged "sympathy and aid in securing political rights and privileges which belong to us as free men." *The Liberator* followed their progress as John Mercer Langston, the Equal Rights League's national leader, came to Missouri, giving a well-attended speech in St. Louis and addressing the Missouri legislature in its chambers. Yet the efforts elicited social rather than political progress, with resolutions on streetcar access and marriage licenses but none for African-American citizenship or political rights.[29]

While the Equal Rights League urged the state's Radicals to grant them the franchise, conservative white Missourians renewed their own criticism of the Drake Constitution, intent on fighting the Radicals' perceived overreaching and fighting for a different version of Lincoln's legacy. Though Lincoln's name remained anathema to many Confederate sympathizers and former Confederates, after his assassination they stressed the ambiguity of the political and social program Lincoln left behind. Integral to this effort was Frank Blair, one of the first politicians to reclaim the mantle of the Democratic Party, championing free white labor rights grounded in an end to slavery but no sympathy for African-American rights. In fall 1865 Blair refused to take a loyalty oath at the polls because, he argued, his Wide Awakes had defended the Union at Camp Jackson by taking up arms against the duly elected—if secession-minded—state government. Were both sides to be excluded under the "ironclad" provisions, or should neither be? Blair engineered a test case to find out, while John Cummings, an Irish-born Catholic priest, challenged the clergy oath in a parallel case.[30]

Opponents also challenged the constitution's tax policies. Radicals had removed the traditional exemptions for churches and schools as an undue privilege. In protest, Washington University, the Mercantile Library, and city churches refused to pay their tax bills, choosing to sue instead; the case was soon heard by the Missouri Supreme Court. Blair and Cummings took their appeals to the U.S. Supreme Court, nationalizing their challenge to Reconstruction. In January 1867 the U.S. Supreme Court sent a jolt through political circles, ruling the test oaths unconstitutional, as ex post facto bills of attainder.

Radicals ruefully noted that antebellum justices—including three who had also ruled on the *Dred Scott* case—formed the majority, while four Lincoln appointees dissented.[31]

The fight to define Reconstruction was a continuation of the Civil War's struggles by other means. St. Louis remained a "political cauldron . . . boiling over," Moses Dickson noted in October 1866, "fed by the fires of the two great political parties, Union and Rebel, or as they are generally called, Radical and Conservative." In contrast, Thomas W. Cunningham, a War Democrat from central Missouri, believed that President Johnson could bring about the necessary and necessarily delimited change. "I was never for Lincoln but now *am* a Johnson Man," Cunningham wrote, "and do believe a White man as good as a Negro." Reacting to talk of African-American citizenship, Cunningham mockingly added a definition for those former slaves as "an American citizen of AFRICAN DE-Sent"—a phrase indicating that he still maintained hope for colonization.[32]

Throughout Andrew Johnson's presidency, the Radicals in Missouri wielded tremendous but uncertain power. As a minority pressure group reliant on convincing other parts of the wartime Republican coalition, their advances were often followed by emotional flare-ups or behind-the-scenes power brokering. In March 1867 Charles Drake became a U.S. senator, replacing the more moderate Benjamin Gratz Brown, who had been forced to resign. Drake's prickly personality and impetuous style alienated both colleagues and voters, but local politicians felt "it will end the political career of any union men that oppose his [Drake's] election." Despite his ascension to the pinnacle of state power, ready to dole out patronage and to participate in the impeachment trial of President Johnson, Drake himself still sensed reluctance from the "little knot of German leaders" in St. Louis, who had opposed ratification of his state constitution. Neither side had forgotten the bitterness, and the division between Drake and St. Louis's German politicians left the Radical coalition vulnerable.[33]

In Washington moderate senators recoiled from the zeal with which Drake and his fellow Radicals prosecuted the President. In May 1868, on the final vote for conviction, Senator John B. Henderson of Missouri turned against his state and national party leaders to maintain Johnson in office. Radical leaders were despondent: "If you remember how you and the Loyal men of Mo. felt when Lincoln was assassinated," a national Republican Party official wrote to a Radical colleague in St. Louis, "you can have some idea of the feeling here when Impeachment became a matter of doubt." Drake reflected on the Radical's difficulties, finding he had "a great deal to learn" if he were to influence national, rather than mere state, matters.[34]

Despite the increasingly organized opposition, the Radical state legislature authorized a referendum for fall 1868 on extending the franchise to African Americans and even put women's suffrage under consideration. Yet Drake's power in his home state also began to fade. By July 1868 James Rollins and James O. Broadhead, both former Whigs and conservative Unionists, were exchanging confidential letters on how best to end Radical rule in Missouri and weighing the merits of Blair's resurgent Democratic Party. Change could come, Rollins understood, but he insisted that "no man . . . who was not thoroughly identified with the Government" should be on the ticket, as the war's symbolic battle lines remained drawn. He considered a proposal to include a former rebel prisoner as candidate for a lower office a particularly egregious mistake.[35]

Given this dissent among Republicans, Frank Blair and the Democrats eagerly stepped into the vacuum, challenging racial inclusion and the pieties of Reconstruction. In 1868 Blair was a candidate for the presidency, hoping to run against Grant and make the election a referendum on the war's suffering; though the party convention chose Horatio Seymour, the governor of New York, after twenty-one deadlocked ballots, Blair was chosen as the vice presidential nominee, pledging to unite moderate Unionists and ex-Confederates—and to oppose the suffrage amendment.[36]

"We need the ballot to protect us from being re-enslaved," Moses Dickson wrote in November 1868, appealing to the white electorate that would decide the question of African-American rights. Assuaging concerns, Dickson readily admitted that the right to vote did not make men equal, citing how the dregs of white society were not equal to its best gentlemen simply because they could all vote in Missouri. Yet Dickson hinted at the power that suffrage would offer, as he pledged that African-American men would "promise to use the ballot as we did the bayonet, to uphold the honor and dignity of our common country." Some of his protégés already knew that power. For example, that same year Blanche Bruce left the St. Louis region for Mississippi. Politically active as a newspaper editor and drawing on his experience with the Missouri Equals Rights League, in 1874 Bruce became the first African-American elected to a full term in the U.S. Senate, following Hiram Revels, the first African-American U.S. senator, also elected from

Mississippi and also a veteran of the civil rights and education circles in Civil War St. Louis.[37]

Yet in Missouri in the fall 1868 elections, Dickson's expansive vision was denied: though Radicals were narrowly returned to office and Ulysses S. Grant won the presidency, Missouri's African-American suffrage amendment failed. Opponents had successfully tarnished this granting of rights as an injustice visited upon still-disfranchised ex-Confederate whites. The Germans, who had so fervently opposed slavery, began to line up behind Frank Blair, championing white free labor by limiting the competition for jobs from freemen. Though no one sector of the Republican coalition in Missouri had spoken out against the suffrage amendment, its failure demonstrated the remaining doubts about African-American fitness that pervaded the white voting population in this former slave state. Radicals had understood that the future for African Americans—protected as equal citizens or discriminated back into an inferior role—would determine the success of national reintegration. Yet after a half-decade of attempts to envision the nation completely anew, many Missourians embraced the easy answers of white supremacy.[38]

Even as the campaign for political rights faltered, African Americans and their supporters secured gains in education. It began with Charlotte Scott, a lone freedwoman reflecting on Lincoln's legacy.

Charlotte Scott heard the news of Lincoln's assassination in her master's house, in Marietta, Ohio. Scott, her children, and her grandchildren were all slaves, held first in her birthplace of Lynchburg, Virginia, then all through western Virginia and—Northwest Ordinance be damned and Justice Taney rot in hell—in Marietta, where she was taken by the Rucker family, Union sympathizers who had fled the Confederacy but not their slaveholding ways. "Of course, she is now a free woman," the newspapers had noted in 1865, but they gave no indication whether her freedom had come early or at the last minute, through the action of the Ruckers (with whom she still lived at that date) or through Lincoln's emancipation policies. With Lincoln's assassination "the colored people have lost their best friend," Scott told the local minister; in her estimation, they had lost the greatest man who ever lived.[39]

And so Charlotte Scott handed the minister $5, asking that he put it toward a monument for Abraham Lincoln. "A noble offering by a grateful heart," the newspaper called it—a gesture that touched James Yeatman, reading the account of Charlotte Scott in the *Missouri Democrat*. As president of the Western Sanitary Commission, founding president of the Mercantile Library, bank director, and Washington University trustee, Yeatman stood at the opposite end of society, yet he reached out to Charlotte Scott. Writing to the *Democrat* to commend Scott's effort, Yeatman offered in June 1865 to collect funds under the aegis of the Sanitary Commission for a Lincoln memorial, under partnership with Reverend Eliot and Wayman Crow. He requested that Scott's photograph, her life story, and her "*foundation $5*" be forwarded to him.[40]

The money poured in for the memorial to Lincoln. Freedwomen and freedmen added their sums, paltry and substantial. The U.S. Colored Troops did the most: $4,200 from colored troops at Vicksburg; $3,200 from another colored regiment; $500 from a battery unit; and more, until more than $16,000 was amassed. "In the fullness of their hearts the colored soldiers would push out their *last* 'greenback,' saying, '*Take it all,*'" the officers told Yeatman, saying they had instituted a policy of no more than $5 apiece to curtail the exuberance. After a lifetime without money, without rights, and without access to the political arena, these colored troops offered tribute to Lincoln, mourning their fallen president in a serious and open way that their lives as slaves had never allowed for on any previous occasion. These funds were another legacy of Abraham Lincoln, and Yeatman wondered how they could be spent appropriately.[41]

In the first years of Reconstruction, while the question of African-American citizenship remained unresolved, both advocates and opponents saw the value in universal public education for all children, white and black. Linking education to political rights, William Greenleaf Eliot was at once sympathetic and patronizing. "I am opposed to negro suffrage, until those who are to enjoy it are better prepared for its exercise," Eliot had informed the 1865 constitutional convention, "not because of their color, but because of their ignorance." Properly implemented, reformers urged, a public school system would transform St. Louis's political as well as social structure—for African Americans, the foreign-born, and the poorly educated of all colors. The Radical Republicans who controlled city and state government passed education taxes, and a dozen schools—separated by race—were built in St. Louis. By October 1866 locals referred to the first "African school" as a local landmark, and newspapers followed the exertions of the Freedmen's Bureau to bring education to African Americans in other parts of the state.[42]

Yet these government efforts were ultimately overshadowed by the gift begun with Charlotte Scott's $5, and the educational innovations of the colored troops themselves.

The Civil War had not ended definitively for all Union troops in April 1865. Because of communication gaps and the need for troops to occupy formerly Confederate areas, demobilization proceeded unevenly. For the 62nd, 63rd, and 65th regiments of the U.S. Colored Troops, the order to muster out did not come until January 1866. These regiments, formed at Benton Barracks in December 1863, hardly saw the fight. They had spent the war marching from Baton Rouge to Port Hudson to Brazos, burying Confederate dead and digging defensive trenches, and performing whatever heavy labor was required of them. They had lined up for battle at Palmito Ranch, Texas, on May 12, 1865—only after the first day's fighting did Union commanders learn the war was over. Preparing to process the Confederate surrender, the troops were surprised to see a never-say-die contingent, led by Missouri's Confederate commander Sterling Price and its Confederate governor Thomas C. Reynolds, strike out for Mexico instead of admitting defeat.[43]

In the long, uneventful stretches, Missouri's colored troops had spent nights around the campfire learning to read and write. The Western Sanitary Commission had provided lessons in St. Louis when the troops waited to be deployed, and their progress so impressed the regiment's first lieutenant, Richard Baxter Foster, that he decided to continue instruction himself throughout the war. At Fort McIntosh, Texas, as the units were ordered to disband, Foster remarked that "it was a pity these men should find no schools when they returned to Missouri, and that the education so happily commenced should cease," and he wondered whether that need be the case. "The past was dead and must soon be buried," Foster recalled thinking in those first days after Lincoln's assassination and the Confederate surrender. "An era had commenced in which all things should become new." Officers and enlisted soldiers conferred, and resolutions were drawn up and signed. The 62nd Regiment would establish a school in Missouri "for the special benefit of freed blacks."[44]

The resolutions written by the 62nd Regiment on January 14, 1866, expressed a clear goal for their new school: "Emancipated slaves, who have neither capital to spend nor time to lose, may obtain an education." Speaking from experience, they wrote how "the freedom of the black race has been achieved by war, and its education is the next necessity thereof." Both colored troops and their white officers contributed to this completely new proposition—an institute of higher education for African Americans—not only by signing commitments but also by offering up funds. Foster and the other officers contributed more than $1,000 while their soldiers managed $4,000. The 65th Regiment offered an additional $1,300—once again, a tremendous sum for the time, let alone for enlisted men. Decades later Foster still recalled the generous contribution of Samuel Sexton, an African-American soldier who managed to give $100 from a salary of $13 per month.[45]

One month later Foster took the funds to St. Louis, ready to organize his school and conduct further fund-raising in the city. As he later told F. A. Seely, the Freedman's Bureau representative for Missouri, the officers of the 62nd had set a high bar, as they "imposed upon themselves the obligation that if the sum of $20,000 were not raised for the school by July 1, 1867, the contributions of the colored soldiers should be refunded." Almost immediately Foster held a meeting that demonstrated the tenuous situation of African Americans in the still-fragile Union. "To day [I] consulted Gen. Fisk, Mr. Fishback, Dr. Post, Dr. Eliot and Mr. Yeatman," Foster reported on February 18, 1866, "all of whom are warmly interested in the education of the colored race, and all seem to think that our enterprise will fail." Foster, rejecting their logic, did not elaborate, but the reluctance of these prominent white educators and officers suggested how shallow the support for African-American education could be.[46]

Could this not be the perfect memorial to Abraham Lincoln, the best use of Charlotte Scott's funds? Money gathered from the U.S. Colored Troops would underwrite the proposed schooling, but white educators and reformers such as General Clinton B. Fisk and Eliot still saw Foster's plan as unfeasible. Without excuse, Eliot later recalled the disposition of Charlotte Scott's memorial funds at about this time in an offhand way: "Then came a revulsion of feeling, from various causes, . . . which checked the movement, and could not afterwards be renewed." Meanwhile, with no irony, Eliot and the other members of the Western Sanitary Commission raised funds for a statue of James Yeatman to be added to a planned Lincoln memorial in Washington. It called for bronzes of seventy-five white men to surround Lincoln as he signed the Emancipation Proclamation.[47] Some legacy indeed.

Foster and his education committee initially intended to donate the funds to a school that would take their African-American veterans as students. Foster approached the Methodist church, which was establishing a "Central

University" in St. Louis, but its administrators rejected the proposal for an integrated school. Eliot's Washington University was also not interested; as James Yeatman later noted, the "present generation, with its prejudices," would shrink from participation in an integrated school system. After these denials, Foster decided to move the effort from St. Louis to Jefferson City. The records are unclear as to why, but suggestions include the chance to form a productive industrial school in the smaller town, to partner with a small school for African Americans already opened there by a committee of "benevolent ladies," or to seek favor with the steadfastly Radical state legislature. Whatever the reason, no partner was easily found: the colored Methodist church objected to housing an American Missionary Association school with white teachers, and the white Methodist church objected to lending a basement to a school with black pupils. Foster only found success lobbying the Freedmen's Bureau, which offered $2,000.[48]

Unable to find an educational partner and convinced that "my best course was to establish the school, and make it at least deserve to live," Foster opened Lincoln Institute, now Lincoln University, for classes on September 16, 1866. Though the exact story of the naming seems lost, the choice was obvious: "The institution bears the grandest name in American history," a Chicago newspaper later remarked. "We trust its career may prove as beneficial to the colored race as Lincoln's act of emancipation." Lincoln University became the nation's only institution of higher education established by U.S. Colored Troops, financed by former slaves, and open to all men, white or black—a dramatic gesture, even compared with the white-initiated black schools of the era, such as Howard and Fisk universities. African Americans and their allies argued that rights for ex-slaves should be Lincoln's most important legacy.

The colored troops sought to memorialize their hero with their continued successes. Whether he could gather funds in the dire postwar economy, Foster clearly could muster institutional support from the state's white community: Governor Thomas C. Fletcher was the school's first president; state superintendent of schools Thomas A. Parker was vice president; James Yeatman served as treasurer; and Foster appointed himself secretary and "general agent." Arnold Krekel, the German-born president of the constitutional convention and a former slaveholder, was another board member who also taught "civil order, self-control, and morality" at the school for years, without salary. Yet it was the presence of Henry Brown, a veteran of the 62nd, as both a student and a member of the board of trustees that was truly groundbreaking. On both accounts, Brown embodied the dreams of his fellow African-American veterans, and demonstrated the power of the experiment Foster wished to nurture in Lincoln's name.[49]

The school's first location was "a shell, a wreck, a ruin" of a former schoolhouse, donated by the township directors, with only two rooms. Brown and his fellow student, Cornelius Chappell, learned reading and writing, and worked on house repairs. Yet the school grew quickly, and ground was soon broken for a new building. Within the first year, Foster reported, "we have thus given instruction to 235 different pupils with an average attendance of 70." Gaining wider notice, Foster and his college-educated African-American recruitment and publicity agent, Charles A. Beal, sought funds and students with the hearty endorsements of Frederick Douglass, Henry Ward Beecher, and Massachusetts Governor William Claflin, among others.[50]

Buoyed by his success, Foster sought to find permanent public support for the Lincoln Institute, and eyed the funds of the Morrill Act, a part of the

This recent sculpture expresses the highest hopes of Lincoln University's founders: that ex-slaves could provide a proper legacy for the assassinated president by seeking education for all. Ed Dwight, *Soldier's Memorial*, 2007. Lincoln University. Photograph by Ed Dwight.

western agenda passed during the Civil War to provide government land for sale to fund public higher education. Since every Missouri county was duty-bound to provide at least one white and one colored school, the need for African-American teachers should have been acute, yet Superintendent Parker's reports indicated that these schools had not been built and teachers not hired. Foster's efforts to make Lincoln University a publicly supported land-grant institution and a state normal school for educating teachers failed in two consecutive legislative sessions, but he persevered, producing report after report on the African-American education gap in Missouri, pressing the state legislature to force the counties to fulfill the mandate.[51]

In April 1868, as Johnson's impeachment and African-American suffrage still hung in the balance, the St. Louis Radical Wesley Watson took a novel approach, suing the city's District Two school board on behalf of the state's colored children. He appealed as far as the Missouri Supreme Court—which dismissed his claim. Despite being Republican appointees, the judges would not force such change; education guarantees would not be established by court decisions until another century and another civil rights struggle had come to pass.[52]

Even as the suffrage amendment failed and efforts to sue for equality in St. Louis faltered, Lincoln Institute became a state-supported normal school. On February 14, 1870, Missouri Governor Joseph McClurg signed the bill—providing that Foster and his supporters first could raise $15,000. With the help of the Western Sanitary Commission—using funds tied to Charlotte Scott's original donation—and from the nearly defunct Freedmen's Bureau, Foster scraped together the necessary money by the deadline, making it possible to dedicate the new building in 1871. Foster's hard work had achieved an amazing success: "Only in Missouri is there a STATE normal school for training colored teachers, and Missouri owes it to the 62nd regiment," he wrote.[53]

By 1870 the window for change was closing. Establishing Lincoln Institute as a state school was the act of a lame-duck governor with the support of remnant Radical legislators. Intimidation and violence returned as everyday threats to freedmen, and officers of the 62nd Regiment noted with sadness the news that one of their former soldiers had been lynched. In January 1871 Foster complained how the *planned* normal schools for white teachers, in Sedalia and Kirksville, had been mentioned in Governor McClurg's outgoing message, while the *extant* Lincoln Institute was ignored, doing "a great injustice by the omission." The new governor did not respond, and Foster's break with the new political leadership led to his dismissal as principal of the school.[54]

Richard Baxter Foster had accomplished what he had promised his troops: together they established an institute that educated African-American veterans and served as a monument both to the efforts of the Missouri colored troops and to the leadership of Abraham Lincoln. Yet as Radical Reconstruction collapsed in Missouri, the school found many of its supporters out of office and its future uncertain.

African Americans and Radical Republicans in St. Louis entered the national conversation about Lincoln's legacies but ultimately struggled with the ambiguous standards of Reconstruction's politics, and the narrow possibilities of Reconstruction's social transformation. All the while, ex-Confederate and other conservative white St. Louisans constructed their own memory of the Civil War—one subtle, false, and ultimately very pervasive. Their myths fostered a conversation about local as well as national identity, one that indicated a shift in regional alliances for longtime St. Louisans from the West to the South, from high hopes for westward expansion to a nostalgia for the slave society lost.

Living in a place where the war went mostly unfought, St. Louisans both hungered for memories of the conflict and more easily forgave its participants. In the fall of 1865, Professor La Rue's "Great War Show" of Kansas City appeared in the Mercantile Library Hall, and the troupe of "Carter's Zouaves" also played a number of shows in years following. In August 1866 Alexander Stephens, former vice president of the Confederacy, was again invited to speak, a sign of the changing politics and debate over the place of former Confederates. Stephens, with his positions known, and these war shows, with their scripted action, were safe, reassuring thrills, an easy escape from Reconstruction. Yet in the months after Lee's surrender, at St. Louis Mercantile Library the librarian "was instructed to respectfully decline the proposal made him to rent the Hall to Frederick Douglass." African-American leaders raised uncomfortable questions in the present, about the planned extent of societal changes.[55]

White St. Louisans commemorated the end of slavery by remembering an event that probably did not occur. It was the "last slave sale" in St. Louis history. As later accounts had it, the slaves were brought to the courthouse steps on January 1, 1861, to be auctioned off in an end-of-the-year probate sale. "Three dollars!" the assembled crowd of two thousand young men roared again and again, drowning out the auctioneer. "Three dollars, and no more!" Disgusted at the low bid for a young boy without blemish—worth thousands despite Lincoln's election—the auctioneer canceled the public sale and sold the slaves in a quieter venue.[56]

This supposed memory was intense, with many histories repeating the incident as fact. It is touted as a point of pride in the elimination of slavery, a palpable St. Louis connection to the Civil War and Lincoln's Emancipation Proclamation. Yet newer investigations suggest that these events are imagined. Emancipation did not come in Missouri until 1865, and slave sales continued at the courthouse intermittently, throughout the war. Jim, a forty-year-old slave, was sold at the courthouse on January 1, 1861, in an auction held without interruption.[57] And rather than celebrating the end of slavery, this memory of the "last slave sale" is intertwined with opposition to Lincoln and to Radical Reconstruction.

It was August 1866 when Thomas Satterwhite Noble first displayed his powerful painting *The Slave Mart*. Depicting a group of slaves for sale on the steps of the St. Louis courthouse, the genre painting captured the sentimental scene when a slave family was divided on the auction block. Like Lincoln's body, the painting caused a sensation, and viewing it was an experience to be sought after, from Chicago to Boston to Washington, where it was displayed in the Capitol rotunda. Not intended to mark any specific historical event, Noble's image was interpreted as showing one "last sale," to demonstrate the end of what had once been an everyday occurrence.[58]

Yet more than a memory of slavery, the painting was seen by reviewers as a commentary on the politics of Reconstruction. In a review titled "The Last Slave Sale," the *St. Louis Times,* an unapologetically antebellum-minded Democratic paper, described how the slave auction should be interpreted in light of the three white men gesturing in the foreground, "the three shades of our political ethics—old fogyism, conservatism and radicalism." The reviewer noted with approval that the antebellum gentleman "has said his say," telling of "the grand 'old times,'" while "the radical (a young man) is earnestly advancing some one of the theories . . . perhaps the 'equality of races.'" The sentimental scene behind them must be understood as mere irony, the reviewer argued; after all, he wrote, "the historian and the painter work out the same end by different means."[59]

That Thomas S. Noble was the painter only added to the ambiguity of the painting's message. Reviews said Noble "first conceived his subject six years ago," in January 1861, just as he was enlisting in St. Louis—for the Confederate army, to fight against Abraham Lincoln and emancipation. After the Civil War Noble painted what were understood as sympathetic images of African Americans, but during the war he designed guns and operated pontoon bridges for the Confederacy. The *Times's* reviewer found no need to mention Noble's military service; he viewed Noble as the new master of western art, whom even George Caleb Bingham would have to emulate. In another column, however, the *St. Louis Times* editors doubted their critic, reminding him that "art has no right to distort history."[60]

Whether Noble's work was originally intended to show a last slave sale or simply interpreted that way, the painting became the touchstone for St. Louisans to remember an iconic scene in their city's history—whatever the records might indicate about its reality. Forgetting their funeral without a body

After the war, Thomas Satterwhite Noble painted this ambiguous scene of an old slave mart. Marking the end of slavery, it fueled false memories of a "last slave sale." Thomas S. Noble, *Last Sale of the Slaves on the Courthouse Steps*, 1880. Missouri History Museum, St. Louis, repainting of the destroyed *The Slave Mart*, 1865.

for Abraham Lincoln and neglecting their connection to Lincoln University, those who doubted the Radical Republican program ultimately enshrined their vision of the war; slavery had ended but racial discrimination continued. Both the champions of Radical Reconstruction and its opponents sought advantage by invoking Lincoln's name. The legacy that could have united the country only proved how deep its divisions remained.

In these years of tumult, the Radicals' results were mixed: Lincoln Institute had been established, yet political rights for African Americans denied and Radical strictures on ex-Confederates challenged. Buoyed by the years of war administration and the dramatic actions of Radical Reconstruction, the city's economic, political, and cultural class cherished their experience of St. Louis as a national city. They maintained its antebellum ambitions: St. Louis could still unite the nation's three regions, still resolve the lingering questions of slavery politics and grasp the promise of Manifest Destiny, its boosters argued. Whether the method of doing so would honor or denigrate Abraham Lincoln's legacy, however, remained an open question.

9

The Capital Failures of Reconstruction

It is not wise for a Church, a political party, a nation, to change its base. Its loss is certain, not the gain. It enters on some sphere already held by others to better advantage.

Do your work better. Never divert it.

—William Greenleaf Eliot, personal notebook, n.d. [August 1870].

On paper, it all made sense. After the trauma of the Civil War years and the contentious changes of Radical Reconstruction, the United States needed a new start. And Logan Uriah Reavis had a plan. As he reasoned, the newly reunited states should fully embrace the nation's continental reach, stretching not only from the Atlantic to the Pacific but from the Gulf of Mexico up to frigid Alaska, recently purchased from Russia. Reavis compiled agricultural and climate data. He analyzed settlement patterns and political trends. He cited esoteric theories, describing isothermal zodiacs and concentric circles of settlement. Reavis took in geography and politics and economics and found one answer for renewing the promise of the United States: capital removal. Rather than from Washington—that "distant place on the outskirts of the country, with little power or prestige," Reavis called it—the nation should be led from "a central position in the Mississippi Valley," he argued, where "the great vitalizing heart of the Republic beats." And Reavis knew the perfect place: St. Louis should become the national capital.[1]

Reavis's scheme was no mere local promotion. With a wide array of supporters from around the nation, the campaign for capital removal precipitated a crisis for Reconstruction. In the years after Lincoln's assassination, it was increasingly obvious that the old ways of governing the United States were no longer adequate. Given the dramatic changes, many observers considered a completely new U.S. constitution likely and believed that some form of capital removal would be inevitable. At the moment Congress was passing the sweeping Reconstruction Amendments, Reavis thought that the seat of government, too, should be reconsidered. Reavis found Washington, D.C., "an utter failure to be a representative city," and St. Louis a far better choice. In such pamphlets as *A Change of National Empire* (1869), *St. Louis, the Future Great City of the World* (1870), and *The Capital Is Movable* (1871), he made his case for relocation.[2]

The program of Reconstruction had caused Americans to question the fundamental precepts of their society. Economically, the imminent completion of the transcontinental railroad line would transform shipping routes

Inveterate in his support for St. Louis as the national capital, Logan Reavis analyzed settlement patterns and traced isothermal zodiacs; this later *Central Magazine* cover continued to emphasize the power of his plan. *Central Magazine* cover, January 1874. Missouri History Museum, St. Louis.

and costs; politically, the sweeping Fourteenth and Fifteenth amendments promised to exclude ex-Confederates and enshrine African-American suffrage. Yet the path to economic prosperity was not smooth, and fights over ratification of the Reconstruction Amendments threatened to launch a new counterrevolution, with distinct echoes of the antebellum order.[3]

Amid all this uncertainty, the quixotic Logan Reavis spearheaded the most serious attempt at capital removal in the nation's history.[4] Urging an economic, political, and cultural rebirth for St. Louis, Reavis and his allies promised a wholesale recovery from the physical and psychological ravages of the Civil War. Once and for all, St. Louis advocates argued boldly for their city's place as the nation's geographic, demographic, economic, and political center. Would St. Louis be a backwater or a capital? Reavis's capital removal campaign encapsulated the challenges of Reconstruction. The cultural civil war pressed on, and St. Louis leaders would try one last time to unite the representatives of the West, North, and South.

On May 10, 1869, the golden spike clanged into place at Promontory Point in the Utah Territory, completing the federally funded transcontinental railroad and connecting the Mississippi River valley to the Pacific. St. Louisans marked the accomplishment in their diaries, but, as the *Democrat* noted glumly, "no general celebration of the event was provided for in our own city." Despite renewed construction after the Civil War, St. Louis railroads did not connect directly to the road's terminus, in Omaha, in time for the celebration. The long-held dream of a transcontinental railroad stood ready to enrich Chicago, as that city—though still smaller than St. Louis—grew at a meteoric rate.[5]

What had happened? Historians have long thrust and parried over the reasons for Chicago's rise and St. Louis's relative decline. Some have blamed St. Louis's old-timers, painting them as indolent antebellum grandees, overconfident about steamboat power, anxious to protect slaveholdings, and eager to curtail Yankee influence in the city. Yet this is just so much smoke, for in the 1840s and 1850s St. Louis's merchant-entrepreneurs, newly arrived or well-established, invested in railroad joint-stock companies. If not for the 1855 disaster at Gasconade, St. Louis would have entered the years of Lincoln's presidency in an equal or better position than Chicago. During the Civil War, both state officials and military leaders affirmed the importance of continuing railroad work, as a war measure and a bounty for peacetime. Confederate forces recognized the power of the rails—and hence they made a point of routinely attacking them, seeking to sabotage this symbol of the Union.[6]

During Reconstruction St. Louis faced the rebuilding of a railroad network damaged but not defeated. The transcontinental route itself, going through Omaha, favored Chicago, yet snow interruptions in 1869 convinced St. Louis advocates that a southern route was preferable. In Washington John C. Frémont emerged once again, lobbying for a second federally financed railroad heading west from St. Louis along the 32nd parallel. St. Louis leaders still envisioned the time when Missouri's Pacific Railroad Company would run all the way to the ocean.[7]

It was not accidents but finances that delayed Missouri's railroads after the war. During the fighting, some of the state's railroad companies had stopped paying interest on their bonds, and during Reconstruction creditors sued to seize assets. The state's most successful rail line, the Hannibal and St. Joseph, was purchased by John Murray Forbes and placed in the service of the Chicago rail system. Missouri's Radical Republicans sought to prevent more sales to eastern financiers, yet they themselves were forced to sell the state's Pacific Railroad shares in March 1868 at a discounted rate. The legislators could neither solve the railroads' financial worries nor lessen their competitive disadvantage.[8]

While markets to the southwest—in southern Missouri, Arkansas, Texas, and New Mexico—remained a successful area for St. Louis companies, investments there tied St. Louis to the ruined economies of the Confederacy. This reorientation strengthened the identification of St. Louis with the interests of the South, after generations of profitable business ties to frontiers in the West. Yet St. Louis had not abandoned its national ambitions. Seeking more residents, the state appointed a Board of Immigration, sending German-speaking recruiters to Europe to find the next generation of Missourians. And the hopes for St. Louis's economic future were pinned to petitions to the state, as more than two hundred local leaders urged construction of James B. Eads's bridge across the Mississippi.[9]

A self-taught engineer, James Buchanan Eads spent a lifetime along the Mississippi River. Before the war, he had invented a diving bell, to aid in his salvaging of steamboat wrecks; during the fighting he managed construction of ironclad gunboats for the U.S. Army, providing the Union an insurmountable advantage on inland waterways. During Reconstruction Eads became interested in the challenges of constructing a bridge across the Mississippi River at the St. Louis levee, where the river was 1,500 feet wide. His knowledge of deep diving and the intricacies of steel construction were crucial to his success in converting decades of discussion about such a bridge into a workable plan.[10]

When Eads's design was revealed in 1867, it caused a sensation. The planned Mississippi River bridge would allow for both vehicular and railroad traffic and the roadway would cross two lengthy steel arches.[11] The novel design would revolutionize the region's transportation—hence those who lorded over the current shipping lines immediately objected. Steamboat and barge companies sought injunctions, arguing that the bridge would endanger their work on the levee, and they worked with Chicago interests to deny the necessary permits in the Illinois legislature. When the St. Louis bridge company began construction, it had not received permission; opponents laughed at the vision of Eads's bridge extending only halfway across the river. Illinois's U.S. senators sponsored legislation to regulate the bridge's dimensions; in 1873 one final steamboaters' challenge found a sympathetic ear in the War Department offices, urging a review by the Army Corps of Engineers. Only after President Ulysses Grant personally intervened did the meddling stop and Eads's bridge get finished.[12]

The bridge opened in a ceremony on July 4, 1874, just the sort of national spectacle Logan Reavis and other St. Louis boosters had envisioned. More than 200,000 celebrants attended the fourteen-mile-long parade, with cavalrymen, trade unionists, members of fraternal orders, and German turners and singing societies marching between the floats. The invited dignitaries proudly—and safely—crossed the bridge in Pullman cars, and the governors of Illinois, Indiana, and Missouri spoke, along with a Michigan senator. Young women from the old French families christened the bridge, and Benjamin Gratz Brown gave the dedicatory address. A fifty-foot-tall banner celebrated Eads's accomplishment, his portrait above the proud caption "St. Louis founded by Laclede, 1764: crowned Queen of the West, 1874." The city celebrated as the completion of Eads's bridge vanquished the ghosts of the Gasconade disaster. But railroad success had come too late: "It does seem ridiculous that the whole United States is to be disturbed and annoyed about a bridge being built over the Mississippi," William Barclay Napton noted in his diary, "there being thousands of just such bridges all over Europe and America." Crowned in 1874, the bridge appeared eighteen years after the Chicago railroads got their bridge over the Mississippi at Rock Island, five years after the rail lines connected Chicago to the Pacific. Again, a lesson in hindsight. While Eads's bridge was under construction, however, the city maintained its national ambitions. Cheering them along was Logan Reavis, with his wild declarations in support of capital removal.[13]

Logan Uriah Reavis justly considered himself a prophet of Manifest Destiny. Born in Sangamon Bottom, Illinois, in 1831, Reavis always walked with a cane, the result of a childhood illness that had crippled one of his legs. Hipshot and hunchbacked his whole life, Reavis wore his red beard long and scraggly, adding to his already unusual appearance. An early effort to be a schoolteacher failed when the students ridiculed him ceaselessly. In the 1850s Reavis tried and failed to establish local newspapers in a number of Illinois and Nebraska towns. Throughout, he had sought advice from Horace Greeley, editor of the influential *New York Tribune,* who kindly wrote to Reavis, recommending that he not go to St. Louis and not establish a newspaper there. Reavis went nevertheless, arriving in 1866 by his own account "a stranger without friends and without means," and began championing the merits of the city.[14]

As early as 1829, visitors and local boosters had predicted that the Mississippi River valley would soon outstrip the East Coast as the center of American culture. In 1846, as troops massed in the city, St. Louis newspapers argued that moving the capital would be essential to governing the newly continental United States after the war with Mexico was concluded. The Mexican Cession and the gold and silver rushes only strengthened the case for moving the national center to the West—as, of course, did the completion of the transcontinental railroad. Thomas Hart Benton had been the St. Louis visionary a generation before, turning his advocacy of the railroad— "There is the East! There is India!"—into a transformative reality. In May 1868 twenty thousand assembled in St. Louis's Lafayette Park for the dedication of a bronze statue of the statesman, his memorable words engraved on the pedestal. Clothed in a toga, eyes to the horizon, Benton urged on his city even in death.[15] Logan Reavis wondered: could capital removal succeed where the transcontinental railroad had failed, uniting the nation culturally as well as technologically, and bringing prosperity and influence to succeed for St. Louis? With his army of facts and his practical plans at the ready, Reavis spoke of capital removal any chance he had.

Reavis's books and pamphlets soon gained a remarkable following, as his ideas resonated with the wide-open possibilities of Reconstruction politics. The *Boston Daily Advertiser* noted when, in February 1868, U.S. Representative from St. Louis Carmen Newcomb introduced legislation to move the capital to his city—though the House Ways and Means Committee promptly buried the proposal. Reavis was undeterred. Like Benton before him, Reavis arranged for a national convention in St. Louis in October 1869, drawing ninety delegates from seventeen states and territories—including a delegation from Alaska—to the Mercantile Library Hall. Given the country's continental reach, Reavis found it "absurd" to still govern from Washington, and predictably support was greatest west of the Appalachian Mountains, in territories and states more naturally oriented to St. Louis. Yet Reavis saw capital removal as a way to make Manifest Destiny and the agenda of the West work again for the benefit of the entire nation.[16]

Reavis canvassed widely for support, and so received statements of support from many prominent correspondents. Senator Charles Sumner of Massachusetts declined the invitation to be keynote speaker, but former President Andrew Johnson planned to attend. Newspapers from Sacramento to Cincinnati joined the chorus of support: Horace Greeley wrote that St. Louis "advances steadily and surely to her predestined station of first inland city on the globe." Joseph Medill, editor of the *Chicago Tribune,* endorsed the plan— arguing that St. Louis was an appropriate political capital, at just the right proximity to enhance Chicago's commercial prospects. In a public debate, members of the St. Louis University Philalethic Society laid out the issues: Washington was "a gloomy little retreat on the banks of the Potomac," one student said, and even those chosen to argue against the proposal voiced their belief that "St. Louis is the centre of the Mississippi Valley—that this Valley is the centre of the United States—and the United States the centre of the whole world." In his book *Democratic Vistas,* Walt Whitman also embraced the plan for an inland national capital in the Mississippi Valley, anchoring the continental nation. In their glee, supporters even approved of Reavis's most radical suggestion, that the nation's public buildings—the White House, the newly completed Capitol, and the other government offices—be disassembled and freighted to St. Louis. (Reavis's ideas may be jarring, but the National Mall and its architecture of authority did not yet exist; the national capital remained a swampy, humid city.)[17] For reasons congruent and complementary, many in St. Louis and around the nation saw capital removal as an idea whose time had come.

General William Tecumseh Sherman, however, had his doubts. Having recently left his Reconstruction command in St. Louis for a promotion to commanding general of the entire army, Sherman wrote back to the *Missouri Republican* to praise how St. Louis was "full of life," in marked contrast to Washington's "mere . . . office routine." But when it came to capital removal, Sherman raised some practical concerns. Apart from financial barriers, there was the jurisdictional issue. Would St. Louis city or county be turned over completely to a federal district? Sherman found it unlikely and unadvisable. Could a relatively open and accessible patch of land, such as oft-mentioned Jefferson Barracks, serve as a capital site? The barracks were a dozen miles south of the city center of St. Louis, Sherman argued, and hence placing the Capitol grounds there would not benefit the city. Instead of fitting the needs of the federal government into the spaces left in a burgeoning city, Sherman advocated selecting an empty site, somewhere along the Mississippi, where a new capital district could be constructed from scratch.[18]

As Reavis's pamphlets and transcripts of the debate sold steadily, the paper torrent of arguments and options for St. Louis continued. "Is it necessary that there should be a second District of Columbia?" asked the *Irving Union,* Washington University's fledgling student newspaper. "Why not a second Paris, or a second London?" its editors argued, suggesting a federal district, outside of existing cities, was not required. Reavis and his allies, including a twenty-three-year-old reporter at the *Westliche Post* named Joseph Pulitzer, prepared for all possibilities by urging the state legislature to grant St. Louis home rule, separate from its county and autonomous within the state, as a step toward ceding land to federal control. Other boosters combined personal and political opportunities. The former congressman Henry T. Blow was a large landholder in Carondelet, the community between St. Louis and Jefferson Barracks. Blow wrote to state and federal officials with a deal: he would donate five hundred acres for the Capitol grounds, if he was permitted to build two hundred tenements alongside, "perfectly adapted" for federal employees. Though Blow was eager to begin construction, his letter received no reply.[19]

Buoyed by the local praise and national attention, Reavis's forces concluded their convention with a resolution to meet again a year later, to measure their progress toward relocating the capital and reinvigorating the nation. They concluded their sessions with a steamboat outing to Carondelet, to view the Jefferson Barracks and Henry Blow's lands. St. Louis's representatives kept the idea active in Congress, and the *Missouri Republican,* which had initially opposed the effort, called the attention from all quarters "positively refreshing." In January 1870 Representative John Logan of Illinois urged Congress to create a commission to study the practical and constitutional questions involved with capital removal, and some western legislators blocked further appropriations for D.C. construction until the removal question was resolved.[20]

When the *Missouri Democrat* endorsed the capital removal plan, its editors urged members of all political parties in St. Louis to "become as one family . . . working together most earnestly and unitedly in every measure." Capital removal could heal the lingering scars of the Civil War and end the contentiousness of Radical Reconstruction, Reavis and his supporters argued. Yet the proposal for capital removal remained bottled up in committee. After the defeat of the 1868 suffrage amendment, the opposition to Charles Drake's Radical proposals grew militant; behind a banner of rights for all, many Americans, including German voters, became convinced that the political and economic rehabilitation of ex-Confederates was essential to national progress and should precede further recompense to the former slaves. Missourians hungered for change, and disillusioned voters nationwide sought a new political program.[21]

Carl Schurz became the catalyst for Missouri's political transformation. Born in Germany, Schurz first gained fame during the 1848 revolutions, as he masterminded the rescue of a dissident leader. After himself fleeing to America, Schurz settled among his fellow German speakers in Wisconsin, where he garnered enough of a following to be nominated for lieutenant governor even before his U.S. citizenship was finalized. An early and ardent Republican, Schurz led the German delegation that rejected Edward Bates's candidacy and favored the nomination of Abraham Lincoln. After lackluster military service in the Civil War and a frustrating experience reporting on the former Confederacy for Andrew Johnson's administration, Schurz moved to St. Louis and returned to editing political newspapers, using the *Westliche Post* to influence the powerful St. Louis German voting bloc.[22]

When Schurz was chosen to fill Missouri's open U.S. Senate seat in January 1869, George Engelmann and Frederich Adolphus Wislenzus, politically conservative fellow Germans, could hardly believe Schurz's rapid rise. "Last week the nomination of this cunning demagogue and carpetbagger who has lived only 1½ years in Missouri, passed in caucus," Wislenzus wrote to Engelmann. "These are golden times for political adventurers and cheaters of every kind!" he concluded. Yet Engelmann, Wislenzus, and other political opponents were pleasantly surprised when the newly elected Schurz advocated a new approach to local prosperity and national recovery. "The civil war, which once absorbed all our thoughts," Schurz declared in June 1869, "is day after day receding into a deeper past. New wants, new problems, connected with the *future* of the country, press irresistibly into the foreground."[23]

Enumerating what would become the tenets of a new movement, Liberal Republicanism, Schurz pledged allegiance to the Union but doubted the honesty of Grant's administration. He firmly believed in granting African Americans rights, but he felt the goals of Reconstruction had been achieved, with amnesty for ex-Confederates and national reconciliation all that remained to be done to heal the nation and finally end the cultural civil war. Liberal in the nineteenth-century sense—placing laissez-faire economics before all, and looking askance at social transformation—the movement quickly attracted those Republicans who doubted the Radicals' programs. Democrats also welcomed the new movement, and not only because it split the opposition. Liberal Republicans urged Democrats to accept the Reconstruction Amendments and the finality of emancipation in exchange for loosening restrictions on ex-Confederates and blocking further rights for African Americans. Through their new compromises, Missouri politicians were reconfiguring the national political parties, calling for an end to Reconstruction, and challenging President Grant from within his own party. Editors of the *Boston Daily Advertiser* observed these developments with alarm, watching former enemies unite along regional lines, "West and South."[24]

Though Charles Drake vehemently denounced these efforts as reactionary, Schurz's circle charged the Radicals with corruption and had their own reforms in mind. Liberal Republicans denounced Missouri Governor Joseph McClurg for requiring state employees to "donate" to the Radicals' campaign funds; his practice was to purge those who did not comply. In the spring of 1869, a St. Louis city councilman proposed allowing women to vote, arguing that they could be a virtuous and presumably conservative counterbalance to African Americans. Though his colleagues merely laughed at the suggestion, a woman's suffrage conference did convene later that year in St. Louis, and Virginia Minor, one of the local suffragist leaders, petitioned in the St. Louis courts for her right to vote as a citizen under the Fourteenth Amendment. Minor's test case, filed at the Old Courthouse, would reach the U.S. Supreme Court.[25]

Joining Carl Schurz in leadership of the Liberal Republicans was Benjamin Gratz Brown. A founder of the Republican Party in Missouri and a Radical during the war, as early as September 1866 Brown broke with Drake's faction to support rights both for African Americans and for ex-Confederates. Forced to retire from his Senate seat in 1867, Brown reemerged on Decoration Day in May 1870 to offer a speech in Jefferson City, ready to condemn the Radical movement. The 1865 state constitution was "a timid, vacillating, shameful compromise," Brown wrote—as much for its punishment of ex-Confederates as for its retention of race-based citizenship. Drake and his cronies had betrayed the true revolution of the past decade, Brown said, interested in personal aggrandizement rather than the needs of their constituents, black and white. Boldly criticizing the Radicals, Brown made his reborn political ambitions clear: he planned to challenge Governor McClurg in the fall elections.[26]

Schurz and Brown also won support from a number of formally Radical newspapers. The *Missouri Democrat,* now run by William Grosvenor and William McKee, joined its former editor Brown in shifting course. So did the *Westliche Post,* which Schurz had turned over to Emil Preetorius, its longtime manager, and the new city editor, Joseph Pulitzer. "The utmost," the *Democrat* declared, "is that color may be forgotten as a basis of legislation or civil institutions." Each newspaper continued to support the Grant administration only as much as necessary to maintain government-printing contracts, and cheered political conversions under way at other newspapers around the country. In August 1870 Horace Greeley's *New York Tribune* narrowed its expectations for African Americans, urging them to seek good trades and abandon political ambition. "Wait and serve," Greeley's printed advice concluded. "Shave and black boots while you must."[27]

The Liberal Republican movement became a global counterrevolution with the outbreak of the Franco-Prussian War. Most German-American leaders were refugees of the 1848 liberal revolutions, yet along with their shift in U.S. politics, they now cheered as King Wilhelm's authoritarian government crushed the French republic and Otto von Bismarck declared the birth of the German empire from the palace of Versailles. Even President Grant congratulated Bismarck on his conquest, ignoring the undemocratic nature of German unification to stay in good graces with the powerful German voting bloc in America. The former liberal partisans had twisted their beliefs until they were unrecognizable.[28]

Grappling with the new nomenclature and the seeming opportunism of the new politics all around him, Reverend William Greenleaf Eliot noted in his journal that "Liberal sometimes means indifferent Radical, without root." As the 1870 elections neared, Radical leader Charles Drake returned to Missouri to rail against Schurz's reform policies. After a state-by-state struggle, the Fifteenth Amendment to the U.S. Constitution had been ratified, making the debate over the 1868 African-American suffrage campaign in Missouri obsolete. Yet Drake could not resist laying blame. In September 1870 he prattled on about how "it was the German vote in the state that killed that amendment," despite vote totals suggesting that voters of all ethnicities had brought about the defeat. Capital removal was all but forgotten as the fall contest between the Radical incumbent McClurg and the Liberal Republican Brown offered the key test of the new movement.[29]

Satirical magazines have flourished in moments of political uncertainty, when their power to aid or destroy candidates is multiplied. *Die Vehme,* or "The Star-Chamber," was the brainchild of Joseph Keppler, a skilled German engraver who found success in the United States with an illustrated satire magazine, rooted in the comedic traditions of his homeland and adapted to local circumstances. Nothing was sacred. Not only did Keppler lampoon the newly dedicated Benton statue, he also used imagery from the Gasconade disaster, showing a Pacific railroad train crashing through a bridge, as a symbol of the era's uncertainty and corruption. In his bilingual magazine, Keppler tackled national issues, questioning why African-American, Irish, and even Chinese men were granted the vote under the Fifteenth Amendment while white women who "read and write and pay taxes" were still denied suffrage. Yet Keppler was not above altering positions to mollify his audience. When his patrons turned against votes *both* for women and for nonwhite Americans, Keppler's cartoons followed suit.[30]

In May 1870 Keppler captured the state of Missouri politics with an image declaring capital removal dead by decree of *Die Vehme.* The cartoon "Verlor'ne Liebesmüh, or Love's Labor Lost," depicted the capital-removal booster Logan

Reavis hunched over his cane, huffing and puffing, wild beard matching wild ideas as he directed the two U.S. senators from Missouri in pulling the Capitol building westward toward St. Louis. In the image, the new Liberal Republican leader, Carl Schurz, eagerly strode forward, ready for anything, while the Radical Charles Drake appeared reluctant, unsure where Schurz and Reavis were leading him. As he attacked Schurz and Brown, Drake also broke rank with his fellow Missouri legislators, arguing that fewer than a hundred men in Missouri would "give up the city of St. Louis to the nation for a capital."[31] Yet to the cynical observer's surprise, the political alliances formed in the capital removal fight lived on.

The Grant administration, the Radicals, the capital removal activists, and the Liberal Republicans all wished to maintain St. Louis's influence on the national stage and struggled to find the correct policy to make it happen.

Die Vehme mocked Logan Reavis, huffing and puffing over his cane, as he directed the two U.S. senators from Missouri in pulling the Capitol building westward toward St. Louis. Carl Schurz eagerly strode forward while Charles Drake appeared reluctant; where were these two leading him, and the country? Keppler, "Verlor'ne Liebesmüh/Love's Labor Lost," *Die Vehme,* May 21, 1870. Missouri History Museum, St. Louis.

Ahead of the second capital removal convention, Reavis published *St. Louis, the Future Great City of the World,* the greatest compendium yet of his arguments for the city's growth and importance. William Greenleaf Eliot was among those infected with its enthusiasm. Saying it reflected his experience of more than forty years in St. Louis, Eliot approved of Reavis's insistence that St. Louis should "no longer be content with remaining far behind when it is in our power to be equally far in advance." Reavis's supporters thronged a city council meeting, urging that a second edition of *St. Louis the Future Great City of the World* be printed at the city's expense, to boost the city at this crucial time. Yet when the capital removal convention gathered in Cincinnati in October 1870, the steering committee could report little progress. With reluctance, they decided to indefinitely postpone the effort; more territories in the American West needed to become states and be represented, they reasoned, before Congress would approve.[32]

Yet convention goers remained hopeful that the results of the 1870 decennial Census, due any day, might prove that the West had arrived, and St. Louis was still ahead of its urban rivals. As with most government hiring before the 1883 Civil Service Act, those chosen as census-takers in St. Louis were patronage employees of Republican political boss and *Missouri Democrat* editor William McKee. Cognizant of the rivalry, McKee encouraged his workers not to tally their numbers until the total population for Chicago had been officially announced. Toward the end of summer, the Illinois bureau announced its figures, with Chicago increasing its tallied population by 166 percent, from 112,172 in 1860 to 298,977 in 1870. McKee was dismissive: "Our neighbor on the lakes has reached its maximum in relative importance," the *Democrat* declared, and "we believe that Chicago will never again approach as near this city in population."[33]

On October 2, 1870, McKee's *Democrat* broke the news: "St. Louis is the fourth city of the country in population," the editors crowed, "and Chicago . . . is beaten by over thirteen thousand." According to the figures, St. Louis had ballooned from 160,773 in 1860 to reach the improbable height of 312,963 residents in 1870. This growth occurred despite the Civil War, and despite "the lack of railroad and other facilities for commerce, which had grown up rapidly in rival cities," the *Democrat* noted. In a decade of strife, St. Louis had passed Baltimore, Boston, Cincinnati, and New Orleans, and remained ahead of Chicago. The *Democrat* averred that since New York and Brooklyn were practically the same city (they did not merge until 1898),

St. Louis was truly the third city of the nation, just behind Philadelphia, and the unchallenged metropolis of the United States over the Appalachians.[34]

In the heady celebration that followed, the *St. Louis Times* joined the celebratory chorus, repeated the population figure in every paragraph, placing the triumphant number—**312,963**—in large bold type. The newspaper congratulated Logan Reavis for urging the city to fulfill its destiny, and ribbed him for underestimating the population gain occurring due to the forces he had predicted. When the number was announced, Horace Greeley happened to be in St. Louis, speaking at the Agricultural and Manufacturing Fair and the St. Louis Mercantile Library. He declared himself pleased to witness history, and praised the ever-more-important links between St. Louis and its sister cities of progress in the East. When Francis Amasa Walker, the superintendent of the 1870 Census, published his vast *Statistical Atlas of the United States,* it seemed to merely confirm Reavis's boldest predictions for St. Louis, the West, and the national destiny.[35]

Only the *Missouri Republican* puzzled how smaller cities could have larger school enrollments. Only later would Reverend Eliot notice that, for the numbers to be accurate, St. Louis would have had ten years with the lowest death rate ever recorded. Another decade would pass before the city's manuscript census pages would be at the center of controversy over the true population of St. Louis.[36] For now, St. Louis was the fourth city, Reavis was a hero, and his political supporters rejoiced. Liberal Republicanism had its first triumph, boosting St. Louis in the month before the Missouri general election.

For much of 1870, Liberal Republicanism remained just another wild idea from Missouri. Like capital removal, it was an informal movement at best, with popular and press endorsements but no party structure, no patronage or ballot lines of its own. That changed in August 1870, as competing slates of Liberal and Radical delegates appeared for the state Republican Party convention.[37]

African Americans were the most fearful of Schurz and Brown's program, and their leader, James Milton Turner, fervently sought reconciliation for the squabbling Republicans. With their chance to vote guaranteed by federal amendment and his constituents loyal to Lincoln's party, ready to "vote as we fought," Turner merely asked for a fair share of patronage appointments and action against the unsettling rise in anti-black violence by ex-Confederates. Turner denounced even the contemplation of amnesty. "It is unsafe to loyal men, white or black, to entrust the potency of the ballot to men who have not avowed a single sentiment of regret or repentance," Turner charged, his words answered with cries of "that's so, that's so." Yet Turner could not even bridge the divide within the African-American community, as Charlton Tandy, a cofounder of the Missouri Equal Rights League, declared his support for Benjamin Gratz Brown's movement, bringing with him a small coterie of African-American Liberal delegates. Turner became so disgusted with the defections that, one month before the election, he declared himself a candidate for Congress, determined not to let either white candidate co-opt the votes of his supporters.[38]

Divisions among African Americans mirrored the general strife among all the former political allies. In hotel lobbies and in the streets, backers of McClurg and Brown argued, with words and on many occasions with fists. After the Liberal Republicans lost a key test vote, they withdrew their delegates and finally formed their own party, nominating Benjamin Gratz Brown for governor. Supporting the effort, the *Missouri Democrat* ran an obituary for the Radical Republican party in Missouri, saying the remnant that supported McClurg was merely a ghost. Meanwhile, the Missouri Democrats observed a "possum policy," running no candidate in the gubernatorial race and merely playing dead in order to support Brown. Erasing the Civil War's political battle lines, Democrats toasted the Liberal Republican policies and declared it time to call another state constitutional convention.[39]

Though President Grant attempted to use federal favor to aid Governor McClurg's reelection campaign, Benjamin Gratz Brown won a commanding victory in November 1870. Brown's victory was hailed around the nation as the clarion call for reform, as Radical Republicans were defeated in the president's home state. Yet while Liberal Republicans were triumphant at the state level, their silent partners in the Democratic Party swept local elections, gaining control of the statehouse and an influential segment both in the state senate and the congressional delegation. Together they effectively ended Reconstruction in Missouri years before it ended elsewhere. A state constitutional amendment to reenfranchise ex-Confederates passed by a recorded vote of 127,000 to 16,000. In December 1870, when Charles Drake resigned his Senate seat to accept the security of a judicial appointment, it was Frank Blair of the resurgent Democratic Party who filled the final years of his term.[40]

Reconstruction had effectively ended in Missouri. Like other states along the former border of slavery—Kentucky, Maryland, Delaware, Tennessee,

Arkansas, and Texas—Missouri saw relatively few African-American state legislators and city and county officers during Reconstruction. In Deep South states, there had been dozens, while in Missouri fewer than ten African-American officials were elected to city, county, or state office, none of them from St. Louis. James Milton Turner been appointed as assistant superintendent of schools, but he failed in his 1870 bid at election and, disgusted with these failures, sought influence elsewhere. In March 1871 Turner became the Grant administration's ambassador to Liberia.[41]

In May 1871, just more than six months after the census figures were announced, Chicago had the good fortune of having a Great Fire. Just like the conflagration that had cleared the center of St. Louis in 1849, the Chicago fire became an impetus for rebuilding and reshaping the city's geography to the newest market needs. Echoing the words of encouragement then offered to St. Louis, Joseph Medill of the *Chicago Tribune* was adamant that "upon the ashes of thirty years' accumulation ... CHICAGO SHALL RISE AGAIN!" St. Louisans were familiar with the opportunities such a fire offered. Local newspapers were filled with advice for Chicago and reminiscences of St. Louis's own fond destruction. By the time Mrs. O'Leary's cow was being blamed for kicking over a lantern, Currier & Ives had already produced a dazzling print to frame the moment of a disaster past. Chicago's leaders rebuilt, reorienting everything to the railroads, catering to their booming trade across a vast hinterland.[42]

With the sweeping political change of Liberal Republicanism and the shift of investment to rebuilding Chicago, there was much to worry St. Louis's leaders. The city's cultural stewards, however, remained optimistic that they could protect their institutions. The Civil War had almost shut Washington University before anyone had graduated, and the Mercantile Library struggled financially during the war years. Despite their antebellum involvement in the Whig Party and their embrace of moderate Unionism during the war, those in Eliot's circle eschewed Reconstruction politics. Instead, they redoubled their efforts to generously endow St. Louis's cultural institutions.[43]

"May the time soon come," the student newspaper wrote in February 1869, "when it will be sufficient testimony of a full college education to say, 'I am a graduate of Washington University.'" Easterners misunderstood Washington University, the editors argued, maintaining a mental image of rough-hewn schools and unprepared pupils that was decades outdated. Yet, when the chancellor, William Chauvenet, resigned because of illness in September 1869, the directors worried about this setback, when outlays were being made to hire a half-dozen new professors and to open a law school. William Greenleaf Eliot reluctantly resigned as pastor of his church to become the university's interim chancellor, leaving his ministry of thirty-three years.[44]

While searching for a capable leader, Eliot worked overtime to build the university endowment and raise its national profile. Within two years, more than $240,000 was pledged by supporters in St. Louis and throughout the nation. In his role as president of the Western Sanitary Commission (which continued as a charitable organization after the war), Eliot provided Washington University with an additional $40,000 in scholarships for the children of white Union soldiers. The *Missouri Democrat,* alongside the columns advocating Liberal Republican positions, praised the effort to "build up in St. Louis a grand seat of generous culture." Eliot became so identified with his university that the search for another chancellor was fruitless; planning to serve a year or two, Eliot remained president of the board of directors and chancellor of Washington University until his death.[45]

The St. Louis Mercantile Library reached its own milestone in the spring of 1871, celebrating its twenty-fifth anniversary with marches, speeches, and a banquet. Many of the founders and former presidents, now eminent men retired from their successful businesses, served on the planning committee. They invited ministers, school principals, judges, and doctors—and the most prominent St. Louisan, President Ulysses S. Grant, who sent regrets. Despite having just renovated its building, the Mercantile Library considered creating a new grand structure to house the St. Louis Academy of Science, the fledgling Missouri Historical Society, and the Mercantile Library on the grounds of a city park. Amid the whirlwind of political and economic change, directors of these twin institutions, Washington University and the Mercantile Library, sought to secure their influence on the city and the nation forever.[46]

Logan Reavis embraced one final wild notion in 1871 when he nominated Horace Greeley for president. Writing in the *Missouri Democrat,* Reavis argued that Greeley was no longer a mere newspaper editor but a true national leader, "the representative of American nationality and civilization" and a candidate with "universal popularity." Even as Reavis kept advocating for capital removal, his championing of Greeley suggested that he was aware of how changing the politics in the capital, rather than changing the capital it-self, would be a far more effective way to change the nation.[47]

Reavis nominated Greeley when Ulysses Grant had hardly begun his third year as president, doing so in an era when it was unimaginable to ad-vocate for a presidential nominee eighteen months before an election. As for Greeley, he had almost no political experience, having served a single U.S. House term twenty years before and never having sought another public of-fice. Greeley had been a Lincoln supporter and a staunch antislavery voice before the Civil War, but afterward had questioned the harsh treatment of ex-Confederates. In 1867 Greeley dramatically demonstrated his disapproval of Radical Reconstruction by joining those posting bond for former Con-federate president Jefferson Davis. Hearing news of Liberal Republican vic-tories in Missouri, and then in Virginia and Tennessee, Greeley cheered the emerging movement, though he still considered himself merely an observer. This made for an unusual political résumé. But Reavis was hardly a conven-tional individual, and the 1872 contest no longer seemed like a conventional election.[48]

As Reavis campaigned for Greeley, writing and publishing a campaign biography, he bypassed a handful of Missouri leaders with political experi-ence and the potential to garner a national audience. "In the event of liberal-ism, we are all Republicans—we are all Democrats," Missouri Governor Benjamin Gratz Brown declared at his inauguration on January 9, 1871, mak-ing his own case for leadership and persuading many around the country. Frank Blair was serving in the U.S. Senate as a Democrat, maneuvering the old party apparatus to fight the Reconstruction Amendments. And Carl Sch-urz could be a kingmaker, himself not the presidential frontrunner only be-cause he was disqualified by his German birth. In September 1871 Schurz announced a national Liberal Republican platform, advocating civil-service reform, reduced tariffs, freedom from regulation, acceptance of the Fifteenth Amendment, and a greater reliance on local control rather than military oc-cupation for what was nominally a reunited country at peace. At national rallies and in widely distributed pamphlets, Missouri politicians expressed their confidence that Reconstruction could be defeated at the ballot box, state by state.[49]

St. Louis wished to host the national convention of Liberal Republicans in 1872, but the city was not ready. Eads's bridge was not yet completed, and even Reavis found the mud and stench of the city during spring rises and sweltering summers to be revolting. Instead, promises were made about the next convention, in four years' time, while Liberal Republicans gathered in the German-American sister city of Cincinnati and the Democrats chose the fellow border-state metropolis of Baltimore. Away from Missouri, the local leaders could not unite behind one candidate; Carl Schurz split from Governor Brown, pledging his support instead to Charles Francis Adams, the U.S. ambassador to Britain and the descendant of two presidents, for the nomination. As Brown broke protocol and arrived to address the convention himself, he shocked his delegates by withdrawing from the race and announcing his support for Greeley. Schurz and his fellow insiders were aghast, but Logan Reavis got his wish: Horace Greeley for president, with Benjamin Gratz Brown the proud vice presidential nominee. In July the Democrats in Baltimore quickly ratified the Liberal Republicans' choices as their own.[50]

As a Liberal Republican nominee, Greeley was an imperfect choice. The movement backed tariff elimination and civil-service reform; Greeley showed no passion for either. While the party needed the votes of antitemperance Irish and German immigrants, Greeley was a temperance supporter. Brown made up for this particular shortcoming, but not in a way that was likely to help the ticket: long rumored to be a drunkard, the Missouri governor was sloppy and insulting on the campaign trail. For a while the Greeley-Brown ticket drew large crowds, but soon their drawbacks, in policy and personal behavior, became evident. After the conventions, Schurz wrote to Greeley, urging that he step aside for the good of the movement. When Greeley declined to do so, Schurz gave a few halfhearted speeches before distancing himself from the movement he had created. On election day 1872, Greeley and Brown carried Missouri, Texas, Georgia, Kentucky, Tennessee, and Maryland, but President Grant handily won reelection without support of his hometown. When Horace Greeley, exhausted and bereft, died a few weeks after the election, the Liberal Republican movement seemed to die with him.[51]

The ambitious plans to cement St. Louis's place at the heart of the republic—with the first transcontinental railroad link, the national capital, and a new political party—had failed. Yet St. Louis leaders did not consider the question settled. In 1872 the new Democratic mayor, Joseph Brown, again sought federal funding for a railroad route along the 35th parallel, reaching from St. Louis to San Francisco, though he knew it would be a difficult campaign. "To-day, although geographically in the center, we are made to appear as off to one side," Mayor Brown wrote, as "another city," Chicago, "grasped the prize" of transcontinental trade. At another local railroad convention, he focused on routes to the still-underdeveloped transportation networks of the Gulf South, and the still-isolated desert Southwest. But some wondered whether it was already too late for yet another grand vision for St. Louis's place in the nation, another scheme built only on promises.[52]

10

Separating the City, County, and Nation

Give over to us those matters of business and vital necessity to the city of St. Louis. Do not interfere, let us govern ourselves, carry out the true principles of local self-government; that is all we want. . . .

—Joseph Pulitzer, *Debates of the Missouri Constitutional Convention,* July 30, 1875.

On June 24, 1876, the carriages flowed west out of St. Louis, filling the dusty roads for miles. Amid the country estates and working farms, gravel paving suddenly appeared, leading to park drives and artificial lakes, all perfectly arranged. It was opening day for Forest Park, a 1,293-acre expanse meant to be, as one longtime promoter described it, "to St. Louis what New York has in Central Park." Extra trains began running early in the morning, and by the time of the ceremony, tens of thousands of people had gathered— including not only St. Louis's mayor and Missouri's governor, but also U.S. senators from California and Wisconsin and the lieutenant governor of New York. They were delegates to the Democratic National Convention, held for the first time in St. Louis. Four days later they would nominate New York governor Samuel J. Tilden for president.[1]

At the gates of Forest Park, both St. Louis leaders and Tilden partisans looked ahead to the fall elections, confident in their call for home rule. Governor Tilden sought the White House on a platform that promised the removal of the federal troops who had been guaranteeing Republican rule in Louisiana and South Carolina; local leaders pressed for ratification of a new city charter and a so-called scheme of separation for the city and county of

St. Louis. The debate over separation reshaped St. Louis politics as had no issue since slavery. In tones once reserved for the promise of the transcontinental railroad or the crowning of St. Louis as the national capital, advocates lauded separation as the paragon of local reform and a chance to begin St. Louis anew. Intended as the accomplishment of a great metropolis, the creation of Forest Park was also a turn inward, toward city beautification and the consolidation of power, at the end of the cultural civil war.[2]

The cultural civil war had begun with a question of unity: How could the vast lands and diverse peoples of the Mexican Cession be integrated into the United States? Under what conditions, if any, would slavery be allowed, and what priority would the national government give this territory, under its professed banner of Manifest Destiny? Advocates from each region of the country—North, West, and South—provided their own answers, and the disagreements over the new territory precipitated a political crisis that led to a fighting war. Signs of unity and signals of the political, economic, and cultural successes seemed to abound that summer. As St. Louisans reveled in the delights of Forest Park, the nation prepared to celebrate its centennial with a grand exposition in Philadelphia. Yet separation won the day: the events of 1876 revealed a nation altered but not transformed. The denouement of Reconstruction revealed how divided the United States remained.

The Panic of 1873 struck soon after the contentious 1872 presidential election, and the economic contraction did not lift easily. As the final phase of Reconstruction opened, St. Louis leaders would not be deterred: "No city has suffered greater reverses by fire, pestilence and flood, by financial crises, by internal dissensions and civil war," declared Wayman Crow, author of the Washington University charter, injured investor at the Gasconade disaster, and a dedicated member of the Western Sanitary Commission. "And yet we have passed through all, chiefly by the sturdy strength and steadfastness of our business men." Edward King, a journalist touring all fifteen former slave states for *Scribner's Monthly,* agreed that St. Louis, "free from the major evils attendant upon reconstruction," would prosper. With projections that would make Logan Reavis proud, King predicted that St. Louis would be the capital of the reborn South, a city of one million residents in less than a generation, and a perennial competitor with Chicago.[3]

As the Panic deepened, however, and the promised economic recovery did not materialize, angry voters turned against the Republican leadership and

Reconstruction. Workers demonstrated for jobs and wages across the nation, and populist "antimonopoly" parties rose up in many western states, adding the complaints of hard-pressed farmers to the general calls for corruption prosecutions and reform. Benjamin Gratz Brown, founder of the Liberal Republicans, led the party remnants into the Democratic Party, and Carl Schurz lost his reelection bid in 1874 to Francis Cockrell, who became the only former Confederate officer to be elected to the U.S. Senate from a state that had not seceded. These "Redeemer" politicians enacted racially discriminatory laws, uniting white constituencies by canceling African-American votes.[4]

Disillusion with Reconstruction was complete, and newspapers regularly announced newly discovered scandals among its remaining adherents. Federal investigations brought down the last vestiges of Republican power in St. Louis by cracking the so-called Whiskey Ring. Though based in St. Louis, the ring had a national reach, skimming profits from liquor production in Chicago, Milwaukee, New Orleans, and as far as away as Colorado, and allegedly including members of President Grant's closest circle of advisers. Pioneering investigative journalists found a national audience for exposés, as Americans grew suspicious of being swindled at every turn.[5]

By 1874 Democrats had free rein in St. Louis and in state government, but they still felt constrained by the provisions of Charles Drake's 1865 Missouri state constitution. In that document, Radical Republicans had centralized power, providing strict state control over local planning and finances. This had long annoyed St. Louis city officials, as all of their decisions were tied to those of the county court, where apportionment favored rural areas and officials had both executive and judicial duties. "Imagine the representatives from rural districts gathered in her [St. Louis's] council chambers to decide and vote upon her necessities, bridges, wharf, ferries, railroad depots," the exasperated *Missouri Democrat* wrote. "What will they know of these things?" From the start of the 1874 session, citizen petitions poured into the state Senate, complaining about tax burdens and demanding that state expenditures be reduced, while city councils lobbied for a greater taxation authority.[6]

To resolve these issues and raise others, the Democrats asked Missourians to approve a constitutional convention, to reconsider all aspects of the Drake constitution. The fall 1874 referendum narrowly passed, approved by 283 votes out of more than 444,000 cast throughout the state. This ambiguous mandate reflected uncertainty about what changes a convention might bring, and hinted at the contentiousness of the elections to come, two years later. On May 5, 1875, the state constitutional convention assembled in Jefferson

City. Representing St. Louis were Thomas Gantt, James Broadhead, and Henry C. Brokmeyer, all longtime local lawyers and Union Democrat office-holders, and the passionate *Westliche Post* editor Joseph Pulitzer.[7]

Though the convention did not follow precedent and adjourn to the comforts of St. Louis, this was one of the few inconveniences faced by the St. Louis delegation. While others debated how best to thoroughly disman-tle the Radical Republicans' constitution, the St. Louis delegates were allowed their own committee to remake the relationship of city, county, and state government. When their proposal was presented to the full convention, as sweltering July turned to August, most committee members approached the task gingerly, but Pulitzer could not be contained. St. Louis was "a small state by itself," he crowed, claiming that the city had half a million residents and a budget rivaling that of the state as a whole. The proposal offered home rule and jurisdictional independence for all Missouri cities over 100,000 resi-dents, but the specific circumstances of St. Louis guided the deliberations. On August 2, 1875, delegates approved the proposed text and scheduled a ratification vote.[8]

Would the exhausted and distrustful electorate approve the new constitu-tion? The proposed separation procedure received little attention amid a general indifference toward the document. William Barclay Napton, the for-mer Missouri Supreme Court justice and Confederate sympathizer, gave a succinct summary of the new constitution: "It was a poor affair," he recorded in his diary, "but was in some respects an improvement on the old one." Nevertheless, that fall the state electorate approved the new constitution by a seventy-point margin. Once again the state had a new constitution, and the ambitions of St. Louis were now enshrined in the state constitution itself. In April 1876, in yet another election, St. Louis city and county residents chose members of the mandated Board of Freeholders to draw up the proposed boundaries and terms of separation for the "scheme and charter" proposal to expand the city's boundaries and create a new home-rule entity. If the plan passed in both jurisdictions, the city of St. Louis would be surrounded by St. Louis County but completely independent of its concerns, separating the forward-looking metropolis from what one proponent called the "diverse and sundry cornfields and melon patches" of its hinterland.[9]

That spring, as the national centennial neared, St. Louis leaders could fi-nally welcome a national political convention to town. As tens of thousands of Democratic Party delegates gathered, William Greenleaf Eliot looked over the faces uneasily. "The very same men in 1861–4 met at Secession Hd. Qu.," Eliot noted to himself, "& some of them w^d put Slavery in again if they could." The correspondent of the *Philadelphia North American,* listening to the Democrats' rhetoric, agreed that the Party "made a leap from 1860 to 1876," as if "for sixteen years the muse of history slumbered" while these partisans resisted the Civil War, emancipation, and Reconstruction. Eliot was happy to see these party leaders now praising the Union, but he remained uncertain whether it would be a case where "necessity makes virtue."[10]

American flags were stretched over Fourth Street in front of the newly built Merchants' Exchange Hall, where the convention gathered. They made quick work of the official business, nominating Samuel J. Tilden on the second ballot. With a message of national reconciliation, reform, and local control—and a disregard for ex-slaves—the Democratic Party courted former southern Whigs as well as the Liberal Republican and German vote. Running a northern candidate but actively seeking to revive support in the South, the Democratic Party worked to regain its antebellum advantages and bridge the Civil War divide. Before and after the sessions, delegates rode the city's railroads, stayed in city hotels, dined in city restaurants, and walked the city's fashionable avenues. St. Louis businessmen hoped to profit from all the excitement. Despite the economic worries and the dramatic political transformations, the city's best was on display—and the opening of Forest Park was the perfect time to celebrate.[11]

Forest Park's creation had been an uncertain dream for decades. From St. Louis's earliest days, residents and visitors alike commented on the lack of parks in the otherwise respectable town. City founders Pierre Laclède and Auguste Chouteau provided for commons but no parks along their avenues; when in 1826 St. Louis aldermen renamed the streets in the manner of Philadelphia (Chestnut, Pine, Olive, Locust), trees were on city-dwellers' lips but the leafy names provided no shade or comfort. The mill basin at Chouteau's Pond seemed an idyllic locale, until the cholera epidemic; then city leaders drained its polluted, stagnant water. Even after the Great Fire, no parks were added to the downtown district. As in New York's commercial district, the blocks were deemed too valuable for mere public amusement.[12]

In the 1850s the need for parks became urgent, as planners worried that the belching smoke of industry might strangle a city without room for amusement. In 1851 St. Louis officials dedicated the modest thirty acres of Lafayette Park, south of downtown, within easy reach of the streetcars. In New York, however, the state legislature considered plans on a vastly larger scale. They envisioned a seven-hundred acre outlet for Manhattan's population, which had recently tripled. In 1857 the Central Park Commission began clearing squatter camps, slaughterhouses, and glue factories to make room for parkland, its workers digging artificial lakes, reshaping hills, and carving meandering paths. Central Park's construction took fifteen years, by which time the park's southern, western, and eastern edges were on their way to becoming sought-after addresses. Planners in St. Louis took note, and discussions about besting New York with a larger, grander Central Park for the West were well under way long before the eastern park's completion.[13]

The Missouri Botanical Garden was the city's first parklike respite. In 1849 the English-born Henry Shaw invested part of his mercantile and land fortune in constructing a country home, Tower Grove, and in 1856 he commissioned a world-class botanical garden, corresponding with Harvard botanist Asa Gray and Kew Gardens designer Sir William Jackson Hooker and employing local doctor George Engelmann as his chief scientific adviser. In 1859 Shaw constructed a museum building, added to his botanical library, and opened his gardens to the public. Frederick Law Olmsted, Central Park's designer, hoped that Shaw's philanthropic gesture would inspire other city leaders to create "a park of noble breadth and delicious repose" to surround it. But an 1864 referendum to approve a 350-acre "Central Park" for St. Louis failed at the wartime polls.[14]

After the war, as Logan Reavis championed capital removal, local real-estate developer Hiram Leffingwell proposed a gigantic three-thousand acre park along the western edge of the city. Lobbying legislators, the *Missouri Democrat* envisioned a "grand new park," to be the city's "municipal lungs." Promoters noted that the distance from the iconic Old Courthouse downtown to the planned Forest Park would be the same as that from City Hall in New York to the gates of Central Park, and thus a fitting addition for a future metropolis. Leffingwell's park plan made it onto Reavis's updated maps, showing the parklands within reach of the imagined capital. Near the height of their heated 1872 election campaigns, Liberal Republican Carl Schurz and Democrat Frank Blair even set aside their differences to both give addresses at the initial park dedication. While "all of the great cities of this country have outgrown anticipation," Blair declared, it would be St. Louis that "will continue increasing in population and developing in size until it will outgrow all the other cities in the country."[15]

After the 1872 dedication, however, state legislators failed to approve Leffingwell's plan. Three thousand acres was too large a park, and the finances of Reconstruction were too tight to purchase the rights from landholders. They compromised on a 1,370-acre reserve, funding the proposal with a special tax district. The Missouri Supreme Court declared this arrangement unconstitutional in 1873, but in the meantime, the city park plan had gathered momentum. In 1874 a Forest Park of 1,326 acres was approved, along with plans for grand parks in each of St. Louis's expanding neighborhoods—Carondelet Park to the south and O'Fallon Park to the north—and a proposal to connect all three with tree-lined avenues. City leaders saw these parks as a way to imitate the intensive growth of such mature metropolises as New York, Boston,

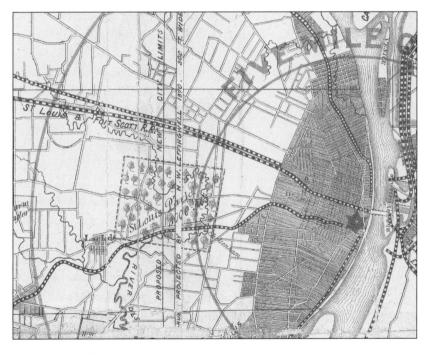

Forest Park succeeded where other park schemes had failed: Reavis and Hiram Leffingwell had imagined a 3,000-acre park "to be to St. Louis what New York has in Central Park." Reavis, map showing Leffingwell's Park, *The Future Great City of the World*, 1871. St. Louis Public Library, Special Collections.

and Philadelphia rather than the extensive spread of such upstart rivals as Chicago and San Francisco. With the "grand system" in place, wrote Nathan Cole, the president of Merchants' Exchange, St. Louis could now claim the motto "City of Parks."[16]

Though real-estate promoters actively lobbied for the proposal—and sold real estate conditional on the park's realization—others doubted whether the city would ever truly surround the Forest Park site. "The extension of city improvements into the wilderness is a piece of folly," the *Globe-Democrat* editors wrote, "which will ruin the most flourishing municipality in the country." Would St. Louis expand to the west, while riverfront property to the south and north remained available? Four landholders, descendants of the founding French families, challenged the plan by suing the state in 1874, using their wealth to fund multiple depositions, documents, maps, and charts to defend their claims and creating one of the largest case files in the history of the St. Louis courts. Even the park's superintendent and landscape gardener, Maximilian G. Kern, noted how "tracts of land, already dedicated for public parks, surrounded on all sides by populated streets, remain uncared for, or are only shabbily improved," while city leaders pushed the development of a remote and extravagant parkland. Yet in June 1876, with the lawsuits settled and incorporation into the newly expanded city planned, the landowners prospered as the neighborhood just to the north of the park developed in lavish style.[17]

As he prepared for the June 1876 opening, Superintendent Kern bragged he could open "a Forest Park defacto," given the tract's upland plateaus and perfect valley meadows. The River des Pères nourished a lush forest, an oasis in the unrelenting prairie. The grounds featured some of the last American Indian mounds in St. Louis County. Yet, in proper Victorian style, Kern oversaw the construction of follies: a "model dairy," "large and commodious rustic structures," and "a castle of the middle ages," to be enjoyed on carriage rides.[18]

Given the size of the park and its distance from the center of the city, most working-class St. Louisans might only visit Forest Park on a rare train excursion. Yet the presiding justice of the county court, Chauncey F. Shultz, wished to include all St. Louis residents in his dedicatory remarks. "The rich and the poor, the merchant and mechanic, the professional man and the day laborer, each with his family and lunch basket, can come here and enjoy his own," Schultz said, "and there will be no notice put up, 'Keep Off the Grass.'" The park was open, he said, "for the enjoyment of yourselves, your children, and your children's children forever." Your white children, and their white children, Shultz might have said. By the end of the nineteenth century, tightening Jim Crow laws made Forest Park amusements available to St. Louis's sizable African-American population only on a restricted schedule. It came to be seen as the "natural" result of Reconstruction's half measures, a retreat from efforts at social or political equality.[19]

Such future failures were already evident on June 17, 1876. While St. Louis politicians detailed the scheme of separation for the city-county split, while businessmen readied downtown for the Democratic National Convention, and while gardeners prepared the ground for the Forest Park dedication, Harriet Scott died. No newspaper noted her passing, no grand procession was held at her funeral, no dedication was made. In fact, Harriet Scott eventually slipped so far from the public eye that historians long thought she had died soon after her husband, before the Civil War. Harriet and Dred Scott were not buried together. By 1876 Dred Scott's remains had been reburied in Calvary Cemetery, through the kindness of Taylor Blow; Harriet Scott was buried in Greenwood Cemetery, an African-American graveyard farther west. Well into the twentieth century, both Scott graves remained unmarked, their court case known to every American but their resting places obscured along with their fight for rights. It has recently been revealed that the Scotts' youngest daughter, Lizzie, slipped even deeper into hiding: she walked the streets of St. Louis, her identity concealed, until her death on December 19, 1945, at around ninety-nine years of age.[20] As slavery politics returned to fuel Jim Crow laws, African Americans would endure humiliation after humiliation—even when commemorating emancipation.

Two months before the opening of Forest Park, national officials and St. Louis dignitaries gathered in Washington, D.C., on the eleventh anniversary of President Lincoln's assassination. On April 14, 1876, President Grant, his cabinet, and a few justices of the U.S. Supreme Court assembled a few blocks east of the U.S. Capitol. The invitation, reprinted in the *New York Times* and other newspapers, augured high hopes: "We respectfully invite the friends of impartial freedom, equal rights, and free institutions our country over to join in the interesting and appropriate exercises," the committee wrote. They dedicated *Freedom's Memorial,* a bronze statue of two figures: a confident Abraham Lincoln stood erect, his left arm outstretched. His right hand grasped the Emancipation Proclamation as it rested upon a pedestal festooned with symbols of federal power. Meanwhile, Lincoln looked down at the second figure, a slave, clothed only at the loins. Forever in half-crouch beneath Lincoln's arm, the slave's arm was outstretched over the broken manacles at his feet. Did the slave grasp pieces of the chain? Did he rise into freedom or kneel below the arm of benevolent Union authority? Given the classical equipoise and the figures' lifeless expressions, the statue's composition and symbolism remained opaque—but, to William Greenleaf Eliot, enthralling.[21]

Eliot had discovered a model of the sculpture in 1869 as he vacationed in Italy. Thomas Ball, a Boston-born artist working in Florence, said he had designed it as a first reaction to Lincoln's assassination, out of "duty . . . to the memory of so great and good a man"—but also with an eye to that day when "it would be required for some city in our union." With a similar mix of idealism and pragmatism, Eliot remembered Charlotte Scott's $5 donation, the Western Sanitary Commission's subsequent fund-raising, and the failed efforts to build a commemoration to emancipation. Eliot did not think of Lincoln Institute, the most powerful memorial to Abraham Lincoln yet created, founded by U.S. Colored Troops and funded in part by the same Western Sanitary Commission funds. Only with this statue, he reasoned, could he provide a "great success."[22]

Armed with photographs of the statue, Eliot returned to St. Louis and secured support from the Western Sanitary Commission. The directors suggested two changes for the final sculpture: that the slave grasp the chain, to indicate his own role in seeking freedom, and that the slave's face include a "likeness . . . as correct as that of Mr. Lincoln himself." Eliot provided Ball with photographs of Archer Alexander, the once-fugitive slave working for the Eliot family who had been freed by a direct order of President Lincoln to the St. Louis provost marshals. (Later, Eliot related how, when told of the statue, Alexander "laughed all over" and thanked God for his living to see this. Yet what did the laughter mean? Eliot's recounting left Alexander's reaction— whether intended as humbled, confident, obliging, or reassuringly subservient— unknown.) Surely Eliot did approve of one final touch: a bas-relief profile of George Washington carved into the pedestal, hinting in an appropriately modest way at founding principles and the connection with Washington University.[23]

On that spring day in Washington, James Yeatman recounted this origin story on behalf of the Western Sanitary Commission. He spoke at length, delaying the remarks of Frederick Douglass, the nation's most prominent African American. When Douglass finally arose to address the crowd, he declared the dedication "something like a national act—an act which is to go into history," a moment when African Americans and their allies were "doing honor to the memory of our friend and liberator." But Douglass mixed encomia with a frank assessment of Lincoln's legacy. Reflecting on the lessons of Reconstruction, Douglass said that Lincoln, too, was "entirely devoted to the welfare of white men," listing the times the president had delayed emancipation, whether for military advantage or political gain. "If war among the whites brought peace and liberty to the blacks," Douglass had wondered the previous year, "what will peace among the whites bring?" Douglass's fervor for Lincoln's accomplishments was tempered by the experience of living through its aftermath.[24]

At events such as the statue dedication, Frederick Douglass maintained his dedication to freedom, honoring the memory of those such as Harriet Scott. But all around him were signs of a devolution in race relations, a selfishness in business, and a scandal in politics that would deny his vision of the cultural civil war. Pointedly, Douglass said nothing about the statue itself in his remarks, and his mild words were reprinted for the St. Louis audience to cherish. Only later did he reveal his disgust for the monument, as it "showed the Negro on his knees." Words in praise of emancipation fell into disrepute against the background of the crouching slave—yet the hypocrisy continued as the statue was used as a symbol of national accomplishment. As one postcard later depicted, the kneeling slave bowed to both Lincoln and Lady Liberty. Leaders from St. Louis had designed the statue as a monument to African-American freedom, yet all around them that freedom was eroding.[25]

On July 4, 1876, the Declaration of Independence was read in front of Independence Hall in Philadelphia and a replica Liberty Bell was rung amid a shower of fireworks. The Centennial Exposition showcased the nation's best agricultural products and its most dazzling technological marvels. Here were the newest inventions: the telephone and the typewriter, the lightbulb and the internal combustion engine. Among the exhibits was a display book from the Lincoln Institute: samples of classwork in geology, zoology, history, arithmetic and more prefaced a photograph of the school's students and teachers, sitting proudly in front of the school building. Though fairgoers would soon recoil at the news of General George Armstrong Custer's death during his battle with Sitting Bull's alliance of Cheyenne, Arapaho, and Lakota warriors, and of the murder of African Americans by former Confederates in

Hamburg, South Carolina, that very day, the Fourth was all celebration, all the "Progress of the Age."[26]

In St. Louis the Board of Freeholders chose the centennial to formally announce the terms of the expanded city charter and the proposed scheme of separation. While consolidation was a possibility under the law—St. Louis city could have attempted a merger with its county—city leaders never seriously considered this option as anything but a backup to annexing the desired territory and then cutting the rest of the county loose. Under the plan, the city of St. Louis would triple in area with annexations, taking all three of the new parks and the commercially viable waterfront, from the confluence of the Mississippi and Missouri rivers in the north to the mouth of the River des Pères in the south. James Broadhead, long a prominent local politician, had been a conservative provost marshal and a loyal opponent of Drake's; in

William Greenleaf Eliot chose a statue to honor emancipation, but it showed a slave kneeling before President Lincoln. This hollow depiction of freedom added to the hypocrisy of claiming progress on racial justice at the nation's centennial. Cyrus Durand Chapman, "Abraham Lincoln Presenting the Proclamation of Freedom to a Slave," postcard for the International Art Publishing Company, 1908. James E. Schmick Collection.

June he both served with the Freeholders and fancied himself a dark-horse candidate for the Democratic nomination. Defending the plan's boundaries, Broadhead reasoned that this "symmetrical contour" was "capable of holding a population of several millions," thus allowing the city to reach its potential without worrying about the meddling county.[27]

With the creation of "the County of the City of St. Louis," as it would formally be known, residents of the existing St. Louis County would lose access to tax revenues from the city's industries. In return, the city of St. Louis would assume the existing county debt, pay for planned road and bridge construction, and provide a good price for the old county courthouse complex in the center of town, with its copper dome and triumphant Wimar murals. The charter outlined civic administration and new ward lines, while the scheme of separation set the timeline for county court and city council resolutions and the necessary city and county elections. The first vote would be in thirty days. With a charter of 239 sections and more than 43,000 words, debate on its approval was necessarily general, not specific.[28]

The vote on scheme and charter permanently fractured the city's political coalitions. Party bosses on both sides formed the opposition, worrying that civil-service appointments and reformulated ward boundaries would erode their patronage power. The Grant-supporting *Globe-Democrat* and the rock-hard-Democratic *St. Louis Times* both raised the hue and cry. In response, Henry Overstolz, the city's first German mayor, elected as an independent, gathered a coalition of property owners, growth proponents, and German speakers in favor of the plan, mirroring the Liberal Republican coalition of years past.[29]

The city and county of St. Louis voted on August 22, 1876, in a special election that drew a tremendous turnout. When first announced, the results indicated that the scheme of separation failed by a vote of 14,142 to 12,726. Mayor Overstolz admitted defeat, though he did not rule out an investigation. On October 13, Overstolz's allies filed suit, claiming that the scheme and charter had actually passed and a true accounting of the vote would show any other outcome to be the result of fraud.[30]

In the evidentiary hearings, the underbelly of St. Louis politics went on display: party bosses, ignorant voters, bribes, and thievery. Some disqualifications were technical: unsworn election judges or unnumbered ballot blanks. Other results seemed irregular, as when 128 of the 132 "no" ballots in one precinct showed evidence of erasures. And then there were whoppers: more votes recorded than voters present in the district; hundreds of identical unfolded "no" votes found at the bottom of ballot boxes; and testimony from polling officials about instructions from party bosses to count ballots hourly and add "no" votes as needed. As the inquiry continued, proponents became ever more confident that the skullduggery and the vote fraud could be reversed. "The imperial municipality will not submit to be disturbed," the *Missouri Republican* argued forcefully, as one way or another "the city will swallow up the county." The contentiousness lasted all through the fall as the national contest between Tilden and Hayes grew heated.[31]

On election night, after the largest turnout of voters in American history, Samuel J. Tilden won the popular vote and all but one of the needed electors to become president. Yet Rutherford B. Hayes would not concede, as three states—Florida, Louisiana, and South Carolina—had not returned results. These were the last three southern states governed by Reconstruction governments, so the outgoing Grant administration hoped that a troop presence, the promise of patronage, and the chance for African Americans to vote freely had provided another victory for the party of Lincoln. Other observers were not so sure: Judge Napton considered the success of Democratic "Redeemer" governments throughout the South and noted in his diary, "It is not clear that elections can be carried by the bayonet now."[32]

William Tecumseh Sherman, then commanding the U.S. Army out of his St. Louis home, was worried. On Washington's Birthday 1876, Sherman had reflected on the strength of the Union for the crowd gathered at Washington University, but eight months later he observed it fraying over the unfinished election. On November 18, Sherman wrote to his subordinate to guard against the unthinkable. "Enjoining great prudence," Sherman ordered four artillery companies from Missouri to redeploy to the arsenal in Washington, D.C., in order to protect the city "with as little display as possible."[33]

"Tilden or Fight!" came the call from the Democratic Party, unwilling to concede the electoral college to Hayes or to submit to the judgment of the president of the Senate, a Republican. Newspapers filled with allegations of intimidation, repeating the ugliness of the St. Louis election on a national scale. As the months dragged on without resolution, Carl Schurz proposed a constitutional amendment to give the U.S. Supreme Court authority to serve as the election returns board in presidential contests. The recount commissioners in St. Louis completed their work in December 1876. The "corrected" vote totals now indicated that 11,309 supported the charter in the city and 8,088 opposed, while throughout the county now 12,181 approved the scheme and 10,928 opposed. Unsurprisingly, their decision was immediately appealed.[34]

It took until March 1877 for the two contentious 1876 elections to be re-solved. When the new Congress gathered in January 1877, it created an Elec-toral Commission, drawing five members from the Democratic-controlled House and five from the Republican-controlled Senate, plus five justices of the U.S. Supreme Court. Its final membership was eight Republicans and seven Democrats, and they decided the election with a series of party-line votes, giving Hayes the presidency. Bolstering their action was the so-called Com-promise of 1877, in which Democratic and Republican party bosses agreed to accept the result if the remaining federal enforcement troops were removed from the South, and the federal government would fund the Texas & Pacific along a southern transcontinental railroad route. On March 5 the Missouri Court of Appeals unanimously accepted the new vote totals in St. Louis and certified the passage of the scheme and charter. The day before, Rutherford B. Hayes had been inaugurated at a small ceremony inside the White House, president of the nominally United States.[35]

The lived experience of the cultural civil war had no specific end date, but 1877 was an important dividing line in both national and St. Louis history. Though multiracial office-holding continued in some states, President Hayes extinguished federal Reconstruction policies and discouraged government officials from further involvement in state affairs. For supporting Hayes and the flagging Republican cause, Carl Schurz was made secretary of the inte-rior. It was a move away from Missouri that would become permanent.[36]

Upon considering the 1876 election result and the end of Reconstruction, Adam von Hammer, for one, had seen enough. A German still committed to the Radical platform, Hammer was a veteran of the secret Home Guards who had saved Camp Jackson for the Union. Yet after Hayes's inauguration, Ham-mer sold his home and abandoned the United States, feeling he had won the battle but, since Appomattox, somehow lost the war. Others merely saw op-portunities: another German Union veteran, Augustus Busch, bought Ham-mer's property and expanded his brewery operations. His company and its sig-nature product, Budweiser, became a lasting symbol of St. Louis industry.[37]

In the summer of 1877, as the recession continued, railroad lines across the country cut employee pay and frustrations boiled over. Rail workers called for a national strike, camping out on rail lines to block traffic. On July 22,

1877, St. Louis factory workers and African-American stevedores joined the pickets, stopping work, seizing railcars, and beginning the first general strike in U.S. history. Officials in St. Louis feared mayhem, and former Union and Confederate militia leaders consulted one another on whether to call out troops to protect the city's businesses. Though the strike collapsed in less than a week, it left behind proclamations of radical defiance issued in English and German against "the overbearing oppression of capitalists and monopolists."[38]

The general strike also claimed Eads's bridge over the Mississippi as a casualty. From the start of the Panic, when railroads had cut rates, the fierce competition led to operating losses, and the bridge company fell into receivership, unable to make its bond payments. In 1878, unable to attract enough traffic, the directors declared bankruptcy. New York financiers took control: J. P. Morgan purchased the bridge, revalued the existing bonds, and signed an agreement with Jay Gould for the bridge to serve the needs of his railroad monopoly. While St. Louis soon controlled the nation's greatest number of railroad connections—back East, throughout the Midwest, and especially into the Southwest—by the end of the decade, their control had been transferred to the boardrooms of New York, and profits mostly flowed through Chicago.[39]

In 1880 St. Louis leaders pinned their hopes on the release of the census numbers, envisioning a gain of another one hundred thousand or perhaps two hundred thousand residents in the boundaries of the expanded city. Instead, the census indicated St. Louis had not grown at all—an impossibility, but a result that revealed the frauds committed by and on St. Louisans a decade before. Joseph Pulitzer described the moment when Washington University professors examined the 1870 census manuscripts: page after page without any emendations, corrected spellings, or misheard items. The fraud was as obvious as a stack of identical unfolded ballots. Perhaps St. Louis had 220,000 residents in 1870, they concluded, enough to be the seventh but not the fourth largest city in America; to be sixth now and ahead of Baltimore was an accomplishment, but disbelieving residents did not see it that way.[40]

Such fraud and deception made St. Louis the butt of Gilded Age humor. Aghast at the behavior of his hometown "friends" in the Whiskey Ring, President Grant had ordered the sale of his St. Louis properties, in preparation for life in New York after the White House. Joseph Keppler's satire magazine, now renamed *Puck,* was also reinvented there, and both Carl Schurz and Joseph Pulitzer would bring their political acumen and cultural influence to New

York City in the decade to come. In contrast, Logan Reavis remained a faithful prophet for St. Louis, still lecturing on capital removal. The *St. Louis Times* solicited funds to offer the bankrupt and ailing Reavis a home in the city he had so long promoted—but the effort failed. Local artists, politicians, and intellectuals gained notoriety and influence, but they turned their backs on St. Louis and the claims they once made for its greatness.[41]

Forest Park was also implicated in the city's disappointments. Once separation was effected, the new county seat was established in Clayton, along the city boundary near the western edge of Forest Park. The roads along the north and south edges of the park became the main thoroughfares between city and county offices—and the source of conflict between the two governments. The Board of Park Commissioners, its appointments between city and county, soon complained that park improvements were sliding into neglect. Mayor Overstolz, overseeing a suddenly cash-strapped city, even suggested selling park lands for development.[42]

Before the separation vote, one newspaper correspondent had wondered whether the scheme of separation would be "fencing in the city of St. Louis," creating "all along our border suburban villages which will grow into cities." Even with the city removed, St. Louis County had 22,000 residents in 1876, as new communities, such as Kirkwood, sprung up along commuter rail lines. In less than a decade, rival cities elsewhere in the United States continued annexing their suburbs, but St. Louis could only grow within its circumscribed boundaries, hemmed in by the state boundary to the east and unable to garner support from the prosperous west-county towns for any further expansion.[43]

In the early twentieth century, the automobile promoted a less-dense style of living, filling the previously undeveloped lands within the city of St. Louis and making the suburbs beyond Forest Park an increasingly attractive alternative. Promoters of these new developments used housing-restriction covenants, highway construction, and favorable tax guidelines to give their residents the benefits of working in St. Louis but returning at night to the suburbs, thereby decimating the tax base of the city itself. In the years after World War II, the city of St. Louis lost one hundred thousand residents each decade while the county more than doubled its population. By the 2000 Census, the St. Louis metropolitan region held 2,603,607 residents, while the city itself stabilized at a population of 348,189—within the margin of error of the 1880 figure. While Forest Park still symbolically unites city and county residents as St. Louisans, its origin is intertwined with the costs of their separation.[44]

The opening of Forest Park provided St. Louis with a stately civic space, its grandeur nationally known. Yet, in the same moment, St. Louis separated itself—first from its county, but then from its quest to unite the North, South, and West. The promise of Manifest Destiny proved fleeting, and the redemptive possibilities of Reconstruction met their final defeat in an ever more divided nation. Through altered vote totals, the home rule was upheld, locally and nationally. The resurgent Democratic Party removed the rights and concerns of African Americans from the national agenda, brokering a new consensus between former Confederate officers and northern industrial interests. The nation prospered from its transcontinental railroad, its political unity, its ignorance of racial justice, and its economic bounty, but in each case St. Louis had lost out, victim of local failures, overpowering rivals, and the sheer misfortune of economic, cultural, and political setbacks, gathering one upon the other.

In the fall of 1879, the poet Walt Whitman came to St. Louis to visit his brother, Thomas, the city's water commissioner. Upon arrival, the great poet could still see St. Louis's promise, as a city that "fuses northern and southern qualities, perhaps native and foreign ones, to perfection." Considering the nation's great cities, Whitman remained convinced that "the wand of future prosperity, future empire, must soon surely be wielded by St. Louis, Chicago, beautiful Denver, perhaps San Francisco," but then admitted, "I see the said wand stretch'd out just as decidedly in Boston."[45] Thus Whitman included St. Louis in his grand celebration of American society. It was a city with enough industry, respectable politics, and typical culture—but no longer any special insight, no national vision, and no solutions to the cultural civil war that still raged.

St. Louis was a great city of the United States, Whitman implied, but simply one among many.

The Forgotten Civil War

St. Louis IS the most UNTOLD—most UNAWARE—most UNDER-ADVISED—most UNDER-ADVERTIZED—and the most UNDER-DOG Big City in America! . . . St. Louis acts like it does NOT want to know its true *identity!* . . . It seems to wish to AVOID the TRUTH and CAMARADIE of its long Past!—which it keeps stored and guarded in basement archives!

—Judge Nathan Benjamin Young Jr., "Speech for the Forty-One
Fellows of the Danforth Foundation," January 30, 1979.

Forty years after emancipation, a young slave girl was sold on the steps of St. Louis's Old Courthouse.

The *St. Louis Post-Dispatch* revealed how it happened: it was two in the morning in the second week of the Louisiana Purchase Exposition, St. Louis World's Fair. And no less an authority than a fair commissioner mounted the courthouse steps, announcing that he had a young slave girl for sale. She was "of unusual beauty," the commissioner said, she was trained as a domestic, and she was ready for maid duties. The bidding began: $25, $100, $125, up to $500, higher, until the slave girl was sold for $750, a bargain by antebellum prices. For a day, at least, it was the talk of the fair.[1]

In May 1904 the world turned with wonder to Forest Park. One hundred years after the Louisiana Purchase ended the French empire in North America, the World's Fair announced the revival of Manifest Destiny, fueling the global empire of the United States. Along the fair's midway, exhibits of old-time French-American fur-trading practices shared space with Eskimo villages and Filipino huts, in a tableau of U.S. conquests past and present. As scholarly congresses assembled and international art competitions were judged, local residents mingled with notables in pavilions illuminated by electric light. And if the fair did not provide enough excitement, the third modern Olympic Games—the first held in the United States—were conducted concurrently, just to the west, on athletic fields intended for the new campus of Washington University.[2]

The 1904 World's Fair is remembered as a moment of cultural rebirth in St. Louis. The city had tried and failed to host the Columbian Exposition, held in Chicago in 1893; the failure motivated a decade-long campaign, the fruit of which was the 1904 extravaganza. Alongside the international spectacles, a rejuvenated St. Louis celebrated its origins and its future. In the decades since the Civil War, organizers of the Missouri Historical Society had gathered heirlooms from St. Louis's first families and sponsored speeches on the city's French past. Just after the Compromise of 1877, the Veiled Prophet festival sailed into St. Louis. This annual high-society masquerade borrowed traditions from New Orleans's Mardi Gras krewes—and robes and weapons from the rites of the Ku Klux Klan. This renewal of interest in the colonial history of the city reversed the fervent Americanization that had followed the Great Fire. Yet even while delving into the past, St. Louis leaders cherished one very recent event: the population counts of the 1900 Census finally confirmed St. Louis's place as America's fourth largest city.[3]

On the night of the slave auction, the fair commissioner returned to the Planters' Hotel and guffawed as the "slave girl" was delivered: no girl at all, it turned out, but simply one fair commissioner "buying" another. The story of the purported slave sale spread quickly; the commissioners had played the bitter realities of slavery for a farce, desecrating both local and national history. Even by the racist standards of the day, it was judged a sordid spectacle and reported in the newspaper in disapproving tones.[4]

Yet the mock auction's message was hardly out of line with the World's Fair, as both ignored the preceding century of St. Louis history. At the fair, Civil War artifacts were displayed in a haze of heroism and valor that negated the war's causes and consequences. The exhibits emphasized the French and regional identities of the city, as if the rise and fall of a national St. Louis between the Mexican Cession and the end of Reconstruction had never occurred. Indians and Europeans, fur traders and riverboatmen were cast as the city's historic heroes, a narrative that was repeated at the 1914 Pageant and Masque, celebrating the city's 150th anniversary.[5] These adventures replaced slavery compromises, railroad advances, and civil war as the key moments in local history.

Cities do not exist in isolation, yet the stories of their success are often told that way. New York and Chicago, San Francisco and Seattle, Los Angeles and Las Vegas rose less as exceptional, exclusively local successes, but rather as national achievements, national stories of immigration, industry, technological innovation, and creative vision. Cities prosper or suffer within national and transnational webs of politics, economy, and culture, and we should judge their significance within these larger contexts. Urban failures are also national stories, containing valuable lessons about American society. The lasting trauma of slavery, the corrosive effects of corruption, and the failures of planning policies and of deindustrialization are both local and national stories. Such histories are never contained in merely one location.[6]

The cultural civil war was a decades-long struggle over national priorities and regional agendas, one that stretched beyond any single city, state, or region. Its confrontations, parceled out over three decades, reveal a national

In 1914, the Pageant and Masque retold St. Louis's history—leaving out the cultural civil war to avoid the painful story of slavery and the failures of Manifest Destiny. St. Louis Pageant and Masque poster, 1914. Missouri History Museum, St. Louis.

convulsion over slavery—one that neither Manifest Destiny nor emancipation could mitigate.

Even historians miss the failures of Manifest Destiny, yet they were multiple.[7] In the mid-nineteenth century, each region of the United States saw a possibly decisive advantage in the newly conquered Mexican lands, in the full embrace of Manifest Destiny. Would new plantations and the greater enslavement of nonwhite races support the South's idyll? Would free land provide every white male settler with prosperity, as the North envisioned? Would a federally financed railroad provide easy transcontinental living and reward the bountiful West with its rightful chance at national control? The competition between these parallel but ultimately conflicting ideologies led the nation into Civil War and left a bitter memory in the decades that followed.

Though William H. Seward engineered the purchase of Alaska in 1867, at the height of Radical Reconstruction, Manifest Destiny seemed a hollow thought indeed for a federal government nearly bankrupt from the cost of the Civil War and barely grasping the consequences of emancipation. Conquest of American Indian nations in the West continued, but Congress rejected the annexation of Santo Domingo (now the Dominican Republic) in 1870, and the surrounding discussions made a mockery of Reconstruction's language of equal rights. As with so many other colonial ideologies, the promises of Manifest Destiny proved hard to secure: grabbing new lands was always easier than truly integrating these conquests—and their people—into the story of the United States.[8]

In the 1890s Manifest Destiny was renewed, its logic of continentalism replaced by a justification that all the globe should be ruled by the world's Anglo-Saxon powers.[9] Under this new banner, the United States invaded Cuba, Puerto Rico, Guam, and the Philippines, and would continue to flex its military might into Latin America throughout the twentieth century. Yet this later reuse of the term should not obscure how the "classic," limited, continental Manifest Destiny as named in the 1840s had failed the nation during the cultural civil war, at great cost to all of its regional adherents. The conquest of new lands had not provided the South with the ability to extend and secure slaveholding. Manifest Destiny did not give Free-Soilers in the North the basis for making society more equal through small landholdings. And the bounty of the West did not translate into that region's chance for cultural, political, and economic dominance until late in the twentieth century.

St. Louis was located at the junction of the North, South, and West, and hence it suffered with all three regions' failures during the cultural civil war. After touting St. Louis as the next great city of the United States—the nation's transportation hub, its commercial metropolis, and the national capital—its leaders had to settle for merely provincial successes. Why? No one event can be blamed, the result caused by a combination of predictable processes and unforeseen contingencies. But more than anything else, the entrenched realities of slavery—its economics, its politics, its racial conceptions, and its culture—squelched the transformations offered by emancipation and Reconstruction. Through Manifest Destiny, leaders in St. Louis imagined an easy path to a new national future that would stretch across the continent and erase the old patterns, but this vision faltered, and the ghostly grip of slavery politics constrained U.S. society for another century.

The larger history of the cultural civil war remains written on the landscape of St. Louis. At Washington University and in Forest Park, at the St. Louis Mercantile Library and the Anheuser-Busch brewery, the stories of the cultural civil war are integral if not always obvious. The local history is national history, and St. Louisans sense it. On radio shows and in barbershops, walking through museum exhibits and sitting in stadium bleachers, they consider again why Thomas Hart Benton fell from power, why Dred and Harriet Scott lost their case, why the Mississippi River bridge was not completed until 1874, and why the city-county split occurred. Their history is cherished but confused, because the tri-regional fight over slavery politics and Manifest Destiny is mostly submerged.[10]

St. Louis began on the banks of the Mississippi River, on the city blocks now buried beneath the reflecting pools and sloping green lawns of Eero Saarinen's Gateway Arch. Silently beautiful, the Arch is an architectural marvel—but one that uses those lawns (and an interstate highway) to cut itself off from the contemporary city, while simultaneously erasing its history. Thankfully, the rest of the Jefferson National Expansion Memorial provides a counterbalance, beginning with the totems of Manifest Destiny—peace medals, buffalo hides, covered wagons—on display underground beneath the Arch in the Museum of Westward Expansion.[11]

But the true message of the cultural civil war comes to life across the street, in the memorial's other building. The Old Courthouse is the site of Thomas Hart Benton's railroad speech, the *Dred Scott* case, Logan Reavis's capital removal convention, the former county courts, and Virginia Minor's suffrage suit. Standing under its dome, gazing up at Carl Wimar's murals, one can feel the intersection of local and national history, the promise and cost of the cultural civil war.

The two symbols—courthouse and Arch—often appear together, carrying within them the national story. They speak forth from National Park Service posters and from the outfield grass of Busch Stadium, broadcast around the world as President Barack Obama threw out the first pitch for Major League Baseball's All Star Game in July 2009. This history reaches out from St. Louis, touching Lincoln University in Jefferson City, the Freedmen's Memorial in Washington, D.C., the *Puck* building in New York City, and countless other sites in the North, West, and South.

Seen in this way, the history of St. Louis becomes more than just the story of another American city. St. Louis is the great heart of the republic, the capital that never was, the hub of unbuilt railroads, the forum of incomplete political compromises, and the place where dramatic cultural gestures were not fulfilled. Impossible or visionary, unfortunate or impractical, these events define the cultural civil war, the conflict at the center of U.S history.

Abbreviations

Cengage	Cengage (Thomson-Gale) 19th Century Newspaper Collection
JNEM	Jefferson National Expansion Memorial Archives, National Park Service, St. Louis
MHM	Missouri History Museum, St. Louis
MHR	*Missouri Historical Review*
MSA	Missouri State Archives, Jefferson City and St. Louis
SLML	St. Louis Mercantile Library Association Archives, on the campus of the University of Missouri–St. Louis
SLPL	St. Louis Public Library, Special Collections
SLU	St. Louis Room, St. Louis University Archives
WHMC	Western Historical Manuscript Collections, Columbia and St. Louis
WU	Department of Special Collections, Washington University Libraries, St. Louis

Notes

Introduction

1. Mark Twain, "The Private History of a Campaign that Failed," 1885, para. 2; as reprinted in *Collected Stories, Sketches, Speeches & Essays* (New York: Library of America, 1992), 863; middle quote is Twain, speech at the Putnam Phalanx Dinner for the Ancient and Honorable Artillery Company of Massachusetts, held in Hartford, October 2, 1877, as reprinted in Paul Fatout, ed., *Mark Twain Speaking* (Iowa City: University of Iowa Press, 1976), 108.

2. Mark Twain, *Life on the Mississippi* (1883), Chapter 45, para. 4, via docsouth. unc.edu/southlit, accessed July 2009; he claims to be overhearing the comment. Thanks to Brian Yothers for emphasizing Twain's links to multiple regions. For Twain's regional ambiguities and the Civil War era, Peter Messent, *The Short Works of Mark Twain: A Critical Study* (Philadelphia: University of Pennsylvania Press, 2001), Chapter 8; and Lawrence Howe, "Transcending the Limits of Experience: Mark Twain's *Life on the Mississippi*," *American Literature* 63, no. 3 (September 1991): 439; and the recent biography Roy Morris Jr., *Lighting Out for the Territory: How Samuel Clemens Headed West and Became Mark Twain* (New York: Simon & Schuster, 2010).

3. Some of the best cultural histories of the Civil War era broadly understood are David W. Blight, *Race and Reunion: The Civil War in American Memory* (Cambridge, Mass.: Belknap Press of Harvard University Press, 2001); Drew Gilpin Faust,

This Republic of Suffering: Death and the American Civil War (New York: Knopf, 2008); Louis Menand, *The Metaphysical Club* (New York: Farrar, Straus, and Giroux, 2001). For the evolution of cultural history, see also the work of cultural anthropologist Clifford Geertz, intellectual historian Lawrence Levine, and Gertrude Himmelfarb, "History with the Politics Left Out," in *The New History and the Old* (Cambridge, Mass.: Belknap Press of Harvard University Press, 1987), 13–32.

4. Differing definitions of the West and the significance of regions in American history go back to Frederick Jackson Turner's essays: John Mack Faragher, ed., *Rereading Frederick Jackson Turner: "The Significance of the Frontier in American History" and Other Essays* (New Haven, Conn.: Yale University Press, 1999), and William Cronon, "Turner's First Stand: The Significance of Significance in American History," in *Writing Western History: Essays on Major Western Historians,* ed. Richard Etulain (Albuquerque: University of New Mexico Press, 1991), 73–101, esp. pp. 93–94. See also Stephen Aron, *American Confluence: The Missouri Frontier from Borderland to Border State* (Bloomington: Indiana University Press, 2006); Christopher Morris, *Becoming Southern: The Evolution of a Way of Life, Warren County and Vicksburg, Mississippi, 1770–1860* (New York: Oxford University Press, 1995); William Cronon, George Miles, and Jay Gitlin, "Becoming West: Towards a New Meaning for Western History," in *Under an Open Sky: Rethinking America's Western Past,* ed. William Cronon, George Miles, and Jay Gitlin (New York: W. W. Norton, 1992), 3–27; Edward L. Ayers, et al., *All Over the Map: Rethinking American Regions* (Baltimore: Johns Hopkins University Press, 1996).

For the evolution of regional politics and identities, David Waldstreicher, *In the Midst of Perpetual Fetes: The Making of American Nationalism, 1776–1820* (Williamsburg and Chapel Hill: Omohundro Institute of Early American History and Culture—University of North Carolina Press, 1997), 247, 249, 262. See also John Craig Hammond, *Slavery, Freedom, and Expansion in the Early American West* (Charlottesville: University Press of Virginia, 2007).

Abraham Lincoln particularly focused on this "great interior region" as determinative of the Civil War's result; see discussion in Martin J. Hershock and Christine Dee, "Series Editors' Preface," in *Missouri's War: The Civil War in Documents,* ed. Silvana R. Siddali (Athens: Ohio University Press, 2009), xv. For a recent discussion of Lincoln as "a man of the [western] territories," Stephanie McCurry, *Confederate Reckoning: Power and Politics in the Civil War South* (Cambridge, Mass.: Harvard University Press, 2010), 67–68. For an emphasis on Lincoln's southern roots and Douglas's Vermont birth instead of their western careers, as well as references to the work of David Moltke-Hansen on southern regional definitions, see Orville Vernon Burton, *The Age of Lincoln* (New York: Hill and Wang, 2007), especially Chapter 5 and its online footnotes at http://ageoflincoln.com/Footnotes/Entries/2008/5/9_Chapter_Five.html, accessed May 2010.

For different three-part divisions of the Civil War, see the organization of the American Civil War Center at the Tredegar Iron Works in Richmond, and the volume of essays delivered there, William J. Cooper and John M. McCardell, eds., *In The Cause of Liberty: How the Civil War Redefined American Ideals* (Baton Rouge: Louisiana State University Press, 2009), as well as Eric Foner and Joshua Brown, *Forever Free: The Story of Emancipation and Reconstruction* (New York: Knopf, 2005; Vintage, 2006), 42.

5. For such connections, Elliott West, "Reconstructing Race," *Western Historical Quarterly* 34, no. 1 (Spring 2003): 7–26; Heather Cox Richardson, *West from Appomattox: The Reconstruction of America after the Civil War* (New Haven, Conn.: Yale University Press, 2007); Edward L. Ayers, *In the Presence of Mine Enemies: War in the Heart of America, 1859–1863* (New York: W. W. Norton, 2003); Michael A. Morrison, *Slavery and the American West: The Eclipse of Manifest Destiny and the Coming of the Civil War* (Chapel Hill: University of North Carolina Press, 1999). An important connection between regional economic agendas and the Civil War is explored in Marc Egnal, *Clash of Extremes: The Economic Origins of the Civil War* (New York: Hill & Wang, 2009). For the sense that all Americans sought to convince others of their particular vision of the future see Burton, *The Age of Lincoln*, esp. pp. 4–6.

6. "Selected Historical Decennial Census Population and Housing Counts," www.census.gov/population, accessed July 2009; Daniel Walker Howe, *What Hath God Wrought: The Transformation of America, 1815–1848* (New York: Oxford University Press, 2007); Peter J. Kastor, "'What Are the Advantages of the Acquisition?': Inventing Expansion in the Early American Republic," *American Quarterly* 60, no. 4 (December 2008): 1003–1035; Stephanie LeMenager, *Manifest and Other Destinies: Territorial Fictions of the Nineteenth-Century United States* (Lincoln: University of Nebraska Press, 2004); Anne Baker, *Heartless Immensity: Literature, Culture, and Geography in Antebellum America* (Ann Arbor: University of Michigan Press, 2006). Thanks to Aaron Sachs for alerting me to Baker's work.

7. [John O'Sullivan], "The True Title," *New York Morning News*, December 27, 1845, as quoted in Julius W. Pratt, "The Origin of 'Manifest Destiny,'" *American Historical Review* 32, no. 4 (July 1927): 795–798. For overviews of Manifest Destiny—which, crucially, skip the Civil War years—Anders Stephanson, *Manifest Destiny: American Expansionism and the Empire of Right* (New York: Hill & Wang, 1996); Walter Nugent, *Habits of Empire: A History of American Expansion* (New York: Knopf, 2008). Despite limiting themselves to the years before the Civil War, see also Morrison, *Slavery and the American West;* Amy S. Greenberg, *Manifest Manhood and the Antebellum American Empire* (New York: Cambridge University Press, 2005); Reginald Horsman, *Race and Manifest Destiny: The Origins of American Racial Anglo-Saxonism* (Cambridge, Mass.: Harvard University Press, 1981); Shelley Streeby, *American Sensations: Class, Empire, and the Production of Popular Culture* (Berkeley: University of California Press, 2002); Thomas R. Hietala, *Manifest Design: American Exceptionalism and Empire*, rev. ed. (Ithaca, N.Y.: Cornell University Press, 2003).

8. These studies have served as inspirations: Timothy Mitchell, *Colonising Egypt* (Berkeley: University of California Press, 1988); Catherine Hall, *Civilising Subjects: Metropole and Colony in the English Imagination, 1830–1867* (Chicago: University of Chicago Press, 2002). See also Benedict Anderson, *Imagined Communities: Reflections on the Origin & Spread of Nationalism*, rev. ed. (London: Verso, 1999); David Cannadine, *Ornamentalism: How the British Saw Their Empire* (New York: Oxford University Press, 2001); Paul Rabinow, *French Modern: Norms and Forms of the Social Environment* (Cambridge, Mass.: MIT Press, 1989). Adele Perry, *On the Edge of Empire: Gender, Race, and the Making of British Columbia, 1849–1871* (Toronto: University of Toronto Press, 2001); Frederick Cooper and Ann Laura Stoler, *Tensions of Empire: Colonial Cultures in a Bourgeois World* (Berkeley: University of California Press, 1997); *Haunted by Empire: Geographies of Intimacy in North American History*, ed. Ann Laura Stoler (Durham, N.C.: Duke University Press, 2006); Amy Kaplan and Donald E. Pease, eds., *Cultures of United States Imperialism* (Durham, N.C.: Duke University Press, 1993).

9. For the history of other nineteenth-century cities told through the lens of empire and Manifest Destiny, see David M. Scobey, *Empire City: The Making and Meaning of the New York City Landscape* (Philadelphia: Temple University Press, 2002), and Andrew David Heath, "'The Manifest Destiny of Philadelphia': Imperialism, Republicanism, and the Remaking of a City and its People, 1837–1877" (PhD diss., University of Pennsylvania, 2008), esp. p. 12.

10. Henry David Thoreau, "Economy," in *Walden,* para. 3; via xroads.virginia. edu, accessed July 2009.

11. See for example the metonymic use in the *New York Tribune,* as quoted in the *Fayetteville Observer,* March 12, 1857, no. 589, col. B, via Cengage. This study takes up the challenge of J. Matthew Gallman, "Urban History and the American Civil War," *Journal of Urban History* 32, no. 4 (May 2006): 631–642; see also the use of the local in Jacqueline Jones, *Saving Savannah: The City and the Civil War* (New York: Knopf, 2008); David Quigley, *Second Founding: New York City, Reconstruction and the Making of American Democracy* (New York: Hill & Wang, 2004); Robert Tracy McKenzie, *Lincolnites and Rebels: A Divided Town in the American Civil War* (New York: Oxford University Press, 2006); David R. Goldfield, *Urban Growth in the Age of Sectionalism: Virginia, 1847–1861* (Baton Rouge: Louisiana State University Press, 1977); George Lipsitz, *The Sidewalks of St. Louis: Places, People, and Politics in an American City* (Columbia: University of Missouri Press, 1991).

12. There are exceptions, especially Louis S. Gerteis, *Civil War St. Louis* (Lawrence: University Press of Kansas, 2001), and Eric Sandweiss, ed., *St. Louis in the Century of Henry Shaw: A View Beyond the Garden Wall* (Columbia: University of Missouri Press, 2003); John D. Morton, "'A High Wall and a Deep Ditch': Thomas Hart Benton and the Compromise of 1850," *MHR* 94, no. 1 (October 1999): 1–24; John D. Morton, "'This Magnificent New World': Thomas Hart Benton's Westward

Vision Reconsidered," *MHR* 90, no. 3 (1996): 284–308. The mid-nineteenth-century history of the city has often boiled down to why St. Louis lost the competition over railroads to Chicago. Economic, regional, and environmental ideas have dominated; Jeffrey S. Adler, *Yankee Merchants and the Making of the Urban West: The Rise and Fall of Antebellum St. Louis* (New York: Cambridge University Press, 1991); Wyatt Winton Belcher, *The Economic Rivalry between St. Louis and Chicago, 1850–1880* (New York: Columbia University Press, 1947); James Neal Primm, *Economic Policy in the Development of a Western State, Missouri, 1820–1860* (Cambridge, Mass.: Harvard University Press, 1954); J. Christopher Schnell, "Chicago Versus St. Louis: A Reassessment of the Great Rivalry," *MHR* 71, no. 3 (1977): 245–265. General coverage appears in the synthesis, James Neal Primm, *Lion of the Valley: St. Louis, Missouri, 1764–1980,* 3rd ed. (St. Louis: Missouri Historical Society Press, 1998). Yet, differently, I argue that the most significant changes were cultural and national, encompassing the political, regional, and economic conflicts, and I see the Reconstruction years as when St. Louis finally failed to surmount these challenges. See also the suggestive comments in Holly Zumwalt Taylor, "Neither North nor South: Sectionalism, St. Louis Politics, and the Coming of the Civil War, 1846–1861" (PhD diss., University of Texas at Austin, 2004), esp. pp. v, 245, 342; Earl K. Holt III, *William Greenleaf Eliot—Conservative Radical* (St. Louis: First Unitarian Church, 1985), 53; Eric Sandweiss, *St. Louis: The Evolution of an American Urban Landscape* (Philadelphia: Temple University Press, 2001), 64. For the intersection of place and ideology, Dolores Hayden, *The Power of Place: Urban Landscapes as Public History* (Cambridge, Mass.: MIT Press, 1995).

13. For St. Louis as a borderland, Abraham P. Nasatir, "The Shifting Borderlands," *Pacific Historical Review* 34, no. 1 (February 1965): 1–20; John F. Bannon, S. J., "Missouri, a Borderland," *MHR* 63, no. 2 (January 1969): 227–247; Jay Gitlin, *The Bourgeois Frontier: French Towns in Mid-America and the Course of Westward Expansion, 1763 to 1863* (New Haven, Conn.: Yale University Press, 2009); Aron, *American Confluence.* For gateway cities, A. F. Burghardt, "A Hypothesis about Gateway Cities," *Annals of the Association of American Geographers* 61, no. 2 (January 1971): 269–285. Both concepts build on Richard C. Wade, *The Urban Frontier: The Rise of Western Cities, 1790–1830* (Cambridge, Mass.: Harvard University Press, 1959). See also Edward Conrad Smith, *The Borderland in the Civil War* (New York: Macmillan Co., 1927); William W. Freehling, *The South vs. the South: How Anti-Confederate Southerners Shaped the Course of the Civil War* (New York: Oxford University Press. 2001), 23–24, 54, 61.

14. The nominees were John C. Frémont, Edward Bates, Frémont again, Ulysses S. Grant, Frank Blair Jr., and Benjamin Gratz Brown.

15. Ralph Waldo Emerson, *The Journals and Miscellaneous Notebooks of Ralph Waldo Emerson,* ed. William H. Gilman, et al. (Cambridge, Mass.: Belknap Press of Harvard University Press, 1960–1982), 11:530; for urban promotions, J. Christopher

Schnell and Katherine B. Clinton, "The New West: Themes in Nineteenth Century Urban Promotion, 1815–1880," *Missouri Historical Society Bulletin* 30, no. 2 (January 1974): 75–88. For the importance of failure, Patricia Nelson Limerick, *The Legacy of Conquest: The Unbroken Past of the American West* (New York: W. W. Norton, 1987).

1 The Destruction of the Past

1. The best history of the fire to date is Laura Wilson, *The Great Fire of St. Louis in 1849* (St. Louis: JNEM, U.S. Department of the Interior, National Park Service, September 1938). For the brief references, focusing on loss, not transformation, see also James Neal Primm, *Lion of the Valley: St. Louis, Missouri, 1764–1980,* 3rd ed. (St. Louis: Missouri Historical Society Press, 1998), 167–168, and Jeffrey S. Adler, *Yankee Merchants and the Making of the Urban West: The Rise and Fall of Antebellum St. Louis* (New York: Cambridge University Press, 1991), 2, 86.

2. William M. Hall, St. Louis, to J. W. Brooks, Detroit, May 19, 1849, SLU, Miscellaneous St. Louis and Missouri Manuscript Collection, MSS 0040 0001 0018.

3. Mrs. J. L. Carver, wife of John Leroy Carver, [1909], Saint Louis Volunteer Firemen Collection, MHM, box 1, folder 16. Quote from Sally Smith Flagg, May 18 and 20, 1849, journal entries, Saint Louis Volunteer Firemen Collection.

4. Frederick M. Colburn, secretary of the Union Fire Company No. 2, May 17, 1899, Saint Louis Volunteer Firemen Collection, MHM, box 1, folder 16; see also *St. Louis People's Organ,* May 21, 1849, p. 2, and Michael M. Fitzpatrick, engineer of the Liberty Engine, Saint Louis Volunteer Firemen Collection. For a general description of nineteenth-century firefighting practices, including in St. Louis, see Amy S. Greenberg, *Cause for Alarm: The Volunteer Fire Department in the Nineteenth-Century City* (Princeton, N.J.: Princeton University Press, 1998).

5. *St. Louis Daily Reveille,* May 18, 1849, p. 2. See also Hall to Brooks, May 19, 1849.

6. *St. Louis People's Organ,* May 21, 1849, p. 2. Quote from Hall to Brooks, May 19, 1849. Original orthography.

7. Fitzpatrick and Colburn accounts; *St. Louis People's Organ,* May 21, 1849, pp. 2–3; Flagg, typescript of May 18, 1849, journal entry; John S. Beggs, June 13, 1909, Saint Louis Volunteer Firemen Collection, MHM, box 1, folder 19.

8. Colburn account; Hall to Brooks, May 19, 1849. See also Fitzpatrick account.

9. Hall to Brooks, May 19, 1849. "Wells Colton, Esq. seriously injured, and since dead" was listed alongside Targée in Board of Direction Minutes, First Volume, meeting June 4, 1849, SLML, M-117, Book A-1–1, p. 111. I am unaware of the name of the third fatality. One report suggests four firemen were killed, and another speculates on the death of twenty; "The St. Louis Fire," *New York Herald,* May 27, 1849, col. D, and "The Great Fire at St. Louis," *Boston Daily Atlas,* May 25, 1849, no. 277, col. B via Cengage.

10. Explicit comparisons to fires in New York and Pittsburgh were made in the very first paragraph in the first article on the fire in the *People's Organ,* May 21, 1849, p. 2; see also George Kyler, n.d., Saint Louis Volunteer Firemen Collection, MHM, St. Louis, box 1, folder 16. Recent disaster scholarship draws comparisons between the situations in lower Manhattan and New Orleans and the earlier challenges faced by San Francisco in 1906 and Chicago in 1871; see, for example, Lawrence J. Vale and Thomas J. Campanella, eds., *The Resilient City: How Modern Cities Recover from Disaster* (New York: Oxford University Press, 2005). Only one recent account has even a passing mention of St. Louis's Great Fire. Peter Charles Hoffer, *Seven Fires: The Urban Infernos that Reshaped America* (New York: PublicAffairs, 2006), 84. Thanks to Andrew Hurley for this reference.

11. For the early history of St. Louis, see William E. Foley and C. David Rice, *The First Chouteaus, River Barons of Early St. Louis* (Urbana: University of Illinois Press, 1983); Jay Gitlin, *The Bourgeois Frontier: French Towns in Mid-America and the Course of Westward Expansion, 1763 to 1863* (New Haven, Conn.: Yale University Press, 2009). The classic narratives are gathered in John Francis McDermott, *The Early Histories of St. Louis* (St. Louis: St. Louis Historical Documents Foundation, 1952). On the date as February 15, not February 14, Tim O'Neil, "Has St. Louis Been Celebrating the Wrong Day as Its Founding?" *St. Louis Post-Dispatch,* February 14, 2010.

12. Heather Devine, *The People Who Own Themselves: Aboriginal Ethnogenesis in a Canadian Family, 1660–1900* (Calgary, AB: University of Calgary Press, 2003); Kathleen DuVal, *The Native Ground: Indians and Colonists in the Heart of the Continent* (Philadelphia: University of Pennsylvania Press, 2006); Brian DeLay, *War of a Thousand Deserts: Indian Raids and the U.S.-Mexican War* (New Haven, Conn.: Yale University Press, 2008); Philip Marchand, *Ghost Empire: How the French Almost Conquered North America* (Toronto: McClelland & Stewart, 2005).

13. J. Frederick Fausz, "The 'Accredited Ascendancy' of Auguste Chouteau: Creating the Image of the Fur Trader as City Founder," speech at the "Frontier Cities" conference, St. Louis, March 2008.

14. For mixing types of power in New Orleans and the Caribbean, Joseph R. Roach, *Cities of the Dead: Circum-Atlantic Performance* (New York: Columbia University Press, 1996). For the transitions from globalized culture to a strictly American one, Peter J. Kastor, *The Nation's Crucible: The Louisiana Purchase and the Creation of America* (New Haven, Conn.: Yale University Press, 2004); Edward Rugemer, *The Problem of Emancipation: The Caribbean Roots of the American Civil War* (Baton Rouge: Louisiana State University Press, 2008); Jennifer Louise Turner, "From Savagery to Slavery: Upper Louisiana and the American Nation" (PhD diss., University of Wisconsin, 2008). For imperial rivalries in frontier cities, Carl Abbott, *How Cities Won the West: Four Centuries of Urban Change in Western North America* (Albuquerque: University of New Mexico Press, 2008), 40–41, 22–24, 27.

15. Robert M. Morrissey, "Bottomlands, Borderlands: Empires and Identities in the 18th Century Illinois Country" (PhD diss., Yale University, 2007). Steve Aron traces the long patterns of cultural change in Missouri; his work suggests how the 1849 Great Fire was merely the most recent, and I would argue longest-lasting, re-founding. Stephen Aron, *American Confluence: The Missouri Frontier from Border-land to Border State* (Bloomington: Indiana University Press, 2006).

16. For the centrality of French needs, rather than U.S. desires, in the Louisiana Purchase, see Kastor, *The Nation's Crucible,* and Kastor, "Inventing Expansion in the Early American Republic," *American Quarterly* 60, no. 4 (December 2008): 1013–1015. On the triple flag ceremony, Primm, *Lion of the Valley,* 69, and Father John F. Bannon, *This Was Saint Louis,* Research Report No. 296, JNEM. The ceremony was reenacted throughout the twentieth century and at the Louisiana Purchase bicenten-nial: see *The Three Flags Festival,* National Louisiana Purchase Bicentennial Com-mittee, www.umsl.edu/~loupurch, accessed August 2006.

17. For the importance of these reorientations, Marc Egnal, *Clash of Extremes: The Economic Origins of the Civil War* (New York: Hill & Wang, 2009), 8–9.

18. Lyman Beecher, *A Plea for the West* (Cincinnati: Turman & Smith, 1835); Wil-liam Barnaby Faherty, "Nativism and Midwestern Education: The Experience of St. Louis University, 1832–1856," *History of Education Quarterly* 8, no. 4 (1968): 451. On Missouri as vague for most Americans, Kastor, "Inventing Expansion in the Early American Republic," 1026. On Thomas and Clay as "appropriately" western, Orville Vernon Burton, *The Age of Lincoln* (New York: Hill & Wang, 2007), 16. For an inter-pretation of the statehood debate stressing the importance of suspicion of French Americans as the reason for the embrace of proslavery doctrine, see Turner, "From Savagery to Slavery." For evolving regional distinctions over slavery, start with Ira Berlin, *Generations of Captivity: A History of African-American Slaves* (Cambridge, Mass.: Belknap Press of Harvard University Press, 2003).

19. Charles Dickens, *American Notes for General Circulation,* in *The Works of Charles Dickens* (London: Brainard, 1908), 174. For comments on Tocqueville's missed opportunity, Stephen Aron, "The Centrality of St. Louis," Western History Associa-tion annual meeting, St. Louis, October 2006.

20. Poem appears in J. C. Wild and Lewis Foulk Thomas, *The Valley of the Missis-sippi Illustrated in a Series of Views,* 1948 reprint ed. (St. Louis: J. Garnier, 1841–1842), 30–31. Joseph Nicholas Nicollet, "Sketch of the Early History of St. Louis," in *The Early Histories of St. Louis,* ed. John Francis McDermott (St. Louis: St. Louis Histori-cal Documents Foundation, 1952), 132, 148. See also William E. Foley and C. David Rice, "'Touch Not a Stone': An 1841 Appeal to Save the Historic Chouteau Man-sion," *Gateway Heritage* 4, no. 3 (1984): 14–19; Martha Coleman Bray, *Joseph Nicollet and His Map* (Philadelphia: American Philosophical Society, 1980), 142–147, 255. For Field's affiliation with the *Reveille,* Lee Ann Sandweiss, "Themes and Schemes: The Literary Life of Nineteenth-Century St. Louis," in *St. Louis in the Century of Henry*

Shaw: A View Beyond the Garden Wall, ed. Eric Sandweiss (Columbia: University of Missouri Press, 2003), 230.

21. Quote from the *Missouri Republican,* April 26, 1840, p. 2, emphasis added. Wild and Thomas, *Valley of the Mississippi,* Plate V, 29–31, 65. On J. C. Wild and other Mississippi River panoramists, John Francis McDermott, *The Lost Panoramas of the Mississippi* (Chicago: University of Chicago Press, 1958); Angela Lynn Miller, "'The Imperial Republic': Narratives of National Expansion in American Art, 1820–1860" (PhD diss., Yale University, 1985), Part Two, 264–435; John William Reps, *John Caspar Wild: Painter and Printmaker of Nineteenth-Century Urban America* (St. Louis: Missouri Historical Society Press—University of Missouri Press, 2006); Martha A. Sandweiss, *Print the Legend: Photography and the American West* (New Haven, Conn.: Yale University Press, 2002), 47–86; Dolores Kilgo, *Likeness and Landscape: Thomas M. Easterly and the Art of the Daguerreotype* (St. Louis: Missouri Historical Society Press, 1994), 161–166.

22. Barbara Alice Mann, *Native Americans, Archaeologists & the Mounds* (New York: Peter Lang, 2003); Thomas E. Emerson and R. Barry Lewis, *Cahokia and the Hinterlands: Middle Mississippian Cultures of the Midwest* (Urbana: Illinois Historic Preservation Agency—University of Illinois Press, 1991); Timothy R. Pauketat and Thomas E. Emerson, *Cahokia: Domination and Ideology in the Mississippian World* (Lincoln: University of Nebraska Press, 1997). For nineteenth-century wondering at the mounds, Otis Adams, "Letter in 1849," *Missouri Historical Society Bulletin* 6, no. 3 (April 1950): 370–371; Wild and Thomas, *Valley of the Mississippi,* 52–54 and 133–134; *Daily Missouri Democrat,* April 18, 1869, found in the James S. Thomas Scrapbooks, SLML, M-92, 1869 Scrapbook. The name was also punctuated "Monk's Mound," but seemingly not "Monks' Mound," which only Charles Dickens used in his account.

23. Kilgo, *Likeness and Landscape,* 191, 201–208. On archaeological finds, Wild and Thomas, *Valley of the Mississippi,* 53; lawyer and amateur scientist Nathaniel Holmes did the same, reporting his findings to the Academy of Science, where he was a member; Daniel Goldstein, "Midwestern Naturalists: Academies of Science in the Mississippi Valley, 1850–1900" (PhD diss., Yale University, 1989), 139. On the beer garden, *Missouri Democrat,* July 11, 1858; on the burning of the pavilion, Edward Edwards, *History of the Volunteer Fire Department of St. Louis* (St. Louis: Veteran Volunteer Firemen's Historical Society, 1906), 196. See also Dr. William M. Smit, "Old Broadway, a Forgotten Street, and Its Park of Mounds," *Missouri Historical Society Bulletin* 4, no. 3 (April 1948): 153–163. On discoveries, *Missouri Republican,* November 9, 1841, p. 2; February 12 and 13, 1854, p. 2; September 26, 1858; May 31, 1865, p. 4; April 9, 1868; April 17, 1869. Listed on the Information File cards for the Big Mound, MHM. See also James M. Loring, "The Big Mound Nearly Disappeared—Further Discovery of Bones, Shells, &c," Letter to the *Daily Missouri Democrat,* April 18, 1869, found in the James S. Thomas Scrapbooks, 1869 Scrapbook.

24. For a consideration of the connection between artifacts, the missing American Indian cultures of North America, and the renewed power of American Indian nations, Russell Thornton, *American Indian Holocaust and Survival: A Population History since 1492* (Norman: University of Oklahoma Press, 1987). Max Page builds on Joseph Schumpeter's phrase in Max Page, *The Creative Destruction of Manhattan, 1900–1940* (Chicago: University of Chicago Press, 1999); see also the link between capital and urban growth in David M. Scobey, *Empire City: The Making and Meaning of the New York City Landscape* (Philadelphia: Temple University Press, 2002), 70.

25. Francis Parkman Jr., *The Oregon Trail* (1849; New York: Penguin Classics, 1985), 385, 432–437; William Clark Kennerly and Elizabeth Kennerly Russell, *Persimmon Hill, a Narrative of Old St. Louis and the Far West* (Norman: University of Oklahoma Press, 1949); Mary E. Seematter, "Merchants in the Middle: The Glasgow Brothers and the Mexican War," *Gateway Heritage* 9, no. 2 (1988): 36–47.

26. John S. D. Eisenhower, *So Far from God: The U.S. War with Mexico, 1846–1848* (New York: Random House, 1989); Richard V. Francaviglia and Douglas W. Richmond, *Dueling Eagles: Reinterpreting the U.S.-Mexican War, 1846–1848* (Fort Worth: Texas Christian University Press, 2000). For the impact of victory on the United States, Robert Walter Johannsen, *To the Halls of the Montezumas: The Mexican War in the American Imagination* (New York: Oxford University Press, 1985); Shelley Streeby, *American Sensations: Class, Empire, and the Production of Popular Culture* (Berkeley: University of California Press, 2002); Amy S. Greenberg, *Manifest Manhood and the Antebellum American Empire* (New York: Cambridge University Press, 2005). On the existing networks around St. Louis and their transformation, Timothy R. Mahoney, *River Towns in the Great West: The Structure of Provincial Urbanization in the American Midwest, 1820–1870* (New York: Cambridge University Press, 1990), 124–128.

27. *Report of the Celebration of the Anniversary of the Founding of St. Louis: On the Fifteenth Day of February,* A.D. 1847 (St. Louis: Missouri Republican—Chambers & Knapp, 1847). Eric Sandweiss sees this commemoration in terms of refounding—but also casts doubt on the authenticity of Auguste Chouteau's fragmentary narrative. Auguste Chouteau and St. Louis Mercantile Library Association, *Fragment of Col. Auguste Chouteau's Narrative of the Settlement of St. Louis* (St. Louis: G. Knapp & Co., 1858). Eric Sandweiss, *St. Louis: The Evolution of an American Urban Landscape* (Philadelphia: Temple University Press, 2001), 63–64. French voices in St. Louis were overshadowed, not eliminated, and would reemerge; see the Epilogue and Jay Gitlin, "From Private Stories to Public Memory: The Chouteau Descendants of St. Louis and the Production of History," Western History Association annual meeting, St. Louis, October 2006.

28. For Wilmot's speech, *Congressional Globe,* 29th Cong., 2nd sess., 1847, Appendix, p. 317. For a recent overview of the war, its aftermath, and the Whig reactions, see

Daniel Walker Howe, *What Hath God Wrought: The Transformation of America, 1815–1848* (New York: Oxford University Press, 2007), Chapters 18–20. For the complex mix of territorial extension, racial fears, and claims for free labor, see Amy S. Greenberg, *Manifest Manhood;* Reginald Horsman, *Race and Manifest Destiny: The Origins of American Racial Anglo-Saxonism* (Cambridge, Mass.: Harvard University Press, 1981); Alexander Saxton, *The Rise and Fall of the White Republic: Class Politics and Mass Culture in Nineteenth-Century America* (London: Verso, 1990). Once the Wilmot Proviso was defeated, another racial issue, the question of the citizenship of the former Mexican inhabitants of the territory, became a central question; see Stephen J. Pitti, *The Devil in Silicon Valley: Northern California, Race, and Mexican Americans* (Princeton, N.J.: Princeton University Press, 2003), and more provocatively, Richard Rodriguez, *Brown: The Last Discovery of America* (New York: Viking, 2002).

29. For the connections that the 1848 revolutions revealed, see Timothy Mason Roberts, *Distant Revolutions: 1848 and the Challenge to American Exceptionalism* (Charlottesville: University of Virginia Press, 2009); Steven W. Rowan, "The Continuation of the German Revolutionary Tradition on American Soil," in *Germans for a Free Missouri: Translations from the St. Louis Radical Press, 1857–1862,* trans. and ed. Steven W. Rowan and James Neal Primm (Columbia: University of Missouri Press, 1983), 23–45; Streeby, *American Sensations,* 3–37; Howe, *What Hath God Wrought,* Chapter 20. See also Jonathan Sperber, *The European Revolutions, 1848–1851,* 2nd ed. (New York: Cambridge University Press, 2005). For Mormon migrants experiencing the Great Fire and the cholera epidemic in St. Louis, among other topics, see the *Mormon Immigration Index* CD, 2000, created by Intellectual Reserve in collaboration with the Church of Latter-Day Saints History and Family History Departments. Thanks to Rob Wilson for sharing this reference.

30. Walter D. Kamphoefner, *The Westfalians: From Germany to Missouri* (Princeton, N.J.: Princeton University Press, 1987); Wolfgang Helbich and Walter D. Kamphoefner, *German-American Immigration and Ethnicity in Comparative Perspective* (Madison, Wis.: Max Kade Institute for German-American Studies, 2004); Bruce C. Levine, *The Spirit of 1848: German Immigrants, Labor Conflict, and the Coming of the Civil War* (Urbana: University of Illinois Press, 1992). For some doubts on the power of Duden in motivating immigrants, Walter D. Kamphoefner, "Learning from the 'Majority-Minority' City: Immigration in Nineteenth-Century St. Louis," in *St. Louis in the Century of Henry Shaw,* 82. On Irish and German Catholic immigration, William Barnaby Faherty, *The St. Louis German Catholics* (St. Louis: Reedy Press, 2004); William Barnaby Faherty, *The St. Louis Irish: An Unmatched Celtic Community* (St. Louis: Missouri Historical Society Press—distributed by University of Missouri Press, 2001).

31. Hall to Brooks, May 9, 1849; Mann Butler, "Great Fire of St. Louis," letter to the *Missouri Republican,* May 29, 1849, p. 1. On interconnections, Thomas Bender, *A*

Nation among Nations: America's Place in World History (New York: Hill & Wang, 2006), 122–130. On the interplay of fear and disease in the cholera outbreak, Robert Wilson, "The Disease of Fear: Yellow Fever and Cholera in the Mississippi Valley" (PhD diss., St. Louis University, 2007).

32. William Greenleaf Eliot, "Slow St. Louis: Her Trial by Fire and Pestilence," *Daily Missouri Democrat,* December 2, 1871, found in the James S. Thomas Scrapbooks, Scrapbook 15. See also William Greenleaf Eliot Diary, May 23, 1849, William Greenleaf Eliot Papers, WU.

33. Kilgo, *Likeness and Landscape,* 166–167, 2–3, 27, 201–209. On the technological transformations of the era generally, Howe, *What Hath God Wrought.*

34. *Louisville Courier* quoted in *St. Louis Reveille,* May 23, 1849, p. 2; for list of businesses, "The Latest Particulars of the St. Louis Fire," (New York) *Weekly Herald,* May 26, 1849, p. 165, no. 22, col. E, via Cengage. For tabulations of rebuilt buildings, which imply the destruction of their original locales, see the *Daily Missouri Republican,* June 6, 1849, p. 3, and for contractor, owner, and address, *Annual Review of the Trade and Commerce of St. Louis,* 13–14. For Pittsburgh's donation, Eliot, "Slow St. Louis," and Elihu H. Shepard, "The Later History of St. Louis and Missouri," *Daily Missouri Democrat,* December 10, 1871, both found in the James S. Thomas Scrapbooks, SLML, Scrapbook 15. For Cincinnati, "Large Fire—Meeting to Sympathise," (New York) *Weekly Herald,* May 26, 1849, p. 165, no. 22, col. C, via Cengage.

35. On the thousands affected, *St. Louis Union,* May 22, 1849; Henry Ware Eliot, "A Brief Autobiography, 1843–1919" (1919), in William Greenleaf Eliot Papers, WU, 47. For the life of slaves on the riverfront generally, see Thomas C. Buchanan, *Black Life on the Mississippi: Slaves, Free Blacks, and the Western Steamboat World* (Chapel Hill: University of North Carolina Press, 2004).

36. On Lynch's Slave Pen and the other downtown slave traders, Harrison Anthony Trexler, *Slavery in Missouri, 1804–1865* (Baltimore: Johns Hopkins University Press, 1914), 48–49; Walter Johnson, *Soul by Soul: Life inside the Antebellum Slave Market* (Cambridge, Mass.: Harvard University Press, 1999), 7, 167. James Green, *Green's St. Louis Directory* (St. Louis: J. Green and Cathcart & Prescott, 1850), 3, 38–41. Quote is from p. 40. For updated directories, *St. Louis Deutsche Tribüne,* May 20, 1849, p. 2, and *Missouri Republican,* June 1, 1849, p. 3. For the sampling and the block reconstruction, see Adam Arenson, "Profiting from Disaster: St. Louis' 'Great Fire' in History and Memory." Western History Association annual meeting, St. Louis, October 2006.

37. Green, *1850 St. Louis Directory,* 41–42; *St. Louis Deutsche Tribüne,* May 20, 1849, p. 2; *Daily Missouri Republican,* June 6, 1849, p. 2; Trinity German Evangelical Lutheran Church minutes, vol. 1839–1853. Thanks to Dennis Ratchert for access and help with translation. For how the Great Fire changed the spatial layout of the city, concentrating on the movement of small businesses, see Glen E. Holt, "The Shaping of St. Louis, 1763–1860" (PhD diss., University of Chicago, 1975), 338–344.

38. *Daily Missouri Republican,* May 26, 1849, p. 2. The newspapers were reestablished as follows: the *Deutsche Tribüne,* May 20; the *St. Louis Daily New Era,* May 21; the *People's Organ,* May 21; the *Missouri Republican,* before May 22; the *Reveille,* May 22.

39. *St. Louis Daily Reveille,* May 23, 1849, p. 2; *Daily Missouri Republican,* June 1, 1849, p. 2. Redevelopment resolutions appear in the *St. Louis Daily Reveille,* May 23, 1849, p. 2. Many articles in each paper traced the progress. At year's end, see *Annual Review of the Trade and Commerce of St. Louis,* 2, 3.

40. Frances Sublette to Solomon Sublette, May 21, 1849, 1849 folder, William L. Sublette Papers, MHM. On fears about pregnancy and cholera, see also Frances to Solomon Sublette, May 5, 1849. On slave holdings and tradings with Lynch, see Sublette Papers, as cited in Trexler, *Slavery in Missouri,* 49. Tarver wrote that the sale was for $14,300, estimated to be $7,000 above what they could have received before the fire. Frances to Solomon Sublette, June 17, 1849, and Tarver to Sublette, August 31, 1849, Sublette Papers. On improvements, Frances to Solomon Sublette, August 10, 1849. For women in business in St. Louis, see Martha Saxton, *Being Good: Women's Moral Values in Early America* (New York: Hill & Wang, 2003), 173–182, 214–236.

41. Quotes from Tarver to Sublette, August 31, 1849; "Evening Report—St. Louis Fire," *New York Herald,* May 20, 1849, col. F. On insurance, *St. Louis Deutsche Tribüne,* May 20, 1849, p. 2; *St. Louis People's Organ,* May 21, 1849, p. 3; *Annual Review of the Trade and Commerce of St. Louis,* 3; see also "The Fire at St. Louis," (Boston) *Emancipator & Republican,* May 24, 1849, col. A, via Cengage.

42. Mann Butler, "Great Fire of St. Louis," letter to the *Missouri Republican,* May 29, 1849, p. 1. See also Elihu H. Shepard, "The Later History of St. Louis and Missouri." Later histories agreed: see Thomas Lynch, *The Volunteer Fire Department of St. Louis* (Saint Louis: R. & T. A. Ennis, 1880), 87; Walter B. Stevens, *St. Louis, the Fourth City 1764–1909,* 3 vols. (St. Louis: S. J. Clarke, 1909) 1:770.

43. Richard C. Wade, *The Urban Frontier: The Rise of Western Cities, 1790–1830* (Cambridge, Mass.: Harvard University Press, 1959), 17, 96, 302. For a similar "myth of origins" in New York, Scobey, *Empire City,* 15–17, 90.

44. *Annual Review of the Trade and Commerce of St. Louis,* 14; Adams, "Letter in 1849," 368; *St. Louis Daily Reveille,* May 22, 1849, p. 2. Jeffrey Adler's *Yankee Merchants and the Making of the Urban West* attempted to highlight these years of Yankee ascendancy but focused too exclusively on an antebellum economic change.

45. *Missouri Republican,* August 8, 1849, typescript in Julius Hutawa research binder, compiled by Josh Newby-Harpole, summer 2005, MHM. Thanks to Emily Troxell Jaycox for access to these research notes. Julius Hutawa wrote a new will in July 1849, perhaps reflecting the change in property caused by the fire, or deaths in the family from cholera. Will and testament of Julius Hutawa, June 29, 1849, in Julius Hutawa research binder. For similar treatment of the photograph, see Kilgo, *Likeness and Landscape,* 190.

46. Nathaniel Currier, *Great Fire at St. Louis, Mo,* MHM; Henry Lewis, "The Great Fire in St. Louis, Missouri," Plate 62, *Das Illustrirte Mississippithal,* 1854–1857, and "Lamasson," *St. Louis Riverfront after the Great Fire,* c. 1849, SLML Art Collection. For iconic parallels from other major urban fires, see J. M. W. Turner, *The Burning of the Houses of Parliament,* 1835, and Margaret Sloan Patterson, "Nicolino Calyo and His Paintings of the Great Fire of New York, December 16th and 17th, 1835," *American Art Journal* 12, no. 2 (Spring 1982). Thanks to Alex Nemerov for this reference.

47. William Greenleaf Eliot, "Slow St. Louis."

2 Thomas Hart Benton's Failed Compromise

1. Thomas Hart Benton, "The Progress of the Age," SLML, Thomas Hart Benton Collection, M-8, pp. 1, 2. Leo Kaiser edited a published version of the speech—but he removed many of Benton's italics and other marks of emphasis, and erroneously called it an inaugural speech for the Mercantile Library. Leo M. Kaiser, "An Unpublished Speech of Thomas Hart Benton," *Missouri Historical Society Bulletin* 19, no. 1 (October 1962): 36–48.

2. Benton, "Progress of the Age," 44, 42, 47. Original emphasis and capitalization.

3. "Senator Benton's Lecture before the Mercantile Library Association," *St. Louis Daily Union,* November 15, 1850, p. 2. Comma between "speaking" and "is" removed. For tickets sold and correspondence on the written copy, SLML Board of Direction Minutes, First Volume, end of year report, meeting December 3, 1850, SLML, M-117, Book A-1-1, pp. 210, 205. For mentions of the speech, William Nisbet Chambers, *Old Bullion Benton, Senator from the New West: Thomas Hart Benton, 1782–1858* (Boston: Atlantic Monthly Press—Little, Brown, 1956), 372–373; Elbert B. Smith, *Magnificent Missourian: The Life of Thomas Hart Benton* (Philadelphia: Lippincott, 1958), 280. Mention also appears in Louis S. Gerteis, *Civil War St. Louis* (Lawrence: University Press of Kansas, 2001), 57–58.

4. On veneration of the others, Merrill D. Peterson, *The Great Triumvirate: Webster, Clay, and Calhoun* (New York: Oxford University Press, 1987), and Ken Winn, "Gods in Ruins: St. Louis Politicians and American Destiny, 1764–1875," in *St. Louis in the Century of Henry Shaw: A View Beyond the Garden Wall,* ed. Eric Sandweiss (Columbia: University of Missouri Press, 2003), 25–26. For recent considerations of the era encapsulated by the Missouri Compromise and the Compromise of 1850 that emphasize Benton, see Daniel Walker Howe, *What Hath God Wrought: The Transformation of America, 1815–1848* (New York: Oxford University Press, 2007); Sean Wilentz, *The Rise of American Democracy: Jefferson to Lincoln* (New York: W. W. Norton, 2005); Robert Pierce Forbes, *The Missouri Compromise and Its Aftermath: Slavery & the Meaning of America* (Chapel Hill: University of North Carolina Press, 2007); and Marc Egnal, *Clash of Extremes: The Economic Origins of the Civil War* (New York: Hill & Wang, 2009), 179–183.

5. Chambers, *Old Bullion Benton,* 3–100; William Montgomery Meigs, *The Life of Thomas Hart Benton* (Philadelphia: J. B. Lippincott Co., 1904), 13–22, 73–82, 104–116; Theodore Roosevelt, *Thomas Hart Benton* (Boston: Houghton, Mifflin & Co., 1887), 23–46; Smith, *Magnificent Missourian,* 13–73.

6. Frederika Bremer, letter of July 10, 1850, in Fredrika Bremer and Mary Botham Howitt, *The Homes of the New World: Impressions of America* (New York: Harper & Bros., 1853), 1:465–466 and 481–483, as cited in Chambers, *Old Bullion Benton,* 365–366. For Benton's political origins, Perry McCandless, "The Rise of Thomas H. Benton in Missouri Politics," *MHR* 50, no. 1 (October 1955): 16–29. On dueling and the advantage of a rough image for politicians, see Joanne B. Freeman, *Affairs of Honor: National Politics in the New Republic* (New Haven, Conn.: Yale University Press, 2001), and her forthcoming work. For Benton's run-ins with Clay, see Maurice G. Baxter, *Henry Clay and the American System* (Lexington: University Press of Kentucky, 1995), esp. pp. 115–118 and 196–198.

7. Jefferson had in fact been paying close attention to the proceedings. Thomas Jefferson, Monticello, to John Holmes, April 22, 1820, Thomas Jefferson Papers, Library of Congress, http://memory.loc.gov, accessed fall 2006; John Adams to Louisa Catherine [Johnson] Adams, December 23, 1819, John Adams Papers, Reel 124, as quoted in John R. Howe Jr., "John Adams's Views of Slavery," *Journal of Negro History* 49, no. 3 (July 1964): 202. These events are recounted by Howe, *What Hath God Wrought,* 148–157.

8. Decades later Benton carefully noted his role in ensuring statehood; Thomas Hart Benton, *Thirty Years' View; or, a History of the Working of the American Government for Thirty Years, from 1820 to 1850. Chiefly Taken from the Congress Debates, the Private Papers of General Jackson, and the Speeches of Ex-Senator Benton, with His Actual View of Men and Affairs; with Historical Notes and Illustrations, and Some Notices of Eminent Deceased Contemporaries* (New York: D. Appleton and Company, 1854), 1:8–10. For the authoritative history of the Missouri Compromise, see Forbes, *The Missouri Compromise and Its Aftermath.*

9. Gerteis, *Civil War St. Louis,* 37; Joseph M. Rogers, *Thomas H. Benton* (Philadelphia: G. W. Jacobs & Company, 1905), 33.

10. Benton, speech at Jefferson City, May 26, 1849, printed in *Congressional Globe,* 31st Cong., 1st sess., appendix, 681, as quoted in Meigs, *Life of Thomas Hart Benton,* 324; see also 344–346, 353–355. For Benton citing Jefferson, Benton, *Thirty Years' View,* 2:759. See especially John D. Morton, "'This Magnificent New World': Thomas Hart Benton's Westward Vision Reconsidered," *MHR* 90, no. 3 (1996): 300–301.

11. The railroad could have proceeded on this federal land even before it was incorporated as a territory; also St. Louis acted quickly to preempt a Memphis convention. R. S. Cotterill, "The National Railroad Convention in St. Louis, 1849," *MHR* 12, no. 4 (July 1918): 215, 205–206. For the evolution of Benton's position on railroads, see Meigs, *Life of Thomas Hart Benton,* 414–418; Rogers, *Thomas H. Benton,* 272–273;

Walter B. Stevens, *St. Louis, the Fourth City 1764–1909,* 3 vols. (St. Louis, Mo.: S. J. Clarke, 1909), 1:472, 475.

12. James Neal Primm proclaimed that Benton "equated St Louis with the West, the West with the nation." James Neal Primm, *Lion of the Valley: St. Louis, Missouri, 1764–1980,* 3rd ed. (St. Louis: Missouri Historical Society Press, 1998), 110. See also Egnal, *Clash of Extremes,* 179–183.

13. *Missouri Republican,* September 30, 1840, p. 2. Benton felt it necessary to formally decline interest; *Missouri Republican,* June 26, 1841, p. 2; and see Meigs, *Life of Thomas Hart Benton,* 497–498. For the differences of urban politics in the South, Frank Towers, *The Urban South and the Coming of the Civil War* (Charlottesville: University of Virginia Press, 2004), 13–14, 23.

14. Calhoun to Treat, July 9, 1849, Samuel Treat Papers, MHM, St. Louis, box 1. For this "first secession crisis," see Egnal, *Clash of Extremes,* 121–122 and 166–184; Benton, *Thirty Years' View,* 2:697: Rogers, *Thomas H. Benton,* 215–217; Smith, *Magnificent Missourian,* 249–250; Holly Zumwalt Taylor, "Neither North nor South: Sectionalism, St. Louis Politics, and the Coming of the Civil War, 1846–1861" (PhD diss., University of Texas at Austin, 2004), 110.

15. Gerteis, *Civil War St. Louis,* 50–51; Taylor, "Neither North nor South," 118–119. On the intent to target Benton, see Chambers, *Old Bullion Benton,* 341–342; Meigs, *Life of Thomas Hart Benton,* 409–412; John D. Morton, "'A High Wall and a Deep Ditch': Thomas Hart Benton and the Compromise of 1850," *MHR* 94, no. 1 (October 1999): 7–11.

16. Calhoun to Treat, n.d. (Spring 1849), Samuel Treat Papers; *Missouri Republican,* May 10, 1849, as quoted in Taylor, "Neither North nor South," 123.

17. Cotterill, "The National Railroad Convention," esp. pp. 203–204; Asa Whitney, *A Project for a Railroad to the Pacific* (New York: G. W. Wood, 1849). Cronon does not explicitly mention the Whitney plan; William Cronon, *Nature's Metropolis: Chicago and the Great West* (New York: W. W. Norton, 1991), 57, 65–74. See instead Dorothy Jennings, "The Pacific Railroad Company," *Missouri Historical Society Collections* 6 (1928–1931): 289–290. On the Frémonts, see Sally Denton, *Passion and Principle: John and Jessie Frémont, the Couple whose Power, Politics, and Love Shaped Nineteenth-Century America* (New York: Bloomsbury, 2007).

18. Cotterill, "The National Railroad Convention." For more on the railroad terminus competition, see Chapters 4 and 9.

19. Ibid., 208.

20. Benton's speech is known only from a newspaper transcription: Thomas Hart Benton, speech to the National Railroad Convention, October 16, 1849, as reported in the *Missouri Republican,* October 18, 1849. Transcription provided by Bob Moore, JNEM. Many of the phrases also appear in Thomas Hart Benton, *Highway to the Pacific. Grand National Central Highway. Speech of Mr. Benton on Introducing a Bill for the Construction of a Grand National Central Highway from St. Louis to San Francisco.*

Delivered in the Senate of the United States, Dec. 16, 1850 (Washington, D.C.: Towers, 1850). Speech discussed, with famous sections quoted, in Chambers, *Old Bullion Benton*, 352–353; Meigs, *Life of Thomas Hart Benton*, 419–422; Rogers, *Thomas H. Benton*, 271, 275; Smith, *Magnificent Missourian*, 253–256.

21. Benton, as reported in the *Missouri Republican*, October 18, 1849.

22. Benton explicitly mentioned Washington's financial interest in canals west; as reported in the *Missouri Republican*, October 18, 1849.

23. Benton, as reported in the *Missouri Republican*, October 18, 1849.

24. Elias Lyman Magoon, *Living Orators in America* (New York: Baker and Scribner, 1849), 342; for the squabbling and the plan to meet again, Cotterill, "The National Railroad Convention," 211–215. This paragraph owes some of its framing to Sandra M. Gustafson, "The Rule and Misrule of Law: Constituting Democracy in the 1820s and 1830s," Yale University English Department Americanist Colloquium, New Haven, Conn., September 18, 2006, and my discussion with her. See also Sandra M. Gustafson, *Forms of Democracy: Political Letters in the United States before Emerson, 1815–1837* (forthcoming). On the contrary, Joseph Rogers argued Benton's fame suffered because of his lack of oratorical skill; Rogers, *Thomas H. Benton*, 10, 328–338.

25. Otis Adams, "Letter in 1849," *Missouri Historical Society Bulletin* 6, no. 3 (April 1950): 371.

26. For a now-classic account, David Morris Potter and Don Edward Fehrenbacher, *The Impending Crisis, 1848–1861* (New York: Harper & Row, 1976), 90–120.

27. Ibid., 97–99; James M. McPherson, *Battle Cry of Freedom: The Civil War Era* (New York: Oxford University Press, 1988), 70–72; Gustafson, *Forms of Democracy*.

28. Benton would have agreed with David Potter's description of the Compromise of 1850 as merely an "armistice." Potter and Fehrenbacher, *The Impending Crisis*, 50. See also Rogers, *Thomas H. Benton*, 265, 298; and Morton, "'This Magnificent New World,'" 298–299, 307; Taylor, "Neither North nor South," 17, 76.

29. Benton, *Thirty Years' View*, 2:768, and "Col. Benton's Speech, Delivered in St. Louis, Saturday Evening November 9th," *St. Louis Daily Union*, November 11, 1850, p. 2. On the basis of this stability and Benton's endorsement of it, Egnal, *Clash of Extremes*, 44, 81, 179–183. See also Meigs, *Life of Thomas Hart Benton*, 390; Morton, "'A High Wall and a Deep Ditch,'" 12–16, 21; Rogers, *Thomas H. Benton*, 252–257; Smith, *Magnificent Missourian*, 269–275. For the explanation of the analogy to patent medicine, Meigs, *Life of Thomas Hart Benton*, 389–390.

30. For the Benton-Fillmore-Foote encounter, Chambers, *Old Bullion Benton*, 360–362; Meigs, *Life of Thomas Hart Benton*, 392–399, Rogers, *Thomas H. Benton*, 261–262; Smith, *Magnificent Missourian*, 270–272; Gerteis, *Civil War St. Louis*, 53. For the speeches and events as edited by Benton, see Benton, *Thirty Years' View*, 2: 742–765, 768–787.

31. Benton, *Thirty Years' View,* 1:344; see also 345, 762, 764. On votes, *Missouri Republican,* May 20, 1852, as quoted in Taylor, "Neither North nor South," 168–69; Chambers, *Old Bullion Benton,* 366–367; Gerteis, *Civil War St. Louis,* 56–57. See also Christopher Phillips, *Missouri's Confederate: Claiborne Fox Jackson and the Creation of Southern Identity in the Border West* (Columbia: University of Missouri Press, 2000), 150–157.

32. Benton long maintained his support in St. Louis, while the rest of the state increasingly opposed him. Phillips, *Missouri's Confederate,* esp. pp. 164–178; Taylor, "Neither North nor South," 109–110, citing Benjamin C. Merkel, "The Slavery Issue and the Political Decline of Thomas Hart Benton, 1846–1856," *MHR* 38, no. 4 (July 1944): 406. See also Morton, "'A High Wall and a Deep Ditch.'" For a county-by-county breakdown for 1850, Chambers, *Old Bullion Benton,* 370.

33. *Anzeiger des Westens* Extra, as reprinted from the *Anzeiger* of July 26, 1854, broadside, Thomas Hart Benton Campaign Handbill, 1854, WHMC-Columbia, C2842. For campaigning for Senate before direct election, William H. Riker, "The Senate and American Federalism," *American Political Science Review* 49, no. 2 (June 1955): 455, 463–465.

34. On German votes, Henry Boernstein, *Memoirs of a Nobody: The Missouri Years of an Austrian Radical, 1849–1866,* trans. Steven Rowan (1881; St. Louis: Missouri Historical Society Press, 1997), 124–125, 139–145. For details of the Assembly makeup, Morton, "'A High Wall and a Deep Ditch,'" 23.

35. "Senator Benton's Address to the Democracy," *St. Louis Daily Union,* November 9, 1850, p. 2; "Col. Benton's Speech, Delivered in St. Louis, Saturday Evening November 9th," *St. Louis Daily Union,* November 11, 1850, p. 2; "Colonel Benton," *St. Louis Daily Union,* November 22, 1850, p. 2. On national readership, "Col. Benton's Speech at St Louis," *Boston Daily Atlas,* November 18, 1850, no. 119, col. F, and "Col. Benton's Speech," (Columbus) *Daily Ohio Herald,* November 22 and 23, 1850, p. 2, via Cengage; see also Chambers, *Old Bullion Benton,* 371; Smith, *Magnificent Missourian,* 257–258, 279–280.

36. "Col. Benton's Speech," p. 2.

37. Ibid. For the conciliatory efforts of the *Daily Union,* Taylor, "Neither North nor South," 48; *Burlington Telegraph* editorial as quoted in "Colonel Benton," *St. Louis Daily Union,* November 22, 1850, p. 2; *St. Louis Intelligencer* as quoted in "Whig Spectacles—Benton Contrasted with Clay and Webster," *St. Louis Daily Union,* November 14, 1850, p. 2.

38. "Mercantile Library," *St. Louis Daily Union,* November 14, 1850, p. 2. "St" without period in original. For Benton's speech, women made up about half the audience; the library provided a socially acceptable venue. "Senator Benton's Lecture before the Mercantile Library Association," *St. Louis Daily Union,* November 15, 1850, p. 2. On the importance of "third places" like mercantile libraries, Adam Arenson, "Libraries in Public before the Age of Public Libraries: Interpreting the

Furnishings and Design of Athenaeums and Other 'Social Libraries,' 1800–1860," in *The Library as Place: History, Community, and Culture,* ed. John E. Buschman and Gloria J. Leckie (Westport, Conn.: Libraries Unlimited, 2007), 41–60; Thomas Augst, *The Clerk's Tale: Young Men and Moral Life in Nineteenth-Century America* (Chicago: University of Chicago Press, 2003), 255–267. For white male fraternal bonds amid gender and racial restrictions, see Dana D. Nelson, *National Manhood: Capitalist Citizenship and the Imagined Fraternity of White Men* (Durham, N.C.: Duke University Press, 1998).

39. For guidelines, Peter Powell, report of the Lectures Committee, SLML, M-117, Board of Direction Minutes, First Volume, 6–7, meeting March 10, 1846; for St. Louis's Whig Party, John Vollmer Mering, *The Whig Party in Missouri* (Columbia: University of Missouri Press, 1967), 71–85. Meagher accepted; Thomas F. Meagher, New York, to John A. Douglass, October 20, 1852, Lecture Committee Letterbook, A-3–5, 57. On letters to Emerson, Agassiz, Clay, and Douglas, Board of Direction Minutes, First Volume, 253–254, meeting June 23, 1851; on Fanny Kemble, see Curtis to Floyd Clarkson, New York Mercantile Library Association, December 11, 1856, Letter Book 7, 114. For Benton's arrangements, Thomas Hart Benton, Washington, to Messrs. Van Nostrand & McAllister, August 12, 1850, and October 23, 1850, Lecture Committee Letter Book, A-3–5, pp. 2 and 164, and Board of Direction Minutes, First Volume, 199–200, meeting November 4, 1850.

40. Benton, "The Progress of the Age," 20, 39, 40.

41. Ibid., 37, 14, 18. On Benton's praise for the Founders, see Benton, *Thirty Years' View,* 1: 87–88, 476–477, 678–682.

42. Benton, *Missouri Republican,* May 1, 1854, as quoted in Taylor, "Neither North nor South," 205; "The Election of United States Senator," *St. Louis Daily Union,* November 19, 1850, p. 2; William Barclay Napton, *The Union on Trial: The Political Journals of Judge William Barclay Napton, 1829–1883,* ed. Christopher Phillips and Jason L. Pendleton (Columbia: University of Missouri Press, 2005), 94, entry for September 1850. On expectations of reelection, Chambers, *Old Bullion Benton,* 373; Smith, *Magnificent Missourian,* 256.

43. Wayman Crow, Jefferson City, to John F. Darby, January 28, 1851, Thomas Hart Benton Papers, MHM, box 2, folder 1. Original punctuation and orthography. "Re-Election of Benton—And the Revolt of the Democracy throughout the State," *St. Louis Daily Union,* November 21, 1850, p. 2. See also Abiel Leonard, Fayette, to J. B. Crockett, St. Louis, February 18, 1851, Abiel Leonard Papers, WHMC-Columbia, C1013, folder 252, University of Missouri-Columbia. For discussion of the vote, Chambers, *Old Bullion Benton,* 374–377; Gerteis, *Civil War St. Louis,* 58; Napton, *The Union on Trial,* 96–97; Mering, *The Whig Party in Missouri,* 173–179.

44. *St. Louis Daily Evening News,* June 28, 1852; Clay died June 29, 1852. Benton in *Missouri Republican,* March 8, 1852, as quoted in Taylor, "Neither North nor South," 173; H., "Editorial Correspondence," *Daily Cleveland Herald,* June 26, 1854,

no. 148, col. A, via Cengage. *Missouri Republican,* June 27, 1852, in Stevens, *St. Louis, the Fourth City,* 1:571; Taylor, "Neither North nor South," 170. For further discussion of Clay's death, the local ceremonies, and the talk of a monument, see a string of articles in the *St. Louis Daily Evening News,* June 30–July 24, 1852; Morton, "'A High Wall and a Deep Ditch,'" 23–24; Chambers, *Old Bullion Benton,* 376–377 and 381–382; Smith, *Magnificent Missourian,* 284–285; Rogers, *Thomas H. Benton,* 277–279.

45. Mercantile Library acquisitions included a Daniel Webster daguerreotype, statue, and letters; Board of Direction Minutes, First Volume, pp. 347, 453, 465, meetings January 3, 1853, March 5 and August 6, 1855, and Alfred Carr to J. C. Taylor, March 7, 1860, Letter Book 7, p. 10. For a Henry Clay bust, Board of Direction Minutes, Second Volume, n.p., meeting July 10, 1860, and Carr to J. H. Brown, St. Louis, July 20, 1860, Letter Book 7, 13, on the bust of Clay. On the debates, September 15, 1850, and January 7, 1853, meetings, SLU, Philalethic Society Minutes, 1850–1863, DOC REC 0001 0012 0031, n.p. For Benton's reputation, especially with later politicians, see Roosevelt, *Thomas Hart Benton,* 319, and John F. Kennedy and Theodore C. Sorenson, *Profiles in Courage* (New York: Harper, 1956).

46. Uncited quotation as found in Magoon, *Living Orators in America,* 308. For the railroad, see Chapter 4; for the German vote and the election of Blair and Brown, see Chambers, *Old Bullion Benton,* 382–388; Smith, *Magnificent Missourian,* 284–290; Meigs, *Life of Thomas Hart Benton,* 423–424; Taylor, "Neither North nor South," 105; Boernstein, *Memoirs of a Nobody,* 183–193, and Chapter 3.

3 Building the National Future in the West

1. William Greenleaf Eliot, entry for February 22, 1853, WU, William Greenleaf Eliot Papers, Notebook 4, p. 9. Annual meetings occurred in the afternoon or evening; for example, in 1854, they met at 3 p.m.; in 1856 and 1858, at 7 p.m. WU, Board of Trustee Minutes, February 22 meetings for 1854, 1856, and 1858, 1:5, 23, 67.

On Washington's Birthday celebrations being held at St. Louis University that year, *St. Louis Daily Evening News,* February 24, 1853. On the lack of public gathering space, G. Vietor Davis, "Notes on Block Seven: The Disappearance of St. Louis' Place Publique," February 1939. Research Report No. 38, JNEM; Richard C. Wade, *The Urban Frontier: The Rise of Western Cities, 1790–1830* (Cambridge, Mass.: Harvard University Press, 1959), 29. For national holidays and civic pride, David Waldstreicher, *In the Midst of Perpetual Fetes: The Making of American Nationalism, 1776–1820* (Williamsburg and Chapel Hill: Omohundro Institute of Early American History and Culture—University of North Carolina Press, 1997), esp. pp. 112, 215, and 231.

2. Quotes from Eliot, "A Statement Relating to the Endowment of Washington University," May 11, 1864, Eliot Papers, pp. 16–17, and entry for January 22, 1853, Notebook 4, p. 9–10.

3. Samuel Treat, "The Law: An Inaugural Discourse," October 16, 1867, speech at the inauguration of the Washington University Law School, newspaper transcript, in the Chancellor's Scrapbooks, Scrapbook 1867–1877, WU. Eliot's papers combine church, university, and personal business with recollections; they are the most extensive. No collected papers of James E. Yeatman, Hudson E. Bridge, Wayman Crow, James Smith, George Partridge, or Mann Butler exist. Judge Samuel Treat has collected papers; Seth Ranlett left a diary; and Eunice Smith wrote a biography of her husband, James Smith; they are at MHS. Nine letters from Hudson Bridge on his donations in the 1870s are held by WU.

4. The origin stories of Washington University have often been referenced but have rarely been explored. The most comprehensive and balanced—though by his own admission still a "company history"—is Ralph E. Morrow, *Washington University in St. Louis: A History* (St. Louis: Missouri Historical Society Press, 1996). He only mentions the 1854 nativist riot in passing, p. 7; for his account of the efforts of earlier university historians, and how they ended up unpublished, pp. ix–xi. On the evidence Eliot knew about the charter beforehand, Candace O'Connor, *Beginning a Great Work: Washington University in St. Louis, 1853–2003* (St. Louis: Washington University in St. Louis, 2003), 4–7.

5. Ken Winn has observed, "Clearly Eliot hoped to remake St. Louis into a little piece of New England." Ken Winn, "Gods in Ruins: St. Louis Politicians and American Destiny, 1764–1875," in *St. Louis in the Century of Henry Shaw: A View Beyond the Garden Wall*, ed. Eric Sandweiss (Columbia: University of Missouri Press, 2003), 32; see also Jeffrey S. Adler, *Yankee Merchants and the Making of the Urban West: The Rise and Fall of Antebellum St. Louis* (New York: Cambridge University Press, 1991), and Louis S. Gerteis, *Civil War St. Louis* (Lawrence: University Press of Kansas, 2001), 40–41.

6. Thomas Easterly, *William Greenleaf Eliot*, c. 1850. MHM. For the other images, see, among other places, Charlotte Chauncy Eliot, *William Greenleaf Eliot, Minister, Educator, Philanthropist* (Boston: Houghton, Mifflin & Co., 1904). Eliot, uncited quotation in Earl K. Holt III, *William Greenleaf Eliot Conservative Radical* (St. Louis: First Unitarian Church, 1985), 53.

7. Eliot, "The Church of the Messiah: Its Genesis—Number One," *Gazetteer* clipping, June 1876, in Notebook 9, p. 174; Eliot, "A Statement Relating to the Endowment of Washington University," May 11, 1864, 7. For an overview of Eliot's family background and early life, see William A. Deiss, "William Greenleaf Eliot: The Formative Years (1811–1834)," in Holt, *Eliot Conservative Radical*; C. Eliot, *Eliot, Minister, Educator*, 1–30. Key sources include "William Greenleaf Eliot: For Fifty-Three Years the Minister in St. Louis, Mo.," *Our Best Words* 8, no. 8 (April 15, 1887), and John H. Heywood, "William Greenleaf Eliot," *Unitarian Review*, March 1887, pp. 227–246.

8. Quotes from Eliot to James Freeman Clarke, February 7, 1834, as quoted in Holt, *Eliot Conservative Radical*, 20; *St. Louis Enquirer*, February 19, 1820, as quoted

in Wade, *The Urban Frontier,* 265; for the Irish anecdote, Robert Collyer, "A Tribute from Robert Collyer," *Our Best Words* 8, no. 8 (April 15, 1887), held in Eliot Papers, WU. "Bla-gard" is dialect for blackguard; "'cess" is Irish for luck. See Eliot, "The Church of the Messiah: Its Genesis—Number One," and "The Church of the Messiah: Its Genesis—Number Two," *Gazetteer* clippings, June 1876, in Notebook 9, p. 174; C. Eliot, *Eliot, Minister, Educator,* 7–19; Holt, *Eliot Conservative Radical,* 20, 24; Winn, "Gods in Ruins," 31; William Barnaby Faherty, *The St. Louis Irish: An Unmatched Celtic Community* (Saint Louis: Missouri Historical Society Press: Distributed by University of Missouri Press, 2001), 62; Wade, *The Urban Frontier,* 262–264; James Freeman Clarke, "Character and Work of William Greenleaf Eliot: A Discourse Delivered to the Church of the Disciples, Boston, Jan. 30, 1887," Eliot Papers, WU.

9. Quotes from Charles Dickens, *American Notes for General Circulation,* in *The Works of Charles Dickens* (London: Brainard, 1908), 174; and Eliot to James Freeman Clarke, February 17, 1841, Correspondence, Eliot Papers, WU. William Greenleaf Eliot, *Address Delivered before the Franklin Society of St. Louis on the Occasion of Its First Anniversary, January 7th, 1836* (St. Louis: Charless & Paschall, 1836). Available on Reel 3 of the microfilmed Eliot Papers, WU; Abigail Adams Cranch Eliot to a friend, August 1895, as reprinted in Holt, *Eliot Conservative Radical,* 97–98. The church was dedicated October 29, 1837; Eliot, "The Church of the Messiah: Its Genesis—Number Two," *Gazetteer* clipping, June 1876, in Notebook 9, 187; C. Eliot, *Eliot, Minister, Educator,* 21, 26, 33–36; Holt, *Eliot Conservative Radical,* 26.

10. Quotes from Eliot, November 17, 1847, Notebook 1, pp. 4–5, and Ralph Waldo Emerson, *The Journals and Miscellaneous Notebooks of Ralph Waldo Emerson,* ed. William H. Gilman et al. (Cambridge, Mass.: Belknap Press of Harvard University Press, 1960–1982), xi, and oft-cited descriptions of Eliot. On German churches, Eliot, entry for November 15, 1847, Notebook 1, p. 1, and letter on fortieth anniversary sermon, December 9, 1874, Notebook 8, p. 113; on charity houses and efforts generally, March 1, 1855, Notebook 4, p. 57; after November 1855, Notebook 4, p. 100; C. Eliot, *Eliot, Minister, Educator,* pp. 28, 42; Morrow, *Washington University,* 16. Documents in Eliot's hand and with his signature include Board of Trustees Rules, 1836, and trusteeship letters, 1841, SLU, Medical-Dental Schools, Minutes, DOC REC 0001 0005 0001 and 0014. See also SLU Board of Trustees Minutes, October 4, 1836, October 12, 1841, and 1842 meetings, 17–27, 43–49, 54–56. Though rarely noted or known in WU sources, Eliot's participation is recorded in the commissioned SLU history; William Barnaby Faherty, *Better the Dream: Saint Louis: University & Community.* (St. Louis: SLU, 1968), 60, 112. On cholera, August 1849 article, Notebook 2, p. 180; on ecumenical charity, *Missouri Republican* clipping, March 1853, Notebook 4, p. 14.

11. Quotes from Eliot to Wayman Crow and James E. Yeatman, November 10, 1884, Eliot Papers, WU, and Christopher Rhodes Eliot, "Adventures in Idealism,"

Commencement Address, June 5, 1928, pp. 1–2. On the church membership and joint charitable work of the group, Morrow, *Washington University*, 1, 14–15; O'Connor, *Beginning a Great Work*, 11. For the involvement of Mrs. Abby Cranch Eliot with Mrs. Ranlett, Mrs. Kasson, Mrs. Partridge, Mrs. Teasdale, and Miss Susan Blow, founder of the first public American kindergarten, see the girls' school announcement, n.d. [1853–1854], Notebook 4, 43; and Eliot, church annual report, entry for January 1860, Notebook 4, 149. Time for charity work could also hinge on slave or hired labor; see Martha Saxton, *Being Good: Women's Moral Values in Early America* (New York: Hill & Wang, 2003), 11–12. See also Eliot, "James Smith: His Gifts and Bequests," newspaper article draft, n.d. [October 16, 1883], Eliot Papers, WU; C. Eliot, *Eliot, Minister, Educator*, 20; Morrow, *Washington University*, 103–104; Mike Venso, "James E. Yeatman—St. Louis' Compassionate Philanthropist of the Civil War," (research paper, University of Missouri-St. Louis, 2004). Thanks to the author for providing access to this paper. On the Eliot children's experiences, see also Henry Ware Eliot, "A Brief Autobiography, 1843–1919."

12. Uncited quote from C. Eliot, *Eliot, Minister, Educator*, 35, 34. On church construction, Eliot, notes on 25 years of service, November–December 1859, Notebook 4, 108–110; C. Eliot, *Eliot, Minister, Educator*, 21, 26–27. For a complete list of Mercantile Library officers, see John Neal Hoover, *Cultural Cornerstone, 1846–1998: The Earliest Catalogs of the St. Louis Mercantile Library and the Growth of the Collections for a Varied Community of Readers* (St. Louis: SLML, 1998). On Eliot's lectures, *Missouri Republican*, October 16, 1848, Notebook 1, 179, and William Greenleaf Eliot, *Lectures to Young Men, Delivered in the Church of the Messiah* (St. Louis: Missouri Republican Office, 1852); William Greenleaf Eliot, *Lectures to Young Women* (New York: C. S. Francis and Company, 1855). For accounts of a "clerk's republic," see Adam Arenson, "The Clerk's Republic: Mercantile Libraries, Political Economy and Culture in the Microcosm of New York," (research paper, 2004); Thomas Augst, *The Clerk's Tale: Young Men and Moral Life in Nineteenth-Century America* (Chicago: University of Chicago Press, 2003); David M. Henkin, *City Reading: Written Words and Public Spaces in Antebellum New York* (New York: Columbia University Press, 1998); E. Anthony Rotundo, *American Manhood: Transformations in Masculinity from the Revolution to the Modern Era* (New York: Basic Books, 1993); Michael Zakim, *Ready-Made Democracy: A History of Men's Dress in the American Republic, 1760–1860* (Chicago: University of Chicago Press, 2003).

13. For the earliest schools in St. Louis, C. Eliot, *Eliot, Minister, Educator*, 67–68; James Neal Primm, *Lion of the Valley: St. Louis, Missouri, 1764–1980*, 3rd ed. (St. Louis: Missouri Historical Society Press, 1998), 315. Richard Wade called St. Louis's educational system the weakest in the cities he studied over the first third of the nineteenth century; Wade, *The Urban Frontier*, 247, 249. On founding of the schools, Eliot, entries for November 18 and December 22, 1847, April, June 26, August 2, October 24 and November 2, 6, and 10, 1848, January 3, February 21, and May 1, 1849, Eliot

Papers, WU, Notebook 1, pp. 5, 38, 96, 132, 137–139, Notebook 2, pp. 6–8, 13, 16, 21–22, 54–55, 78, 80–81, 85; C. Eliot, *Eliot, Minister, Educator,* 70–73, 86; John Hogan, *Thoughts about the City of St. Louis: Her Commerce and Manufactures, Railroads, &C* (St. Louis: Missouri Republican Press, 1854), 31–32; Jacob N. Taylor and M. O. Crooks, *Sketch Book of Saint Louis: Containing a Series of Sketches of the Early Settlement, Public Buildings, Hotels, Railroads* (St. Louis: G. Knapp & Co. Printers, 1858), 34–35. The church's own school was closed due to the time and effort put into the public schools; see Eliot, entry for August 28, 1848, Notebook 1, p. 140. For a brief survey of Eliot's innovations in St. Louis educational projects, Charles M. Dye, "William Greenleaf Eliot and Washington University, St. Louis: An Innovation in Nineteenth Century American Higher Education," *Missouri Historical Society Bulletin* 35, no. 3 (April 1979): 131–146.

14. Quotes from October 16, 1838, meeting, SLU, Philalethic Society Minutes, 1836–1850, DOC REC 0001 0012 0029, p. 39; November 7, 1852, meeting; December 6, 1851, meeting; September 15, 1850, November 24, 1850, and December 1, 1850, meetings; January 2, 1856, meeting; SLU Historical Records, Philalethic Society Minutes, 1850–1863, DOC REC 0001 0012 0031, n.p. Membership lists for 1849, 1850, and 1852, SLU Historical Records, Philalethic Society Minutes, 1836–1850, DOC REC 0001 0012 0029, and Philalethic Society Minutes, 1850–1863, DOC REC 0001 0012 0031. See also William Barnaby Faherty, "Nativism and Midwestern Education: The Experience of St. Louis University, 1832–1856," *History of Education Quarterly* 8, no. 4 (Winter 1968): 449; William Hyde and Howard Louis Conard, *Encyclopedia of the History of St. Louis, a Compendium of History and Biography for Ready Reference.* (New York: Southern History Company, 1899), 3:1690–1691, as cited in Ann Gulbransen, "Moses Montrose Pallen," Five Families Person Page 51, www.gulbangi.com, accessed January 2007; Faherty, *Better the Dream,* 83.

15. Eliot, comments on the Catholic *St. Louis Leader* in *Missouri Republican,* March 1853, Eliot Notebook 4, p. 14; H. Eliot, "A Brief Autobiography," 30. On the connection between girls' education and slavery in an earlier era, Saxton, *Being Good,* 14. On churchmember manumissions, November 15, 1853, Notebook 4, p. 39; C. Eliot, *Eliot, Minister, Educator,* 135–139. For Crow family manumissions, Eliot, entry for March 28, 1853, Notebook 4, p. 15. Eliot's family had free black servants, a common arrangement; see Chapter 7 and H. Eliot, "A Brief Autobiography."

16. Eliot, entries for January–February 1849, Notebook 2, pp. 69–70, and December 16, 1851, Notebook 3, p. 115; notes on 25 years of service, November–December 1859, Notebook 4, pp. 110–111. See also C. Eliot, *Eliot, Minister, Educator,* 60, 61; H. Eliot, "A Brief Autobiography," 24; Holt, *Eliot Conservative Radical,* 47–48. On Eliot's pride, Eliot to James Freeman Clarke, March 2, 1852, Eliot Papers, WU. On the church's being paid for, Eliot, entry for December 21, 1852, Notebook 4, p. 1; on the size of the resulting endowment, Holt, *Eliot Conservative Radical,* 48. Eliot said the second church cost $100,000 and notes it came readily from donations; Eliot, "A

Statement Relating to the Endowment of Washington University," May 11, 1864, p. 9. Declining a raise, Eliot to Seth A. Ranlett, January 8, 1853, Eliot Papers, WU. Eliot at times called Washington University a "thank-offering" for his congregation's fortunes; WU Board of Trustee Minutes, March 11, 1864 meeting, as quoted in Morrow, *Washington University*, 17.

17. *Missouri Republican*, June 21, 1857, as quoted in Primm, *Lion of the Valley*, 196; Walter D. Kamphoefner, "Learning from the 'Majority-Minority' City: Immigration in Nineteenth-Century St. Louis," in *St. Louis in the Century of Henry Shaw*, 91.

18. Eric Sandweiss, *St. Louis: The Evolution of an American Urban Landscape* (Philadelphia: Temple University Press, 2001), 66–69, 93; Faherty, "Nativism and Midwestern Education." On Lovejoy and the German response, Primm, *Lion of the Valley*, 175–178; *Missouri Republican*, December 12, 1840, p. 2. January 7, 1846, meeting, SLU Historical Records, Philalethic Society Minutes, 1836–1850, DOC REC 0001 0012 0029, 246; October 1, 1853, and September 24, 1854, meetings, Philalethic Society Minutes, 1850–1863, DOC REC 0001 0012 0031, n.p. Quote from October 8, 1854, meeting. On prosecutions, Henry Boernstein, *Memoirs of a Nobody: The Missouri Years of an Austrian Radical, 1849–1866*, trans. Steven Rowan (1881; St. Louis: Missouri Historical Society Press, 1997), 198–199.

19. Faherty, *Better the Dream*, 95–105; Faherty, "Nativism and Midwestern Education," 452–453; Primm, *Lion of the Valley*, 165. SLU Charter and Board of Direction Minutes, p. 44, as quoted in Faherty, *Better the Dream*, 82. Eliot, entry for February 22, 1853, Notebook 4, p. 9. After the nativist upsurge in 1854, the medical school decided to formally separate from St. Louis University—and, much later, joined Washington University, on the advice of joint board member James Yeatman and joint officer William Greenleaf Eliot.

20. Quotes from *St. Louis Leader*, March 1, 1853, and Eliot's response, as printed in *Missouri Republican* clipping, March 1853, Notebook 4, p. 14. Eliot read German thinkers in divinity school in the original; James Freeman Clarke, "Character and Work of William Greenleaf Eliot: A Discourse Delivered to the Church of the Disciples, Boston, Jan. 30, 1887," Eliot Papers, WU; C. Eliot, *Eliot, Minister, Educator*, 9–11.

21. *Charter and Constitution of the Washington Institute of St. Louis*, 9.

22. Frank Luther Mott, *American Journalism; a History, 1690–1960*, 3rd ed. (New York: Macmillan, 1962); on Fillmore, J. Thomas Scharf, *History of St. Louis City and County, from the Earliest Periods to the Present Day Including Biographical Sketches of Representative Men* (Philadelphia: L. H. Everts, 1883), 2:1835, as quoted in Faherty, *Better the Dream*, 105. For nativism in St. Louis, John C. Schneider, "Riot and Reaction in St. Louis, 1854–1856," *MHR* 68, no. 2 (1974): 171–185, and, with special reference to events at SLU, see Faherty, *Better the Dream*, 95–105. For an eastern perspective, Tyler Anbinder, *Nativism and Slavery: The Northern Know Nothings and the Politics of the 1850s* (New York: Oxford University Press, 1992); Ray Allen Billington,

The Protestant Crusade, 1800–1860; a Study of the Origins of American Nativism (New York: Macmillan, 1938).

23. *Charter and Constitution,* 5, 8; Eliot, "A Statement Relating to the Endowment of Washington University," May 11, 1864, p. 6; Eliot, "Inaugural Address [as Chancellor] before the Government and Alumni of Washington University," February 29, 1872, p. 8. See similar sentiments from Eliot and Treat at the inaugural; *Inauguration of Washington University,* 32, 46.

24. Eliot, March 2, 1853, Notebook 4, p. 11; entries for fall 1853, Notebook 4, p. 35, and Eliot, pp. 80–81; O'Connor, *Beginning a Great Work,* p. 6. Eliot later cited the State University experience as key to his insistence on nonpartisan and nonsectarian education; Eliot, outline of chancellor inaugural address, January 1872, Notebook 8, p. 22; C. Eliot, *Eliot, Minister, Educator,* 83.

25. Eliot, "A Statement Relating to the Endowment of Washington University," May 11, 1864, p. 18. Reverend Truman M. Post had formulated it similarly at the inaugural; *Inauguration of Washington University,* 40. For explicit description of Washington's values to Eliot, drawn from the Farewell Address, see *Inauguration of Washington University,* 46, and *Charter and Constitution,* 15–16. David Waldstreicher makes the important distinction between nonpartisanship and antipartisanship; the practice described here is a combination. Waldstreicher, *In the Midst of Perpetual Fetes,* 230–234. On the name committee, WU Board of Trustee Minutes, February 22, 1854, meeting, 1:5. On the "accident" of a name, Eliot, "A Statement Relating to the Endowment of Washington University," May 11, 1864, p. 18; Holt, *Eliot Conservative Radical,* 49. On the name controversy, Eliot, entry for March 3, 1855, and clipping, April 1855, Notebook 4, p. 61, 74; Morrow, *Washington University,* 3–4; James Thomas Craig, "Origin and History of the Collegiate Department of Washington University, 1853–1870" (master's thesis, Washington University, 1941); Holt, *Eliot Conservative Radical,* 49. On O'Fallon's gifts, Eliot, entry in fall 1853, Notebook 4, p. 35.

26. Eliot, outline of chancellor inaugural address, January 1872, Notebook 8, p. 22; Eliot, "Inaugural Address [as Chancellor] before the Government and Alumni of Washington University," February 29, 1872, p. 12.

27. For such exclusions in the name of universality, Dana D. Nelson, *National Manhood: Capitalist Citizenship and the Imagined Fraternity of White Men* (Durham, NC: Duke University Press, 1998).

28. James M. McPherson, *Battle Cry of Freedom: The Civil War Era* (New York: Oxford University Press, 1988), 121–125; David Morris Potter and Don Edward Fehrenbacher, *The Impending Crisis, 1848–1861* (New York: Harper & Row, 1976), 151–176; Gerteis, *Civil War St. Louis,* 59, 68.

29. Micajah Tarver, "Improvement of Western Rivers," *Western Journal* 6 (April 1851): 1 and 2, as quoted in Holly Zumwalt Taylor, "Neither North nor South: Sectionalism, St. Louis Politics, and the Coming of the Civil War, 1846–1861" (PhD diss., University of Texas at Austin, 2004), 238. See also *Missouri Democrat,* September 9

and 25, 1854, as quoted in Taylor, "Neither North nor South," 242 and 241. On Benton in 1854, Gerteis, *Civil War St. Louis,* 59; William Nisbet Chambers, *Old Bullion Benton, Senator from the New West: Thomas Hart Benton, 1782–1858* (Boston: Atlantic Monthly Press—Little, Brown, 1956), 398–406; William Montgomery Meigs, *The Life of Thomas Hart Benton* (Philadelphia: J. B. Lippincott Co., 1904), 425–433; Theodore Roosevelt, *Thomas Hart Benton* (Boston: Houghton, Mifflin & Co., 1887), 348–354; Elbert B. Smith, *Magnificent Missourian; the Life of Thomas Hart Benton* (Philadelphia: Lippincott, 1958), 294–299.

30. *Anzeiger des Westens* Extra, as reprinted from the *Anzeiger* of July 26, 1854, broadside, Thomas Hart Benton Campaign Handbill, 1854, WHMC-Columbia, C2842; April 24, 1854, meeting, SLU Historical Records, Philalethic Society Minutes, 1850–1863, DOC REC 0001 0012 0031, n.p. See also Benjamin C. Merkel, "The Slavery Issue and the Political Decline of Thomas Hart Benton, 1846–1856," *MHR* 38 (July 1944): 399–406.

31. Quote is G. W. Good to Col. F. Kennett, December 8, 1852, Kennett Family Papers, MHM, from Mark A. Neels, "The Crisis of the Foreign Element: Nativist Suppression of German Radicals in Antebellum St. Louis, 1848–1861," paper delivered at the Missouri Conference on History, Springfield, April 2009, pp. 5–6. Thanks to the author for making this paper available. On Thomas Dawes Eliot, James K. Hosmer, introduction to C. Eliot, *Eliot, Minister, Educator,* xvi; *Biographical Directory of the United States Congress, 1774–2005* (Washington, D.C.: U.S. Government Printing Office, 2005), http://bioguide.congress.gov, accessed January 2007. On Bates and Kennett, Norma Lois Peterson, *Freedom and Franchise; the Political Career of B. Gratz Brown* (Columbia: University of Missouri Press, 1965), 31–32; Boernstein, *Memoirs of a Nobody,* 177–185; Frank Towers, *The Urban South and the Coming of the Civil War* (Charlottesville: University of Virginia Press, 2004), 85. For an emphasis on the antislavery rather than nativist element of Know-Nothing politics, Marc Egnal, *Clash of Extremes: The Economic Origins of the Civil War* (New York: Hill & Wang, 2009), 212–217. This balance would lose the presidency for Bates in 1860; see Chapter 6.

32. Quote is David Rice Atchison, Platte City, to Samuel Treat, May 29, 1853, Samuel Treat Papers, MHM; see also *Anzeiger des Westens* Extra, as reprinted from the *Anzeiger* of July 26, 1854, broadside, Thomas Hart Benton Campaign Handbill, 1854, WHMC-Columbia. For the roots of the nativist violence in the 1852 elections— and the oft-overlooked fact that a German mob attempted to break up a Whig-Democrat unity meeting in the courthouse on March 27, 1852, triggering further electoral violence—see Neels, "The Crisis of the Foreign Element," pp. 6–9.

33. Quote from *Missouri Democrat,* August 11, 1854, as quoted in Taylor, "Neither North nor South," 213. On the early history of the newspaper and its connections to Benton, see Walter B. Stevens, *St. Louis, the Fourth City 1764–1909,* 3 vols. (St. Louis: S. J. Clarke, 1909), 1:863–864.

34. Jonathan A. Dougherty to Dear Sir, August 8, 1854, Thomas Hart Benton Collection, MHM, box 2, folder 1; Faherty, "Nativism and Midwestern Education," 456; Schneider, "Riot and Reaction"; Kamphoefner, "Learning from the 'Majority-Minority' City," 86–89; Primm, *Lion of the Valley,* 170–172; Faherty, *Better the Dream,* 103; Stevens, *St. Louis, the Fourth City,* 1:1072, 1075. On the location of Battle Row, Primm, *Lion of the Valley,* 173. Boernstein compares the riots across the 1852, 1854, and 1856 elections, at times transposing details; Boernstein, *Memoirs of a Nobody,* 177–182, 203–210. New state and city ordinances imposed a nighttime curfew for minors, prohibited the sale of alcohol on election day, and volunteer and regular policemen patrolled the streets in April 1855, when the next election was without incident. Editorial and Mayor John How's proclamation, *Missouri Republican,* April 3, 1855, in Eliot Notebook 4, p. 72.

35. The vote totals were Kennett 6,259; Benton 5,298; Trusten Polk, 378; Peterson, *Freedom and Franchise,* 32. Frank Towers describes the 1854 election as key to the collapse of the Whig Party and considers St. Louis specifically; Towers, *The Urban South,* 84–85, 95, 103, 108. For a national perspective, Potter and Fehrenbacher, *The Impending Crisis,* 249–250, and Anbinder, *Nativism and Slavery.*

36. William E. Gienapp, *The Origins of the Republican Party, 1852–1856* (New York: Oxford University Press, 1987).

37. Dougherty to Dear Sir, August 8, 1854, Thomas Hart Benton Collection, MHM; William Barclay Napton, *The Union on Trial: The Political Journals of Judge William Barclay Napton, 1829–1883,* ed. Christopher Phillips and Jason L. Pendleton (Columbia: University of Missouri Press, 2005), 132–133, 138; Chambers, *Old Bullion Benton,* 409–410; Meigs, *The Life of Thomas Hart Benton,* 414–415. On the school's progress, Morrow, *Washington University,* 32–33; for the beginning of the construction process, a receipt shows payment to George Small as architect for the Eliot Seminary, December 24, 1855, Reel 3, Eliot Papers, WU.

38. Discussing a building, SLML, Board of Direction Minutes, First Volume, p. 98; on canvassing and bonds, Board of Direction Minutes, First Volume, pp. 19, 432. For the mortgage, see the Mercantile Library Hall Company records, Record Group 2, as well as Board of Direction Minutes, Second Volume, pp. 96–99, and n.p., meeting January 28, 1868. The board of directors continued their innovative fund-raising by later urging stockholders to convert their stake to life memberships; see Board of Direction Minutes, Second Volume, n.p., meeting March 19, 1861. For details of the financing and bonds, Clarence E. Miller, "Forty Years of Long Ago: Early Annals of the Mercantile Library Association and Its Public Hall, 1846–1886" (SLML, 1935), typescript pp. 31, 34. On its completion, Board of Direction Minutes First Volume, October 3, 1854, meeting, p. 419; Miller, "Forty Years of Long Ago," typescript pp. 31–35. For the specifications of the halls, see William Curtis to S. Colton, Milwaukee, December 29, 1856, Letter Book 8, A-3–13, 117.

39. Eliot's request mentioned in October 3, 1854, meeting, SLML Board of Direction Minutes, First Volume, p. 419, and declined at the August 6, 1856, meeting, and

then approved, Board of Direction Minutes, Second Volume, August 11, 1856, meeting, p. 54; scholarship from Wayman Crow was accepted, Board of Direction Minutes, Second Volume, August 26, 1856, meeting, pp. 55–56. See also WU Board of Trustee Minutes, September 11, 1856, meeting, 1:46; Crow to Eliot, May 8, 1856, as recorded in WU Board of Trustee Minutes, September 11, 1856, 1:59–60. For correspondence on its establishment and early applicants, see Eliot to William M. Morrison, President, SLML, August 20, 1856; and others in Letter Book 2, A-3–6, pp. 344, 345, 346, 349, and 350. Lease was approved, SLML Board of Direction Minutes, Second Volume, September 2, 1856, meeting, 57. On professors lecturing, entry for February 15, 1855, Notebook 4, p. 51; *Missouri Republican,* December 4, 1854, Notebook 4, p. 48; Miller, "Forty Years of Long Ago," typescript p. 38. On classes meeting there, October 3, 1854, meeting, SLML Board of Direction Minutes, First Volume, p. 419; August 6 and 11, 1856, meetings, Board of Direction Minutes, Second Volume, pp. 53, 54. On membership agreement for stock, Agreement between SLML and WU, December 9, 1863, Mercantile Membership Correspondence, A-12–11. See also WU Board of Trustee Minutes, December 1, 1863, meeting, 1:172–173; *Eighteenth Annual Report of the Board of Directors of the Mercantile Library Association of St. Louis, Missouri* (St. Louis: George Knapp and Co., 1864), 15. For mercantile colleges linked to mercantile libraries, "especially in the West," see Allan Stanley Horlick, *Country Boys and Merchant Princes; the Social Control of Young Men in New York* (Lewisburg, Pa.: Bucknell University Press, 1975), 175–176. On the bust of Crow in the library, "Public Education: Commencement at Washington University," newspaper clipping, June 19, 1868, in the Chancellor's Scrapbooks, Scrapbook 1867–1877, WU; O'Connor, *Beginning a Great Work,* 10; WU Board of Trustee Minutes, June 19, 1868, meeting, 1:238.

40. Rev. Cornelius F. Smarius, SLU, to John T. Douglass and R. C. McAllister, Committee on Lectures, October 13, 1851; Smarius to Theodore Clark, Secretary, SLML, February 10, 1852; James Shannon, University of the State of Missouri, Columbia, to Sir, February 14, 1852; Letter Book 2, pp. 113, 133, 136; *Fifth Annual Report of the Board of Directors of the Mercantile Library Association of St. Louis, Missouri* (St. Louis: Chambers and Knapp, 1851), 15–17. The closeness of the board of directors with Reverend Eliot might explain why requests to him do not exist in letter form. On the recommendation, John B. Druyts, President, SLU, to Gentlemen, April 17, 1852, Letter Book 2, p. 144. Before the establishment of Washington University, Druyts refers to evening classes for clerks, on subjects from languages to practical skills. The student, Raymond Papin, a first cousin to the Chouteaus, is hired; April 11, 1852, and February 7, 1853, meetings, SLML Board of Direction Minutes, First Volume, 315, 361; Miller, "Forty Years of Long Ago," typescript p. 28. For the German report, *St. Louis Kaufmannischen Bibliothek-Vereins* (1853), SLML, A-17–1; for the gift, Henry Boernstein, *Anzeiger des Westens,* St. Louis, to SLML, November 1, 1853, and Boernstein to Curtis, November 11, 1853, Letter Book 2, pp. 209, 210.

41. Quotes from Thomas F. Meagher, New York, to John A. Douglass, October 20, 1852, Lecture Committee Letterbook, A-3–5, p. 57, and "One of your Friends," St. Louis, to Thomas F. Meagher, November 2, 1854, Lecture Committee Letterbook, A-3–5, 94. Original spelling and capitalization maintained. On the Smithsonian publications, Curtis to Spencer Baird, September 28, 1854, Letter Book 8, A-3–13, 46; see also Ashbury Dickens, Secretary of the U.S. Senate, to President, SLML, May 30, 1851, Letter Book 2, A-3–6, 98. For similar efforts by Hungarian revolutionary Louis Kossuth to appear outside of politics, Donald S. Spencer, *Louis Kossuth and Young America: A Study of Sectionalism and Foreign Policy 1848–1852* (Columbia: University of Missouri Press, 1977), 127.

42. Quotes from *Inauguration of Washington University,* 7, and *Inauguration of Washington University,* 61. (Philadelphia) *North American and United States Gazette,* May 4, 1857, no. 20,007, col. J, via Cengage. Comparisons to Harvard began in the founding address and continued regularly. *Charter and Constitution,* 13; see Morrow, *Washington University,* 25.

43. This is emblematic of the fantasy and denial often shaping St. Louis's "psychic history"; e-mail conversation with Nanora Sweet, June 12, 2006.

4 Antislavery Derailed

1. Thomas Hart Benton, speech to the National Railroad Convention, October 16, 1849, as reported in the *Missouri Republican,* October 18, 1849. Transcription provided by Bob Moore, JNEM. See Chapter 2.

2. "The Railway Disaster," *St. Louis Leader,* November 10, 1855; this and many of the newspaper accounts mentioned below are reproduced and transcribed in Timothy C. Klinger et al., "Union Pacific Railroad Gasconade River Crossing: Cultural Resources Documentation" (submitted to the Missouri Department of Natural Resources—Division of Historic Preservation, July 2002), a copy of which resides at the Gasconade County Historical Society, Hermann, Missouri. "Highly Interesting Incidents of the Gasconade Disaster from Jefferson City," *Daily Missouri Democrat,* November 5, 1855; Hannah Ramsay, Jefferson City, to Meredith T. Moore, November 3, 1855, Meredith T. Moore Papers, MHM, folder 2.

Hardly known today outside of central Missouri, the Gasconade disaster was the first serious railroad-bridge collapse in American history, killing thirty passengers and injuring more than a hundred. Scholars have mostly overlooked the Gasconade disaster and its wider significance; an exception is J. Christopher Schnell, "Chicago Versus St. Louis: A Reassessment of the Great Rivalry," *MHR* 71, no. 3 (1977): 245–265. The fullest account, though riddled with inaccuracies, is R. John Brockmann, *Twisted Rails, Sunken Ships: The Rhetoric of Nineteenth Century Steamboat and Railroad Accident Investigation Reports, 1833–1879* (Amityville, N.Y.: Baywood, 2005), 153–173. Among the many primary documents available, see especially Karl Roider, ed., "Eyewitness: Letters about the Gasconade Bridge Disaster," *Railroad History* 184 (Spring 2001): 62–65.

3. For the impractical nature of railroads in the nineteenth century, and their tendency to corruption, see Richard White, "Information, Markets, and Corruption: Transcontinental Railroads in the Gilded Age," *Journal of American History* 90, no. 1 (June 2003): 19–43, and White's forthcoming book on transcontinental railroads. On the difficulties of suboptimal operation, George Rogers Taylor and Irene D. Neu, *The American Railroad Network, 1861–1890* (Cambridge, Mass.: Harvard University Press, 1956).

4. For background information on all these men, see entries in the *Dictionary of Missouri Biography,* ed. Lawrence O. Christensen (Columbia: University of Missouri Press, 1999).

5. James Neal Primm, *Economic Policy in the Development of a Western State, Missouri, 1820–1860* (Cambridge, Mass.: Harvard University Press, 1954), 77–78; Paul W. Gates, "The Railroads of Missouri, 1850–1870," *MHR* 28, no. 2 (January 1932): 128; Schnell, "Chicago Versus St. Louis," esp. pp. 252–256.

6. Schnell, "Chicago Versus St. Louis," 258; James Neal Primm, "The Economy of Nineteenth-Century St. Louis," in *St. Louis in the Century of Henry Shaw: A View Beyond the Garden Wall,* ed. Eric Sandweiss (Columbia: University of Missouri Press, 2003), 104, 117.

7. "St. Louis and the Extension of Slavery," *Boston Daily Atlas,* October 20, 1854, no. 95, col. H, reprinted from the *St. Louis Democrat,* via Cengage, "complee" corrected to "complete." For the reasons for anti-railroad sentiment among slaveholders, see Orville Vernon Burton, *The Age of Lincoln* (New York: Hill & Wang, 2007), 24.

8. Sextus Shearer, San Francisco, to James Bissell, St. Louis, October 15, 1854, Daniel Bissell Papers, MHM.

9. William Walker, Wyandott, to Sir [David Rice Atchison], July 6, 1854, and Atchison, Platte County, to [Jefferson] Davis, September 24, 1854, both in David Rice Atchison Papers, WHMC-Columbia, C71, folder 4. See Kenneth H. Winn, "The Missouri Context of Antebellum Mormonism: Mormonism and Its Legacy of Violence," in *The Missouri Mormon Experience,* ed. Thomas M. Spencer (Columbia: University of Missouri Press, 2010), 19–26.

10. "Dr. Aristides Rodrigue: Passing through Cambria County on the Way to 'Bloody Kansas,'" *Cambria County Heritage* 26, no. 2 (Spring 2006), www.cambria countyhistorical.com, accessed May 2007; Massachusetts Emigrant Aid Company, *Nebraska and Kansas. Report of the Committee of the Massachusetts Emigrant Aid Company, with the Act of Incorporation, and Other Documents.* (Boston: For the Massachusetts Emigrant Aid Co., 1854), 18.

11. Andrew Hurley, "On the Waterfront: Railroads and Real Estate in Antebellum St. Louis." *Gateway Heritage* 13, no. 4 (1993): 4–17. For a brief discussion of the political roadblocks, see also William Cronon, *Nature's Metropolis: Chicago and the*

Great West (New York: W. W. Norton, 1991), 300. For Davis's antipathy toward internal improvements generally, Marc Egnal, *Clash of Extremes: The Economic Origins of the Civil War* (New York: Hill & Wang, 2009), 111.

12. U.S. Army Corps of Topographical Engineers, *U.S. Pacific Railroad Exploration and Surveys* (1855); quote from John Milton Bigelow, Lancaster, Ohio, to Engelmann, September 21, 1855, George Engelmann Papers, Missouri Botanical Garden Archives; Natural Resource Conservation Service, "Plants Profile: Echinocereus Viridiflorus Engelm. Var. Davisii (Davis' Hedgehog Cactus)," U.S. Department of Agriculture, http://plants.usda.gov, accessed May 2006. Thanks to Andrew Colligan for helping to confirm this connection.

13. Letters between Jefferson Davis, War Department, and Thomas L. O'Sullivan, consulting engineer, St. Louis and Iron Mountain Rail Road Company, September 20, October 13 and 20, 1853; held in Records of the War Department, Office of the Secretary, Letters Sent, Military Book 35, marked 13–20, 54–57, and 63 by the National Archives and Records Service, in copies held at SLPL. Quotes are from sheet marked 20; then Mayor John How, G. Taylor, President of the Board of Alderman and Samuel Simmons, Chairman of the Board of Delegates, St. Louis, to President Franklin Pierce, marked 82; and also Missouri General Assembly and C. C. Ziegler, *Report of the Committee to Examine into and Report Upon the Condition of the Various Railroad Companies in the State of Missouri* (Jefferson City: J. Lusk, public printer, 1855), 112, as cited in Hurley, "On the Waterfront," 61–63.

14. *Missouri Democrat,* February 12, 1855, p. 2, and September 21, 1854, as quoted in Holly Zumwalt Taylor, "Neither North nor South: Sectionalism, St. Louis Politics, and the Coming of the Civil War, 1846–1861" (PhD diss., University of Texas at Austin, 2004), 225.

15. John Locke Hardeman, Saline Co., to George R. Smith, June 10, 1855, George R. Smith Papers, MHM. See William Earl Parrish, *David Rice Atchison of Missouri, Border Politician* (Columbia: University of Missouri Press, 1961); Christopher Phillips, *Missouri's Confederate: Claiborne Fox Jackson and the Creation of Southern Identity in the Border West* (Columbia: University of Missouri Press, 2000).

16. Beecher's congregation provided embossed Bibles as well as matching the gift of twenty-five rifles. Debby Applegate, *The Most Famous Man in America: The Biography of Henry Ward Beecher* (New York: Doubleday, 2006), 281–282; Louis S. Gerteis, *Civil War St. Louis* (Lawrence: University Press of Kansas, 2001), 42. For recent overviews and interpretations, see Nicole Etcheson, *Bleeding Kansas: Contested Liberty in the Civil War Era* (Lawrence: University Press of Kansas, 2004), and Jeremy Neely, *The Border between Them: Violence and Reconciliation on the Kansas-Missouri Line* (Columbia: University of Missouri Press, 2007). On Sumner, Visitor Register 1846–1856, SLML, M-117, A-13–1, n.p.

17. Louisa B. Hull, Monticello Seminary, Godfrey, Illinois, to uncle, August 31, 1855, Hull Family Papers, MHM.

18. *Missouri Republican,* November 2, 1855.

19. Excursion train ticket, November 1, 1855, Railroads Collection, MHM; "The Railway Disaster," *St. Louis Leader,* November 10, 1855. *Anzeiger* editor Heinrich Boernstein also declined, staying home in protest, he said later, because he felt too few Germans had been invited due to the influence of the Know-Nothing city government. Henry Boernstein, *Memoirs of a Nobody: The Missouri Years of an Austrian Radical, 1849–1866,* trans. Steven Rowan (1881; St. Louis: Missouri Historical Society Press, 1997), 209.

20. *Report of the Committee Appointed by the Directors of the Pacific Railroad to Investigate the Cause of the Accident at Gasconade Bridge* (St. Louis: Missouri Republican Book and Job Office, 1855), 3, 14–15, 5, as quoted in Brockmann, *Twisted Rails,* 158; Francis T. Bryan, St. Louis, to Mary Bryan Pettigrew, Raleigh, North Carolina, November 3, 1855, P. Taylor Bryan Papers, MHM; "Further Particulars," *Daily Missouri Democrat,* November 2, 1855. Quotes from "The Bridges on the Pacific Railroad," *Daily Missouri Democrat,* November 6, 1855.

21. "Further Particulars," *Daily Missouri Democrat,* November 2, 1855.

22. "Most Disastrous Accident," *Missouri Republican,* November 2, 1855, and "The Disaster," *Missouri Republican,* November 3, 1855; Bryan to Pettigrew, November 3, 1855, P. Taylor Bryan Papers. Quotes from the eyewitness account from the *St. Louis Daily Evening News,* reprinted in the *St. Louis Leader* and the November 14, 1855, *Bangor* (Maine) *Daily Whig & Courier,* no. 116, col B, via Cengage, accessed November 2006; and "Further Particulars," *Daily Missouri Democrat,* November 2, 1855.

23. *St. Louis Leader,* November 3, 1855; "Most Disastrous Accident," *Missouri Republican,* November 2, 1855; eyewitness account from Mr. Pollard, editor of *Weekly Mirror* and survivor of the crash, as quoted in the *St. Louis Leader,* November 10, 1855; "The Great Catastrophe," *Daily Missouri Democrat,* November 3, 1855, and "The Disaster," *Missouri Republican,* November 3, 1855.

24. "The Great Catastrophe," *Daily Missouri Democrat,* November 3, 1855; and "The Disaster," *Missouri Republican,* November 3, 1855; Howard Wight Marshall and James W. Goodrich, *German-American Experience in Missouri: Essays in Commemoration of the Tricentennial of German Immigration to America, 1683–1983* (Columbia: Missouri Cultural Heritage Center, 1986); Inquest, November 2, 1855, Gasconade County Historical Society.

25. Summons and Inquest, November 2, 1855, Gasconade County Historical Society. All spellings and German in original. Obituaries in "The Disaster," *Missouri Republican,* November 3, 1855; *Daily Missouri Democrat,* November 6, 1855. On O'Sullivan, quote from Bryan to Pettigrew, November 3, 1855, P. Taylor Bryan Papers.

26. Quotes from *Daily Missouri Democrat,* November 5, 1855; *Daily Cleveland Herald,* November 9, 1855, no. 267, col. B, via Cengage, accessed November 2006; On Abeles, Boernstein, *Memoirs of a Nobody,* 124 and 209.

27. Isabella Wells was just a few months pregnant with Rolla Wells, the future railroad executive, mayor, and Federal Reserve Bank chair, born June 1, 1856. Ramsay to Moore, November 3, 1855, Meredith T. Moore Papers; "The List of Killed and Wounded," *Daily Missouri Democrat,* November 5, 1855; Deposition transcript, signed by Erastus Wells, Gasconade County Historical Society, also partially transcribed in Brockmann, *Twisted Rails,* 161. See also survivor accounts in "Gasconade Horror Almost a Parallel to the Ashtabula Calamity," *St. Louis Globe-Democrat,* January 4, 1877, p. 4, no. 229, col. E, via Cengage, accessed November 2006.

28. James Neal Primm, *Lion of the Valley: St. Louis, Missouri, 1764–1980,* 3rd ed. (St. Louis: Missouri Historical Society Press, 1998), 209; "The Great Catastrophe," "The Latest," and "A Third Bridge Gone," *Daily Missouri Democrat,* November 3 and 5, 1855; "Postscript—Arrival of the Train," *Missouri Republican,* November 3, 1855.

29. Quotes from "The Great Catastrophe," *Daily Missouri Democrat,* November 3, 1855, and "The List of Killed and Wounded," *Daily Missouri Democrat,* November 5, 1855. For a less complete list, but with further details on some victims, see "Most Disastrous Accident," *Missouri Republican,* November 2, 1855.

30. W. S. Eager, St. Louis, to Lizzie W. Marsh, Batavia, Illinois, "Monday evening before ten," [November 5,] 1855, held privately by Karl Roider. Transcribed in Roider, ed., "Eyewitness," 65. Post, account in *New York Intelligencer,* November 3, 1855, reprinted in Truman Augustus Post, *Truman Marcellus Post, D.D., a Biography, Personal and Literary* (Boston and Chicago: Congregational Sunday-School and Publishing Society, 1891), 225.

31. "The Great Catastrophe," *Daily Missouri Democrat,* November 3, 1855;; Lecture committee report, SLML, Board of Direction Minutes, Second Volume, n.p., meeting January 7, 1856; WU Board of Trustees Minutes, February 22, 1856, meeting, p. 23; William Wall & Sons, New York, to William C. Hull, St. Louis, November 7, 1855, and William P. Cowles, New York, to Hull, St. Louis, November 6, 1855, Hull Family Papers; "Adjourned Meeting of the St. Louis Bar," *Daily Missouri Democrat,* November 6, 1855. See also Roider, ed., "Eyewitness," 62. Quote from "Meeting of the Board of Directors of the Pacific Railroad," *Daily Missouri Democrat,* November 6, 1855.

32. King's proclamation appears alongside "Mourning for the Dead," *Daily Missouri Democrat,* November 5, 1855; *St. Louis Leader,* November 10, 1855. Quotes from "Mourning for the Dead," *Daily Missouri Democrat,* November 5, 1855, and "The Funeral Ceremonies," *Daily Missouri Democrat,* November 6, 1855.

33. *Daily Cleveland Herald,* November 12, 1855, no. 269, col. D, via Cengage; Hudson Bridge to the *St. Louis Intelligencer,* as reprinted in the *Daily Cleveland Herald,* November 13, 1855, no. 270, col. C; "The Gasconade Bridge," (Philadelphia) *North American and United States Gazette,* November 10, 1855; no. 19,554, col. J, via Cengage, accessed November 2006; *Report . . . Accident at Gasconade Bridge,* 14, 760, as quoted in Brockmann, *Twisted Rails,* 164–167. "The Bridges on the Pacific Railroad," *Daily*

Missouri Democrat, November 6, 1855; "Meeting of the Board of Directors of the Pacific Railroad," *Daily Missouri Democrat,* November 6, 1855.

34. "The Railway Disaster," *St. Louis Leader,* November 10, 1855, p. 9; Brockmann, *Twisted Rails,* 164.

35. *St. Louis Leader,* November 10. 1855.

36. Quotes from B. Hornsay, Big Creek, Kansas, to George R. Smith, December 11, 1855, George R. Smith Papers; Charles Sumner, "The Crime against Kansas," May 19–20, 1856, *Congressional Globe* 34th Cong., 1st sess., Appendix, 530. See David Morris Potter and Don Edward Fehrenbacher, *The Impending Crisis, 1848–1861* (New York: Harper & Row, 1976), 208; William Barclay Napton, *The Union on Trial: The Political Journals of Judge William Barclay Napton, 1829–1883,* ed. Christopher Phillips and Jason L. Pendleton (Columbia: University of Missouri Press, 2005), 149.

37. More people died in the Gasconade River disaster than from any single event in Kansas. Historians have raised the question of whether the situation in Kansas benefited from manufactured hype when compared to the number of homicides in nativist riots or the deaths of slaves fighting more directly for their freedom. See for example Robert Taft, "Review of Bleeding Kansas by Alice Nichols," *Mississippi Valley Historical Review* 41, no. 3 (December 1954): 517–519, and Dale E. Watts, "How Bloody Was Bleeding Kansas?: Political Killings in Kansas Territory, 1854–1861," *Kansas History* 18 (Summer 1995): 116–129, who counts a total of fifty-six killed. As Potter asserted, "For purposes of understanding what took place in the nation, it is possibly less important to know what happened in Kansas than to know what the American public thought was happening in Kansas." Potter and Fehrenbacher, *The Impending Crisis,* 217. Also quoted in Taylor, "Neither North nor South," 228. For the events mentioned, David S. Reynolds, *John Brown, Abolitionist: The Man Who Killed Slavery, Sparked the Civil War, and Seeded Civil Rights* (New York: Knopf, 2005), 165–180; James M. McPherson, *Battle Cry of Freedom: The Civil War Era* (New York: Oxford University Press, 1988), 150–152; Potter and Fehrenbacher, *The Impending Crisis,* 209–211 and 220–221. On Sumner and this signal moment, David Herbert Donald, *Charles Sumner and the Coming of the Civil War* (New York: Knopf, 1960); William E. Gienapp, "The Crime against Sumner: The Caning of Charles Sumner and the Rise of the Republican Party," *Civil War History* 25 (September 1979): 218–245; Manisha Sinha, "The Caning of Charles Sumner: Slavery, Race, and Ideology in the Age of the Civil War," *Journal of the Early Republic* 23, no. 2 (2003): 233–262.

38. For a similar reflection on the meaning of Sumner's vacant chair, see James McPherson and James Hogue, *Ordeal by Fire: The Civil War and Reconstruction,* 4th ed. (New York: McGraw-Hill, 2009), 104.

39. *St. Louis Leader,* December 22, 1855, p. 7; *North American and United States Gazette,* November 17, 1855, no. 19,560, col. A, via Cengage, accessed November 2006. For the economic evidence of this loss and the Hannibal and St. Joseph Railroad, Cronon, *Nature's Metropolis,* 300; see also Timothy R. Mahoney, *River Towns in the*

Great West: The Structure of Provincial Urbanization in the American Midwest, 1820–1870 (New York: Cambridge University Press, 1990), 205, 234, and 248.

40. On Davis's objections, "Rock Island Bridge," *Boston Daily Atlas,* February 1, 1855, no. 182, col. H, via Cengage, accessed November 2006. For the history of the Rock Island Bridge, Ira Oliver Nothstein, "Rock Island Arsenal: Its History and Development," (Rock Island, Ill.: Rock Island Arsenal Museum, 1937), 66–67; Thomas J. Slattery, "An Illustrated History of the Rock Island Arsenal and Arsenal Island" (Rock Island, Ill.: Historical Office, U.S. Army Armament, Munitions and Chemical Command, 1990), 1:60–62. Chicago already had railroad connections to Alton (1853) and Rock Island (1854) before the Rock Island Bridge was completed, but the symbolism of this feat helped reorient regional patterns; Cronon, *Nature's Metropolis,* 295–300. On the resulting St. Louis setback, Maury Klein, "Dreams of Fields: St. Louis and the Pacific Railroad," *SLML Fellowship Reports* 2003, p. 10. See "Completion of the Great Bridge at Rock Island," *Daily Cleveland Herald,* April 14, 1856, no. 89, col. D, and *Bangor Daily Whig & Courier,* April 24, 1856, no. 253, col. A, via Cengage, accessed November 2006.

41. *Missouri Democrat,* May 7, 1856; "Rock Island Bridge," *Daily Missouri Republican,* November 2, 1858, no. 252, col. C, via Cengage, accessed November 2006; Slattery, "An Illustrated History of the Rock Island Arsenal," 1:65–66; Steven J. Keillor, *Grand Excursion: Antebellum America Discovers the Upper Mississippi* (Afton, Minn.: Afton Historical Society Press, 2004); Curtis C. Roseman and Elizabeth M. Roseman, *Grand Excursions on the Upper Mississippi River: Places, Landscapes, and Regional Identity after 1854* (Iowa City: University of Iowa Press, 2004). Thanks again to the Rosemans for all their help during my research in the Quad Cities. On the arson attempt, "The Rock Island Bridge Case," *Milwaukee Daily Sentinel,* December 19, 1860, no. 287, col. A, via Cengage, accessed November 2006.

42. J. D. F., "The Gasconade," *St. Louis Leader,* November 17, 1855; "Gasconade Horror Almost a Parallel"; Joseph Keppler, "They Both Break their Necks" and "Starting Westward," *Die Vehme* 23 (January 29, 1870) and 43 (June 18, 1870).

43. Bonnie Stepenoff, "Kate Chopin," in *Dictionary of Missouri Biography,* 165; Chopin's story often appears under her revised title, "The Story of an Hour"; Kate Chopin and Per Seyersted, *The Complete Works of Kate Chopin* (Baton Rouge: Louisiana State University Press, 1970), 352–354.

44. Benjamin Gratz Brown, *Speech of the Hon. B. Gratz Brown, of St. Louis, on the Subject of Gradual Emancipation in Missouri* (St. Louis: Missouri Democrat Book and Job Office, 1857), 18. See mention in Frank Towers, *The Urban South and the Coming of the Civil War* (Charlottesville: University of Virginia Press, 2004), 143–144.

5 The Limits of Dred Scott's Emancipation

1. Telegraph lines reached from the East Coast to St. Louis by the end of 1852; see John E. Sunder, "St. Louis and the Early Telegraph, 1847–1857," *MHR* 50, no. 3

(April 1956): 248–258. For an overview of the decision, Paul Finkelman, "The Dred Scott Case, Slavery and the Politics of Law," *Hamline Law Review* 20 (Fall 1996): 1–42. For a similar opening scene, Adam Arenson, "Dred Scott vs. the *Dred Scott Case:* History and Memory of a Signal Moment in American Slavery, 1857–2007," in *The Dred Scott Case: Historical and Contemporary Perspectives on Race and Law,* ed. Paul Finkelman, David Konig, and Christopher Bracey (Athens: Ohio University Press, 2010), 25.

2. "The Dred Scott Case," *New York Herald,* March 9, 1857, p. 1. Non-Missouri newspapers throughout this chapter via Cengage, accessed January 2007. Quotes are from the newspaper transcript, not the later revised and printed version of Taney's decision. For a discussion of the differences, Walter Ehrlich, *They Have No Rights: Dred Scott's Struggle for Freedom* (Westport, Conn.: Greenwood Press, 1979), 137–143 and notes.

3. The newest work addresses these problems; Arenson, "Dred Scott vs. the *Dred Scott Case*"; and Lea VanderVelde, *Mrs. Dred Scott: A Life on Slavery's Frontier* (New York: Oxford University Press, 2009). See also Ehrlich, *They Have No Rights;* Don Edward Fehrenbacher, *The Dred Scott Case, Its Significance in American Law and Politics* (New York: Oxford University Press, 1978); Louis S. Gerteis, *Civil War St. Louis* (Lawrence: University Press of Kansas, 2001), 17–29, 60–64; Lea VanderVelde and Sandhya Subramanian, "Mrs. Dred Scott," *Yale Law Journal* 106, no. 4 (January 1997): 1033–1122; Barbara Bennett Woodhouse, "Dred Scott's Daughters: Nineteenth Century Urban Girls at the Intersection of Race and Patriarchy," *Buffalo Law Review* 48 (Fall 2000): 669–701.

4. For slaves and free blacks in St. Louis generally, see Donnie Duglie Bellamy, "Slavery, Emancipation, and Racism in Missouri 1850–1865" (PhD diss., University of Missouri, 1971); Donnie Duglie Bellamy, "The Education of Blacks in Missouri Prior to 1861," *Journal of Negro History* 59, no. 2 (April 1974): 143–157; Judy Day and M. James Kedro, "Free Blacks in St. Louis: Antebellum Conditions, Emancipation, and the Postwar Era," *Missouri Historical Society Bulletin* 30, no. 2 (1974): 117–135; Lloyd A. Hunter, "Slavery in St. Louis 1804–1860," *Missouri Historical Society Bulletin* 30, no. 4 (1974): 233–265; Harrison Anthony Trexler, *Slavery in Missouri, 1804–1865* (Baltimore: Johns Hopkins University Press, 1914); and Maximilian Reichard, "Black and White on the Urban Frontier: The St. Louis Community in Transition, 1800–1830," *Missouri Historical Society Bulletin* 33, no. 1 (October 1976): 3–17. For specific cases of black semi-independence through the rivers, Ira Berlin, *Slaves without Masters: The Free Negro in the Antebellum South* (New York: Pantheon Books, 1975); Thomas C. Buchanan, *Black Life on the Mississippi: Slaves, Free Blacks, and the Western Steamboat World* (Chapel Hill: University of North Carolina Press, 2004); Frank Towers, *The Urban South and the Coming of the Civil War* (Charlottesville: University of Virginia Press, 2004).

5. This chapter must be different than others because there are fewer slave voices recorded in the archives; for some reflections on the topic, see James Oliver Horton

and Lois E. Horton, *Slavery and Public History: The Tough Stuff of American Memory* (New York: New Press, distributed by W. W. Norton, 2006); Walter Johnson, *Soul by Soul: Life inside the Antebellum Slave Market* (Cambridge, Mass.: Harvard University Press, 1999), 8–53. For marvelous examples of those reconstructions, Ruth Ann (Abels) Hager, *Dred and Harriet Scott: Their Family Story* (St. Louis: St. Louis County Library, 2010), and VanderVelde, *Mrs. Dred Scott.*

6. David Thomas Konig, "The Long Road to Dred Scott: Personhood and the Rule of Law in the Trial Court Records of St. Louis Slave Freedom Suits," *University of Missouri–Kansas City Law Review* 45, no. 1 (Fall 2006): 43–50.

7. George Byron Merrick, *Old Times on the Upper Mississippi: The Recollections of a Steamboat Pilot from 1854 to 1863* (Cleveland: A. H. Clark Co., 1909), 64. All but last line quoted in Hunter, "Slavery in St. Louis," 234. On the Chouteaus, VanderVelde, *Mrs. Dred Scott,* 133, 191–196. Thomas T. Pitts to James Tower Sweringen, December 20, 1856, Ruth Ferris Collection, Herman T. Pott National Inland Waterways Library, SLML. Thanks to Bette Gorden for bringing these letters to my attention. For a consideration of the pain hiding behind brief mentions of enslaved women, see Wendy Warren, "'The Cause of Her Grief': The Rape of a Slavewoman in Early New England," *Journal of American History* 93, no. 4 (March 2007): 1031–1049. For the internal slave trade, Ira Berlin, *Generations of Captivity: A History of African-American Slaves* (Cambridge, Mass.: Belknap Press of Harvard University Press, 2003), Chapter 4.

8. William Wells Brown, *Narrative of William W. Brown, a Fugitive Slave— Written by Himself* (Boston: Anti-Slavery Office, 1847), 26, 28–29. Eliot confirmed Harney's actions: William Greenleaf Eliot, *The Story of Archer Alexander from Slavery to Freedom March 30, 1863* (Boston: Cupples Upham & Co., 1885), 91–92.

9. J. C. Wild and Lewis Foulk Thomas, *The Valley of the Mississippi Illustrated in a Series of Views,* 1948 reprint ed. (St. Louis: J. Garnier, 1841–1842), 118–119 (italicized in original); Abraham Lincoln, "The Perpetuation of Our Political Institutions: Address before the Young Men's Lyceum of Springfield, Illinois, January 27, 1838," in *Collected Works. The Abraham Lincoln Association, Springfield, Illinois,* ed. Roy P. Basler (New Brunswick, N.J.: Rutgers University Press, 1953), 1: 110. See Daniel A. Graff, "The Lynching of Francis McIntosh and the Boundaries of Labor Solidarity in 1830s St. Louis," conference paper, Western History Association Annual Meeting, St. Louis, 2006, and David W. Blight, "The Martyrdom of Elijah P. Lovejoy," *American History Illustrated* 12, no. 7 (1977): 20–27.

10. The tree where McIntosh was hanged became a community landmark; Gerteis, *Civil War St. Louis,* 30–32, 121–129; VanderVelde, *Mrs. Dred Scott,* 129–132. The 1843 ordinance is mentioned in Frances Hurd Stadler, *St. Louis Day by Day* (St. Louis: Patrice Press, 1989), 43–44. Anecdote from John O'Hanlon, *Life and Scenery in Missouri: Reminiscences of a Missionary Priest* (Dublin: J. Duffy & Co., 1890), as reprinted in "The Light Fingered Gentry," *Missouri Historical Society Bulletin* 6, no. 1 (October 1949): 43.

11. For the newest and most thorough reconstruction of family information, see Hager, *Dred and Harriet Scott*. Many have connected the name of Dred Scott to General Winfield Scott's successes in Mexico: Fehrenbacher, *The Dred Scott Case*, 240, 652n2. For more recent and persuasive research suggesting Dred is a shortened version of Etheldred, a family name among the Blow family, VanderVelde, *Mrs. Dred Scott*, 197–198, 384n44,45. See also John Albury Bryan, "The Blow Family and Their Slave Dred Scott—Part One," *Missouri Historical Society Bulletin* 4 (July 1948): 223–231; John Albury Bryan, "The Blow Family and Their Slave Dred Scott—Part Two," *Missouri Historical Society Bulletin* 5 (October 1948): 19–33. For a discussion of the Rock Island railroad bridge, see Chapter 4.

12. Hager, *Dred and Harriet Scott*, 8–11. See also VanderVelde, *Mrs. Dred Scott*, esp. pp. 134–136.

13. Hager, *Dred and Harriet Scott*, 13–14; "The Original Dred Scott a Resident of St. Louis—a Sketch of His History," *St. Louis [Daily Evening] News*, April 3, 1857; "Selections from the Westminster Review: Manifest Destiny of the American Union," *The Liberator*, November 6, 1857. The frequency of emancipations and freedom bonds in St. Louis peaks in 1847, when the fighting was fiercest, but emancipations do show an upward trend in the few years before as well. My analysis of this data is ongoing; a first presentation was Adam Arenson, "The Local Impact of the *Dred Scott Case*: 1857–2007," paper presented at "The *Dred Scott Case* and Its Legacy: Race, Law, and Equality" conference, Washington University School of Law, St. Louis, March 2007. The underlying data is now available at www.nps.gov/jeff/historyculture, accessed October 2008.

14. Blow sisters married Joseph Charless Jr. and Charles Drake, and the Blow men also married into influential local families. Hager, *Dred and Harriet Scott*, 7; Ehrlich, *They Have No Rights*, 10–11; VanderVelde, *Mrs. Dred Scott*, 249–254, 274.

15. *Scott v. Emerson*, 15 Mo. 576 (1852) (majority opinion), 11–12. On appeal to the Missouri Supreme Court, the parties agreed that only the case of Dred Scott would be considered, with the decision considered binding on Harriet's case as well—despite the different basis for her claims. For Napton and judicial elections, see Christopher Phillips, introduction to William Barclay Napton, *The Union on Trial: The Political Journals of Judge William Barclay Napton, 1829–1883*, ed. Christopher Phillips and Jason L. Pendleton (Columbia: University of Missouri Press, 2005), 44–46, 49, and Napton, entry for June 20, 1857, p. 182.

16. Hager, *Dred and Harriet Scott*, 29–36. On Chaffee, see Ehrlich, *They Have No Rights*, 55–56, 180; Fehrenbacher, *The Dred Scott Case*, 274, 659n21. Eliza Irene Sanford Emerson Chaffee's marriage left her with no legal standing; see Lea VanderVelde, "The Legal Ways of Seduction," *Stanford Law Review* 48 (1996): 876–883, as cited in VanderVelde and Subramanian, "Mrs. Dred Scott," 1041. Even more complex became the question of who actually owned the Scotts; Hager, *Dred and Harriet Scott*, 35; Ehrlich, *They Have No Rights*, 75–77; Fehrenbacher, *The Dred Scott Case*, 270–276, VanderVelde, *Mrs. Dred Scott*, 229.

17. J. Orville Spreen, photographs of Dred Scott case historical markers, 486.2862–486.2871, 1938–1941, box 58, J. Orville Spreen Papers, WHMC-St. Louis. On refiling in federal court, Ehrlich, *They Have No Rights*, 73–82; Fehrenbacher, *The Dred Scott Case*, 267–283. For the close ties between Sanford and his Chouteau in-laws, VanderVelde, *Mrs. Dred Scott*, 189–191. For earlier freedom suits involving the Chouteaus, Hunter, "Slavery in St. Louis," 263–264; Konig, "The Long Road to Dred Scott," 61n42; VanderVelde, *Mrs. Dred Scott*, 133, 191–196; Hager, *Dred and Harriet Scott*, 22–23.

18. Dred Scott suffered so serious illness in the winter of 1856 that he was expected to die; VanderVelde, *Mrs. Dred Scott*, 307. "Curious Slave Case," *Frederick Douglass' Paper*, July 20, 1855, no. 31, col. B, reprinted from *St. Louis Democrat*, via Cengage, accessed November 2006. On Harriet Scott and her daughters, the most compelling arguments are made in Hager, *Dred and Harriet Scott*, esp. pp. 25–26. See also Martha Saxton, *Being Good: Women's Moral Values in Early America* (New York: Hill & Wang, 2003), 23–24; VanderVelde and Subramanian, "Mrs. Dred Scott"; VanderVelde, *Mrs. Dred Scott;* Woodhouse, "Dred Scott's Daughters." For the independence of laundresses, before and after the Civil War, Tera W. Hunter, *To 'Joy My Freedom: Southern Black Women's Lives and Labors after the Civil War* (Cambridge, Mass.: Harvard University Press, 1997). For the sale of childbearing female slaves in St. Louis, "The Slave Sale in St. Louis," *The Liberator*, December 10, 1858. Calculations over the daughters also mentioned in Adam Arenson, "Freeing Dred Scott: St. Louis Confronts an Icon of Slavery, 1857–2007," *Common-place* 8, no. 3 (April 2008), www.common-place.org, accessed April 2008. Reports of the daughters in Canada appear in "Selections from the Westminster Review" and "The Original Dred Scott." On Canada as unlikely, Vandervelde, *Mrs. Dred Scott*, 230, 322, and notes.

19. For a recent overview, VanderVelde, *Mrs. Dred Scott*, 305–219. Ironically, Henry Geyer had been one of the plaintiff's lawyers in the *Winny v. Whitesides* precedent-setting case, another example of shifting politics. Konig, "The Long Road to Dred Scott," 72.

20. *New York Herald*, January 1, 1857, col. F, p. 4. "Tertoriries" corrected. "The Dred Scott Case at Washington," *New York Herald*, January 5, 1857, p. 4; col. A. Both were widely reprinted and discussed. Napton, *The Union on Trial*, 179, entry for February 12, 1857; see also Christopher Phillips, *Missouri's Confederate: Claiborne Fox Jackson and the Creation of Southern Identity in the Border West* (Columbia: University of Missouri Press, 2000), 232–233. On the death of Justice Daniel's wife, *Cincinnati Enquirer*, reprinted in the *Charleston Mercury*, February 23, 1857, no. 9856, col. C.

21. B. Gratz Brown to George R. Smith, March 3, 1857, George R. Smith Papers, MHM. For Blair, free labor ideology, and the evolution of the Republican Party in slave-state cities, see Marc Egnal, *Clash of Extremes: The Economic Origins of the Civil War* (New York: Hill & Wang, 2009), 299; Towers, *The Urban South*, esp. pp. 109–148; and also Eric Foner, *Free Soil, Free Labor, Free Men: The Ideology of the Republican*

Party before the Civil War with a New Introductory Essay (New York: Oxford University Press, 1970; 1995 reprint).

22. *Westliche Post* editorial statement in premiere edition, September 27, 1857, as translated in Steven W. Rowan and James Neal Primm, *Germans for a Free Missouri: Translations from the St. Louis Radical Press, 1857–1862* (Columbia: University of Missouri Press, 1983), 50–51; "A Fire-Eater's Meditations on the St. Louis Emancipation Victory," *Richmond South,* April 11, 1857.

23. Kris Zapalac is completing a study of Meachum; see also VanderVelde, *Mrs. Dred Scott,* 224–230 and notes; John Richard Anderson, *Sermon on the Life, Character, and Death of Rev. John B. Meachum, Late Pastor of the First African Baptist Church, Saint Louis, Mo.* (Saint Louis: Charless, 1854). The story of the floating school first appears in twentieth-century sources; see for example Christopher K. Hays, "John Berry Meachum," in *Dictionary of Missouri Biography,* 543–544. Thanks to Louis Gerteis and Ken Winn for raising doubts about it with me. Blacks freed by blacks appear asterisked in the list of emancipations registered in the St. Louis Circuit Court, 1817–1865, available online, www.nps.gov/jeff/historyculture, accessed October 2008.

24. See the database of freedom bonds and emancipation records, available online, www.nps.gov/jeff/historyculture, accessed October 2008.

25. James F. Clarke, Meadville, Pennsylvania, to William Greenleaf Eliot, February 9, 1852; Eliot's address to the Colonization Society, December 1847 and January 1848, Notebook 1, pp. 24, 39–42, 46; a fund-raiser for slave emigration, March 26, 1848, Notebook 1, pp. 91, 94; a pseudonymous letter, September 20, 1848, Notebook 1, pp. 154–155, 160, 162; on the need for emancipation law, December 26, 1848, Notebook 2, p. 52; splitting churches, January 8, 1852, Notebook 3, p. 133; WIDE AWAKE [William Greenleaf Eliot], "Unitarian conference at Alton–Explosion upon the Slavery Question," *Missouri Republican,* May 18, 1857, Reel 4; on Negritia, Eliot, entry for early 1860, Notebook 4, p. 159; Eliot Papers, WU. Eliot also obtained a permit for the school to meet even under martial law; entry for April 12, 1861, Notebook 6, p. 6. See also Earl K. Holt III, *William Greenleaf Eliot Conservative Radical* (St. Louis: First Unitarian Church, 1985), 66.

26. *Uncle Tom's Cabin,* April 24, 1854, playbill, New Varieties Theater, Theater Programs Collection, box 113, MHM. See Louis Gerteis, "Shaping the Authentic: St. Louis Theater Culture and the Construction of American Social Types, 1815–1860," in *St. Louis in the Century of Henry Shaw: A View Beyond the Garden Wall,* ed. Eric Sandweiss (Columbia: University of Missouri Press, 2003), 215–217. For a critique of minstrelsy as "racial theft," Eric Lott, *Love and Theft: Blackface Minstrelsy and the American Working Class, Race and American Culture* (New York: Oxford University Press, 1993). For a more sympathetic look at the white-black interactions in the theater, Louis Gerteis, "St. Louis Theatre in the Age of the Original Jim Crow," *Gateway Heritage* 15, no. 4 (1995): 32–41.

27. Benjamin Gratz Brown, *Speech of the Hon. B. Gratz Brown, of St. Louis, on the Subject of Gradual Emancipation in Missouri* (St. Louis: Missouri Democrat Book and Job Office, 1857), [1]. For the length, George M. Williams, Jefferson City, to Dr. John F. Snyder, February 12, 1857, Dr. John F. Snyder Papers, MHM.

28. Brown, *Speech . . . on the Subject of Gradual Emancipation,* 5, 23. Also quoted in Gerteis, *Civil War St. Louis,* 72, and Holly Zumwalt Taylor, "Neither North nor South: Sectionalism, St. Louis Politics, and the Coming of the Civil War, 1846–1861" (PhD diss., University of Texas at Austin, 2004), 292. Richard Wade made a similar argument about the replacement of slave labor in maturing cities; see Richard C. Wade, *Slavery in the Cities; the South, 1820–1860* (New York: Oxford University Press, 1964); Towers, *The Urban South,* 143; Eric Burin, *Slavery and the Peculiar Solution: A History of the American Colonization Society* (Gainesville: University Press of Florida, 2005); Daniel A. Graff, "Forging an American St. Louis: Labor, Race, and Citizenship from the Louisiana Purchase to Dred Scott" (PhD diss., University of Wisconsin–Madison, 2004); John Stauffer, *The Black Hearts of Men: Radical Abolitionists and the Transformation of Race* (Cambridge, Mass.: Harvard University Press, 2002).

29. George M. Williams, Jefferson City, to Dr. John F. Snyder, February 12, 1857, Dr. John F. Snyder Papers, box 1; A. W. Mitchell, Philadelphia, to James Tower Sweringen, February 7, 1857, Ruth Ferris Collection; B. Gratz Brown to George R. Smith, March 3, 1857, George R. Smith Papers. For the duel and the broader political landscape, Gerteis, *Civil War St. Louis,* 69–72; Towers, *The Urban South,* 143–44. See also the Brown-Reynolds Duel Collection, MHM.

30. *Scott v. Sandford,* 60 U.S. 393 (McLean dissent), 550; (Curtis dissent), 582. For the characterizations, Ehrlich, *They Have No Rights,* 137, 160–168.

31. *Cincinnati Gazette,* as cited in *Daily Cleveland Herald,* March 10, 1857, no. 58, col. B; *New York Tribune* as quoted in *Fayetteville Observer,* March 12, 1857, no. 589; col. B (italicized in original); *New York Herald* as reprinted in the *Charleston Mercury,* March 16, 1857, no. 9874, col. C. The patterns of reprinting, with and without commentary, would provide an interesting analysis of political and sectional alliances and divides.

32. Donn Pratt, Cincinnati, to George R. Harrington, March 18, 1857, George R. Harrington Papers, MHM. Abraham Lincoln, "Fragment on the Dred Scott Case," in *Collected Works,* 2:388. Original capitalization. See also Orville Vernon Burton, *The Age of Lincoln* (New York: Hill & Wang, 2007), 87–88.

33. "The Original Dred Scott." For similar estimations of appearance and age, "Visit to Dred Scott—His Family—Incidents of His Life—Decision of the Supreme Court," *Frank Leslie's Illustrated Newspaper,* June 27, 1857. For the sense of not being seen, Horton and Horton, *Slavery and Public History;* Woodhouse, "Dred Scott's Daughters," 397; see also Arenson, "Dred Scott vs. the *Dred Scott Case*" and "Freeing Dred Scott." For more on the first wife or dead sons, Hager, *Dred and Harriet Scott,* 7, 14.

34. "The Original Dred Scott."

35. Arenson, "The Local Impact," preliminary analysis of court records now available at www.nps.gov/jeff/historyculture, accessed October 2008; March 18, 1857, and January 1, 1858, meetings, SLU Historical Records, Philalethic Society Minutes, 1850–1863, DOC REC 0001 0012 0031; T., "Correspondence of the Daily Sentinel," *Milwaukee Daily Sentinel,* May 19, 1857, printed May 27, 1857. For the best picture of the slave market, Johnson, *Soul by Soul;* for further analysis and description of St. Louis slave markets, Hunter, "Slavery in St. Louis," 258–261.

36. Gerteis, *Civil War St. Louis,* 65; Brown, *Missouri Democrat,* April 8, 1857, as quoted in Taylor, "Neither North nor South," 293–294.

37. "A Fire-Eater's Meditations"; *Ripley* (Ohio) *Bee,* April 18, 1857; *The Liberator,* Friday, April 17, 1857, p. 63, no. 16, col. A, via Cengage, accessed November 2006; "The Anti-slavery Triumph in St. Louis," *New York Herald,* April 14, 1857, p. 4; col. B, via Cengage, accessed November 2006.

38. Contemporaneous notation by unknown author on letters from Calvin C. Chaffee to Montgomery Blair and Montgomery Blair to Roswell Field, April 11 and 13, 1857, as printed and transcribed in Hager, *Dred and Harriet Scott,* 123–125. Hager, *Dred and Harriet Scott,* 33–44; Ehrlich, *They Have No Rights,* 180–181; Fehrenbacher, *The Dred Scott Case,* 420–421, 473, 663n20; VanderVelde, *Mrs. Dred Scott,* 306, 320, 322. Chaffee may have sought a ruling as a test decision; Albert P. Blaustein and Robert L. Zangrando, *Civil Rights and African Americans: A Documentary History* (Evanston, Ill.: Northwestern University Press, 1991), 147. After emancipation, "Dred Scott Free at Last: Himself and His Family Emancipated," *St. Louis Daily Evening News* May 26, 1857; "General News," *Hartford Daily Courant,* May 28, 1857.

39. "The Original Dred Scott"; Charles Elliott, "Correspondence. [Letter to Brother Haven]," *Zion's Herald and Wesleyan Journal,* July 25, 1857 (printed September 23, 1857); "Visit to Dred Scott." See also VanderVelde, *Mrs. Dred Scott,* 323.

40. On Düsseldorf and American artists, Barbara S. Groseclose, *Emanuel Leutze, 1816–1868: Freedom Is the Only King* (Washington, D.C.: National Collection of Fine Arts—Smithsonian Institution Press, 1975); Lynda Joy Sperling, "Northern European Links to Nineteenth Century American Landscape Painting: The Study of American Artists in Duesseldorf" (PhD diss., University of California, Santa Barbara, 1985). On Bingham's letters from Düsseldorf, Albert Christ-Janer, *George Caleb Bingham of Missouri; the Story of an Artist* (New York: Dodd, Mead & Co., 1940), 90–95.

41. George Caleb Bingham, Düsseldorf, to James Rollins, June 3, 1857, James Rollins Papers, WHMC-Columbia, C1026, folder 39. For the melding of western and national sensibilities, Angela Miller, "The Mechanisms of the Market and the Invention of Western Realism: The Example of George Caleb Bingham," in *American Iconology: New Approaches to Nineteenth-Century Art and Literature,* ed. David C. Miller (New Haven, Conn.: Yale University Press, 1993), 112–134.

42. The connection between *Jolly Flatboatmen at Port* and the *Dred Scott* decision has not been made by others. For a brief discussion of Bingham's black dancing figures in relation to Mount and minstrelsy—but not politics—see Louis Gerteis, "Shaping the Authentic: St. Louis Theater Culture and the Construction of American Social Types, 1815–1860," in *St. Louis in the Century of Henry Shaw*, 212–215. Thanks to Alex Nemerov for conversations that helped me develop this reading. George Caleb Bingham, *The Jolly Flatboatmen at Port*, 1857, St. Louis Art Museum; *The Jolly Flatboatmen*, 1846, The Manoogian Collection. On Bingham's "type" sketches, Christ-Janer, *George Caleb Bingham*, esp. pp. 35–91; see also Nancy Rash, *The Painting and Politics of George Caleb Bingham* (New Haven, Conn.: Yale University Press, 1991). For the flatboat as outdated, Stephen Aron, *American Confluence: The Missouri Frontier from Borderland to Border State* (Bloomington: Indiana University Press, 2006), 171.

43. See for example William Sidney Mount, *The Dance of the Haymakers* (1845) and *The Power of Music* (1847). On Mount, racial meaning, and American genre scenes, Albert Boime, *The Art of Exclusion: Representing Blacks in the Nineteenth Century* (Washington, D.C.: Smithsonian Institution Press, 1990), 88–101, and Martin A. Berger, *Sight Unseen: Whiteness and American Visual Culture* (Berkeley: University of California Press, 2005), esp. Chapter 1. Thanks to Jennie Sutton for mentioning Boime's work. See brief mention in Jonathan Weinberg, "The Artist and the Politician—George Caleb Bingham," *Art in America*, October 2000.

44. Abraham Lincoln, "Speech at Springfield, June 27, 1857," in *Collected Works*.

45. Ibid., 404, 401.

46. Thomas Hart Benton, *Historical and Legal Examination of That Part of the Decision of the Supreme Court of the United States in the Dred Scott Case, Which Declares the Unconstitutionality of the Missouri Compromise Act and the Self-Extension of the Constitution to Territories, Carrying Slavery Along with It* (New York: D. Appleton & Co., 1857), 5. See William Nisbet Chambers, *Old Bullion Benton, Senator from the New West: Thomas Hart Benton, 1782–1858* (Boston: Atlantic Monthly Press—Little, Brown, 1956), 433–436; Elbert B. Smith, *Magnificent Missourian; the Life of Thomas Hart Benton* (Philadelphia: Lippincott, 1958), 322.

47. Napton, *The Union on Trial*, 183, entry for June 20, 1857; "Elihu Burritt Proposes Compensated Emancipation," in William H. Pease and Jane H. Pease, eds., *The Antislavery Argument* (Indianapolis: Bobbs-Merrill, 1965), 203, as quoted in Betty L. Fladeland, "Compensated Emancipation: A Rejected Alternative," *Journal of Southern History* 42, no. 2 (May 1976): 183. See also James L. Huston, "Property Rights in Slavery and the Coming of the Civil War," *Journal of Southern History* 65, no. 2 (May 1999): 264, 272.

48. Heinrich Boernstein, *Memoirs of a Nobody: The Missouri Years of an Austrian Radical, 1849–1866*, trans. Steven Rowan (1881; St. Louis: Missouri Historical Society

Press, 1997), 205; A. W. Mitchell, Philadelphia, to James Tower Sweringen, December 24, 1857, Ruth Ferris Collection. See also *Germans for a Free Missouri*, 53–58. On Brown's initiatives, George M. Williams, Jefferson City, to Dr. John F. Snyder, November 6, 1857, Dr. John F. Snyder Papers, box 1.

49. Massey, Jefferson City, to Snyder, December 28, 1858, and April 18, 1859, Dr. John F. Snyder Papers; James S. Green, Canton, Missouri, to Samuel Treat, September 29, 1858, Samuel Treat Papers, MHM; *Mississippi Blätter* (Sunday edition of *Westliche Post*), March 8, 1858, in *Germans for a Free Missouri*, 65. The small cadre of Democrats against the expansion of slavery held the balance in many southern cities; see Towers, *The Urban South*, 23–24, and Taylor, "Neither North nor South," 300–313.

50. Cyprian Clamorgan, *The Colored Aristocracy of St. Louis*, ed. Julie Winch (1858; University of Missouri Press, 1999). For background, Julie Winch, "The Clamorgans of St. Louis," in *The Colored Aristocracy*, 21–36. For African-American biographical dictionaries, Henry Louis Gates Jr., "Revealing African American Lives," New-York Historical Society, February 14, 2008, made available as a podcast by the Gilder Lehrman Institute for American History. See also Day and Kedro, "Free Blacks in St. Louis"; Towers, *The Urban South*, 47.

51. Clamorgan, *The Colored Aristocracy*, 48; see also 49 and 52, as well as all the other remarkable word portraits.

52. Clamorgan, *The Colored Aristocracy*, 47. Winch notes that no standard Taney biography corroborates Clamorgan's claim, but given his slaveholding ancestors and slave knowledge about parentage, I find it plausible. Clamorgan, *The Colored Aristocracy*, 69n16. For the prosperous if precarious free black urban elite, Wade, *Slavery in the Cities*; Berlin, *Slaves without Masters*; Buchanan, *Black Life on the Mississippi*; Towers, *The Urban South*.

53. Thomas Hart Benton, ed., *Abridgment of the Debates of Congress, from 1789 to 1856* (New York: D. Appleton & Co., 1857). On finishing the day before and Benton's final days, Chambers, *Old Bullion Benton*, 436–439; William Montgomery Meigs, *The Life of Thomas Hart Benton* (Philadelphia: J. B. Lippincott & Co., 1904), 517–518; Smith, *Magnificent Missourian*, 322–324.

54. On the funeral in Washington, Associated Press report, April 12, 1858, reprinted in *New York Times*, April 13, 1858, p. 1; Chambers, *Old Bullion Benton*, 439; Meigs, *Life of Thomas Hart Benton*, 519; Smith, *Magnificent Missourian*, 324. Brown as quoted in Chambers, *Old Bullion Benton*, 443. "Funeral of Col. Benton," *Chicago Daily Tribune*, April 17, 1858. See excerpt of the same report in the April 17, 1858, *New York Times*.

55. On the St. Louis funeral generally, Chambers, *Old Bullion Benton*, 440–444; "Funeral of Col. Benton"; Meigs, *Life of Thomas Hart Benton*, 519–520; Smith, *Magnificent Missourian*, 324–325. Rogers says that the ceremonies were rivaled only by those for Henry Clay before and Lincoln afterward. Joseph M. Rogers, *Thomas*

H. Benton (Philadelphia: G. W. Jacobs & Co., 1905), 345. Section of inscription quoted without citation in Smith, *Magnificent Missourian,* 324; it excerpts and places in the past tense the description of Benton in George Washington Bungay, *Nebraska: A Poem Personal and Political* (Boston: John P. Jewett and Co., 1854), lines 582–610, via Antislavery Literature Project, http://antislavery.eserver.org, accessed August 2007. For political rivals, Taylor, "Neither North nor South," 278–280. Not all was forgiven, however; see the anecdote on Nathaniel Paschall's reaction in Walter B. Stevens, *St. Louis, the Fourth City 1764–1909,* 3 vols. (St. Louis: S. J. Clarke, 1909), 1: 220.

56. For Sanford's death notice, *New York Times,* May 6, 1857, p. 5, via ProQuest Historical Newspapers. Walter Ehrlich, "John F. A. Sanford," in *Dictionary of Missouri Biography,* 665–666; Fehrenbacher, *The Dred Scott Case,* 569; VanderVelde, *Mrs. Dred Scott,* 322; Hager, *Dred and Harriet Scott,* 38.

57. "Dred Scott," *New York Times,* September 21, 1858; *Daily National Intelligencer,* September 22, 1858, no. 14,395; col. D. "Ineffacebly" corrected. Similar sentiments and even the same metaphors appear in "Dred Scott Gone to Final Judgment," reprint of *New York Herald* in *The Liberator,* October 1, 1858, pp. 28, 40, via APS Online. For other mentions of Dred Scott's death, see *Weekly Raleigh Register,* September 29, 1858, no. 45, col. D, and "Dred Scott Dead," *Daily Cleveland Herald,* September 20, 1858, no. 222, col. G.

58. *Daily National Intelligencer,* September 22, 1858, no. 14,395, col. D; Abraham Lincoln, "Seventh and Last Debate with Stephen A. Douglas at Alton, Illinois," in *Collected Works,* 305.

59. Massey, Jefferson City, to Snyder, June 14, 1859, Dr. John F. Snyder Papers. Blair contested the extremely narrow victory of Democrat John Richard Barret and was eventually seated for the last nine months of the term, beginning June 1860; William Earl Parrish, *Frank Blair: Lincoln's Conservative* (Columbia: University of Missouri Press, 1998), 73, 83, 85–86. See also Norma Lois Peterson, *Freedom and Franchise: the Political Career of B. Gratz Brown* (Columbia: University of Missouri Press, 1965), 87–88. For specifics of the Illinois vote totals and elections, "Lincoln Chronology," www.nps.gov, accessed August 2007. On indirect election of U.S. senators, see Chapter 2. For claiming the mantle of uniters not dividers, Taylor, "Neither North nor South," 311.

60. Waldo P. Johnson, Osceola, to Snyder, December 21, 1859, Dr. John F. Snyder Papers.

61. Eliot, entry for May 22, 1860, Notebook 5, p. 34, Eliot Papers, WU.

62. On the various possibilities for slavery's future in the opening days of Lincoln's administration, see Foner, *Free Soil, Free Labor, Free Men;* Willie Lee Nichols Rose, *Rehearsal for Reconstruction: The Port Royal Experiment* (Indianapolis: Bobbs-Merrill, 1964); Doris Kearns Goodwin, *Team of Rivals: The Political Genius of Abraham Lincoln* (New York: Simon & Schuster, 2005).

6 Germans and the Power of Wartime Union

1. "Open Letter from Prof. Joseph N. McDowell to Rev. Henry Ward Beecher," dated December 8, 1859, *St. Louis Daily Morning Herald,* December 15, 1859, broadside attached to Benjamin F. Massey to John F. Snyder, July 27, 1859, Dr. John F. Snyder Papers, MHM. McDowell discusses the actual crossing, not Leutze's image.

2. For Leutze's transnational message, Barbara S. Groseclose, *Emanuel Leutze, 1816–1868: Freedom Is the Only King* (Washington, D.C.: National Collection of Fine Arts—Smithsonian Institution Press, 1975), esp. p. 37. For a response to literalists' objections to the painting, see David Hackett Fischer, *Washington's Crossing* (New York: Oxford University Press, 2004), 1–6.

3. "Open Letter from Prof. Joseph N. McDowell." Given the conversion from Julian to Gregorian calendars, McDowell is marking the anniversary as transposed from the Julian (December 24, 1776) to Gregorian (December 8, 1859) date.

4. While some German Americans sided with the Confederacy, the vast majority proved loyal and active partisans for the Union. For McDowell's life, William C. Winter and Civil War Round Table of St. Louis, *The Civil War in St. Louis: A Guided Tour* (St. Louis: Missouri Historical Society Press, 1994), 127. For a recent overview of German contributions to the war effort, Walter D. Kamphoefner, "Comments and Context," *Journal of American Ethnic History* 28, no. 1 (Fall 2008): 70–76.

5. Heinrich Boernstein, *Memoirs of a Nobody: The Missouri Years of an Austrian Radical, 1849–1866,* trans. Steven Rowan (1881; St. Louis: Missouri Historical Society Press, 1997), 262.

6. Bates began his diary with the start of his campaigning; Edward Bates, *The Diary of Edward Bates, 1859–1866,* ed. Howard K. Beale and Mary Parker Ragatz (Washington, D.C.: U.S. Government Printing Office, 1933), with his newspaper articles on pp. 1–10. On chairing the convention, Beale's introduction to Bates, *Diary,* xii; for the portrait, Bates, *Diary,* 30, and the quite damaged original, MHM, Museum Collections, 1940 034 0001. *Louisiana* (Missouri) *Journal,* July 25, 1859, as quoted in Bates, *Diary,* 38. See Reinhard H. Luthin, "Organizing the Republican Party in the 'Border-Slave' Regions: Edward Bates's Presidential Candidacy in 1860," *MHR* 38, no. 2 (January 1944): 138–161, and Doris Kearns Goodwin, *Team of Rivals: The Political Genius of Abraham Lincoln* (New York: Simon & Schuster, 2005).

7. Boernstein, *Memoirs of a Nobody,* 213; *Mississippi Blätter* (Sunday edition of the *Westliche Post*), April 29, 1860, in *Germans for a Free Missouri: Translations from the St. Louis Radical Press, 1857–1862,* trans. and ed. Steven W. Rowan and James Neal Primm (Columbia: University of Missouri Press, 1983), 104. On the 1854 visit, see Chapter 3. For Bates's pandering in a questionnaire from Benjamin Gratz Brown and the St. Louis Germans and the general response, Bates, *Diary,* 111–114, and Goodwin, *Team of Rivals,* 221–228. See also William E. Parrish, "Edward Bates," in

Dictionary of Missouri Biography, ed. Lawrence O. Christensen (Columbia: University of Missouri Press, 1999), 40–41.

8. Gustav Philipp Körner and Thomas J. McCormack, *Memoirs of Gustave Körner, 1809–1896: Life-Sketches Written at the Suggestion of His Children,* 2 vols. (Cedar Rapids, Iowa: Torch Press, 1909), 2:88–89, as quoted in Goodwin, *Team of Rivals,* 242; *Anzeiger des Westens,* May 17, 1860, in *Germans for a Free Missouri,* 107–108. On Schurz and Körner's influence and Bates's defeat, Bates, *Diary,* 131 and 131n1,2; see also Goodwin, *Team of Rivals,* 253–256; Holly Zumwalt Taylor, "Neither North nor South: Sectionalism, St. Louis Politics, and the Coming of the Civil War, 1846–1861" (PhD diss., University of Texas at Austin, 2004), 327.

9. Carl Schurz, *Speech of Carl Schurz delivered at Verandah Hall, August 1, 1860* (St. Louis: Missouri Democrat Book and Job Office, 1860), as quoted in Boernstein, *Memoirs of a Nobody,* 265n4; and "The Free Labor Movement—Great Speech of Carl Schurz, of Wis., Delivered at St. Louis, Wednesday Eve. Aug. 1," (Atchison, Kan.) *Freedom's Champion,* August 11, 1860, no. 25, col. A, and "Carl Schurz's Speech at Verandah Hall, St. Louis, August 1st, 1860," *Milwaukee Daily Sentinel,* August 11, 1860, no. 178, col. A, via Cengage, accessed May 2008. For Seward and Reynolds, Boernstein, *Memoirs of a Nobody,* 265–266. See also Bates, *Diary,* 132; See also Stevens, *St. Louis, the Fourth City,* 1:864, 867; Lawrence O. Christensen, "Thomas Caute Reynolds," in *Dictionary of Missouri Biography,* 647–648.

10. Douglas, *Missouri Republican,* October 20, 1860, and Barret, *Missouri Republican,* June 20, 1860, as quoted in Taylor, "Neither North nor South," 337–338, 331. See also Bates, *Diary,* 154; Stevens, *St. Louis, the Fourth City,* 1:634.

11. Half of New Jersey's electors were also pledged to Douglas. Lincoln won in St. Louis by seven hundred ballots, with Douglas coming in second. Frances Hurd Stadler, *St. Louis Day by Day* (St. Louis: Patrice Press, 1989), 211–212. Eric Foner has challenged the notion that German voters were the deciding factor in the St. Louis vote; see Eric Foner, *Free Soil, Free Labor, Free Men: The Ideology of the Republican Party before the Civil War* (New York: Oxford University Press, 1970), 259, as cited in Frank Towers, *The Urban South and the Coming of the Civil War* (Charlottesville: University of Virginia Press, 2004), 47n37. See also Taylor, "Neither North nor South," 342.

12. Claiborne Fox Jackson, inaugural address, January 3, 1861, as found in *The Messages and Proclamations of the Governors of the State of Missouri,* comp. and ed. Buel Leopard and Floyd C. Shoemaker (Columbia: State Historical Society of Missouri, 1922), 3:334; Louis S. Gerteis, *Civil War St. Louis* (Lawrence: University Press of Kansas, 2001), 79. See also Charles B. Dew, *Apostles of Disunion: Southern Secession Commissioners and the Causes of the Civil War* (Charlottesville: University Press of Virginia, 2001), 19, 56; and Christopher Phillips, *Missouri's Confederate: Claiborne Fox Jackson and the Creation of Southern Identity in the Border West* (Columbia: University of Missouri Press, 2000). For a detailed firsthand account of the secessionists'

maneuvering, Thomas Lowndes Snead, *The Fight for Missouri: From the Election of Lincoln to the Death of Lyon* (New York: C. Scribner's Sons, 1886).

13. Boernstein, *Memoirs of a Nobody,* 266–274; Gerteis, *Civil War St. Louis,* 79–89; quote from *Mississippi Blätter* (Sunday edition of *Westliche Post*), March 31, 1861, in *Germans for a Free Missouri,* 170. See also Henry T. Blow, St. Louis, to Richard Yates, Washington, March 2, 1861, in the Logan Uriah Reavis Papers, Chicago History Museum.

14. "Letter from St. Louis," (San Francisco) *Daily Evening Bulletin,* March 30, 1861, no. 146, col. D, via Cengage, accessed January 2007; Basil W. Duke, *Reminiscences of General Basil W. Duke* (Garden City, N.Y.: Doubleday, Page & Co., 1911), 37–42; Gerteis, *Civil War St. Louis,* 78–79, 87–88; Towers, *The Urban South,* 187; Winter, *The Civil War in St. Louis,* 31–33.

15. *Anzeiger des Westens,* December 3, 1860, in *Germans for a Free Missouri,* 143.

16. *St. Louis Daily Evening News,* March 4 and 5, 1861, also cited in Winter, *The Civil War in St. Louis,* 32; Gerteis, *Civil War St. Louis,* 73, 87.

17. William Earl Parrish, *Frank Blair: Lincoln's Conservative* (Columbia: University of Missouri Press, 1998), 85; James Edwin Love, autobiography, transcript p. 11, James Edwin Love Papers, MHM; Boernstein, *Memoirs of a Nobody,* 278, 275; Gerteis, *Civil War St. Louis,* 80, 84, 85; Stevens, *St. Louis, the Fourth City,* 1:830.

18. Boernstein, *Memoirs of a Nobody,* 278n11, 277n8, 344; Stephen D. Engle, "Franz Sigel," and Christopher Phillips, "Nathaniel Lyon," in *Dictionary of Missouri Biography,* 699–700, 509–510; Gerteis, *Civil War St. Louis,* 87–89; Taylor, "Neither North nor South," 362.

19. Boernstein, *Memoirs of a Nobody,* 275; Gerteis, *Civil War St. Louis,* 90–92; *Germans for a Free Missouri,* 172–174; Mark A. Neels, "The Crisis of the Foreign Element: Nativist Suppression of German Radicals in Antebellum St. Louis, 1848–1861," paper delivered at the Missouri Conference on History, Springfield, April 2009, p. 12. On seizing the arsenals, Love, autobiography transcript p. 11; Boernstein, *Memoirs of a Nobody,* 276–277.

20. *The War of the Rebellion: A Compilation of the Official Records of the Union and Confederate Armies,* Series 3 (Washington, D.C.: U.S. Government Printing Office, 1899), 1:82–83, as quoted in Boernstein, *Memoirs of a Nobody,* 274–275. From the original (not retranslated); Gerteis, *Civil War St. Louis,* 93.

21. Boernstein, *Memoirs of a Nobody,* 276; Gerteis, *Civil War St. Louis,* 102, 107, 95.

22. Boernstein, *Memoirs of a Nobody,* 276, 282–284, 287–291, 290n2; quote from 295–296. See also Gerteis, *Civil War St. Louis,* 93, 103–104.

23. From April 14–29, 1861, 334 bonds were registered; the 1,080 extant span February 1843–May 1863. See the database of freedom bonds from the Dexter P. Tiffany Collection, MHM, available online, www.nps.gov/jeff/historyculture, accessed October 2008. For Eliza Scott's April 23, 1861, bond, Ruth Ann (Abels) Hager, *Dred and Harriet Scott: Their Family Story* (St. Louis: St. Louis County Library, 2010), 54. For

patterns of noncompliance in Virginia and North Carolina, see Luther P. Jackson, "Manumission in Certain Virginia Cities," *Journal of Negro History* 15 (1930): 278; John Hope Franklin, *The Free Negro in North Carolina, 1790–1860* (Chapel Hill: University of North Carolina Press, 1943), 198; Ira Berlin, *Slaves without Masters: The Free Negro in the Antebellum South* (New York: Random House, 1974), 327–330. These citations thanks to Ellen Eslinger, who is researching how partial compliance may still give evidence to the strength, not the gaps, of slavery's surveillance system.

24. Peregrine Tippett, "In the Matter of Granting Licensee to Free Negroes and Mulattoes," protest to the St. Louis Board of County Commissioners, presented May 27, 1861, for consideration on June 3, 1861, with amendment by William Taussig. Dexter P. Tiffany Collection, MHM, box 63, folder 10. For a discussion of Tippett, Taussig, and the court, John Fletcher Darby, *Personal Recollections of Many Prominent People Whom I Have Known, and of Events—Especially of Those Relating to the History of St. Louis—During the First Half of the Present Century* (St. Louis: G. I. Jones & Co., 1880), 225. For slaves' awareness of war events, James Thomas, *From Tennessee Slave to St. Louis Entrepreneur: The Autobiography of James Thomas,* ed. Loren Schweninger (Columbia: University of Missouri Press, 1984), 158; David W. Blight, "They Knew What Time It Was: African-Americans and the Coming of the Civil War," in *Why the Civil War Came,* ed. Gabor Borritt (New York: Oxford University Press, 1996), 51–78.

25. Philip D. Stephenson, "My War Autobiography," manuscript in the Louisiana State University archives, p. 2, as quoted in Winter, *The Civil War in St. Louis,* 42. Many first-person accounts exist, including published views of Heinrich Boernstein, *Memoirs of a Nobody,* 292–311; Thomas, *From Tennessee Slave,* 160–161; Duke, *Reminiscences of General Basil W. Duke;* Robert J. Rombauer, *The Union Cause in St. Louis in 1861; An Historical Sketch* (St. Louis: Press of Nixon-Jones Printing Co., 1909); Thomas L. Snead, *The Fight for Missouri, from the Election of Lincoln to the Death of Lyon* (New York: C. Scribner's Sons, 1886). For extensive, detailed analyses of the skirmish, see Gerteis, *Civil War St. Louis,* 97–116; Winter, *The Civil War in St. Louis,* 40–53.

26. Frost to Lyon, Camp Jackson, May 10, 1861, as quoted in Gerteis, *Civil War St. Louis,* 106–107. See also Boernstein, *Memoirs of a Nobody,* 297; Winter, *The Civil War in St. Louis,* 48.

27. Gerteis, *Civil War St. Louis,* 107–115; Winter, *The Civil War in St. Louis,* 49–53.

28. *Missouri Republican* headline from Boernstein, *Memoirs of a Nobody,* 302–303; *Westliche Post,* May 15, 1861, as translated in *Germans for a Free Missouri,* 206.

29. William T. Sherman, *Memoirs of General William T. Sherman,* 2nd ed., 2 vols. (New York: D. Appleton & Co., 1886), 1:191–192, and Ulysses S. Grant, *Personal Memoirs of U.S. Grant* (New York: Century Co., 1885), 1:231–238, as cited in Gerteis, *Civil War St. Louis,* 110, 112.

30. Boernstein, *Memoirs of a Nobody,* 307. See also Gerteis, *Civil War St. Louis,* 115; *Germans for a Free Missouri,* 236–239.

31. Newspaper clipping and correspondence of Mary Gempp Fruth, n.d. [April 1861], Civil War Collection, B140, MHM; for flag presentations, *Westliche Post,* May 1 and 8 and August 28, 1861, in *Germans for a Free Missouri,* 186–187, 195–197, 277–279, and *Daily Missouri Democrat,* April 30, 1861, in *Missouri's War: The Civil War in Documents,* ed. Silvana R. Siddali (Athens: Ohio University Press, 2009), 73–74. For John P. Couran, Provost Marshal records, September 30, 1861, and May 28, 1863, F1242, National Archives, microfilm accessed at MSA. For similar charges, which continued throughout the war, see Chapter 7.

32. Gerteis, *Civil War St. Louis,* 124; Winter, *The Civil War in St. Louis,* 67–68.

33. For troop numbers—and a claim St. Louis had the largest percentage fighting of any city—Walter B. Stevens, *St. Louis, the Fourth City 1764–1909,* 3 vols. (St. Louis: S. J. Clarke, 1909), 1:830. On the burned bridges, *Westliche Post,* May 15, 1861, in *Germans for a Free Missouri,* 212. While Belcher notes the advantages to Chicago, away from the battle lines, he misunderstands the ability for government-related business to flourish in St. Louis, even in the war years. Wyatt Winton Belcher, *The Economic Rivalry between St. Louis and Chicago, 1850–1880* (New York: Columbia University Press, 1947), 139–144. See also Margaret Louise Fitzsimmons, "Missouri Railroads during the Civil War and Reconstruction," *MHR* 35, no. 2 (January 1941): 189–197.

For the occupation of Jefferson City, Boernstein, *Memoirs of a Nobody,* 315, 324–325, 325n2.

34. Minerva Blow, Carondelet, to Susie Blow, December 18, 1860, Blow Family Papers, MHS; Records of the Second Baptist Church, Volume 1850–1885, meeting minutes from May 22, 1861, pp. 183–185; see also Neola McCorkle Koechig, *The Story of the Second Baptist Church of Greater St. Louis* (St. Louis: A. C. Lithograph, 1982), 19–21. For the Second Presbyterian scuffle, Winter, *The Civil War in St. Louis,* 63–64. On Catholic churches and St. Louis University, Boernstein, *Memoirs of a Nobody,* 282; correspondence with *Globe-Democrat* staff, March 27, 1961, in Bannon Papers, SLU Archives. Trinity German Evangelical Lutheran Church, Volume 1856–1869, meeting September 9, 1861, in 1992 translation by Dennis Ratchert. This mention of German prayers follows Frémont's dismissal, but the enthusiasm for the Union is evident throughout. For other St. Louis churches, Marcus J. McArthur, "Sins of Omission: Rev. Samuel B. McPheeters and St. Louis Civil War Politics," Missouri Conference on History, St. Louis, 2007; unpublished paper was provided by its author. For the Civil War fights elsewhere in Missouri, Michael Fellman, *Inside War: The Guerrilla Conflict in Missouri during the American Civil War* (New York: Oxford University Press, 1989); Donald L. Gilmore, *Civil War on the Missouri–Kansas Border* (Gretna, La.: Pelican Publishing Company, 2006); Gerteis, *Civil War St. Louis;* Winter, *The Civil War in St. Louis.*

35. Gerteis, *Civil War St. Louis*, 136–161. See also Sally Denton, *Passion and Principle: John and Jessie Frémont, the Couple Whose Power, Politics, and Love Shaped Nineteenth-Century America* (New York: Bloomsbury USA), 2007; Tom Chaffin, *Pathfinder: John Charles Frémont and the Course of American Empire* (New York: Hill & Wang), 2004.

36. Boernstein, *Memoirs of a Nobody*, 372, 370; quote from p. 372. For breathless coverage of Frémont's arrival, *Anzeiger des Westens*, July 25 and August 1, 1861, in *Germans for a Free Missouri*, 273–274.

37. For full text of Frémont's declaration, *The Destruction of Slavery*, Series 1, Vol. 1 of *Freedom: A Documentary History of Emancipation, 1861–1867*, ed. Ira Berlin, Barbara J. Fields, Thavolia Glymph, Joseph P. Reidy, and Leslie S. Rowland (New York: Cambridge University Press, 1985), 415. The counterinsurgency and emancipation policy applied below the line connecting Leavenworth, Kansas; Jefferson City; Rolla; Ironton; and Cape Girardeau; Gerteis, *Civil War St. Louis*, 149. "Gen. Fremont's Proclamation," *The Liberator*, September 6, 1861, p. 143, no. 36, col. E, via Cengage, accessed May 2008; for one celebration, *Anzeiger des Westens*, December 4, 1861, in *Germans for a Free Missouri*, 291–292. Alexander Badger, Fort Vancouver, to Mother, October 14, 1861, Badger Family Collection, MHM. For Lincoln's reaction, Abraham Lincoln to Orville Browning, September 22, 1861, and editor's notation in Michael P. Johnson, *Abraham Lincoln, Slavery, and the Civil War: Selected Writings and Speeches* (Boston, Mass.: Bedford/St. Martin's, 2001), 185.

38. Quoted in Gerteis, *Civil War St. Louis*, 151 (italicized in original). For a detailed account of Blair's role in Frémont's removal, see Parrish, *Frank Blair*, 115–136.

39. For the freed slaves, Gerteis, *Civil War St. Louis*, 153, 355n53. Provost Marshal records, Robert S. McDonald, November 23, 1861, F1198, and Provost Marshal records, F. M. Colburn, December 17, 1861, F1141. Colburn wrote an account of fighting the Great Fire; see notes to Chapter 1.

40. *Anzeiger des Westens*, November 13, 1861, in *Germans for a Free Missouri*, 289–290; Schuyler Colfax, *Fremont's Hundred Days in Missouri. Speech of Schuyler Colfax, of Indiana, in Reply to Mr. Blair, of Missouri, Delivered in the House of Representatives, March 7, 1862* (Washington, D.C.: Scammell & Co., 1862), 15. Thanks to John Maurath for alerting me to this source.

41. William Greenleaf Eliot to Salmon Chase, November 1, 1861, Chase Papers, as quoted in Gerteis, *Civil War St. Louis*, 159–160.

42. Provost Marshal records, Ada Clifford, October 1, 1862, F1239; Boernstein, *Memoirs of a Nobody*, 370–378.

43. Samuel Cupples to John McAllister, December 24, 1861, Alphabetical Files, MHM; for which part of Frémont's order was rescinded and what was renewed in January 1862, Gerteis, *Civil War St. Louis*, 169–174. For new research on antislavery and the motivation of soldiers, Chandra Manning, *What This Cruel War Was Over: Soldiers, Slavery, and the Civil War* (New York: Knopf, 2007).

44. "Completion of the St. Louis Court House," *Daily Missouri Democrat*, July 4, 1862, typescript in JNEM Collections. Patent #35,630, dated June 17, 1862, copy at JNEM. Image of the dome test, carte-de-visite, 1860, MHM Prints and Photographs Collection. This section has benefited from multiple conversations with Alex Nemerov. On relation to the U.S. Capitol and the courthouse as a civic icon during the Civil War, see also Angela L. Miller, "Carl Wimar: A Muralist of Civic Ambitions," in *Carl Wimar: Chronicler of the Missouri River Frontier*, ed. Rick Stewart, Joseph D. Ketner, and Angela L. Miller (Fort Worth, Tex., and New York: Amon Carter Museum—H. N. Abrams, 1991), 187–226.

45. "That Glorious Flag on the Court House Dome," June 17, 1861, typescript at JNEM from the scrapbook of Antoinette Taylor. For the visibility for miles, Thomas S. Hawley to parents, August 3, 1866, Thomas S. Hawley Papers, MHM. For an evocative image, Th. Anders, large flag over the St. Louis courthouse, "Old Courthouse" file, MHM Prints and Photographs Collection. Though the newspapers have June 22, 1862, the actual date was January 22; see St. Louis County Records, 11:71, JNEM; and Miller, "Carl Wimar: A Muralist of Civic Ambitions," 192. On Wimar's hiring, *Missouri Republican*, July 4, 1862, typescript in JNEM.

46. Carl Wimar to parents, August 27, 1854, and December 6, 1853, translations from Carl Wimar Papers, MHM. See also Joseph D. Ketner, "The Indian Painter in Düsseldorf," in *Carl Wimar: Chronicler of the Missouri River Frontier*, 30–79.

47. Wimar to parents, March 23, 1853, as quoted in Ketner, "The Indian Painter in Düsseldorf," 40; Wimar to parents, October 23, 1854, and February 20, 1855, translations from Wimar Papers. See also Carl to Parents, n.d. (c. 1855): "Leutze is very helpful."

48. Joseph D. Ketner, "Charles 'Carl' Ferdinand Wimar," in *Dictionary of Missouri Biography*, 809–811; Ketner, "The Indian Painter in Düsseldorf," 65–66; Rick Stewart, "An Artist on the Great Missouri," in *Carl Wimar: Chronicler of the Missouri River Frontier*, 81–162.

49. Miller, "Carl Wimar: A Muralist of Civic Ambitions," 191–192.

50. Boernstein, *Memoirs of a Nobody*, 297n8; Stewart, "An Artist," 84–85. We know these figures from descriptions and sketches; they were destroyed by later overpainting and alterations. John H. Lindenbusch, *Historic Structure Report, Historic Data Section, Part I, and Historic Grounds Study, Old Courthouse, JNEM* (Denver: Denver Service Center, National Park Service, U.S. Department of the Interior, 1982), 209–211.

51. In 1780 St. Louis was actually governed by the Spanish and outside the United States, but a scene from the American Revolution helped connect St. Louis to history paintings of American past. William Taussig to Emil Preetorius of the *Westliche Post*, September 26, 1862, English typescript in Wimar Papers; Miller, "Carl Wimar: A Muralist of Civic Ambitions," 193–202. Taussig is mentioned on a committee to determine themes; St. Louis County Court Records, January 22, 1862, 11:71, JNEM.

For a suggestion lunettes were a secondary consideration for decoration, Linden-busch, *Historic Structure Report,* 82. On harkening back to a pre-American St. Louis, see the Epilogue.

52. For connections to Bierstadt as well as Leutze, Miller, "Carl Wimar: A Mu-ralist of Civic Ambitions," 202–209. See also Mary Zundo, "Westward Buffalo and Vanishing Americans: Manifest Destiny on the Picture 'Plain,'" Huntington–USC Institute on California and the West, Bill Lane Center, and Autry National Center Joint Dissertation Workshop, Los Angeles, 2007. On the transcontinental railroad link, Chapter 9.

53. Miller, "Carl Wimar: A Muralist of Civic Ambitions," 211–212. Wimar sup-posedly told his wife, "This is my last work, when the dome is finished I shall be finished too." William R. Hodges, *Carl Wimar, a Biography* (Galveston, Tex.: Charles Reymershoffer, 1908), 26.

54. St. Louis County Court Records, entry for July 28, 1862, 11:161, JNEM.

55. Adalbert John Volck, *Sketches from the Civil War in North America, 1861, '62, '63* ("London" [likely Baltimore], 1863), online at www.gettysburg.edu/special_col-lections, accessed November 2007. See also James Barber, *Faces of Discord: The Civil War Era at the National Portrait Gallery* (Washington, D.C.: National Portrait Gallery–Collins, 2006); Adalbert John Volck and George M. Anderson, *The Work of Adalbert Johann Volck, 1828–1912, Who Chose for His Name the Anagram V. Blada* (Baltimore, 1970). Thanks to Steve Rowan for alerting me to the musical allusion.

56. George Engelmann, St. Louis, to Alexander Carl Heinrich Braun, fragment, n.d. [1865; mentions "after four such years of devastating war"], George Engelmann Papers, Missouri Botanical Garden Archives, transliteration by Denison 1994, Westin 1996, Eliasson 1997, Taubel 1997; translation by "SGE." See also Daniel Goldstein, "Midwestern Naturalists: Academies of Science in the Mississippi Valley, 1850–1900" (PhD diss., Yale University, 1989), 143. George Julius Engelmann, "Civil War Diary of a Washington University Student," transcript pp. 6a, Insert, and 20, February 18, 1862, and January 20, 1863, George Julius Engelmann Papers, MHM. Thanks to Carmen Brooks for mentioning this incident. Provost Marshal records, Jacob Miller, August 4, 1862, F1157; testimony from J. H. Sherman, M. Tanenbaum, and Jacob Floret.

7 Building Union from Neutrality

1. Provost Marshal records, Hennessey, June 2, 1862, F1471, National Archives, as accessed at MSA.

2. Provost Marshal records, Hennessey, June 2, 3, and 5, 1862, F1471, National Archives.

3. See Amy Murrell Taylor, *The Divided Family in Civil War America* (Chapel Hill: University of North Carolina Press, 2005); for rich historical parallels, Michel

Foucault, *Discipline and Punish: The Birth of the Prison* (New York: Pantheon Books, 1977); Carlo Ginzburg, *The Cheese and the Worms: The Cosmos of a Sixteenth-Century Miller* (Baltimore: Johns Hopkins University Press, 1980).

4. Charlotte Chauncy Eliot, *William Greenleaf Eliot, Minister, Educator, Philanthropist* (Boston: Houghton Mifflin, 1904), 254–255; Louis S. Gerteis, *Civil War St. Louis* (Lawrence: University Press of Kansas, 2001), 174–190; Michael Fellman, *Inside War: The Guerrilla Conflict in Missouri during the American Civil War* (New York: Oxford University Press, 1989), 94–95. On the most arrests, Mark E. Neely, *The Fate of Liberty: Abraham Lincoln and Civil Liberties* (New York: Oxford University Press, 1991), 39, as cited in Gerteis, *Civil War St. Louis,* 186–187.

5. Provost Marshal records, A. R. Cazauran, November 2, 1863, F1140, and statement of L. P. Eldridge against George Mathews, September 19, 186? (no year provided), F1485, National Archives.

6. Provost Marshal records, sworn statement of Louis Weil in the case of Peter Helle, July 29, 1862, F1470, National Archives. Particularly interesting is the charge brought against U.S. Army Captain John Austerick for threatening the Germans in his neighborhood; Provost Marshal records, John Austerick, October 7, 1861, F1220. See also Fellman, *Inside War,* esp. pp. 26–34, 41–50.

7. Provost Marshal records, sworn statement of Margaret J. Knapp in the case of Margaret Gay, July 13, 1863, F1323; Mary Reed against Maggie Melvin, July 11, 1863, F1372; Anna Fliegen and Kate Merrick against Mary Ann Fitzgerald, May 19 and July 11, 1863, F1318, National Archives. For an extended consideration, Gerteis, *Civil War St. Louis,* 202–235; and see also Catherine Clinton and Nina Silber, eds., *Divided Houses: Gender and the Civil War* (New York: Oxford University Press, 1992).

8. William Carr Lane, St. Louis, to Mrs. Sarah Lane Glasgow, Wiesbaden, February 7, 1862, from transcription in William Carr Lane Papers, MHM. On the Lane family and the strains of the Civil War, William G. B. Carson, "Anne Ewing Lane," *Missouri Historical Society Bulletin* 21, no. 2 (January 1965): 87–99, and " 'Secesh,' " *Missouri Historical Society Bulletin* 23, no. 2 (January 1967): 119–145. Carson cites many of the same letters quoted below.

9. List of assessed from Lane to Glasgow family, January 15, 1862, and fragment c. January 1862, both from transcription in William Carr Lane Papers; quotes from Lane to Glasgow, February 7, 1862, and Lane to Sarah and William Glasgow and family, January 15, 1862. Martha Farrar Sweringen and family, Milwaukee, to James Tower Sweringen, St. Louis, July and August 1864, Ruth Ferris Collection, Herman T. Pott National Inland Waterways Library, SLML. Thanks to Bette Gorden for locating these letters. On Lane's protection and Farrar's appointment, see also Gerteis, *Civil War St. Louis,* 173, 176.

10. Auntie [Sarah Lane Glasgow] to Nannie [?? Ewing], March 9, 1864, from transcription in William Carr Lane Papers.

11. Anne Lane to Sarah Lane Glasgow, April 19, 1863 ("making faces"), c. 1863 fragment (O'Flaherty garden), and June 21, 1863 ("nice country"), from transcriptions in William Carr Lane Papers. See also Gerteis, *Civil War St. Louis,* 176, 178–181.

12. William T. Sherman, *Memoirs of General William T. Sherman,* 2nd ed., 2 vols. (New York: D. Appleton & Co., 1886), 1:190–191, as quoted in Gerteis, *Civil War St. Louis,* 105 and 115.

On the flowers, unidentified newspaper clipping transcribed in William M. McPheeters, *I Acted from Principle: The Civil War Diary of Dr. William M. Mcpheeters, Confederate Surgeon in the Trans-Mississippi,* ed. Cynthia DeHaven Pitcock and Bill J. Gurley (Fayetteville: University of Arkansas Press, 2002), 46–47. Benjamin F. Massey, Jefferson City, to John F. Snyder, July 9, 1859, Dr. John F. Snyder Papers, MHM; Christopher Phillips, introduction to *The Union on Trial: The Political Journals of Judge William Barclay Napton, 1829–1883,* ed. Christopher Phillips and Jason L. Pendleton (Columbia: University of Missouri Press, 2005), 61. See also James Thomas, *From Tennessee Slave to St. Louis Entrepreneur: The Autobiography of James Thomas,* ed. Loren Schweninger (Columbia: University of Missouri Press, 1984), 165; Gerteis, *Civil War St. Louis,* 175–182.

13. Clarence E. Miller, "Forty Years of Long Ago: Early Annals of the Mercantile Library Association and Its Public Hall, 1846–1886," (SLML, 1935), typescript p. 65; Adam Arenson, "A Cultural Barometer: The St. Louis Mercantile Library as National Institution, 1846–1871," *MHR* 102, no. 2 (January 2008): 96.

14. "An Old Member and an Unconditional Union Man," letter to the *Missouri Republican,* February 21, 1862; see also Minerva Blow to Susie Blow, December 18, 1860, Blow Family Papers, MHM, and Walter B. Stevens, *St. Louis, the Fourth City 1764–1909,* 3 vols. (St. Louis: S. J. Clarke, 1909), 1:686.

15. Quotes from Schuyler Colfax, *Fremont's Hundred Days in Missouri. Speech of Schuyler Colfax, of Indiana, in Reply to Mr. Blair, of Missouri, Delivered in the House of Representatives, March 7, 1862* (Washington, D.C.: Scammell & Co., 1862), 2–3; and James Edwin Love, Camp Hunter, Fort Leavenworth, Kansas, to Eliza Molly Wilson, February 9, 1862, James Edwin Love Papers, MHM. See also Gerteis, *Civil War St. Louis,* 176; Board of Direction Minutes, Second Volume, n.p., meetings January 28, 1862; Miller, "Forty Years of Long Ago," typescript p. 65; John W. McKerley, "Citizens and Strangers: The Politics of Race in Missouri from Slavery to the Era of Jim Crow" (PhD diss., University of Iowa, 2008), 66–67; Love to Wilson, February 16, 1862, Love Papers.

16. Board of Direction Minutes, Second Volume, n.p., meeting March 4, 1862, SLML; Miller, "Forty Years of Long Ago," typescript p. 65; Edward Johnston file, SLML; *Missouri Republican,* January 21, 1862; Johnston to President and Directors, January 28, 1862, Board of Direction Minutes, Second Volume, n.p., meeting February 4, 1862, SLML; Clarence E. Miller, "Edward William Johnston, Roving Scholar,"

Missouri Historical Society Bulletin 9, no. 1 (October 1952): 81–87. A painting of Johnston still hangs in the library.

17. Anna Ella Carroll, "Plan of the Tennessee Campaign," *North American Review* 142, no. 353 (April 1886): 343; Provost Marshal records, Edward W. Johnston, St. Louis, to Major General John Schofield, Commanding Officer, August 4, 1863, F1348, National Archives. See also Janet L. Coryell, *Neither Heroine nor Fool: Anna Ella Carroll of Maryland* (Kent, Ohio: Kent State University Press, 1990). For cramped handwriting, Provost Marshal records, Johnston, July 3, 1863, F1350; on Mercantile work, Miller, "Edward William Johnston, Roving Scholar," 85–86.

18. Phrase from Johnston to Schofield, August 4, 1863, F1348.

19. On Halleck's promotion, James M. McPherson, *Battle Cry of Freedom: The Civil War Era* (New York: Oxford University Press, 1988), 502–504; on his slave policy, Gerteis, *Civil War St. Louis,* 262–269, 276–278. Samuel T. Glover, St. Louis, to James O. Broadhead, Jefferson City, June 4, 1862, James Overton Broadhead Papers, MHM.

20. *Missouri Democrat,* May 10, 1862. For a full consideration, see Louis Gerteis, "The Legacy of the *Dred Scott* Case: The Uncertain Course of Emancipation in Missouri," in *The* Dred Scott Case: *Historical and Contemporary Perspectives on Race and Law,* ed. Paul Finkelman, David Konig, and Christopher Bracey (Athens: Ohio University Press, 2010), 68–82. See also McKerley, "Citizens and Strangers," Chapter Three; Gerteis, *Civil War St. Louis,* 263–265; Willie Lee Nichols Rose, *Rehearsal for Reconstruction: The Port Royal Experiment* (Indianapolis: Bobbs-Merrill, 1964).

21. James Neal Primm, *Lion of the Valley: St. Louis, Missouri, 1764–1980,* 3rd ed. (St. Louis: Missouri Historical Society Press, 1998), 248; Gerteis, *Civil War St. Louis,* 180–181. For Drake, David D. March, "Charles Daniel Drake of St. Louis," *Missouri Historical Society Bulletin* 9, no. 2 (April 1953): 291–310, and "Charles D. Drake and the Constitutional Convention of 1865," *MHR* 47, no. 2 (January 1953): 110–123.

22. For the oaths, Dexter P. Tiffany Collection, boxes 64 to 70, MHM. Provost Marshal records on Taylor Blow, October 1863, F1466, National Archives. For the failed business, Minerva Blow, Carondelet, to Susie Blow, April 29, 1861; Minerva Blow, Southampton, to Susie Blow, May 18, 1861; Henry T. Blow to Minerva Blow, Southampton, December 1861; Blow Family Papers, MHM.

23. Provost Marshal records, Abraham Lincoln, Executive Mansion, to Oliver Filley, St. Louis, December 22, 1863, F1371, National Archives. See also Gerteis, *Civil War St. Louis,* 182–186; McPheeters, *I Acted from Principle;* Marcus J. McArthur, "Sins of Omission: Rev. Samuel B. McPheeters and St. Louis Civil War Politics," Missouri Conference on History paper, St. Louis, 2007; and cases against minister W. C. Dawson, the Reformed Presbyterian Church, and the Grace Episcopal Church, Provost Marshal records, March 15, 1864, February 6, 1864, and May 26, 1864, respectively, F1297, F1237, and F1198.

24. Eliot, draft of letter to Chancellor Hoyt, December 19, 1860, Notebook 5, pp. 125–126, Eliot Papers, WU; Eliot, *The Story of Archer Alexander from Slavery to Freedom March 30, 1863* (Boston: Cupples Upham & Co., 1885), 55. For the complaints to Lincoln, Eliot to Gamble, December 1, 1862, folder 8, William Greenleaf Eliot Papers, MHM. Halleck, Head Quarters of the Army, Washington, to Major General Curtis, St. Louis, December 15, 1862, Eliot Papers, MHM, and related in C. Eliot, *William Greenleaf Eliot,* 174–181.

25. Eliot, sermon notes for August 22, 1862, Notebook 6, p. 121, Eliot Papers, WU; Gerteis, *Civil War St. Louis,* 94; Ralph E. Morrow, *Washington University in St. Louis: A History* (St. Louis: Missouri Historical Society Press, 1996), 44–46. Frank Eliot was killed at Chancellorsville. For an exemption, Provost Marshal records, Edward G. Martin, September 15, 1862, F1368, National Archives; H. Eliot, "A Brief Autobiography, 1843–1919," 45–49, 52–53. On the drills, C. W. Marsh, Assistant Adjutant General, to Librarian, September 21, 1862, Special Orders, No. 245, on behalf of General Schofield, SLML, Letterbook 3, A-3–7, p. 8.

26. George Julius Engelmann, "Civil War Diary of a WU Student," transcript pp. 6a Insert, and 20, February 18, 1862, and January 20, 1863, George Julius Engelmann Papers, MHM. Thanks to Carmen Brooks for mentioning this incident. On worries, Engelmann, St. Louis, to Alexander Carl Heinrich Braun, fragment, n.d. [1865], George Engelmann Papers, Missouri Botanical Garden Archives. Transliteration by Denison 1994, Westin 1996, Eliasson 1997, Taubel 1997; translation by "SGE."

27. For Eliot's forays, entries for September 3–8, 1861, Notebook 6, pp. 59–68, Eliot Papers, WU. For establishment, notation on the original order, J. C. Frémont, September 5, 1861, box 2, folder 21, Eliot Papers, MHM. See also Gerteis, *Civil War St. Louis,* 203–206. On the wounded and dead, see Drew Gilpin Faust, *This Republic of Suffering: Death and the American Civil War* (New York: Knopf, 2008).

28. Oath of Allegiance for George Partridge, September 21, 1862, Dexter P. Tiffany Collection, MHM, box 64, folder 10. For the Commission, C. Eliot, *William Greenleaf Eliot,* 212–278; Robert Patrick Bender, "Old Boss Devil: Sectionalism, Charity, and the Rivalry between the Western Sanitary Commission and the United States Sanitary Commission During the Civil War" (PhD thesis, U. of Arkansas, 2002); Bender, " 'This Noble and Philanthropic Enterprise': Mississippi Valley Sanitary Fair of 1864 and the Practice of Civil War Philanthropy," *MHR* 95.2 (2001), 117–139.

29. Yeatman and Olmsted, as quoted in Gerteis, *Civil War St. Louis,* 206 and 226, respectively; see also *Civil War St. Louis,* 205–208, 226–228.

30. Eliot to James Freeman Clarke, November 14, 1861, box 2, folder 21, Eliot Papers, MHM; Eliot, reprint of a *North American Review* article on the Western Sanitary Commission, April 1864, Eliot Papers, MHM. Mentioned in Eliot, *William Greenleaf Eliot,* 272–274. On requests and collections, see also Sylvester Waterhouse to Amos Lawrence, Harvard, June 22, 1861, Sylvester Waterhouse Papers, MHM; *The*

Daily Cleveland Herald, June 11, 1862, issue 137; col. D, via Cengage; Eliot, *Archer Alexander,* 119.

31. Correspondence between John Napier Dyer and Mrs. Anna Lansing Wendell Clapp, Ladies Union Aid Society, September 27, November 7, 8, and 14, 1862, SLML, Letter book 9, pp. 51, 54, 68, 70, 75–6; and the Ladies Union Aid Society report, 1862–1863, WHMC-Columbia, C1936; Eliot to Clarke, November 14, 1861, Eliot Papers, MHM; Gerteis, *Civil War St. Louis,* 202–204 and 211–214; Katharine T. Corbett, *In Her Place: A Guide to St. Louis Women's History* (St. Louis: Missouri Historical Society Press, 1999), 85–86. "Memorial—St. Louis Missouri Ladies' Union Aid Society, 1865," Major & Knapp, engravers, New York, 1870. Print Image D-1, MHM, also discussed in Gerteis, *Civil War St. Louis,* 202.

32. Playbill for 300th Anniversary of the Birth of Shakespeare benefit, April 23, 1864, MHM; quilt, MHM Museum Collections, 1941 020 0001; "The St Louis Sanitary Fair," *Bangor Daily Whig & Courier,* May 24, 1864, issue 276, col. C, via Cengage; W. S. Stedman, and Co., *Catalogue of Autographs, Letters, Documents, and Signatures, Relics and Curiosities, Photographs, Portraits, &C., Donated to the Mississippi Valley Sanitary Fair, and to Be Sold at Auction for the Benefit of the Western Sanitary Commission* (St. Louis: R. P. Studley, 1864). Thanks to Mike Venso for providing a photocopy of this catalogue. Clock, notes from acquisition, MHM Museum Collections, 1948 039 0001. See also C. Eliot, *William Greenleaf Eliot,* 269–274; Gerteis, *Civil War St. Louis,* 230–232.

33. Mississippi Valley Sanitary Fair circular, February 5, 1864, St. Louis Sanitation Papers, MHM, in *Missouri's War: The Civil War in Documents,* ed. Silvana R. Siddali (Athens: Ohio University Press, 2009), 78. On the poll, Gerteis, *Civil War St. Louis,* 231; for a similar vote at the New York City Sanitary Fair, Mark E. Neely, Jr., *The Boundaries of American Political Culture in the Civil War Era* (Chapel Hill: University of North Carolina Press, 2005), 71. For photographs, see the collections of SLML and MHM. For accounting, Western Sanitary Commission, General Report of the Mississippi Valley Sanitary Fair, August 16, 1864; copy in box 2, folder 21, Eliot Papers, MHM.

34. Calculations in Western Sanitary Commission, General Report of the Mississippi Valley Sanitary Fair, August 16, 1864; copy in box 2, folder 21, Eliot Papers, MHM. Also mentioned in Gerteis, *Civil War St. Louis,* 232. See also "St. Louis Sanitary Fair," *The Daily Cleveland Herald,* June 6, 1864, issue 132, col. C; and *The Ripley Bee,* June 16, 1864, issue 49, col. B, via Cengage; "The Mississippi Valley Sanitary Fair," *New York Times* April 26, 1864, p. 9, via ProQuest Historical Newspapers.

35. Mackwitz, "A Scene at the Sanitary Fair in St. Louis," *Missouri Republican,* June 27, 1864, clipping found in the Ludlow-Field-Maury Family Papers, MHM; Gerteis, *Civil War St. Louis,* 232–233.

36. Thomas Mitchell, Huntsville, Missouri, to James Tower Sweringen, January 11, 1863, Ruth Ferris Collection, Herman T. Pott National Inland Waterways Library,

SLML. Thanks to Bette Gorden for locating these letters. See also the sale in Goode to Sweringen, September 17, 1863, Sweringen Papers, MHM. For an argument that neutrality was surrendered earlier in these crucial Unionist slave states, William W. Freehling, *The South vs. The South: How Anti-Confederate Southerners Shaped the Course of the Civil War* (New York: Oxford University Press. 2001), Chapter Four.

37. Love, Union City, Tennessee, to Eliza, June 11, 1862, box 1, Love Papers, MHM.

38. For Eliot's church and education activities, see Chapter 5. Bond of indemnity from John A. Kasson to William Greenleaf Eliot, April 15, 1850, for slave Lydia; Reel 3, Eliot Papers, WU. Quote from Eliot, *Archer Alexander,* 123. For Eliot's thoughts and actions in 1862, entries and sermon notes for August 22, 1862, Notebook 6, pp. 120–126, Eliot Papers, WU. See also Joseph M. Thomas, "The Post-Abolitionist's Narrative: William Greenleaf Eliot's the Story of Archer Alexander," *New England Quarterly* 73, no. 3 (September 2000): 464–465.

39. Eliot, St. Louis, to Thomas Dawes Eliot, January 14, 1863, Eliot Papers, MHM. Passage is quoted in C. Eliot, *William Greenleaf Eliot,* 185; Mitchell to Sweringen, January 11, 1863, Ruth Ferris Collection, Herman T. Pott National Inland Waterways Library, SLML.

40. Eliot, *Archer Alexander,* 39–42, quotes from pp. 40–41, 42. For the narrative's unusual qualities, Thomas, "The Post-Abolitionist's Narrative."

41. Eliot, *Archer Alexander,* 54–60, 65–73, 88; quote is from p. 58. For slaves using the tropes of slave narratives and abolitionist literature—as well as Eliot's own appropriations of the tradition—see Thomas, "The Post-Abolitionist's Narrative." For Gabriel Chouteau chasing his slave, see Provost Marshal records, James F. Dwight, March 24, 1863, F1186; S. R. Curtis, March 3, 1863, F1236; National Archives.

42. Silas Bent to Sweringen, August 18, 1864, Ruth Ferris Collection, Herman T. Pott National Inland Waterways Library, SLML. For rural sales, Lucie Acock, Greenwood, to Snyder, June 11, 14, and 30 and August 4, 1864, Dr. John F. Snyder Papers, MHM. On Blow, Gerteis, *Civil War St. Louis,* 281; on the end of loyal master allowances, Gerteis, *Civil War St. Louis,* 289.

43. Quotes from draft order, n.d., Eliot to Schofield, accompanying Eliot, St. Louis to Schofield, November 9, 1863, folders 9 and 10, Eliot Papers, MHM (quoted in full, C. Eliot, *William Greenleaf Eliot,* 196–199); and sermon notes for August 22, 1862, Notebook 6, p. 126, Eliot Papers, WU. Louisa and her youngest, Nellie, arrived in the wagon; the other two came earlier on their own.

Eliot, to Sir, n.d. [after August 4, 1863] and Eliot, St. Louis, to Governor Andrew, November 15, 1863, folders 6 and 9, Eliot Papers, MHM; Eliot, *Archer Alexander,* 74–82; C. Eliot, *William Greenleaf Eliot,* 200–204.

44. Original orthography. Spotswood Rice, Benton Barracks Hospital, St. Louis to Kittey Diggs, September 3, 1864, in Ira Berlin et al., *Freedom,* 2: 289–290, as quoted in Gerteis, *Civil War St. Louis,* 290; Lane to Glasgow, June 8 [section dated

June 12], 1863, from transcription in William Carr Lane Papers, MHM. For brokers, Provost Marshal records, James Anderson, April 8, 1865, F1217; Alexander Hill, April 8 and 10, 1865, F1193, National Archives.

45. Thomas, *From Tennessee Slave,* 163; Edward L. Woodson, testimony to American Freedmen's Inquiry Commission, Berlin et al., *Freedom,* 2:580–581, in Gerteis, *Civil War St. Louis,* 286. "The Incredible Lindell Hotel Ball," *Missouri Historical Society Bulletin* 6, no. 2 (January 1950): 161; on the Colored Ladies' Union Aid Society, Gerteis, *Civil War St. Louis,* 224.

46. Yeatman, Partridge, Johnson, Greeley, and Eliot, St. Louis, to Abraham Lincoln, November 6, 1863, printed version of the open letter, Eliot Papers, MHM. On the Missouri Hotel, Samuel J. May to Sir, March 24, 1863, Eliot Papers, WU; Thomas, *From Tennessee Slave,* 168, 173; Gerteis, *Civil War St. Louis,* 273–276; and Leslie Schwalm, *Emancipation's Diaspora: Race and Reconstruction in the Upper Midwest* (Chapel Hill: University of North Carolina Press, 2009), 77–78. On AMA efforts, Provost Marshal records, Joseph McCracken, February 6, 1864, F1198, National Archives; C. Eliot, *William Greenleaf Eliot,* 260–273; Gerteis, *Civil War St. Louis,* 216, 218–219, 225, 275.

47. See Fellman, *Inside War,* 110–111; T. J. Stiles, *Jesse James: Last Rebel of the Civil War* (New York: Knopf, 2002); Maury Klein, "Dreams of Fields: St. Louis and the Pacific Railroad," *SLML Fellowship Reports,* ed. Gregory P. Ames (St. Louis: SLML, 2003), 21; Margaret Louise Fitzsimmons, "Missouri Railroads during the Civil War and Reconstruction," *MHR* 35, no. 2 (January 1941); 196–198. For a new perspective, see Mark W. Geiger, "Indebtedness and the Origins of Guerrilla Violence in Civil War Missouri," *Journal of Southern History* 75, no. 1 (February 2009): 49–82.

48. Fellman, *Inside War,* 95–96. For its shadow, Jennie Sutton, "St. Louis as a Theater of the South African War," American Studies Association annual meeting, Philadelphia, 2007; Benjamin Madley, "From Africa to Auschwitz," *European History Quarterly* 35, no. 3 (July 2005): 429–464; I thank both Sutton and Madley for our conversations on this subject.

49. George Caleb Bingham, *An Address to the Public, Vindicating a Work of Art Illustrative of the Federal Military Policy in Missouri During the Late Civil War* (Kansas City, 1871), 11, as quoted in Sutton, "St. Louis as a Theater of the South African War"; Albert Christ-Janer, *George Caleb Bingham of Missouri; the Story of an Artist* (New York: Dodd, Mead & Company, 1940), 101–110 and notes; Kenneth H. Winn, "George Caleb Bingham," in *Dictionary of Missouri Biography,* ed. Lawrence O. Christensen (Columbia: University of Missouri Press, 1999), 70–74.

50. George Caleb Bingham, *Order #11* (1865–c.1868), versions held by the State Historical Society of Missouri and the Cincinnati Art Museum. See also the reading in Aaron Astor, "Belated Confederates: Black Politics, Guerrilla Violence, and the Collapse of Conservative Unionism in Kentucky and Missouri, 1860–1872" (PhD diss., Northwestern University, 2006), 277–278.

51. *Daily Missouri Democrat,* September 1, 1863, as quoted in Sutton, "St. Louis as a Theater of the South African War." See also Charles R. Mink, "General Orders, No. 11: The Forced Evacuation of Civilians During the Civil War," *Military Affairs* 34, no. 4 (December 1970): 134.

52. Gerteis, *Civil War St. Louis,* 201. See also *Harper's Pictorial History of the Civil War,* September 1864; William J. Wooden Letters, MSA, also described in Gerteis, *Civil War St. Louis,* 193–195. On further refugees, Eliot to Mrs. E. S. Emmons's students, July 27, 1865, Eliot Papers, WU; C. Eliot, *William Greenleaf Eliot,* 256–259.

53. John Davis, Wood Lawn near Fayette, Missouri, to Col. Broadhead, May 10, 1864, James Overton Broadhead Papers, MHM; [Eliot], unsigned draft of memorial to Lincoln, n.d. [1864 by internal references], folder 8, Eliot Papers, MHM. On Frémont's bid, Gerteis, *Civil War St. Louis,* 307–308; Jörg Nagler, *Frémont contra Lincoln: Die deutsch-amerikanische Opposition in der Republikanischen Partei während des amerikanischen Bürgerkriegs* (New York: Peter Lang, 1984). On the 1864 election, Adam I. P. Smith, *No Party Now: Politics in the Civil War North* (New York: Oxford University Press, 2006); Jennifer L. Weber, *Copperheads: The Rise and Fall of Lincoln's Opponents in the North* (New York: Oxford University Press, 2006). Thanks to Ari Kelman for mentioning these books.

54. "Germans Arouse!" poster, rally announced for October 25, 1864, MHM Prints and Photographs Collection. For a St. Louis soldier's confidence, Love, Marine Hospital, Charleston, S.C., to Molly, September 10, 1864, Love Papers, MHM. On the 1864 election in Missouri, McKerley, "Citizens and Strangers," 77–78.

55. For the link between economic advancement and Republican war policies, see Marc Egnal, *Clash of Extremes: The Economic Origins of the Civil War* (New York: Hill & Wang, 2009), 13, 320–325. See also Eric Foner, *Reconstruction: America's Unfinished Revolution, 1863–1877* (New York: Harper & Row, 1988), Chapter Two; Orville Vernon Burton, *The Age of Lincoln* (New York: Hill & Wang), Chapter Ten.

56. Isaac Sturgeon, St. Louis, to Charles H. Branscomb, January 9, 1867, John F. Darby Papers, MHM. The letter is retrospective, recalling key events since 1860.

8 Abraham Lincoln's Lost Legacies

1. Handwritten transcript of St. Louis County records, April 18, 1865, 18:213, JNEM; *Missouri Democrat,* April 20, 1865, p. 2.

2. For the hearse, "St. Louis Closely Linked with Lincoln," *St. Louis Star-Times,* February 12, 1934, Abraham Lincoln Papers, MHM. Thanks to John Maurath of the Missouri Civil War Museum for this reference. For the courthouse decorations, *Daily Missouri Democrat,* April 22, 1865, reprinted in John Albury Bryan, *The Rotunda, 1839–1955: Its Changing Styles of Architecture, Its Historic Events and Mural Paintings, Its Restoration* (St. Louis: s.n., 1956), 32.

3. William E. Gienapp, *Abraham Lincoln and Civil War America: A Biography* (New York: Oxford University Press, 2002); Doris Kearns Goodwin, *Team of Rivals:*

The Political Genius of Abraham Lincoln (New York: Simon & Schuster, 2005); Orville Vernon Burton, *The Age of Lincoln* (New York: Hill & Wang, 2007). For the important connection between African Americans and Lincoln's legacy, see Burton, *The Age of Lincoln,* esp. p. 5.

4. Louis S. Gerteis, *Civil War St. Louis* (Lawrence: University Press of Kansas, 2001), 1–2, 308; William Earl Parrish, *Missouri under Radical Rule, 1865–1870* (Columbia: University of Missouri Press, 1965). For crosscurrents between westward expansion and southern rehabilitation, Heather Cox Richardson, *West from Appomattox: The Reconstruction of America after the Civil War* (New Haven, Conn.: Yale University Press, 2007).

5. *Missouri Democrat,* January 16, 1865, as cited in Gerteis, *Civil War St. Louis,* 310. On celebrations, George E. Stevens, *The History of the Central Baptist Church: Following Her Influence upon Her Times* (St. Louis, 1927), 10. Album of 1865 convention, MHM. For coverage, "Emancipation Jubilee in St. Louis," *Milwaukee Daily Sentinel,* January 18, 1865, no. 14, col. B, and "Emancipation Celebration in St. Louis," *Bangor Daily Whig & Courier,* January 22, 1865, no. 173, col. A, via Cengage, accessed May 2008. See also Louis Gerteis, "The Legacy of the *Dred Scott* Case: The Uncertain Course of Emancipation in Missouri," in *The* Dred Scott Case: *Historical and Contemporary Perspectives on Race and Law,* ed. Paul Finkelman, David Konig, and Christopher Bracey (Athens: Ohio University Press, 2010), 77–78.

6. For the fundamental reformulation of Reconstruction, see George P. Fletcher, *Our Secret Constitution: How Lincoln Redefined American Democracy* (New York: Oxford University Press, 2001); Amy Dru Stanley, *From Bondage to Contract: Wage Labor, Marriage, and the Market in the Age of Slave Emancipation* (New York: Cambridge University Press, 1998); Alison Efford, "New Citizens: German Immigrants, African Americans, and the Reconstruction of Citizenship, 1865–1877" (PhD thesis, Ohio State University, 2008), 74–76.

7. David D. March, "Charles Daniel Drake of St. Louis," *Missouri Historical Society Bulletin* 9, no. 2 (April 1953): 291–310, and David D. March, "Charles D. Drake and the Constitutional Convention of 1865," *MHR* 47, no. 2 (January 1953): 110–123. On uncertainty about Lincoln's thinking, see George M. Fredrickson, "A Man but Not a Brother: Abraham Lincoln and Racial Equality," *Journal of Southern History* 41, no. 1 (February 1975): 39–58.

8. Petition to the Convention, January 31, 1865, MSA.

9. Gerteis, *Civil War St. Louis,* 307–322; Parrish, *Missouri under Radical Rule,* 53–60; March, "Charles Daniel Drake"; Efford, "New Citizens," Chapter Two; John W. McKerley, "Citizens and Strangers: The Politics of Race in Missouri from Slavery to the Era of Jim Crow" (PhD diss., University of Iowa, 2008), 102–107, 113; Walter D. Kamphoefner, "St. Louis Germans and the Republican Party, 1848–1860," *Mid-America* 57, no. 2 (April 1975): 74–76, as cited in Kristen L. Anderson, "German Americans, African Americans, and the Republican Party in St. Louis, 1865–1872,"

Journal of American Ethnic History 28, no. 1 (Fall 2008), www.historycooperative.org/journals/jaeh/28.1/anderson.html, para. 17.

10. Husmann, *Missouri Constitutional Convention, Journal,* 48, as quoted in Efford, "New Citizens," 84; Anderson, "German Americans," paras. 2, 10–12. See also Efford, "New Citizens," Chapter Two; James Thomas, *From Tennessee Slave to St. Louis Entrepreneur: The Autobiography of James Thomas,* ed. Loren Schweninger (Columbia: University of Missouri Press, 1984), 176–178. On the specter of *laïcité* (enforced secularism), McKerley, "Citizens and Strangers," 85; Gerteis, *Civil War St. Louis,* 314.

11. Quoted in Parrish, *Missouri under Radical Rule,* 117–118; for "Draconian," Efford, "New Citizens," 71. See also Efford's Chapter Two generally.

12. On the closing of the convention, Gerteis, *Civil War St. Louis,* 313–314; for the howitzers, James H. Rollins to Dear Friend, April 13, 1865, Letter Book 3, p. 9, SLML. On the search for Booth, orders for telegram from E. B. Alexander, St. Louis, to commanders in Ironton, Macon, Hannibal, Lexington, Jefferson City, St. Joseph, and St. Charles, Abraham Lincoln Papers, MHM. For the most complete account of Lincoln's assassination as experienced in St. Louis, Louis Fusz Diary, MHM, entries for April 17 and 19, 1865, typescript pp. 69–77; for arrests and his suspicions of a new attack in entry for April 17, 1865, typescript p. 73, and Provost Marshal records, April 1865, F1139, F1201, F 1225, F1347, F 1391, and June 1865, F 1246, F 1317, National Archives, as accessed at MSA.

13. Excerpt from Eliot sermon in *Missouri Republican,* April 18, 1865; *Missouri Democrat,* April 20, 1865, p. 2. On Catholic actions and other church services, *Missouri Republican,* April 19 and 20, 1865. On the trauma of Lincoln's assassination, Barry Schwartz, "Mourning and the Making of a Sacred Symbol: Durkheim and the Lincoln Assassination," *Social Forces* 70, no. 2 (December 1991): 343–364; Kevin R. Hardwick, "'Your Old Father Abe Lincoln Is Dead and Damned': Black Soldiers and the Memphis Race Riot of 1866," *Journal of Social History* 27, no. 1 (Autumn 1993): 109–128; David W. Blight, *Frederick Douglass and Abraham Lincoln: A Relationship in Language, Politics, and Memory,* Frank L. Klement Lectures (Milwaukee: Marquette University Press, 2001).

14. Gerteis, *Civil War St. Louis,* 313–314.

15. Telegram reprinted in *Missouri Democrat,* April 20, 1865. St. Louis's funeral attempt has been forgotten almost completely. While mentioned in Bryan, *The Rotunda,* 31–33, and in a footnote of Lloyd A. Hunter, "Slavery in St. Louis 1804–1860," *Missouri Historical Society Bulletin* 30, no. 4 (1974): 260n89, it is not mentioned in Gerteis, *Civil War St. Louis;* James Neal Primm, *Lion of the Valley: St. Louis, Missouri, 1764–1980,* 3rd ed. (St. Louis: Missouri Historical Society Press, 1998); or William C. Winter and Civil War Round Table of St. Louis, *The Civil War in St. Louis: A Guided Tour* (St. Louis: Missouri Historical Society Press, 1994); and it was unknown to the Lincoln Museum librarian and archivist, though he knew of a similar

effort in Decatur, Illinois. Phone conversation with Kim Bauer, curator, Abraham Lincoln Presidential Library and Museum, March 30, 2006. On Lincoln and ties to Missouri, Richard W. Etulain, "Abraham Lincoln: Political Founding Father of the American West," *Montana: The Magazine of Western History* 59, no. 2 (Summer 2009): 5–6.

16. James Blaine to George R. Harrington, March 17, 1865, memoranda to Harrington, April 16, 1865, list of diplomatic corps and draft of funeral procession; James Wormley et al., Colored Committee of Washington, to Sir, April 17, 1865; Otis Swan, New York, to Harrington, April 17, 1865; Bishop Simpson, Philadelphia, to Harrington, April 17, 1865; Philip Speed, Louisville, to James Speed, April 17, 1865; George R. Harrington Papers, MHM.

17. William P. Smith, Camden Station, to Harrington, April 18, 1865; William B. Thomas to Harrington, April 17, 1865; George R. Harrington Papers. For early discussion of a more direct route, see the April 17, 1865, note to General Dix over the signature of Edwin Stanton; Henry J. Raymond and F. B. Carpenter, *The Life and Public Services of Abraham Lincoln. Together with His State Papers, Including His Speeches, Addresses, Messages, Letters, and Proclamations, and the Closing Scenes Connected with His Life and Death. To Which Are Added Anecdotes and Personal Reminiscences of President Lincoln* (New York: Derby & Miller, 1865), 788.

18. *Anzeiger des Westens,* April 21, 1865, author's translation; Althea [Mrs. Stephen Pierce Johnson], St. Louis, to Parents, April 23, 1865, Abraham Lincoln Papers, MHM.

19. Althea [Mrs. Stephen Pierce Johnson], St. Louis, to Parents, April 23, 1865, Abraham Lincoln Papers; for the hearse, see article on its destruction, "Fire in St. Louis. Three or More Men Crushed to Death by Falling Walls," *Philadelphia Inquirer,* February 11, 1887. On the Springfield funeral, Alexander M. Block, Springfield, to Sister, [Lee, Mass.], May 21, 1865, Hagaman Family Papers, MHM.

20. No recorded correspondence from Mary Todd Lincoln, George Harrington, or other White House representatives was found—nor, indeed, any mention beyond the letter from Blow, Taussig, and Thomas. On embalming Lincoln, Gary Laderman, *The Sacred Remains: American Attitudes toward Death, 1799–1883* (New Haven, Conn.: Yale University Press, 1996), 157–163.

21. Blow, Thomas, and Taussig were among those pressing for the Mississippi Bridge to be completed as soon as possible; see for example the James S. Thomas Scrapbooks, SLML, and advocacy for the bridge before the 23rd General Assembly, MSA.

22. *Daily Missouri Democrat,* April 22, 1865, reprinted in Bryan, *The Rotunda,* 32; *Anzeiger des Westens,* April 21, 1865, author's translation. For an article describing the bust, once damaged by Booth, "Wilkes Booth—His Treatment of a Bust of Lincoln," *Daily Cleveland Herald,* [May 25, 1869], no. 124, col. B, reprinted from the *St. Louis Dispatch,* May 3, 1869, via Cengage, accessed November 2006.

23. Sarah Williams, entries for April 14 and May 29, 1865, Sarah Cornelia Williams Diary, WHMC–St. Louis, SL 177; Frank B. Cressy, Cambridge, Mass., 1908, annotation in the copy of Galusha Anderson's *The Story of a Border City* held in the Snyder Collection of Americana, University of Missouri–Kansas City, as quoted in Hunter, "Slavery in St. Louis," 260n89.

24. Transcript of St. Louis County records, April 18, 1865, 12:247, JNEM.

25. Fusz Diary, entries for April 17 and 19, 1865, typescript pp. 72, 73, 75. For the influence of fear on the shape of Reconstruction, see Mark W. Summers, *A Dangerous Stir: Fear, Paranoia, and the Making of Reconstruction* (Chapel Hill: University of North Carolina Press, 2009).

26. Henry Boernstein, *Memoirs of a Nobody: The Missouri Years of an Austrian Radical, 1849–1866,* trans. Steven Rowan (1881; St. Louis: Missouri Historical Society Press, 1997), 397. For the complexities of Reconstruction, Eric Foner, "Reconstruction Revisited," *Reviews in American History* 10, no. 4 (December 1982): 82–100. For Johnson's clash with the Radicals, Michael Les Benedict, *The Impeachment and Trial of Andrew Johnson* (New York: W. W. Norton, 1973); Pamela Brandwein, "Slavery as an Interpretive Issue in the Reconstruction Congresses," *Law & Society Review* 34, no. 2 (2000): 315–366.

27. George Engelmann, St. Louis, to Alexander Carl Heinrich Braun, March 18, 1866, George Engelmann Papers, Missouri Botanical Garden. Translation by Edgar Denison, January 1988. On Germans and the 1865 vote, Efford, "New Citizens," 101–105; Anderson, "German Americans," paras. 11–17.

28. *An Address by the Colored People of Missouri to the Friends of Equal Rights* (St. Louis: Missouri Democrat Book and Job Office, 1865), appendix p. 23, held by SLPL. For the Missouri Equal Rights League and its leaders, McKerley, "Citizens and Strangers," 88–96; Gerteis, *Civil War St. Louis,* 292–293, 322–324; Gary R. Kremer, *James Milton Turner and the Promise of America: The Public Life of a Post–Civil War Black Leader* (Columbia: University of Missouri Press, 1991); Cyprian Clamorgan, *The Colored Aristocracy of St. Louis,* ed. Julie Winch (1858; Columbia: University of Missouri Press, 1999), 59, 95; William Patrick O'Brien, "Moses Dickson," in *Dictionary of Missouri Biography,* ed. Lawrence O. Christensen (Columbia: University of Missouri Press, 1999), 240–241.

29. *An Address by the Colored People of Missouri,* appendix p. 25; *Missouri Democrat,* January 15, 1867, as cited in Kremer, *James Milton Turner,* 23. On Langston's campaign and the resulting laws, *The Liberator,* October 13, 1865, p. 163, no. 41, col. A, via Cengage, accessed June 2007; Isaac Sturgeon, St. Louis, to Hon. Charles H. Branscomb, January 9, 1867, John Fletcher Darby Papers, MHM, and McKerley, "Citizens and Strangers," 94–99.

30. Gerteis, *Civil War St. Louis,* 316–322; Parrish, *Missouri under Radical Rule,* 53–60.

31. For the tax assessments, see the Dexter P. Tiffany Papers, box 52, folder 8. *Cummings v. Missouri* (1867), 71 U.S. 277. Chase, Miller, Swayne, and Davis dissented; one

Lincoln appointee, Justice Field, joined Wayne, Nelson, Grier, and Clifford in over-turning the oath. See Gerteis, *Civil War St. Louis,* 320.

32. Dickson to the *Christian Recorder,* October 13, 1866, as quoted in McKerley, "Citizens and Strangers," 102; Thomas W. Cunningham, Bolivar, to John F. Snyder, September 6, 1866, Dr. John F. Snyder Papers, MHM.

33. On opposing Drake, R. H. Cooper, St. Louis, to Charles H. Branscomb, January 1, 1867, Darby Papers; on the Germans, C. D. Drake to Aleck H. McGuffey, Cincinnati, January 18, 1867, Charles D. Drake Papers, MHM.

34. J. H. Clendening, Washington DC, to Major [William K. Patrick], May 12, 1867, William K. Patrick Papers, MHM; Drake to McGuffey, Cincinnati, January 23, 1867, Drake Papers. On Henderson's vote, Parrish, *Missouri under Radical Rule,* 240.

35. James Rollins, Omaha, to Samuel Glover and James Broadhead, St. Louis, July 28, 1868, James Overton Broadhead Papers, MHM, box 2. For the effort at women's suffrage, Gerteis, *Civil War St. Louis,* 233.

36. William Earl Parrish, *Frank Blair: Lincoln's Conservative* (Columbia: University of Missouri Press, 1998), 254–260.

37. Dickson, "A Plea for Impartial Suffrage," *Missouri Democrat,* November 1, 1868, Moses Dickson vertical file, MHM. For Bruce, Eric Foner, *Reconstruction: America's Unfinished Revolution, 1863–1877* (New York: Harper & Row, 1988), 357; Samuel Shapiro, "A Black Senator from Mississippi: Blanche K. Bruce (1841–1898)," *Review of Politics* 44, no. 1 (January 1982): 83–109. For Revels, McKerley, "Citizens and Strangers," 150.

38. For analysis of the 1868 amendment voting, McKerley, "Citizens and Strangers," esp. pp. 107–123, Table A1, and Figure B1; Anderson, "German Americans," paras. 18–22. For national comparisons, Efford, "New Citizens," 115.

39. "Monument to Lincoln—Energy of Colored Persons," *The Liberator,* August 18, 1865, via APS Online, accessed February 2007. Eliot's later account has Charlotte giving the money to Rucker, who gave it to General T. H. C. Smith, who forwarded it to Yeatman with a letter on April 26, 1865. Story retold in William Greenleaf Eliot, *The Story of Archer Alexander from Slavery to Freedom March 30, 1863* (Boston: Cupples Upham & Co., 1885), 12–13.

40. "Monument to Lincoln"; Eliot, *Archer Alexander,* 12.

41. Eliot, *Archer Alexander,* 12; "Monument to Lincoln."

42. William Greenleaf Eliot, *Education as Connected with the Right of Suffrage. An Address Delivered before the Constitutional Convention of the State of Missouri Jan. 24th, 1865* (n.p., n.d.), as quoted in Gerteis, *Civil War St. Louis,* 311. For the "African school," M. J. Hull, St. Louis, to J. F. Hull, October 25, 1866, Hull Family Papers, MHM. See also Gerteis, *Civil War St. Louis,* 275–276.

43. On recruitment and enrollment, Gerteis, *Civil War St. Louis,* 282–283; Antonio Frederick Holland, "Richard Baxter Foster," in *Dictionary of Missouri Biography,* 311–312. On Missouri Confederates in Mexico, Gerteis, *Civil War St. Louis,* 334;

William M. McPheeters, *I Acted from Principle: The Civil War Diary of Dr. William M. McPheeters, Confederate Surgeon in the Trans-Mississippi,* ed. Cynthia DeHaven Pitcock and Bill J. Gurley (Fayetteville: University of Arkansas Press, 2002), 292; Andrew F. Rolle, *The Lost Cause; the Confederate Exodus to Mexico* (Norman: University of Oklahoma Press, 1965), 8–18.

44. Richard Baxter Foster, *Historical Sketch of Lincoln Institute, Jefferson City, Missouri . . . Upon the Dedication of the New Building* (July 4, 1871), 6; 62nd Regiment, Fort McIntosh resolutions [January 19, 1866], as quoted in W. Sherman Savage, *The History of Lincoln University* (Jefferson City, Mo.: Lincoln University, 1939), quote from p. 2; see also pp. 1–18. Some of the primary sources Savage relied on are no longer available. For an earlier account from Foster, see Antonio F. Holland and Gary R. Kremer, eds., "Some Aspects of Black Education in Reconstruction Missouri: An Address by Richard B. Foster," *Missouri Historical Review* 92, no. 4 (July 1998): esp. pp. 415–416. See also Parrish, *Missouri under Radical Rule,* 128–132; and Holland, "Richard Baxter Foster."

45. 62nd Regiment, Fort McIntosh resolutions [January 19, 1866], as quoted in Savage, *History of Lincoln University,* 2; Foster, *Historical Sketch,* 7.

46. Richard Baxter Foster to F. A. Seely, April 16, 1867, Freedmen's Bureau Field Office Records for Missouri, Letters Received, M1908, roll 11, frames 226–232, accessed at the St. Louis County Library. Thanks to Ruth Ann Hager for alerting me to this letter. On the meeting with Eliot and others, Foster, *Historical Sketch,* 8.

47. Eliot, *Archer Alexander,* 13; Eliot uses a very similar phrase in the *St. Louis Democrat,* July 4, 1873, William Greenleaf Eliot Papers, WU, Notebook 8:83, 94. "Honor to a St. Louis Citizen: A Bronze Statue proposed of James E. Yeatman, at Washington, D.C.," [fall 1869] in Thomas Scrapbooks, SLML, Scrapbook for 1869, p. 256. See also Chapter 10.

48. Foster, *Historical Sketch,* 8–9; Savage, *History of Lincoln University,* 3–4. On the prejudices, *Missouri Republican,* April 18, 1868, reprinting an article from the *Missouri Democrat,* James S. Thomas Scrapbooks, SLML, Vol. 7, p. 163. On the move to Jefferson City, "Some Aspects of Black Education," 412; Holland, "Richard Baxter Foster," 312; Savage, *History of Lincoln University,* 4; "Snapshots of Old Lincoln— Continued," *Lincoln University Quarterly* 1–2 (March/April/May 1922): 4. On the AMA and the Freedmen's grant, Foster, *Historical Sketch,* 8–10.

49. Foster, *Historical Sketch,* 10; "Lincoln Institute," (Chicago) *Inter Ocean,* August 19, 1875, p. 4, no. 126, col. C, via Cengage, accessed November 2006. No explanation for the name is given in the earliest available records, despite the fact that they record the switch from "the Educational Institute" in January 14, 1866, to "Lincoln Institute" seemingly by the time of the first meeting, February 20, 1866. Savage, *History of Lincoln University,* 3–5; "Snapshots of Old Lincoln—Continued," 3. For board members, Sixth Annual Report of State Superintendent for Schools, MSA, General Assembly report appendix, 1872, report p. 22; Adolf E. Schroeder, "Arnold Krekel," in

Dictionary of Missouri Biography, 463–465. On Brown as a student, Foster, *Historical Sketch,* 10, and as a member of the board, Lincoln Institute Constitution, William Bishop Papers, WHMC-Columbia, C3894. Lincoln University is rarely mentioned in accounts of historically black colleges founded by whites, such as Fisk, Howard, and Lincoln University of Pennsylvania. See "The Origin and Development of the Negro Public College, with Especial Reference to the Land-Grant College," *Journal of Negro Education* 31, no. 3 (Summer 1962): 240–250; J. M. Stephen Peeps, "Northern Philanthropy and the Emergence of Black Higher Education—Do-Gooders, Compromisers, or Co-Conspirators?" *Journal of Negro Education* 50, no. 3 (Summer 1981): 251–269. For the briefest mention, see Donald Robert Shaffer, *After the Glory: The Struggles of Black Civil War Veterans* (Lawrence: University Press of Kansas, 2004), 33.

50. Foster, *Historical Sketch,* 10; Foster to Seely, April 16, 1867, Freedmen's Bureau Field Office Records for Missouri. For the endorsements, Savage, *History of Lincoln University,* 8; "Snapshots of Old Lincoln—Continued," 3–4.

51. Foster, *Historical Sketch,* 11; Savage, 12–15; McKerley, 98. Quote from Foster to Seely, April 16, 1867, Freedmen's Bureau Field Office Records for Missouri. For the reports, Superintendent Reports, 1869–1872, MSA, Kremer, *James Milton Turner,* 28–29.

52. See files on *State of Missouri v. Michael Schisler et al.,* box 619, folder 8, Missouri Supreme Court, MSA, as well the mention in *Missouri Democrat,* April 21, 1868, Thomas Scrapbooks, SLML, Vol. 7, p. 167. See also Elinor Mondale Gersman, "The Development of Public Education for Blacks in Nineteenth Century St. Louis, Missouri," *Journal of Negro Education* 41, no. 1 (Winter 1972): 35–47; Kurt F. Leidecker, "The Education of Negroes in St. Louis, Missouri, during William Torrey Harris' Administration," *Journal of Negro Education* 10, no. 4 (Fall 1941): 643–649.

53. Bill #688, 25th House Session, Adjourned, 1870, pp. 95–96, MSA; Foster, *Historical Sketch,* 11–12; Foster, entry for Lincoln Institute, Fifth Annual Circular to the 62nd Regiment, July 25, 1861 [1871], appendix p. 33, as found in Lincoln University Archives. See also "Lincoln Institute," (Chicago) *Inter Ocean;* and Kremer, *James Milton Turner,* 26–39.

54. Foster to Benjamin Gratz Brown, January 8, 1871, Governor's Papers, MSA. On the lynching, entry for Captain J. N. Gott, Boonville, Third Annual Circular to the 62nd Regiment, March 10, 1869, appendix p. 23, as found in Lincoln University Archives. On Foster's dismissal, Holland, "Richard Baxter Foster."

55. Dyer to D. C. LaRue, Kansas City, October 2 and 3, 1865, Letter Book 7:496 and 498, SLML; Dyer to J. H. Carter, August 21 and September 2, 1867, Letter Book 10:35, 45, 47; Dyer to A. H. Stephens, Philadelphia and Milledgeville, August 17 and 18, 1866, Letter Book 9:612, 619–620; on Douglass, Board of Direction Minutes, SLML, Second Volume, n.p., meeting August 1, 1865.

56. Paraphrase of Galusha Anderson, *The Story of a Border City during the Civil War* (Boston: Little, Brown, 1908), 28–31. For a similar account, Homer Bassford,

"Boisterous Group of Young Men Broke up Slave Auction at Steps of Old Court-house Here in 1861," August 4, 1933, as found in Bassford Scrapbook, 130A, MHM, which cites Winston Churchill, *The Crisis* (New York: Macmillan, 1901)—though in fact the sale there is of a Confederate's piano.

57. For a detailed investigation, see the internal report of Miel Wilson and Robert Moore, JNEM, Summer 2007. They suggest that Galusha Anderson, Winston Churchill, and the painting discussed here were melded into fact by popular memory. E-mail correspondence with Bob Moore, JNEM, National Park Service, to author, July and November 2007. For repetition as fact, Jo-Ann Morgan, "Thomas Satterwhite Noble's Mulattos: From Barefoot Madonna to Maggie the Ripper," *Journal of American Studies* 41, no. 1 (April 2007): 87–88; Hunter, "Slavery in St. Louis," 260n89; Primm, *Lion of the Valley*, 233; Winter, *The Civil War in St. Louis: A Guided Tour*, 27.

58. The original painting was purchased and then lost in a fire in the 1870s. Noble then completed a smaller replica copy, and this copy was donated in 1939 to MHM. James D. Birchfield, "Thomas S. Noble: 'Made for a Painter,'" *Kentucky Review* 6, no. 1 (Winter 1986): 44–45. For its tour, Henry T. Tuckerman, *Book of the Artists—American Artist Life* (New York: G. P. Putnam & Son, 1867), 488, also cited in Morgan, "Thomas Satterwhite Noble's Mulattos," 88. For linking the review to the renaming as a "last slave sale" after emancipation, see Albert Boime, "Burgoo and Bourgeois: Thomas Noble's Images of Black People," in James D. Birchfield, Albert Boime, and William J. Hennessey, *Thomas Satterwhite Noble, 1835–1907* (Lexington: University of Kentucky Art Museum, 1988), 38–44, and "A St. Louis Artist," *St. Louis Guardian*, March 16, 1867, as quoted in Boime, "Burgoo and Bourgeois," 39–40.

59. Alfred Jingle [pseudonym], "Fine Arts: Noble's 'Last Sale,'" *St. Louis Daily Times*, August 12, 1866, p. 2.

60. Ibid. Final quote from *St. Louis Daily Times*, August 12, 1866, p. 2, cited in Boime, "Burgoo and Bourgeois," 40. On Noble's ambiguous perspective, Birchfield, "Thomas S. Noble," and Morgan, "Thomas Satterwhite Noble's Mulattos," 83.

9 The Capital Failures of Reconstruction

1. L. U. Reavis, *A Pamphlet for the People: Containing Facts and Arguments in Favor of the Removal of the National Capital, to the Mississippi Valley* (St. Louis: E. P. Gray, 1869), 6. For Reavis's plan, without link to Liberal Republicanism, Patrick E. McLear, "Logan U. Reavis: Nineteenth Century Urban Promoter," *MHR* 66, no. 4 (July 1972): 567–588. For similarly "scientific" theories to promote western cities, see J. Christopher Schnell and Katherine B. Clinton, "The New West: Themes in Nineteenth Century Urban Promotion, 1815–1880," *Missouri Historical Society Bulletin* 30, no. 2 (January 1974): 75–88; Elliott West, *The Contested Plains: Indians, Goldseekers & the Rush to Colorado* (Lawrence: University Press of Kansas, 1998), 237–238; William

Cronon, *Nature's Metropolis: Chicago and the Great West* (New York: W. W. Norton, 1991), 32; Carl Abbott, *How Cities Won the West: Four Centuries of Urban Change in Western North America* (Albuquerque: University of New Mexico Press, 2008), 1–5; Henry Nash Smith, *Virgin Land: The American West as Symbol and Myth* (Cambridge, Mass.: Harvard University Press, 1950), 35–40.

2. Reavis, *A Pamphlet for the People*, 7. Reavis, *The New Republic, or, the Transition Complete, with an Approaching Change of National Empire, Based upon the Commercial and Industrial Expansion of the Great West Together with Hints at National Safety & Social Progress* (St. Louis: J. F. Torrey, 1867); *A Change of National Empire; or, Arguments in Favor of the Removal of the National Capital from Washington City to the Mississippi Valley* (St. Louis: J. F. Torrey, 1869); *Saint Louis: The Future Great City of the World* (St. Louis: By the order of the St. Louis County Court, 1870); *The National Capital Is Movable; or, Facts and Arguments in Favor of the Removal of the National Capital to the Mississippi Valley* (St. Louis: Missouri Democrat Book and Job Printing House, 1871). See Lee Ann Sandweiss, "Themes and Schemes: The Literary Life of Nineteenth-Century St. Louis," in *St. Louis in the Century of Henry Shaw: A View Beyond the Garden Wall*, ed. Eric Sandweiss (Columbia: University of Missouri Press, 2003), 234–235. On inevitability, Richard Yates, *Congressional Globe*, 41st Cong., 2nd sess., May 10, 1870, p. 3341, as quoted in Whit Cobb, "Democracy in Search of Utopia: The History, Law, and Politics of the National Capital," *Dickinson Law Review* 95 (Spring 1995): 574n224; thanks to Kate Masur for this source. See also *Missouri Republican*, October 23, 1869, as found in the James S. Thomas Scrapbooks, 1869 Scrapbook, p. 219.

3. On resistance to the amendments, William Gillette, *Retreat from Reconstruction, 1869–1879* (Baton Rouge: Louisiana State University Press, 1979); Michael Perman, *The Road to Redemption: Southern Politics, 1869–1879* (Chapel Hill: University of North Carolina Press, 1984); Heather Cox Richardson, *The Death of Reconstruction: Race, Labor, and Politics in the Post–Civil War North, 1865–1901* (Cambridge, Mass.: Harvard University Press, 2001). For Missouri's firstness, John W. McKerley, "Citizens and Strangers: The Politics of Race in Missouri from Slavery to the Era of Jim Crow" (PhD diss., University of Iowa, 2008), Chapter Five; Thomas Swain Barclay, *The Liberal Republican Movement in Missouri, 1865–1871* (Columbia: State Historical Society of Missouri, 1926). On Grant's challenges, Brooks D. Simpson, "The Reforging of a Republican Majority," in *The Birth of the Grand Old Party: The Republicans' First Generation*, ed. Robert F. Engs and Randall M. Miller (Philadelphia: University of Pennsylvania Press, 2002), 148–166. See also Andrew L. Slap, *The Doom of Reconstruction: The Liberal Republicans in the Civil War Era* (New York: Fordham University Press, 2006).

4. William Hyde and Howard Louis Conard, *Encyclopedia of the History of St. Louis, a Compendium of History and Biography for Ready Reference* (New York: Southern History Company, 1899), 1:490–491; James Neal Primm, *Lion of the Valley: St. Louis,*

Missouri, 1764–1980, 3rd ed. (St. Louis: Missouri Historical Society Press, 1998), 273–275; Cobb, "Democracy in Search of Utopia," 561–583. See also Olynthus B. Clark, "The Bid of the West for the National Capital," *Proceedings of the Mississippi Valley Historical Association* 3 (1909–1910): 214–290. For capital removal attempts, Cobb, "Democracy in Search of Utopia," and Kevin P. Phillips, *Arrogant Capital: Washington, Wall Street, and the Frustration of American Politics* (Boston: Little, Brown, 1994). Thanks to Carl Luna for this source.

5. *Daily Democrat,* May 11, 1869, as quoted in Maury Klein, "Dreams of Fields: St. Louis and the Pacific Railroad," in *SLML Fellowship Reports,* ed. Gregory P. Ames (St. Louis: SLML, 2003), 27; entries for May 10, 1869, Nathan D. Allen Diary and Seth A. Ranlett Diary, MHM.

6. Wyatt Winton Belcher, *The Economic Rivalry between St. Louis and Chicago, 1850–1880* (New York: Columbia University Press, 1947), esp. pp. 175–179, 193–194, 201; Jeffrey S. Adler, *Yankee Merchants and the Making of the Urban West: The Rise and Fall of Antebellum St. Louis* (New York: Cambridge University Press, 1991); Charles Van Ravenswaay, "Years of Turmoil, Years of Growth: St. Louis in the 1850's," *Missouri Historical Society Bulletin* 23, no. 4 (July 1967): 313–314; Carlos A. Schwantes and James P. Ronda, *The West the Railroads Made* (Seattle: University of Washington Press, 2008). For debunking, J. Christopher Schnell, "Chicago Versus St. Louis: A Reassessment of the Great Rivalry," *MHR* 71, no. 3 (April 1977): 245–265; Dorothy Jennings, "The Pacific Railroad Company," *Missouri Historical Society Collections* 6 (1928–1931): 288–314; Margaret Louise Fitzsimmons, "Missouri Railroads During the Civil War and Reconstruction," *MHR* 35, no. 2 (January 1941): 188–206; Cronon, *Nature's Metropolis;* James Neal Primm, "The Economy of Nineteenth-Century St. Louis," in *St. Louis in the Century of Henry Shaw: A View Beyond the Garden Wall,* ed. Eric Sandweiss (Columbia: University of Missouri Press, 2003), 131. See Chapter 4.

7. On the snow, Frederich Adolphus Wislenzus, St. Louis, to George Engelmann, February 28, 1869, George Engelmann Papers, Missouri Botanical Garden. On Omaha as a defeat, David M. Young, *The Iron Horse and the Windy City: How Railroads Shaped Chicago* (Dekalb: Northern Illinois University Press, 2005), 30; Klein, "Dreams of Fields," 21–22.

8. Primm, *Lion of the Valley,* 272, 282; Cronon, *Nature's Metropolis,* 295–309. For the state's critics, *Governor Thomas Fletcher v. George and John Knapp,* February Term 1867, Case Number 4441, St. Louis Circuit Court Records, MSA.

9. For the Southwest, Belcher, *The Economic Rivalry,* 206; Cronon, *Nature's Metropolis,* 302; Primm, "The Economy of Nineteenth-Century St. Louis," 118–120, 128–129. For shifting regional identity—albeit credited to earlier times—Adler, *Yankee Merchants,* 173–174; Christopher Phillips, *Missouri's Confederate: Claiborne Fox Jackson and the Creation of Southern Identity in the Border West* (Columbia: University of Missouri Press, 2000); Holly Zumwalt Taylor, "Neither North nor South:

Sectionalism, St. Louis Politics, and the Coming of the Civil War, 1846–1861" (PhD diss., University of Texas at Austin, 2004), 11, 389–390. Isidor Bush, Report to the Missouri Senate, 25th General Assembly, Adjourned, 1870, Missouri House and Senate Journals, box 39, MSA. For the petition, Capitol Fire Microfilm, 24th General Assembly, folder 78, items 30 and 31, MSA.

10. Louis S. Gerteis, *Civil War St. Louis* (Lawrence: University Press of Kansas, 2001), 236–252; Joseph E. Vollmer Jr., *The Incomparable James B. Eads, the Eads Bridge and His Great Ship Railway* (St. Louis: SLML and the Herman T. Pott Inland Waterways Library, 2007); Ken Winn, "Gods in Ruins: St. Louis Politicians and American Destiny, 1764–1875," in *St. Louis in the Century of Henry Shaw,* 48–49.

11. Robert W. Jackson, *Rails across the Mississippi: A History of the St. Louis Bridge* (Urbana: University of Illinois Press, 2001); Vollmer, *The Incomparable James B. Eads;* John A. Kouwenhoven, "The Designing of the Eads Bridge," *Technology and Culture* 23, no. 4 (October 1982): 535–568.

12. Primm, *Lion of the Valley,* 279–292. The bridge was to be known as the St. Louis Bridge; locals called it Eads's Bridge, which in the twentieth century became Eads Bridge.

13. Engraving of the banner, MHM Prints and Photographs; William Barclay Napton, *The Union on Trial: The Political Journals of Judge William Barclay Napton, 1829–1883,* ed. Christopher Phillips and Jason L. Pendleton (Columbia: University of Missouri Press, 2005), entry for June 18, 1874, p. 480; John A. Kouwenhoven, "Eads Bridge: The Celebration," *Missouri Historical Society Bulletin* 30, no. 3 (April 1974): 159–180; Primm, *Lion of the Valley,* 290–291.

14. Denton Jacques Snider, *The St. Louis Movement in Philosophy, Literature, Education, Psychology, with Chapters of Autobiography* (St. Louis: Sigma Publishing Co., 1920), 87; see also pp. 82–89. See also McLear, "Logan U. Reavis"; Logan Uriah Reavis Papers, Chicago History Museum; Logan Uriah Reavis Papers, MHM.

15. Caleb Atwater's 1829 comments, as quoted in Selwyn K. Troen and Glen E. Holt, *St. Louis* (New York: New Viewpoints, 1977), 45–49; *People's Organ,* January 21, 1846, p. 2, cols. 1–4, as held in RU106, Series 9, Subseries 9–2, Old Courthouse Material, JNEM; see also Schnell and Clinton, "The New West," 79–80; for statue dedication, Father and Mother [William and Abigail Eliot] to Etta Eliot, May 23, 1868, Eliot Papers, WU; Gerteis, *Civil War St. Louis,* 336.

16. Reavis, *A Pamphlet for the People,* 6; *Boston Daily Advertiser,* February 17, 1868, no. 41, col. H, via Cengage, accessed November 2006; Cobb, "Democracy in Search of Utopia," 562n160, 564–575; Hyde and Conard, *Encyclopedia of the History of St. Louis,* 1:490–491. On location, John Napier Dyer, librarian, to Logan Uriah Reavis, September 30, 1869, SLML, Letter Book 10, p. 275.

17. Horace Greeley to Logan Reavis, February 4, 1870, as reprinted in Reavis, *Saint Louis: The Future Great City of the World,* 6,7; *A Debate by the Philalethic Society of SLU, on Monday, February 21, 1870* (St. Louis: G. Knapp & Co., 1870) 5, 6.

Charles Sumner, Washington, to B. Gratz Brown, Erastus Wells, Henry T. Blow, William McKee, et al., June 10, 1869, Reavis Papers, MHM; for Johnson, *Missouri Republican,* September 24, 1869, as cited in Clark, "The Bid of the West," 235. For other newspapers, "St. Louis the National Capital," *Missouri Republican,* [July 7, 1869?], as found in the James S. Thomas Scrapbooks, 1869 Scrapbook, p. 115, SLML; Clark, "The Bid of the West," 240–245; Cobb, "Democracy in Search of Utopia," 563–564. *Chicago Tribune,* July 4, 1869, as found in James S. Thomas Scrapbooks, SLML, M-92, 1869 Scrapbook, p. 115. Walt Whitman, *Democratic Vistas* (1871), online at www.bartleby.com/229 paragraph 44, mentioned in Bryan M. Jack, *The St. Louis African American Community and the Exodusters* (Columbia: University of Missouri Press, 2007), 121. For the connection between capital removal and the eventual 1904 National Mall plan, Cobb, "Democracy in Search of Utopia," 581–582.

18. William Sherman, letter to the *Missouri Republican,* [October 22, 1869], as reprinted in "Capital Removal—A Candid Opinion from General Sherman—A Cold Douch for the St. Louis People," *Milwaukee Daily Sentinel,* October 30, 1869, no. 257, col. D, accessed via Cengage, accessed November 2006, also quoted in Cobb, "Democracy in Search of Utopia," 566–567.

19. "National Capital Convention," *Irving Union,* October 1869, p. 2, WU; Henry T. Blow, St. Louis, to G[ustavus] A[dolphus] Finkelnburg, Jefferson City, February 17, 1868, printed as appendix to Reavis, *A Pamphlet for the People,* 12. On Pulitzer and home rule efforts in 1870, Thomas Swain Barclay, *The Movement for Municipal Home Rule in St. Louis* (Columbia: University of Missouri Press, 1943), 59–68; William Nathan Cassella Jr., "Governing the Saint Louis Metropolitan Area" (PhD diss., Harvard University, 1953), 125–127, 135; and James McGrath Morris, "The Political Education of Joseph Pulitzer," *MHR* 104, no. 2 (January 2010), 78–94.

20. Capital Removal Convention Resolutions, 1869, WHMC-Columbia, C1711; "St. Louis the National Capital," *Missouri Republican,* [July 7, 1869], as found in the James S. Thomas Scrapbooks, 1869 Scrapbook, p. 115; Cobb, "Democracy in Search of Utopia," 565–575.

21. *Missouri Democrat,* October 24, 1869. On local changes, William Earl Parrish, *Missouri under Radical Rule, 1865–1870* (Columbia: University of Missouri Press, 1965), 228–326; McKerley, "Citizens and Strangers," Chapters Four and Five. For racial reunification nationally, David W. Blight, *Race and Reunion: The Civil War in American Memory* (Cambridge, Mass.: Belknap Press of Harvard University Press, 2001), 122–128; Heather Cox Richardson, *West from Appomattox: The Reconstruction of America after the Civil War* (New Haven, Conn.: Yale University Press, 2007), 89–90, 92, 108–110. On capital removal blocked, Cobb, "Democracy in Search of Utopia," 574. On the 1868 amendment, McKerley, "Citizens and Strangers," Chapter Four; Richard Allan Gerber, "The Liberal Republicans of 1872 in Historiographical Perspective," *Journal of American History* 62, no. 1 (June 1975): 40–73.

22. Carl Schurz, *The Reminiscences of Carl Schurz* (New York: McClure Company, 1907); Hans Louis Trefousse, *Carl Schurz, a Biography* (Knoxville: University of Tennessee Press, 1982); Rudolf Geiger, *Der Deutsche Amerikaner: Carl Schurz, Vom Deutschen Revolutionär Zum Amerikanischen Staatsmann* (Gernsbach: Casimir Katz Verlag, 2007).

23. Frederich Adolphus Wislenzus, St. Louis, to Engelmann, January 18, 1869, Engelmann Papers, translated by Edgar Denison, December 1987; "Senator Schurz on Suffrage," *Westliche Post* [June 18, 1869], as translated in the *Daily Missouri Democrat,* June 19, 1869. Emphasis in original. Found in the James S. Thomas Scrapbooks, 1869 Scrapbook. For an examination of how ethnically German the Liberal Republican movement was, see Jörg Nagler, "Deutschamerikaner und das *Liberal Republican Movement* 1872," *Amerikastudien/American Studies* 33 (1988): 415–438, and Alison Efford, "New Citizens: German Immigrants, African Americans, and the Reconstruction of Citizenship, 1865–1877" (PhD diss., Ohio State University, 2008), Chapter Six.

24. "West and South—The St. Louis Republican Supporting the Carl Schurz Republicans," *Boston Daily Advertiser,* September 30, 1870, no. 78, col. F, via Cengage, accessed May 2008. For the "New Departure" and Liberal Republicanism's tenets, Michael F. Holt, *By One Vote: The Disputed Presidential Election of 1876* (Lawrence: University Press of Kansas, 2008), 3–9; Slap, *The Doom of Reconstruction;* Barclay, *The Liberal Republican Movement;* and Marc Egnal, *Clash of Extremes: The Economic Origins of the Civil War* (New York: Hill & Wang, 2009), 337.

25. On McClurg's corruption, McKerley, "Citizens and Strangers," 168. On Virginia Minor, Bonnie Stepenoff, "Disfranchised and Degraded: Virginia Minor's Case for Women's Suffrage," in *History of Missouri Law,* ed. Mark Carroll and Kenneth H. Winn (Athens: Ohio University Press, forthcoming); Adam Winkler, "A Revolution Too Soon: Woman Suffragists and the 'Living Constitution,'" *New York University Law Review* 76, no. 5 (November 2001): 1456–1526.

26. Under the 1865 constitution, McClurg only had a two-year term. *Missouri Republican,* June 1, 1870, as quoted in Norma Lois Peterson, *Freedom and Franchise: The Political Career of B. Gratz Brown* (Columbia: University of Missouri Press, 1965), 176; Parrish, *Missouri under Radical Rule,* 288–289.

27. *Missouri Democrat,* March 18, 1870, as quoted in McKerley, "Citizens and Strangers," 151; "Advice Gratis," *New York Tribune,* as quoted in undated clipping [August 1870] from James S. Thomas Scrapbooks, SLML, Scrapbook 12, p. 48. Thanks to James McGrath Morris and Alison Efford for sharing their insights on the *Westliche Post's* structure at this time.

28. Efford, "New Citizens," Chapters Five and Six; Nagler, "Deutschamerikaner," esp. p. 421; Thomas Bender, *A Nation among Nations: America's Place in World History* (New York: Hill & Wang, 2006), 145.

29. Eliot, entry n.d. [late September 1870], Eliot Papers, WU, Notebook 7, p. 77; Charles Drake, *Speech of Senator C. D. Drake, delivered at Hannibal, Mo., September*

28th, 1870 (n.p.), 9, Rare Book and Special Collections Division, Library of Congress, as quoted in McKerley, "Citizens and Strangers," 122. See also McKerley, "Citizens and Strangers," 135–136, 124, 140–145, Figure A1, and Table B1; Kristen L. Anderson, "German Americans, African Americans, and the Republican Party in St. Louis, 1865–1872," *Journal of American Ethnic History* 28, no. 1 (Fall 2008), www.history cooperative.org/journals/jaeh/28.1/anderson.html, paras. 21 and 22.

30. Joseph Keppler, "The 15th Amendment Illustrated," *Die Vehme,* April 2, 1870, held by MHM. For Gasconade cartoons, see Chapter 5; for parodies of the Benton statue, Keppler, "Die Stadtväter im Anstreichergeschaft/The City Fathers in the Painting Business," *Die Vehme,* July 2, 1870, and "Statue of Senator Reed of Mo., to be erected in Lafayette Park, proposed by Puck," *Puck,* [clipping misdated; from after 1910], MHM. For Keppler's shift, Richard Samuel West, *Satire on Stone: The Political Cartoons of Joseph Keppler* (Urbana: University of Illinois Press, 1988), 52.

31. Keppler, "Verlorne Liebesmüh/Love's Labor Lost," *Die Vehme,* May 21, 1870, MHM; Drake, *Congressional Globe,* May 10, 1870, 41st Cong., 2nd sess., p. 3896, as quoted in Cobb, "Democracy in Search of Utopia," 574.

32. William Greenleaf Eliot, "Reavis' St. Louis the Future Great City of the World," *Missouri Democrat,* July 20, 1870, pasted over the draft version in Eliot Papers, Notebook 7, pp. 25–26, WU. On the council meeting, "The Future Great City," undated [August or September 1870] clipping in James S. Thomas Scrapbook, SLML, Scrapbook 12, p. 68. "St. Louis: The Capital Removal Question,*" Milwaukee Sentinel,* April 27, 1871, no. 98, col. D, via Cengage, accessed November 2006; Cobb, "Democracy in Search of Utopia," 575–580.

33. "The Future Great City," *Missouri Democrat,* October 2, 1870, as found in James S. Thomas Scrapbooks, SLML, Scrapbook 12, p. 149; Primm, *Lion of the Valley,* 272.

34. "The Future Great City," *Missouri Democrat,* October 2, 1870, as found in James S. Thomas Scrapbooks, Scrapbook 12, p. 149.

35. "St. Louis, the First City West of the Atlantic Seaboard," *St. Louis Times,* n.d., as found in James S. Thomas Scrapbooks, SLML, Scrapbook 12, p. 153; R. M. Scruggs, President of the Association, to Horace Greeley, New York City, April 1, 1870, Letterbook 10, SLML, M-117, A-3–15, p. 328. See also letters to Greeley on April 4, 1870, p. 305, and January 7, 1871, p. 393.

Thomas P. Kinnahan, "Charting Progress: Francis Amasa Walker's Statistical Atlas of the United States and Narratives of Western Expansion," *American Quarterly* 60, no. 2 (June 2008): 399–423.

36. Eliot, n.d. [1876], Eliot Papers, WU, Notebook 9, p. 149; Primm, *Lion of the Valley,* 272; Primm, "The Economy of Nineteenth-Century St. Louis," 130; Stevens, *St. Louis, the Fourth City,* 1:988–989.

37. McKerley, "Citizens and Strangers," 162–165; Anderson, "German Americans," para. 23.

38. "The Convention," *Daily Missouri Democrat,* September 4, 1870, as found in the James S. Thomas Scrapbooks, SLML, Scrapbook 12, p. 89. "The Colored Delegates Present an Ultimatum," un-attributed clipping [August 1870] in James S. Thomas Scrapbooks, Scrapbook 12, pp. 76–77. See also McKerley, "Citizens and Strangers," 149, 151–152; Peterson, *Freedom and Franchise,* 180–181. On Tandy, McKerley, "Citizens and Strangers," 157, 164–165. For Turner's candidacy, *Missouri Republican,* October 30, 1870, as cited in McKerley, "Citizens and Strangers," 169–170. On black Liberal Republicans, Leslie Schwalm, *Emancipation's Diaspora: Race and Reconstruction in the Upper Midwest* (Chapel Hill: University of North Carolina Press, 2009), 190–191.

39. "Obituary," *Missouri Democrat,* September 18, 1870, as found in the James S. Thomas Scrapbooks, SLML, Scrapbook 12, pp. 113–114; Peterson, *Freedom and Franchise,* 181; Parrish, *Radical Rule,* 291–299; McKerley, "Citizens and Strangers," 125, 159–174; Richardson, *West from Appomattox,* 109.

40. Parrish, *Radical Rule,* 309–317.

41. Eric Foner, *Freedom's Lawmakers: A Directory of Black Officeholders during Reconstruction* rev. ed. (Baton Rouge: Louisiana State University Press, 1996), as discussed in McKerley, "Citizens and Strangers," 154–155 and 176–178. On Turner, McKerley, "Citizens and Strangers," 171–172; Gary R. Kremer, *James Milton Turner and the Promise of America: The Public Life of a Post-Civil War Black Leader* (Columbia: University of Missouri Press, 1991), 51–56.

42. *Chicago Tribune,* October 11, 1871, as quoted in Schnell and Clinton, "The New West," 84. Images and headlines of Chicago fire and discussion of St. Louis's role in James S. Thomas Scrapbooks, SLML, Scrapbook 15, pp. 0–1, 2 verso, 4 recto. Currier & Ives, *The Great Fire at Chicago, Oct'r 8th* [sic], *1871.* See Cronon, *Nature's Metropolis,* 345–350. For memory of the St. Louis fire, see Chapter 1.

43. Washington University Board of Directors minutes, meetings on April 12, 1861, and June 12, 1861, pp. 130–139, WU; Ralph E. Morrow, *Washington University in St. Louis: A History* (St. Louis: Missouri Historical Society Press, 1996), 44–46; financial reports in the Board of Direction Minutes, SLML, Second Volume, n.p.

44. "Western Colleges," *Irving Union,* February 1869, p. 2, WU; on Chauvenet, Morrow, *Washington University,* 68–69; on hiring, "Changes and Improvements in Washington University," un-attributed clipping, September 1870, in Marshall Snow Scrapbooks, Scrapbook 1869–1874, p. 127, WU. For Eliot's resignation, entries for July 1, September 18, and [November or December] 1870, Notebook 7, pp. 1, 68–69, 91, Eliot Papers, WU.

45. "Washington University," *Missouri Democrat,* March 1871, Marshall Snow Scrapbook for 1869–1874, WU. On fund-raising, M., letter to the *Advertiser,* March 1871, in Marshall Snow Scrapbooks, Scrapbook for 1869–1874, p. 153; Morrow, "Washington University," 127; Charles M. Dye, "William Greenleaf Eliot and Washington University, St. Louis: An Innovation in Nineteenth Century American Higher

Education," *Missouri Historical Society Bulletin* 35, no. 3 (April 1979): 141–145. On Western Sanitary Commissions funds, Washington University Board of Directors minutes, January 20, 1871, pp. 288–289. On chancellorship, Eliot to James Yeatman, Chairman of the Board, September 9, 1871, transcribed in Board of Directors minutes, October 10, 1871 meeting, p. 309, WU.

46. For anniversary planning, S. A. Ranlett, Hudson E. Bridge, John T. Douglass, J. H. Alexander, J. H. Beach, R. A. Barnes, Robert Barth, John C. Tevis, Lafayette Wilson, and Charles Miller to Scruggs, September 17–29, 1870, Letter Book 4(a): 118–129, SLML. For responses to invitations, see December 23, 1870–January 9, 1871, Letter Book 4(a): 173–232. On plans to move, Board of Direction Minutes, Volume 3, pp. 31, 32, 54; Dyer to Bridge, Yeatman, and John M. Krum, June 7, 1871, Letter Book 10, pp. 454, 456, 458.

47. "Reavis Nominates Greeley for President," *Milwaukee Sentinel,* April 13, 1871, no. 86, col. B, via Cengage, accessed November 2006.

48. On Greeley's politics and his thinking, James Lundberg, "Reading Horace Greeley's America, 1834–1872" (PhD diss., Yale University, 2008); Jeter Allen Isely, *Horace Greeley and the Republican Party, 1853–1861, a Study of the New York Tribune* (Princeton, N.J.: Princeton University Press, 1947).

49. Brown as quoted in Peterson, *Freedom and Franchise,* 191; L. U. Reavis, *A Representative Life of Horace Greeley* (New York: G. W. Carleton & Co., 1872). Eugene Lawrence (text) and Thomas Nast (engraving), "Mr. Carl Schurz and His Victims," *Harper's Weekly,* September 7, 1872, p. 693; Nagler, "Deutschamerikaner," 428. For Blair, see Louis Gerteis, "The Legacy of the *Dred Scott* Case: The Uncertain Course of Emancipation in Missouri," in *The* Dred Scott Case: *Historical and Contemporary Perspectives on Race and Law,* ed. Paul Finkelman, David Konig, and Christopher Bracey (Athens: Ohio University Press, 2010), 78–79. For the national platform, Eric Foner, *Reconstruction: America's Unfinished Revolution, 1863–1877* (New York: Harper & Row, 1988), 500.

50. Lewis Bogy, Mayor's Message on Democratic National Convention, April 20, 1872, reprinted in *Missouri Democrat,* May 1, 1872, and Logan Reavis, "A Word to the Board of Health," April 7, 1872, as found in the James S. Thomas Scrapbooks, SLML, 1869 Scrapbook 16, pp. 45, 36. On the conventions, Matthew T. Downey, "Horace Greeley and the Politicians: The Liberal Republican Convention in 1872," *Journal of American History* 53, no. 4 (March 1967): 727–750; Peterson, *Freedom and Franchise,* 213–217, 223–224; Nagler, "Deutschamerikaner," 427; Slap, *Doom of Reconstruction,* Chapters 8, 9, and 10.

51. Holt, *By One Vote,* 3; Peterson, *Freedom and Franchise,* 217, 223–224, 226–227; Nagler, "Deutschamerikaner," 429–431, 435, 437; Anderson, "German Americans," para. 24.

52. "Speech of Mayor Brown," *Missouri Democrat,* June 18, 1872, clipping in the Thomas Scrapbooks, SLML, Scrapbook 16, pp. 83–84. For the 1875 National Railroad

Convention in St. Louis and the Texas & Pacific Railroad, C. Vann Woodward, *Reunion and Reaction; the Compromise of 1877 and the End of Reconstruction* (Boston: Little, Brown, 1951), 90–100.

10 Separating the City, County, and Nation

1. *Daily Missouri Democrat,* August 3, 1873, p. 4, Forest Park Collection, WHMC–St. Louis; Caroline Loughlin, Catherine Anderson, and Junior League of St. Louis, *Forest Park* (St. Louis: Junior League of St. Louis—University of Missouri Press, 1986), 3.

2. The St. Louis home-rule statute had been cited as the first of its kind, but recent research on annexation strategies (and failures) in the Northeast have pushed back that chronology. Richardson Dilworth, *The Urban Origins of Suburban Autonomy* (Cambridge, Mass.: Harvard University Press, 2005), Chapter Five, and Kenneth T. Jackson, *Crabgrass Frontier: The Suburbanization of the United States* (New York: Oxford University Press, 1985), Chapter Eight. Thanks to Michael Ebner for these references. On "firstness" claims, Howard Lee McBain, *The Law and the Practice of Municipal Home Rule* (New York: Columbia University Press, 1916), 113, as quoted in Thomas Swain Barclay, *The Movement for Municipal Home Rule in St. Louis* (Columbia: University of Missouri Press, 1943), 77. See also E. Terrence Jones, *Fragmented by Design: Why St. Louis Has So Many Governments* (St. Louis: Palmerston & Reed, 2000), 6–7. For the politics and the end of an era, Adam Arenson, "A Central Park in the West: Dividing City and County While Creating St. Louis's Forest Park," Western History Association, Oklahoma City, October 2007; Ken Winn, "Gods in Ruins: St. Louis Politicians and American Destiny, 1764–1875," in *St. Louis in the Century of Henry Shaw: A View Beyond the Garden Wall,* ed. Eric Sandweiss (Columbia: University of Missouri Press, 2003), 50, and David M. Scobey, *Empire City: The Making and Meaning of the New York City Landscape* (Philadelphia: Temple University Press, 2002), 251–252.

3. Crow, 1875, quoted without citation in Walter B. Stevens, *St. Louis, the Fourth City 1764–1909* (St. Louis: S. J. Clarke, 1909), 1:651; Edward King, *The Great South; a Record of Journeys in Louisiana, Texas, the Indian Territory, Missouri, Arkansas, Mississippi, Alabama, Georgia, Florida, South Carolina, North Carolina, Kentucky, Tennessee, Virginia, West Virginia, and Maryland* (Hartford: American Publishing Co., 1875), 219 (quote), 244. For the Panic, Michael F. Holt, *By One Vote: The Disputed Presidential Election of 1876* (Lawrence: University Press of Kansas, 2008), 10.

4. For antimonopoly parties, Holt, *By One Vote,* 11–18; Ruth Warner Towne, "Francis Marion Cockrell," in *Dictionary of Missouri Biography,* ed. Lawrence O. Christensen (Columbia: University of Missouri Press, 1999), 197–198; Hans Louis Trefousse, *Carl Schurz, a Biography* (Knoxville: University of Tennessee Press, 1982), 221–223. For the return to Democrats, William Earl Parrish, *Missouri under Radical Rule, 1865–1870* (Columbia: University of Missouri Press, 1965), 323–326.

5. "The St. Louis Whiskey Frauds—The Formation, Constitution and Operations of the Ring," *Boston Daily Advertiser*, July 19, 1875, no. 15, col. B, via Cengage, accessed November 2006; Lucius E. Guese, "St. Louis and the Great Whiskey Ring," *MHR* 36, no. 2 (January 1942): 160–183; James Neal Primm, *Lion of the Valley: St. Louis, Missouri, 1764–1980*, 3rd ed. (St. Louis: Missouri Historical Society Press, 1998), 301–303; William S. McFeely, *Grant: A Biography* (New York: W. W. Norton, 1981), 404–416. For exposés, Eric Foner, *Reconstruction: America's Unfinished Revolution, 1863–1877* (New York: Harper & Row, 1988), 512–524; William Gillette, *Retreat from Reconstruction, 1869–1879* (Baton Rouge: Louisiana State University Press, 1979), 236–251.

6. *Missouri Democrat*, February 2, 1871, quoted in Jones, *Fragmented by Design*, 4. On the constrained city, Jones, *Fragmented by Design*, 1–4, Parrish, *Missouri under Radical Rule*, 323; Barclay, *The Movement for Municipal Home Rule*, 38–42, 50–52, and 59; petition of the citizens of Chariton County, January 23, 1874, Senate Journal, 27th General Assembly, Adjourned, p. 155, MSA.

7. Barclay, *The Movement for Municipal Home Rule*, 74n3; delegates listed in *Debates of the Missouri Constitutional Convention of 1875*, ed. Isidor Loeb and Floyd C. Shoemaker, 12 vols. (Columbia: State Historical Society of Missouri, 1930).

8. Pulitzer, *Debates of the Missouri Constitutional Convention of 1875*, 1:402–403. Cited in Primm, *Lion of the Valley*, 303, and Barclay, *The Movement for Municipal Home Rule*, 80. On proposal to move to St. Louis, Pulitzer and Broadhead, *Debates of the Missouri Constitutional Convention of 1875*, 1:505, 3:249. For St. Louis committee and their proposals, *Debates of the Missouri Constitutional Convention of 1875*, July 20–August 2, 1875, sessions; Barclay, *The Movement for Municipal Home Rule*, 74–118; Jones, *Fragmented by Design*, 5; John W. McKerley, "Citizens and Strangers: The Politics of Race in Missouri from Slavery to the Era of Jim Crow" (PhD diss., University of Iowa, 2008), 174–176. For the St. Louis focus, Bradfield, 20th District, in debate of July 30, 1875, p. 9, as quoted in Barclay, *The Movement for Municipal Home Rule*, 117. For final vote, Barclay, *The Movement for Municipal Home Rule*, 119.

9. William Barclay Napton, *The Union on Trial: The Political Journals of Judge William Barclay Napton, 1829–1883*, ed. Christopher Phillips and Jason L. Pendleton (Columbia: University of Missouri Press, 2005), entry for July 4, 1875, p. 498; on cornfields, David Armstrong, *St. Louis Globe-Democrat*, April 21, 1876, as quoted in Thomas Swain Barclay, *The St. Louis Home Rule Charter of 1876; Its Framing and Adoption* (Columbia: University of Missouri Press, 1962), 21. Also quoted in Jones, *Fragmented by Design*, 11. For details, Article IX, Sections 20–25, of the 1875 Constitution; Barclay, *The Movement for Municipal Home Rule*, 119–120. Across the state, the totals were 76,688 (84.0 percent) for adoption, 14,517 (15.9 percent) opposed; Barclay, *The Movement for Municipal Home Rule*, 124–125. For a similar rhetoric around the 1854 consolidation of Philadelphia, see Andrew David Heath, "'The Manifest Destiny of Philadelphia': Imperialism, Republicanism, and the Remaking of a City and its People, 1837–1877" (PhD diss., University of Pennsylvania, 2008).

10. Eliot, entry for June 28, 1876, Notebook 9, p. 136, William Greenleaf Eliot Papers, WU; *Philadelphia North American,* as quoted in *Inter Ocean,* July 17, 1876, p. 5, no. 98, col. B, via Cengage, accessed November 2006. For longstanding hope for convention, Lewis Bogy, Mayor's Message on Democratic National Convention, April 20, 1872, reprinted in *Missouri Democrat,* May 1, 1872, and Logan Reavis, "A Word to the Board of Health," April 7, 1872, as found in the James S. Thomas Scrapbooks, SLML, 1869 Scrapbook 16, pp. 45, 36.

11. For decorations, abstract of St. Louis County Court Records, Vol. 22, p. 247, June 19, 1876, JNEM; David H. Armstrong, Chairman, Resident Committee, to Rufus J. Lackland, President, Chamber of Commerce, July 5, 1876, Saint Louis Merchants' Exchange Records, MHM. "The St. Louis Convention: Samuel J. Tilden, of New York, Nominated for President on the Second Ballot," *Daily Arkansas Gazette,* June 29, 1876, no. 189, col. B, via Cengage, accessed November 2006; Holt, *By One Vote,* 108–116. For the shifting political alliances, C. Vann Woodward, *Reunion and Reaction; the Compromise of 1877 and the End of Reconstruction* (Boston: Little, 1951), and the rebuttal in Holt, *By One Vote,* 11–14, 277–278n56. On hope for profits, L. A. Pratt, Barnum's Hotel proprietor, to George R. Taylor, owner, July 3, 1876, George R. Taylor Papers, MHM.

12. Primm, *Lion of the Valley,* 16, 122, 145–146; Walter Schroeder, "The Environmental Setting of the St. Louis Region," in *Common Fields: An Environmental History of St. Louis,* ed. Andrew Hurley (St. Louis: Missouri Historical Society Press, 1997), 18–19. St. Louis and Philadelphia streets share names but not the same order.

13. Arenson, "A Central Park in the West." For Lafayette Park, John F. Darby's draft letter to the *Missouri Republican,* July 28, 1876, John F. Darby Papers, MHM. For Central Park, Roy Rosenzweig and Elizabeth Blackmar, *The Park and the People: A History of Central Park* (Ithaca, N.Y.: Cornell University Press, 1992).

14. Frederick Law Olmsted, *Defending the Union: The Civil War and the U.S. Sanitary Commission, 1861–1863,* ed. Jane Turner Censer, The Papers of Frederick Law Olmsted, Vol. 4 (Baltimore: Johns Hopkins University Press, 1986), 585–602, as quoted in Louis S. Gerteis, *Civil War St. Louis* (Lawrence: University Press of Kansas, 2001), 227. For the history of the Botanical Garden and Shaw, William Barnaby Faherty, *Henry Shaw, His Life and Legacies* (Columbia: University of Missouri Press, 1987), and *St. Louis in the Century of Henry Shaw.* For the 1864 vote, Loughlin and Anderson, *Forest Park,* 4–5.

15. *Daily Missouri Democrat,* August 3, 1873, p. 4, Forest Park Collection; Blair, in "Forest Park—A Fete Champetre," [June 30, 1872], clipping in Thomas Scrapbooks, SLML, Scrapbook 16, pp. 88–89. On the distances, Report of the Commissioners of Forest Park, January 1, 1876, typescript p. 8, Forest Park Municipal Reference Collection, RB-M Oversize 352.73, SLPL; L. U. Reavis, *Saint Louis: Die Welt-Stadt Der Zukunft* (St. Louis: County Court, 1870), as copied in Loughlin and Anderson, *Forest Park,* 7–8.

16. Nathan Cole to John F. Darby, August 1, 1871, John F, Darby Papers, MHM; Loughlin and Anderson, *Forest Park,* 4–5, 13; Stevens, *St. Louis, the Fourth City,* I:797–798. See also Kevin C. Kearns, "The Acquisition of St. Louis' Forest Park," *MHR* 62, no. 2 (January 1968): 95–106. For the contrast with the West, Gunther Paul Barth, *Instant Cities: Urbanization and the Rise of San Francisco and Denver* (New York: Oxford University Press, 1975); Eugene P. Moehring, *Urbanism and Empire in the Far West, 1840–1890* (Reno: University of Nevada Press, 2004).

17. "The Size of the City," *St. Louis Globe-Democrat,* May 30, 1876, p. 4, quoted in Loughlin and Anderson, *Forest Park,* 22; Maximilian G. Kern, Report of Superintendent of Public Parks, December 19, 1871, *Mayor's Message,* appendix B, p. 224, Forest Park Collection. For doubts, N., "The Central Park," *Missouri Republican,* April 3, 1864, Forest Park Collection, and Loughlin and Anderson, *Forest Park,* 31. *Charles P. Chouteau v. Hiram Leffingwell* and *City and County of St. Louis v. William D. Griswold,* April Term 1874, case no. 29198. See also the Missouri Supreme Court decisions at 54 Mo. 458 and 58 Mo. 178, respectively. Files held at the St. Louis Circuit Court Files project, MSA, St. Louis. Relative size determined in conversations with Michael Everman, St. Louis Circuit Court Records archivist, July 2007. See also Loughlin and Anderson, *Forest Park,* 8–13.

18. Kern to Andrew McKinley, President of the Board of Commissioners, January 1, 1876, First Annual Report of the Superintendent and Landscape Gardener, typescript pp. 6–8, Forest Park Municipal Reference Collection. On carriages, "Forest Park Opening," *Missouri Republican,* March 21, 1880, p. 6, Forest Park Collection. See also Loughlin and Anderson, *Forest Park,* 15. On Mounds, Stevens, *St. Louis the Fourth City,* 1:921–929.

19. Quoted in Loughlin and Anderson, *Forest Park,* 3, 19. On working-class visitors, Kern to Andrew McKinley, First Annual Report, typescript pp. 7 and 8, Forest Park Municipal Reference Collection. On Jim Crow restrictions, Loughlin and Anderson, *Forest Park,* 110–111, 120, 165, 168–169.

20. Ruth Ann (Abels) Hager, *Dred and Harriet Scott: Their Family Story* (St. Louis: St. Louis County Library, 2010), esp. pp. 61–66, 85–90. See also Adam Arenson, "Freeing Dred Scott: Confronting an Icon in the History of Slavery, 1857–2007," *Common-Place* 8, no. 3 (April 2008), www.common-place.org.

21. Though Eliot maintained the title *Freedom's Memorial* and this title appears on its dedicatory plaque, by March 1876 (a month before its dedication), the statue was being referred to as the *Freedmen's Memorial.* "The Freedmen's Monument," *New York Times,* March 11, 1876, via New York Times Historical Archive; William Greenleaf Eliot, *The Story of Archer Alexander from Slavery to Freedom March 30, 1863* (Boston: Cupples Upham & Co., 1885), 14; Kirk Savage, *Standing Soldiers, Kneeling Slaves: Race, War, and Monument in Nineteenth-Century America* (Princeton, N.J.: Princeton University Press, 1997), especially Chapter Four. See also Christopher R. Eliot, "The Lincoln Emancipation Statue," *Journal of Negro History* 29, no. 4 (October 1944): 471–475.

22. Eliot, undated entry [April 14, 1876], Notebook 9, p. 105, Eliot Papers, WU; Ball to Stille, January 18, 1867, Stille Papers, Historical Society of Pennsylvania, as quoted in Joni L. Kinsey, "Thomas Ball, Freedom's Memorial, 1875," in *A Gallery of Modern Art: At Washington University in St. Louis,* ed. Joseph D. Ketner and Jane E. Neidhardt (St. Louis: WU Gallery of Art, 1994), 58.

23. Eliot, *Archer Alexander,* 88, 89. See also Joseph M. Thomas, "The Post-Abolitionist's Narrative: William Greenleaf Eliot's the Story of Archer Alexander," *New England Quarterly* 73, no. 3 (September 2000): 278–280. For the pedestal, Eliot, *Archer Alexander,* 13–14.

24. Frederick Douglass, *Oration in Memory of Abraham Lincoln: Delivered at the Unveiling of the Freedmen's Monument in Memory of Abraham Lincoln in Lincoln Park, Washington, D.C.* (1876), paras. 3, 24, 9, http://teachingamericanhistory.org, accessed July 2008. Douglass, "The Color Question," delivered July 5, 1875, in Hillsdale, near Washington, as quoted in David W. Blight, *Race and Reunion: The Civil War in American Memory* (Cambridge, Mass.: Belknap Press of Harvard University Press, 2001), 132. Eliot sent Yeatman in his place; Yeatman, St. Louis, to Eliot, March 28, 1876, pasted into Notebook 9, pp. 103–104, Eliot Papers, WU, and quoted in Charlotte Chauncy Eliot, *William Greenleaf Eliot, Minister, Educator, Philanthropist* (Boston: Houghton, Mifflin & Co., 1904), 350–351. See also discussion in David W. Blight, *Frederick Douglass' Civil War: Keeping Faith in Jubilee* (Baton Rouge: Louisiana State University Press, 1989), 51.

25. Frederick Douglass, *Inaugural Ceremonies of the Freedmen's Memorial Monument to Abraham Lincoln. Washington City, April 14, 1876* (Saint Louis: Levison & Blythe, 1876); later quote from David W. Blight, "'For Something Beyond the Battlefield': Frederick Douglass and the Struggle for the Memory of the Civil War," *Journal of American History* 75, no. 4 (March 1989): 1164–1165. See also Savage, *Standing Soldiers, Kneeling Slaves,* 77–81, 114–117. For Douglass's evolving emancipationist vision, see also Blight, "'For Something Beyond the Battlefield,'" and *Frederick Douglass' Civil War.* For fears at the centennial, Blight, *Race and Reunion,* 132–135. For connecting the centennial and the sculpture, Wayne Craven, "Thomas Ball and the Emancipation Group," *Elvehjem Art Center Bulletin* (Madison, Wis., 1976–1977), 45–47.

26. Lincoln Institute centennial exhibit, 1876, Manuscript, Archives, and Rare Book Library, Emory University. Thanks to Michael David Cohen for the reference. On the Centennial generally, John R. Keigher, "Remembering the Revolution: Perceptions of Independence Hall, the Declaration, and the Liberty Bell in 1876," in *The Centennial Exhibition of 1876: A Material Culture Study by Villanova University Students,* www3.villanova.edu/centennial, accessed July 2008; Foner, *Reconstruction,* 564–565; Robert W. Rydell, *All the World's a Fair: Visions of Empire at American International Expositions, 1876–1916* (Chicago: University of Chicago Press, 1984), 9–37.

27. Broadhead, statement in *Missouri Republican,* April 22, 1876, as quoted in Barclay, *The St. Louis Home Rule Charter,* 21; on consolidation, Address of Thomas T. Gantt to the Missouri Historical Society, December 21, 1880, printed in *Missouri Republican,* December 26, 1880, as quoted in Barclay, *The Movement for Municipal Home Rule,* 88n70. For a detailed description, Barclay, *The Movement for Municipal Home Rule;* Barclay, *The St. Louis Home Rule Charter;* William Nathan Cassella Jr., "Governing the Saint Louis Metropolitan Area" (PhD diss., Harvard University, 1953); William Nathan Cassella Jr., "City-County Separation: The 'Great Divorce' of 1876," *Missouri Historical Society Bulletin* 55, no. 2 (January 1959): 85–104; Lana Stein, "Home Rule for St. Louis," *Gateway Heritage* 22, no. 2 (2001): 74; for summaries, Primm, *Lion of the Valley,* 303–308; Jones, *Fragmented by Design,* 2–24. For Broadhead, G. B. Crane, Napa County, California, to Broadhead, June 10, 1876, and Thomas C. Reynolds, St. Louis, to W. D. Porter, Charleston, S. C., June 12, 1876, James Overton Broadhead Papers, MHM, and Kirby Ross, "James O. Broadhead: Ardent Unionist, Unrepentant Slaveholder." www.civilwarstlouis.com/history2/broadhead-profile.htm, 2002, accessed July 2009.

28. St. Louis County Court Records, Vol. 23, p. 173, March 12, 1877, extracted at JNEM. For the requirements, see Article IX of the 1875 Constitution; Barclay, *The St. Louis Home Rule Charter,* 1–9; Jones, *Fragmented by Design,* 6–9. On the length, Barclay, *The St. Louis Home Rule Charter,* 58.

29. Barclay, *The St. Louis Home Rule Charter,* 52–53.

30. For the vote date, Barclay, *The St. Louis Home Rule Charter,* 52. Official returns, *Records of the Registers Office,* City of St. Louis, as cited in Barclay, *The St. Louis Home Rule Charter,* 67. For Overstolz's reaction, pp. 76–77; on the lawsuit, p. 68–69.

31. *Missouri Republican,* February 6, 1877, quoted in Barclay, *The St. Louis Home Rule Charter,* 89. See also pp. 78–80. For national parallels, see Scobey, *Empire City.*

32. Napton, *The Union on Trial,* entry for August 31, 1876, p. 509. For an excellent overview of the election and its controversy, Holt, *By One Vote.* For Republican hope of influence, Holt, *By One Vote,* 128–129.

33. William Tecumseh Sherman to J. C. Audenreid, November 18, 1876, Sherman Papers, Library of Congress, as quoted by Eric Rauchway at http://edgeofthewest.wordpress.com, January 2, 2008. On the speech, Board of Trustees meetings February 8 and 22, 1876, Volume 1, pp. 343–334, WU; Sherman, St. Louis, to William Greenleaf Eliot, February 19, 1876, William Greenleaf Eliot Papers, MHM.

34. On the national election, Holt, *By One Vote,* 183–184, 206–213; Gillette, *Retreat from Reconstruction,* 301–322; on Schurz, Napton, *The Union on Trial,* entry for December 6, 1876, p. 522, and Gillette, *Retreat from Reconstruction,* 327; for St. Louis, Barclay, *The St. Louis Home Rule Charter,* 81–86.

35. The final St. Louis appeal, to the Missouri Supreme Court, was refused April 26, 1877, yet the county court had already dissolved; St. Louis County Records,

meeting March 12, 1877, 23: 173, excerpted in Planning Records, RU106, Series 9, JNEM; Barclay, *The St. Louis Home Rule Charter*, 90–100. For Hayes's election, Holt, *By One Vote*, 214, 220, 223, 232–235. "Compromise of 1877" is C. Vann Woodward's phrase; see Holt, *By One Vote*, 238–240. Funding for the Texas and Pacific Railroad was not approved, but the Southern Pacific Railroad was later supported; James McPherson and James Hogue, *Ordeal by Fire: The Civil War and Reconstruction* 4th ed. (New York: McGraw-Hill, 2009), 653.

36. For 1877 and some dissent on end dates, Thomas J. Brown, ed., *Reconstructions: New Perspectives on the Postbellum United States* (New York: Oxford University Press, 2006); Heather Cox Richardson, *West from Appomattox: The Reconstruction of America after the Civil War* (New Haven, Conn.: Yale University Press, 2007).

37. Henry Boernstein, *Memoirs of a Nobody: The Missouri Years of an Austrian Radical, 1849–1866,* trans. Steven Rowan (St. Louis: Missouri Historical Society Press, 1997), 233n12. Thanks to Steve Rowan for pointing out the connection between Hammer's land and Busch.

38. Strike proclamation, July 25, 1877, State Historical Society of Wisconsin, as reproduced as the frontispiece in David T. Burbank, *Reign of the Rabble: the St. Louis General Strike of 1877* (New York: A. M. Kelley, 1966). See also David Roediger, " 'Not Only the Ruling Classes to Overcome, but Also the So-Called Mob': Class, Skill and Community in the St. Louis General Strike of 1877," *Journal of Social History* 19, no. 2 (Winter 1985): 213–239; David O. Stowell, ed., *The Great Strikes of 1877* (Urbana: University of Illinois Press, 2008).

39. For a comparison of freight rates in St. Louis, Cincinnati, Chicago, and Louisville, Edward Vernon, Transportation Bureau of the Merchants' Exchange, to Michael McEnnis, Chair, Executive Committee, March 18, 1876, Saint Louis Merchants' Exchange Records, MHM. On bankruptcy and sale, John A. Kouwenhoven, "Eads Bridge: The Celebration," *Missouri Historical Society Bulletin* 30, no. 3 (April 1974): 160–161; Primm, *Lion of the Valley*, 292–293. The collapse of St. Louis's rivalry with Chicago was complete; see Robert E. Riegel, "The Missouri Pacific Railroad to 1879," *MHR* 18, no. 1 (October 1923): 15–16, 20–26.

40. Schurz to Eliot, September 27, 1880, Eliot Papers, WU; Primm, *Lion of the Valley*, 272; James Neal Primm, "The Economy of Nineteenth-Century St. Louis," in *St. Louis in the Century of Henry Shaw*, 130–131.

41. John Y. Simon, "Ulysses S. Grant," in *Dictionary of Missouri Biography*, 347; Richard Samuel West, *Satire on Stone: The Political Cartoons of Joseph Keppler* (Urbana: University of Illinois Press, 1988); Trefousse, *Carl Schurz, a Biography;* Chester Verne Easum, *The Americanization of Carl Schurz* (Chicago: University of Chicago, 1929); Denis Brian, *Pulitzer: A Life* (New York: J. Wiley, 2001). For Reavis, continuing editions of *The Future Great City,* and ticket stubs in the L. U. Reavis Papers, MHM; J. Christopher Schnell, "Logan Uriah Reavis," in *Dictionary of Missouri Biography,* 641.

42. Loughlin and Anderson, *Forest Park,* 26–29; Henry Overstolz, *Mayor's Message,* 1877, p. 15, as cited in Loughlin and Anderson, *Forest Park,* 25.

43. *St. Louis Dispatch,* August 18, 1876, as quoted in Barclay, *The Movement for Municipal Home Rule,* 100–101n73. For County settlement, Tim Fox, *Where We Live: A Guide to St. Louis Communities* (St. Louis: Missouri Historical Society Press, 1995). For the history of partial and informal unification, Cassella, "Governing the Saint Louis Metropolitan Area," 166–592; Jones, *Fragmented by Design,* especially Chapters 3 and 5. For the rise of suburbs after annexation, see Heath, "'The Manifest Destiny of Philadelphia,'" 467, and Dilworth, *The Urban Origins of Suburban Autonomy,* Chapter 2.

44. For suburbanization, Dolores Hayden, *Building Suburbia: Green Fields and Urban Growth, 1820–2000* (New York: Pantheon Books, 2003). The metropolitan area also includes adjacent counties in Missouri and Illinois. Population figures from Campbell Gibson, *Population of the 100 Largest Cities and Other Urban Places in the United States: 1790 to 1990* (Washington, D.C.: Population Division, U.S. Bureau of the Census, June 1998), www.census.gov/population, accessed August 2007; Jones, *Fragmented by Design,* 25. On the post–World War II struggles of St. Louis, Colin Gordon, *Mapping Decline: St. Louis and the Fate of the American City* (Philadelphia: University of Pennsylvania Press, 2008).

45. Whitman, "202. St. Louis Memoranda" and "225. A Week's Visit to Boston" in *Specimen Days* (1885), accessed online at www.bartleby.com/229.

Epilogue

1. "Slave Auction on Courthouse Steps," *St. Louis Post-Dispatch,* May 10, 1904, p. 1. Thanks to Jennie Sutton for this source.

2. *Official Directory of the Louisiana Purchase Exposition, 1904,* (St. Louis: Woodward & Tiernan Printing Co., 1904); Tim Fox and Duane R. Sneddeker, *From the Palaces to the Pike: Visions of the 1904 World's Fair* (St. Louis: Missouri Historical Society Press, 1997); Robert W. Rydell, *All the World's a Fair: Visions of Empire at American International Expositions, 1876–1916* (Chicago: University of Chicago Press, 1984), 154–183.

3. The Missouri History Museum centennial exhibit provides good perspective; "The 1904 World's Fair: Looking Back at Looking Forward," sections online, www. mohistory.org, accessed July 2008. On attempts at 1893, James Neal Primm, *Lion of the Valley: St. Louis, Missouri, 1764–1980,* 3rd ed. (St. Louis: Missouri Historical Society Press, 1998), 373–374. Thomas M. Spencer, *The St. Louis Veiled Prophet Celebration: Power on Parade, 1877–1995* (Columbia: University of Missouri Press, 2000); on French memories and the Missouri Historical Society, Jay Gitlin, "From Private Stories to Public Memory: The Chouteau Descendants of St. Louis and the Production of History," Western History Association annual meeting, St. Louis, October 11,

2006. In the 1900 and 1910 Censuses, St. Louis was legitimately the fourth largest, behind New York City, Chicago, and Philadelphia, just ahead of Boston. Campbell Gibson, *Population of the 100 Largest Cities and Other Urban Places in the United States: 1790 to 1990* (Washington, D.C.: Population Division, U.S. Bureau of the Census, 1998) www.census.gov/population, accessed August 2006.

4. "Slave Auction on Courthouse Steps."

5. In the Pageant and Masque, the cultural civil war made a cameo—Thomas Hart Benton and the Western Sanitary Commission nurses rush by and Union victory solves all. St. Louis Pageant Drama Association, *Official Programme. The Pageant and Masque of Saint Louis, Forest Park, Thursday, Friday, Saturday and Sunday, May 28th, 29th, 30th and 31st, 1914* (St. Louis: Nixon-Jones Printing Co., 1914). See also Donald Bright Ostler, "Nights of Fantasy: The St. Louis Pageant and Masque of 1914," *Missouri Historical Society Bulletin* 31, no. 3 (April 1975): 175–205. For the Masque's created history, Sandweiss, *St. Louis: The Evolution of an American Urban Landscape* (Philadelphia: Temple University Press, 2001), 208–209. For the era of forgetting, David W. Blight, *Race and Reunion: The Civil War in American Memory* (Cambridge, Mass.: Belknap Press of Harvard University Press, 2001).

6. See for example Catherine Hall, *Civilising Subjects: Metropole and Colony in the English Imagination, 1830–1867* (Chicago: University of Chicago Press, 2002); Timothy Mitchell, *Colonising Egypt* (Berkeley: University of California Press, 1988); Frank Towers, *The Urban South and the Coming of the Civil War* (Charlottesville: University of Virginia Press, 2004); Carl Abbott, *How Cities Won the West: Four Centuries of Urban Change in Western North America* (Albuquerque: University of New Mexico Press, 2008).

7. For glosses of Manifest Destiny that skip its failures, Anders Stephanson, *Manifest Destiny: American Expansionism and the Empire of Right* (New York: Hill & Wang, 1995); Walter T. K. Nugent, *Habits of Empire: A History of American Expansion* (New York: Knopf, 2008).

8. Walter T. K. Nugent, *The Money Question during Reconstruction* (New York: W. W. Norton, 1967; on Alaska's struggle for approval, Nugent, *Habits of Empire*, 244–245. On western policy after the Civil War, see Elliott West, "Reconstructing Race," *Western Historical Quarterly* 34, no. 1 (Spring 2003): 7–26; Heather Cox Richardson, *West from Appomattox: The Reconstruction of America after the Civil War* (New Haven, Conn.: Yale University Press, 2007); C. Joseph Genetin-Pilawa, "Reconstruction in Indian Country: Ely Parker and the Contentious Peace Policy," American Historical Association annual meeting, San Diego, January 9, 2010.

9. For the newness of the 1890s version, Paul Sabin, "Home and Abroad: The Two 'Wests' of Twentieth-Century United States History," *Pacific Historical Review* 66, no. 3 (August 1997): 305–335; David M. Wrobel, *The End of American Exceptionalism: Frontier Anxiety from the Old West to the New Deal* (Lawrence: University Press of Kansas, 1993).

10. For less St. Louis history and more lore, Ernest Kirschten, *Catfish and Crystal* (Garden City, N.Y.: Doubleday, 1960); Charles Van Ravenswaay, *St. Louis: An Informal History of the City and Its People, 1764–1865* (St. Louis: Missouri Historical Society, 1991).

11. Jefferson National Expansion Memorial, elements online, www.nps/gov/jeff.

Archival Bibliography

Academy of Science of St. Louis
  Academy of Science Minutes
Archdiocese of St. Louis Archives
  Bishop Files
  Parish Files
  Mary E. White, "Archbishop Peter Richard Kenrick and the Civil War"
Beinecke Rare Book and Manuscript Library, Yale University
  St. Louis City Directories
Central Baptist Church Archives, St. Louis
  Church Histories
Chicago History Museum (formerly the Chicago Historical Society)
  L. U. Reavis Papers
Davenport Public Library
  Davenport City Council Minutes
Emory University Manuscript, Archives, and Rare Book Library
  Lincoln Institute Centennial Exhibit
Gasconade County Historical Society, Hermann, Missouri
  1855 Inquest, Deposition, and Subpoena
Harvard University Libraries
Jefferson National Expansion Memorial, National Park Service, St. Louis
  John A. Bryan, "The Rotunda 1839–1955"

Historic Structure Report
Jefferson National Expansion Memorial Administrative History
Mechanics' Institute of St. Louis Records
Old Courthouse Materials
Research Reports
Superintendents' Reports
Lincoln University Archives, Jefferson City, Missouri
Board Minutes
Lincoln Institute Blotter
Subject Files
Mark Twain Boyhood Home and Museum, Hannibal, Missouri
Larry McHenry Research Collection of Rock Island Bridge Materials
Midwest Jesuit Archives, St. Louis
Biographical Files
Missouri Botanical Garden, St. Louis
George Engelmann Papers
Missouri History Museum, St. Louis (formerly the Missouri Historical Society)
Nathan D. Allen Diary
Badger Family Papers
Henry C. Barnard Papers
Bates Family Papers
Nathan Belcher Papers
Thomas Hart Benton Collection
Daniel Bissell Papers
Blow Family Papers
Hudson Erastus Bridge Papers
James Overton Broadhead Papers
P. Taylor Bryan Papers
Chouteau Papers
Civil War Collection
Crow Family Papers
John Fletcher Darby Papers
John Dougherty Papers
Charles D. Drake Papers
William Greenleaf Eliot Papers
George J. Engelmann Papers
Filley Family Papers
Louis Fusz Diary
Daniel B. Gale Papers
Charles Gibson Papers
Hagaman Family Papers

George R. Harrington Papers
Thomas S. Hawley Papers
Hull Family Papers
Hunt Family Papers
Julius Hutawa Binder
Kennett Family Papers
Kensinger Family Collection
Knapp Family Papers
James C. Lackland Papers
William Carr Lane Papers
Abraham Lincoln Papers
James Edwin Love Papers
Ludlow-Field-Maury Family Papers
Mayer Family Papers
A. F. McAlister File
Madison Miller Papers
Missouri Historical Society Museum Collections
Missouri History Collection
Missouri History Museum Scrapbooks
Meredith T. Moore Papers
Morrison Family Papers
Mullanphy Family Papers
Frank P. O'Hare Papers
Paddock Family Papers
William K. Patrick Papers
Charles Peabody Travel Diary
Portraits Collection
Prints and Photographs Collection
Railroads Collection
Seth A. Ranlett Diary
L. U. Reavis Papers
St. Louis Circuit Court Records
St. Louis Merchants' Exchange Records
St. Louis Volunteer Fire Department Collection
Schools Collection
Dred Scott Collection
Slaves and Slavery Collection
George R. Smith Papers
Solomon Franklin Smith Papers
Dr. John F. Snyder Papers
William L. Sublette Papers

James Tower Sweringen Papers
George R. Taylor Papers
Theater Program Collection
Dexter P. Tiffany Collection
Transportation Collection
Samuel Treat Papers
Julius Sylvester Walsh Papers
Sylvester Waterhouse Papers
James Josiah Webb Papers
Willis Family Papers
Carl Wimar Papers
Missouri State Archives, Jefferson City
1875 Constitutional Convention Debates
W. J. Burton Manuscript History of the Pacific Railroad, 1956
Capitol Fire Collection
Governor's Papers
Laws of Missouri
Missouri House and Senate Papers
Missouri Supreme Court Papers
Provost Marshal Papers (National Archives microfilm)
William J. Wooden Letters
Missouri State Archives, St. Louis Circuit Court Records, St. Louis
Civil and Criminal Cases from the Civil War Era
Forest Park Cases
Mechanics' Liens
New York Public Library, Humanities and Social Science Library
Pilgrim Congregational Church, St. Louis
Board Minutes
Church Histories
Rock Island Arsenal Museum
Arsenal Histories
Museum and Artwork Collection
Rock Island County Historical Society, Moline, Illinois
Rock Island Public Library
Rock Island Bridge Files
Second Baptist Church of Greater St. Louis
Church Board Minutes
Church Histories
State Historical Society of Missouri, Columbia
State Historical Society Art Collection
Vertical Files

St. John's Methodist Church Archives
    Church Histories
    St. John's Auxiliary Minutes
St. Louis Art Museum
    Curators' Files
St. Louis County Library
    Church Histories
    Freedmen's Bureau Letters (National Archives microfilm)
St. Louis Mercantile Library
    1856 Letter of Introduction
    Archives of the St. Louis Mercantile Library Association
    Adolphus Benedict Scrapbook
    Thomas Hart Benton Collection
    Emil Boehl Photographs
    Robert Campbell Family Collection
    Gantt et al. Letter to George Vandenhoff
    Alexander Gardner Photographic Prints
    Greve-Fisher Collection
    Records of the St. Louis Lyceum
    Robbins Collection
    St. Louis Fairs Collection
    St. Louis Maps and Guidebooks
    St. Louis Mercantile Library Art and Sculpture Collection
    St. Louis Views and Images Collection
    Elihu Shephard Letter
    Snow-Wherry Papers
    Henry Stoddard Letter
    James Tower Sweringen Letters, Ruth Ferris Collection
    Tevis Civil War Scrapbook Collection
    James S. Thomas Collection
    Daniel Webster Letters
St. Louis Public Library
    Forest Park Collection
    U.S. Department of War Arsenal correspondence
    U.S. Senate Photograph Album for the Western Sanitary Commission
    Winston Churchill Collection
St. Louis University Archives
    John F. Bannon Manuscript Collection
    Clemens-Hardaway Manuscript Collection
    Cyril Clemens Manuscript Collection
    Oscar W. Collet Manuscript Collection

    Walter H. Hill Manuscript Collection
    Laurence J. Kenny Manuscript Collection
    Miscellaneous Autograph Collection
    Miscellaneous St. Louis and Missouri Manuscript Collection
    Mullanphy-Clemens Family Manuscript Collection
    Philalethic Society Records
    St. Louis University Records
    St. Louis University Scrapbooks
    Nathan B. Young Jr. Archive
Trinity German Evangelical Lutheran Church
    Church Board Minutes
    Church Histories
Department of Special Collections, Washington University Libraries, St. Louis
    Chancellor's Scrapbooks
    William Greenleaf Eliot Papers
    Hudson Bridge Papers
    Irving Union
    Alexander S. Langsdorf, "History of Washington University, 1853–1953"
    Holmes Smith, "History of Washington University"
    Marshall Snow Scrapbooks
    Marshall S. Snow, "History of Washington University"
    Washington University Board of Trustees Minutes
Western Historical Manuscript Collections, Columbia and St. Louis
    Alvord Collection
    David Rice Atchison Papers
    J. H. P. Baker Civil War Diary
    G. W. Ballow Letter
    Louis Benecke Papers
    Bennett and Clark Champ Papers
    Thomas Hart Benton Campaign Handbill
    William Bishop Papers
    Griffin Brander Papers
    Boatmen's Savings Bank History
    Lizzie E. Brannock Letter
    B. Gratz Brown Letter
    Capital Removal Convention Resolutions
    Civil War Letter, 1863
    Colman-Hayter Family Papers
    James S. Cowan Letter
    J. C. Crane Letter
    Charles P. Deatherage, "The Rambles of a School Boy in Saint Louis"

Alexander W. Doniphan Letters
W. R. Dyer Letter
Henry C. Fike Diaries
Chauncey Ives Filley Letters
Forest Park Collection
Emory S. Foster Letter
Sarah Guitar Papers
A. L. Hager Diary
John H. Holman Papers
Alexander Inness Letter
Claiborne Fox Jackson Papers
Lilburn A. Kingsbury Collection
Ladies' Union Aid Society Reports, 1862–1863
Charles Lanman Collection
Abiel Leonard Papers
Nathan H. McCausland Papers
Public Works Board
Charles Rannell Papers
Logan Uriah Reavis Papers
A. W. Reese Papers
James Rollins Papers
Francis Asbury Sampson Collection
William Henry Schrader Papers
George R. Smith Papers
J. Orville Spreen Papers
Frederick Starr Jr. Papers
St. Louis Banking Houses Notice
St. Louis Mississippi Bridge Company, Articles of Association
Charles A. Wade Papers
Sarah and Alice Williams Diaries
Yale University Manuscripts and Archives
Nathan B. Young Jr. File

Newspapers and Magazines

Amerika
Anzeiger des Westens
Daily Missouri Democrat
Davenport Daily Gazette
Missouri Daily Argus
Missouri Republican

Moline Workman
New York Times
Rock Island Daily Republican
Rock Island Weekly Advertiser
Rock Islander
St. Louis Daily Evening News
St. Louis Daily New Era
St. Louis Daily Times
St. Louis Daily Union
St. Louis Deutsche Tribüne
St. Louis Globe
St. Louis Intelligencer
St. Louis People's Organ
St. Louis Post-Dispatch
St. Louis Reveille
Die Vehme
Westliche Post (and Sunday edition, *Mississippi Blätter*)

For a full bibliography, please contact the author.

Acknowledgments

"CENTRAL TIME," reads the red-letter reminder, emblazoned over the walkways in Lambert International Airport in St. Louis. I first encountered St. Louis as a layover, a place where all my TWA flights would land in between San Diego and Boston. I never even left the passenger lounges until my final year of college, searching for sources on how Ralph Waldo Emerson experienced the city during his first visit, 150 years before. What I found were rich archives with new stories to tell about the relationship between the North, South, and West during the era of the American Civil War and Reconstruction. In the years that followed, I took the time to make St. Louis central to my understanding of American history.

Writing about the interaction of regional agendas, cultural events, and political forces often means finding ways to use sources that the subject catalogers could not have imagined. A vanguard of archivists and librarians helped me make the intellectual leap. The St. Louis Mercantile Library provided a literal and a figurative home for me through the kind efforts of John Neal Hoover and his staff, including Charles Brown, Gregory Ames, Julie Dunn-Morton, Bette Gorden, Laura Diel, and Jennifer J. Lowe. Day after day, Debbie Cribbs went beyond the call of duty to make my research work easier. Miranda Rechtenwald doubled my thanks after moving to the University Archives, Department of Special Collections, at Washington University, where she assisted Sonya Rooney in finding gleaming historical gems in their subterranean quarters. The collections of the Missouri Historical Society (now renamed the Missouri History Museum) are immense, and without the guidance and patience of Christopher Gordon, Dennis Northcutt, Molly Kodner, Amanda Claunch, and Jeff Meyer, as well as Emily Troxell Jaycox, Duane Sneddeker, Carolyn Gilman, Ellen Thomasson, and Angie Dietz, I would have been lost.

The public servants at the St. Louis Public Library, the St. Louis County Library, and the National Park Service deserve greater recognition for their efforts on behalf of students of history, whether professional or amateur. Jean Gosebrink led me through the caged treasures of the St. Louis Public Library and offered up her desk for my keyword searches; Ruth Ann Hager, assisted by Scott Hall, made the St. Louis County Library the ideal place to search through microfilmed newspapers in three languages and to discuss the tricky work of recovering the family history of Dred and Harriet Scott. Kenneth Johnson provided key images from the Library of Congress. Bob Moore and Jennifer Clark at the archives of the Jefferson National Expansion Memorial aided me within the well-preserved Old Courthouse, a moving setting for St. Louis research.

The book required finding the politics of a cactus name, the pattern of connection in a cemetery plot, and the cultural stakes in a legal filing. Helping me along the way were Mike Everman and Bill Glankler at the St. Louis Circuit Court Records Project of the Missouri State Archives; Andrew Colligan at the Missouri Botanical Garden Archives; John Maurath at the Missouri Civil War Museum; Audrey Newcomer at the Archdiocese of St. Louis Archives; David Miros at the Midwest Jesuit Archives; Jeanette Fausz at the St. Louis Art Museum; and Jerry Garrett, who joined me for a muddy yet educational tromp through the cemeteries of St. Louis. The local collections of St. Louis University consistently offered up new avenues for research, and John Waide, Randy McGuire, and Faye Hubbard always held good cheer. The St. Louis staff of the Western Historical Manuscript Collections saved me days and thousands of dollars by bringing the richness of Columbia to me— William "Zelli" Fischetti quietly works magic, and the late Doris Wesley is sorely missed.

In St. Louis I made a habit of knocking on doors and interrupting perfectly content contemporary lives with questions about history and archives. Many of these journeys led to attics, storage rooms, hidden doors, and forgotten volumes. Among those accommodating these searches were Mary Burke, Mistii Ritter, and Jim Houser at the Academy of Science of St. Louis; Melinda Frillman at the St. Louis Science Center; Fred Eppenberger at Pilgrim Congregational Church; Ethel Miller at Central Baptist Church; Dennis Ratchert at Trinity Evangelical Lutheran; Esley Hamilton's help with the St. Louis map; Suzanne Lee and the church staff at St. John's Methodist Church; and the office staff at Second Baptist Church.

When I jumped into my blue 1988 Honda Accord (thanks, Emily Michelson!) to recapture St. Louis's hinterland, I was consistently impressed by the generosity shown to an itinerant (and hence pressed) researcher. In Hermann, Lois Puchta, Donna Mundwiller, Helen Barks, and Elizabeth Loepfe at the Gasconade County Historical Society; J. D. Kallmeyer of Historic Hermann Inc.; and Cindy Kuhn at the *Hermann Advertiser-Courier* made it possible to capture the record of the Gasconade disaster in the course of one long day. In Columbia, at the State Historical Society, Gary Kremer made time for an impromptu visitor and Todd Christine aided in searches through the vertical files, while Bill Stolz and Mary Beth Brown made the time- and money-saving at the Western Historical Manuscript Collections possible by allowing me a speedy perusal and the chance to leave a very long to-send list.

When I settled into the Missouri State Archives in Jefferson City, Patsy Luebbert, Lynn Morrow, Steven E. Mitchell, Lynne Haake, Dave Snead, and Laura Jolley made the research go swimmingly, and Alana Inman brought a bit of Texas hospitality to the middle of Missouri. On numerous occasions, I was glad to catch up with former state archivist Ken Winn. His expert knowledge of the state's history and its legacies prevented many potential "outsider" mistakes. State Representative Rachel Storch and her assistant Jill Ott, as well as Donna Schulte in state senator Michael Gibbons's office, facilitated a tour of the Capitol and its art collection, while Carmen Beck made heroic strides to aid my recovery of the history of Lincoln University.

When I drove upriver, Curtis and Libby Roseman warmly welcomed me to the Quad Cities. Kris Leinecke and Jennifer Malone at the Rock Island Arsenal Museum and Kristine Cawley at the Rock Island Public Library provided the initial basis for me to compare railroad bridges, but the collection that Larry McHenry has personally amassed blows away any established archive on the subject. Larry's eager help—from my flat tire to discussing the economics of a Prius in ethanol country—was a highlight of the research semester. And Jen Fulham's hospitality brought home that much closer.

St. Louis scholars, students of the Civil War, and St. Louisans who are themselves living history provided camaraderie and many valuable tips throughout my time living in the region. Joseph Heathcott picked some great places for coffee and provided the best advice in grad student connections; Robert Wilson generously shared notes from cholera to work-life balance and joined me for a number of truly exceptional Cardinals games. Peter Kastor, Iver Bernstein, Angela Miller, and David Konig helped me understand the ins and outs of Washington University and where to seek St. Louis's history under its mantle, and Jennie Sutton provided crucial insights on how the 1904 World's Fair has warped the city. At the University of Missouri–St. Louis, Louis Gerteis, Steve Rowan, and Andrew Hurley offered research leads and Davis van Bakergem let me peek into the Virtual City project, while Carlos Schwantes provided perspective on transportation history over great Greek dinners. Mike Venso and I crossed paths early in my time at UMSL, and our conversations about public history and the place of James Yeatman influenced how I approached Mercantile Library history. From Jefferson City to the St. Louis airport, conversations with Antonio Holland, Michael Long, and Michael Whaley added momentum, while Frank Towers and Eric Sandweiss offered advice and encouragement from afar. I cherish how Lynne Madison Jackson opened the personal history of Dred and Harriet Scott's family to me. And Father William Barnarby Faherty, ninety-one years young, amazed me: he both told tales of learning St. Louis history while paddling the Mississippi with John F. McDermott and offered perceptive advice on the shape of my research.

When the archive closed, when the week ended, when Jewish holidays arrived, many generous folks opened their homes to me. Far above and beyond was the generosity of Mikhail Pevzner, who made his apartment my own. Among those others welcoming me, from dinners to kiddush, were Rabbi Ari Vernon and Rabbi Anne Belford, Rabbi Avi Katz Orlow and Adina Frydman, Rabbi Hyim Shafner and Sara Winkelman, Rabbi Hershey Novack and Chana Novack, Sheryl Grossman, Dana Zatman, Kim Margolis, Bryce and Dina Mendelson, Adam and Rachel Lubchansky, Cyndee and Ken Levy, and Heidi Miller and Steve Gunn. And the Bais Abe Congregation and the St. Louis folk-dancing circle run by Rachel Armoza and Gloria Bilchik provided a chance to connect to things familiar but not historical.

This book was conceived in New Haven, written in New York, discussed in San Diego, and edited in El Paso, tracing the circle of professional and personal connections that broadened my consideration of St. Louis's place within the nation. As research continued at the New York Public Library and the Beinecke Rare Book and Manuscript Library at Yale University, I found the chance to continue conversations with writing groups and scholarly mentors. David Blight enthusiastically embraced my research project, carefully commenting on both the tenor and the content of my work while allowing me the space to find the unexpected. John Mack Faragher and Joanne Freeman offered valuable advice, while Jay Gitlin and George Miles consistently opened up new avenues for research. Conversations with Matthew Jacobson, Jean-Christophe Agnew, Barbara Berglund, John Merriman, Ute Frevert, Laura Engelstein, Keith Wrightson, Lloyd Pratt, and Edward Cooke particularly enriched this work. I was particularly glad to catch the eye of Alex Nemerov, who helped me interpret the visual imagery of his hometown, and of Marni Sandweiss, another St. Louisan roped into the cause.

I believe in challenging historians to embrace the power of writing. Before my work with Jana Remy and the Making History Podcast blog, this was mostly done face-to-face, in the waning Connecticut afternoon light. In his ever-modest way, John Demos created a true community of history writers, and those who met as Writing

History—including Wendy Warren, Barry Muchnick, Roxanne Willis, Francesca Ammon, Caitlin Fitz, Scott Gac, Bob Morrissey, Christian McMillen, Kip Kosek, Roger Levine, Elaine Lewinnek, Caitlin Crowell, Christine DeLucia, Paul Shin, and especially Aaron Sachs—have deeply shaped my work. As the work continued, my writing groups provided motivation and care: Caroline Sherman, Sophia Lee, and Katherine Foshko in New York; Gretchen Heefner, Theresa Runstedtler, Jenifer Van Vleck, Helen Veit, and Erin Wood in New Haven; Robert Gunn, Brad Cartwright, Brian Yothers, Dana Wessell Lightfoot, Keith Erekson, Matthew Desing, Joshua Fan, and Aileen El-Kadi in El Paso. These colleagues have become friends; so too have Gerry Cadava, Susie Woo, Amanda Ciafone, Melissa Stuckey, Rebecca McKenna, Jake Lundberg, Jake Ruddiman, Aaron O'Connell, Angela Pulley, R. Owen Williams, Mike Morgan, Ben Madley, Katie Scharf, Karen Marrero, Michael Kral, Daniel Feldman, Dara Orenstein, Jennifer Raab, Crawford Alex Mann, Ethan Lasser, Ezra Cappell, Max Grossman, Julia Schiavone-Camacho, and Jeffrey Shepherd.

Aaron Sachs, Zane Miller, Ken Winn, Iver Bernstein, Kate Unterman, and Irv Rosenthal read the entire manuscript in draft, acts of scholarly or familial kindness for which I am very thankful. Kathleen McDermott, with the assistance of Kathleen Drummy, shepherded the project through publication to your hands. Antoinette Smith provided expert copyediting. I also was fortunate to have Jenny Turner, a historian of a slightly earlier Missouri, offer insights, especially on my early chapters, and I was glad to exchange materials with Robert Forbes, Sandra Gustafson, Alison Efford, John McKerley, and Melanie Kiechle. Presenting my research to the Missouri Civil War Museum board of directors, the St. Louis Area Religious Archivists and Association of St. Louis Area Archivists, the St. Louis Mercantile Library colloquium, and the Washington University History Department workshop asked new questions of my research. And the chance to receive feedback from all the participants at workshops hosted by the Autry Museum in 2007 and the Howard R. Lamar Center for the Study of Frontiers and Borders in 2008 was particularly helpful.

Funding is what kept the lights on and the keys clicking. I was fortunate to receive a Jacob K. Javits Fellowship for the Humanities, a St. Louis Mercantile Library Research Fellowship, a Richard S. Brownlee Fund Grant from the State Historical Society of Missouri, a Gilder Lehrman Center for the Study of Slavery, Resistance, and Abolition Graduate Research Fellowship, an inaugural William E. Foley Research Fellowship from the Missouri State Archives, and funding from Yale University, including being named one of the Lamar Center's Tesoro-Kinney Fellows, with the chance to enjoy the hospitality of Holly Arnold Kinney and Jeremy Kinney at the spectacular re-creation of Bent's Fort outside Denver.

Paul, Penny, and Aliza Arenson, Emma Barron Lefkowitz, and Davi Kutner have supported me for decades. Ruth Jarmul and Irv, Rachel, and Sarah Rosenthal have welcomed me generously and were patient when an academic's office sprouted in their apartment.

Finally and most profoundly, I thank Rebecca Rosenthal for her patience, support, and love throughout, and Simon, who always has time to go to the playground.

Index